The 'Win

Julian Jeffs was born in 1931. After leaving Cambridge, where he read Natural Sciences, in 1956 he got a job (by accident) in the sherry trade in Jerez de la Frontera, where he worked in a bodega and learnt how wine was made. On getting back to England he was called to the bar but took two years off to write a book on sherry (now in its fourth edition and translated into Spanish) before practising. In his early years at the bar he found time to edit *Wine & Food*. As a barrister he became a QC and a bencher of Gray's Inn. He also wrote two more books on wine and others on law. He retired in 1991 and is now a full-time wine writer. He is a Miembro de la Gran Orden de Caballeros del Vino. He has been Chairman and subsequently President of the Circle of Wine Writers and has been general editor of the Faber Books on Wine series since its inception in 1971.

FABER BOOKS ON WINE

**Series Editor: Julian Jeffs**

# THE WINES OF SPAIN

## JULIAN JEFFS

*faber and faber*

LONDON · NEW YORK

First published in 1999
by Faber and Faber Limited
3 Queen Square London WC1N 3AU
This paperback edition first published in 2000

Published in the United States by Faber and Faber Inc.,
a division of Farrar, Straus and Giroux Inc., New York

Photoset by RefineCatch Limited, Bungay, Suffolk
Printed in England by Clays Ltd, St Ives plc

© Julian Jeffs, 1999

Maps © John Flower, 1999
Illustrations © Wendy Jones, 1999

Julian Jeffs is hereby identified as author of this
work in accordance with Section 77 of the Copyright,
Designs and Patents Act 1988

A CIP record for this book
is available from the British Library
ISBN 0-571-17532-5

2 4 6 8 10 9 7 5 3

# Contents

CONTENTS

# Maps

# Acknowledgements

So many Spanish wine growers have helped with information and hospitality that if I were to attempt to list them there would inevitably be unfortunate omissions, so I have taken the easy way and shall name none. My wife Deborah came with me on four long visits to Spain, did a good deal of the driving, and helped in all sorts of ways. Wendy Jones has very kindly prepared the line illustrations. The Spanish Commercial Office in London has given every possible sort of help, especially in digging out information from Spanish sources and in providing me with its invaluable Education Notes, prepared initially by Jeremy Watson and subsequently by John Radford. I have unashamedly made great use of these Notes and have done so with great gratitude. Especial help has been given by the Commercial Counsellor, Juan Calabozo, and by his predecessor Javier Burgos, by Graham Hines, Daniel Brennan and many other friends in the embassy. Many members of the wine trade have also helped, and I should specially mention John Hawes of the specialist importers Laymont & Shaw. I have been to many tastings, notably those given by Harold Heckle and by the Moreno Spanish Wine Club. I am also grateful to Professor Jocelyn Hillgarth for supplying fascinating literary references. Many others have helped with information and advice, and I am grateful to them all. Alan Bell and John Lockwood have very kindly read the proofs. Mistakes are mine alone.

# Spanish names

Readers may be perplexed by the formation of Spanish names. The Spaniard uses the surnames of both parents, putting that of the father first. The two names may or may not be joined by *y* (or in Catalan *e*), meaning 'and'. Thus if Sr Fernández married Sráta Gómez and they had a son whom they christened Pedro, his full name would be Pedro Fernández (y) Gómez. In normal speech and informal writing, the second name is generally omitted unless it is necessary for clear identification. To complicate matters, some Spanish names are double-barrelled.

A Spanish woman retains her maiden name after marriage but adds her husband's surname. Thus if Ana López married Sr Castillo, she would become Ana López de Castillo, and would be referred to as Castillo's señora. If her husband were to die, she would describe herself as his widow, *viuda*.

To the British the system sounds rather complicated, but it is much more logical than ours, and this explanation may help to understand the formation of some of the names mentioned in the text.

# Introduction

———

Writing a book that attempts to cover all Spanish wines has been a fascinating experience and an exhausting one. The area is vast and of course there have been problems. It has been difficult to know whether to use Spanish names or English ones where these are available: Navarra or Navarre, Mallorca or Majorca, Cataluña or Catalonia? Not without hesitation I have decided to use the Spanish names throughout, though I doubt whether I have been absolutely consistent. In many books the Spanish word for pink wine – *rosado* – is translated as *rosé*, but I can see no reason to substitute a French word for a Spanish one. There have been problems, too, with genders. This arises particularly with the names of vines, which can often be either masculine or feminine, depending on where you are and to whom you are talking. I have generally used the masculine form but it should be remembered that growers may use either. For each wine I have given the basic information at the beginning of a chapter: geography, climate, soils, grapes, planting, vineyard area, authorized yield, wines, production and vintages. In a country where the wine scene is changing so rapidly, though, figures are often revised and can never be completely up to date. The Spanish authorities classify vintages as poor, average, good, very good, or excellent. Using my own tasting experience, and following the practice of the International Wine and Food Society, I have attempted a slightly more detailed gradation by using a scale of 0 to 7. Vintage assessments, though, can often be misleading, as those who buy claret, for instance, know only too well. There are always a few disappointing wines in even a very fine vintage, and it is great fun to find really good wines (and there usually are a few) in vintages that have generally failed. This certainly applies to areas such as the Rioja, where the large area and the irregular terrain provide many microclimates. However, Spanish sunshine means that there are far fewer failures than in more northerly countries.

I have not attempted to explain abbreviations, Spanish words or wine-making terms in the text (apart from where necessary in the first chapter) but have attempted to put them all into the Glossary. Spain grows a great many different grape varieties, some of which are unique to a specific area, but most are grown in several areas and often, to complicate matters further, have several different names depending on where they are grown, and sometimes more than one name in a single area. I have set out the grape varieties, all the names for them that I can trace, and the areas in which they are grown (either officially or unofficially) in the last chapter.

# I

# The Spanish wine scene

It has been positively exciting to taste Spanish wines over the last forty years. They have been transformed, and the rate of transformation has been accelerating steadily all the time. Now that so many vineyards have reached their potential it is slowing down, but fine new wines are still emerging. This achievement should be set in its context. The Civil War had left the country bankrupt and with large areas in ruins. This was followed by the Second World War, with most export markets cut off and, for Spain, no hope of recovery. In those days most of the wine was made in conditions that nowadays look primitive, fermenting the must in huge earthenware (or later concrete) *tinajas* that made bodegas look like stage sets for a production of *Ali Baba and the Forty Thieves*, though good wines were made that way, and still sometimes are. By 1960 the only Spanish wine well known outside Spain and acknowledged to be world class was sherry. Vega Sicilia had become legendary but it was very expensive and hard to find, like the Burgundies of Romanée-Conti. Within Spain the great table wines were those of the Rioja, but in the UK they only appeared in their humblest form at the lowest end of the market, mislabelled Spanish Chablis and Spanish Burgundy, while most of the wines so labelled did not come from Rioja at all but were simply table wines of doubtful origin. There was also Spanish Sauternes, which was very sweet and rather nasty. Within Spain you could buy fine Riojas, and if you could not afford them you bought a Valdepeñas. There were some other good wines but, for the most part, these could only be bought locally. And there were some good sparkling wines, now called Cava but in those days mislabelled Champaña.

How things have changed! The first fine wines to break into the UK and US markets were the best Riojas. If you went to the right

Vineyards of Spain

FRANCE

Pamplona

Huesca

Zaragoza

Lerida

Barcelona

Sitges

Teruel

Valencia

Denia

Albacete

Alicante

Murcia

Cartagena

Palma

**Chapter 2**
1   Penedés
2   Alella
3   Ampurdán-Costa Brava
4   Conca de Barberá
5   Costers del Segre
6   Pla de Bages
7   Priorato
8   Tarragona
9   Terra Alta

**Chapter 3**
10  Calatayud
11  Campo de Borja
12  Cariñena
13  Somontano

**Chapter 4**
14  Rioja
15  Navarra

**Chapter 5**
16  Cigales
17  Ribera del Duero
18  Rueda
19  Toro

**Chapter 6**
20  Bierzo
21  The Chacolis
22  Galicia
23  Monterrei
24  Rias Baixas
25  Ribera Sacra
26  Ribeiro
27  Valdeorras

**Chapter 7**
28  Alicante
29  Almansa
30  Bullas
31  Jumilla
32  Utiel-Requena
33  Valencia
34  Yecla

**Chapter 8**
35  Vinos de Madrid
36  La Mancha
37  Méntrida
38  Mondéjar
39  Valdepeñas

**Chapter 9**
40  Ribera del Guadiana

**Chapter 10**
41  Sherry (Jerez)
42  Montilla-Moriles
43  Condado de Huelva
44  Málaga

**Chapter 11**
45  Binissalem

wine merchant in the 1960s you could also find an occasional Valdepeñas or even an Alella, but not much else. The best wines were expected to come from France or Germany. Most of the wines that you can get excited about today simply did not exist or were made only in very small quantities for local sale, just finding their way on to the wine lists of the best restaurants in Madrid and Barcelona. A number of things led to the revolution – for revolution it was. Perhaps the most important was Spain's increasing prosperity, which brought with it an important national market for fine wines and people with money for investment to make them. Another was an increasingly international outlook, so that enologists got their training in such places as Bordeaux and Davis, California. Their values became absolute rather than local and insular. And at the same time they could be provided with the modern tools of their trade, notably cool fermentation in hygienic stainless-steel vessels. These enabled delicate wines of great finesse to be made in hot places. Previously the fermentations had been tumultuous and uncontrolled, so that many elements of flavour and aroma were driven off and lost for ever.

Another, and very important, aspect was a new willingness to experiment with vine varieties and to match them to the soils and microclimates in which they were grown. The acknowledged pioneer in this area was Miguel Torres, who virtually created Penedés as a fine wine area. He brought in foreign vines such as Cabernet Sauvignon, Pinot Noir and Gewürztraminer and found out where to grow them. The introduction of international varieties led to controversy and the debate still goes on hotly. Some international varieties were originally Spanish: the Garnacha, for instance, called the Grenache in France, and the Cariñena, which the French call Carignan. Spain has other grapes of its own which are amongst the best in the world: Tempranillo, for instance. Some Spanish grape varieties practically disappeared, and while a number of these will not be missed, there might well be others that could contribute something special. Some enlightened growers, like Miguel Torres, are cultivating them and trying them out. But the real argument is whether Spain should concentrate on producing wines from native varieties, wines that are uniquely Spanish, or from international varieties that produce yet another Cabernet Sauvignon or Chardonnay. The danger lies in saying 'yet another'. The style of wine that a grape produces depends on four things: the clone, the soil, the microclimate, and the way the wine is made. And quite apart from that, vines are remarkably adaptable plants and develop characteristics of their own, depending on where they are grown. No vine demonstrates this more than the Tempranillo. So just as the Garnacha has produced great wines when transplanted to Châteauneuf-du-Pape, Cabernet Sauvignon has produced great wines in, for instance, Penedés and in Navarra. And an admixture of Cabernet Sauvignon can add backbone and finesse to a Tempranillo in Spain just as it can to a Syrah in Australia. Great wines can never be look-alikes; their greatness lies in their individuality. They come usually from years of devotion and experiment. To adopt either a too nationalistic approach or a too international one can cut off one's nose to spite one's face and prevent the emergence of something special. Spanish wine growers have generally avoided the pitfalls and have produced some very fine wines, adopting the approach best suited to where they are. Growers in areas untrammelled by tradition – Penedés, Somontano or Navarra, for instance – have had most freedom in making good use of international varieties, though they have not neglected the native ones.

Another thing that has had a profound effect on the wines is the way in which they are aged. The traditional way in Spain was to use large oak casks. Sometimes the wine spent years in them. Some were infected and imparted taints. Some made the wines taste very woody. Some had been in use so long that they had become practically impermeable to air and the wine might just as well have been in tanks. The ways in which wines mature became the subject of intense study, and experiments are still going on in all the major vineyards.

There are two ways of ageing table wines. The first is by oxidation, where the wine is in cask and oxygen permeates through the wood and between the staves. The second is by reduction, where the wine is in bottles or airtight tanks. Ageing in oak is quicker than reduction and is also extremely complex. The wine is oxidized and also takes in tannins, vanillin and other flavouring elements from the wood. Just how quickly it is oxidized and what these elements are depend on the wood that is used, how big the casks are, and how they have been made. The larger the cask, the smaller the area of contact between the oak and a given volume of wine. Some wine makers use American oak, some French, and some a combination of the two. There is also some Spanish oak, but this is in such short supply as to be insignificant. In the past there was also oak from Slovenia, which was considered good, but although this has largely disappeared it may come back; there are still a few large old casks of Slovenian oak left.

American oak, *Quercus alba,* is the most popular in Spain and has been for years. It imparts more of an oaky flavour than French, particularly vanillin. Those who favour it say that it is best suited to the native vines. Others use it for an initial part of the ageing and then go over to French, or use French for ageing a part of their wines and blend them together. In American cooperage the staves are sawn while in Europe they are split into shape (if European oak is sawn the staves tend to leak), and this also makes a difference. Amongst the many experiments going on are some making casks from American oak but by European methods.

There are two principal kinds of French oak: Limousin and Allier. Sometimes one finds Nevers or Tronçais referred to but these, like Allier, come from the centre of France and are virtually indistinguishable. French oak is of a different kind from American, or rather of two different kinds, *Quercus sessiliflora* and *Quercus robur*, but in practice no distinction is drawn between them. French oak, of whatever kind, is less aggressive, which may or may not be a good thing: it depends on the wine and what you are looking for.

Other factors influence the effect of casks, regardless of the oak they are made from. The first is the way the oak is seasoned. This can be hastened artificially or left to time and nature. The latter is considered best, and to make sure, some bodegas buy in wood and season it themselves before having it coopered. The second is the degree of 'toast'. In making a cask the staves are bent by placing a partly assembled cask over a fire, which burns in the middle; water is then thrown on, making it possible to bend the staves into shape. The fire chars the wood, to give casks of high, medium or low toast. The higher the toast, the less the penetration of the wine, which therefore tastes less woody and tannic, but the char also imports flavours of its own.

Then there is the question of the size of the cask. In the past the practice was to use enormous casks which provided a low surface-to-volume ratio. Nowadays DO regulations stipulate that casks have to be of less than 1,000 litres, though following French practice most bodegas now use *barricas* of 225 litres. Finally (at any rate for the purposes of this brief description) there is the age of the cask.

New casks impart the most flavour. Indeed, if the wine is very deli-cate (for instance in a light vintage) it may be unwise to use new casks at all. But generally the tannins and vanilla overtones that they bring are desirable and they are used, at least in part, for mat-uration of new wines, and some are actually fermented in new casks. After four or five years, though, the flavouring matters have been absorbed and what is left is simply slow oxidation. Casks can be revived to some extent if they are taken apart and shaved, but this is not often done. Older casks are desirable for some wines and particularly for the later stages of maturation. Too long in a new cask can be altogether too much of a good thing and is a mistake that the new wave of wine makers is learning to avoid, after some unfortunate experiences.

Wines are classified according to the amount of cask ageing they are given. They are as follows:

*Vino joven.* These wines are also called *vino del año, sin crianza,* or (rarely but officially) *con simple garantía de origen,* but the author-ities are encouraging the term *joven.* They are made for drinking immediately and have not spent any time in cask, or less than the time needed to qualify them as *crianzas.*

*Vino de crianza. Crianza* is usually translated as 'breeding', but in this context a better translation might be 'upbringing' or 'education'. Red wines must be aged for at least two full years after the vintage, of which a period, usually at least six months but sometimes a year, as in Rioja, must be in oak. White and *rosado* wines must spend at least a year in the bodega, of which at least six months must be in oak.

*Reserva.* Red wines must have at least three years' ageing, of which at least one must be in oak. Whites and *rosados* must be aged for at least two years, of which at least six months must be in oak.

*Gran reserva.* These are only allowed to be made in good vintages. Reds must be aged for at least five years, of which at least two must be in oak. Whites and *rosados* are rare and must be aged for at least four years, of which at least six months must be in oak.

The above ageing periods must all be in the bodega; time spent at a merchant's does not count, though it can, of course, make a profound difference to the maturity of the wine. The normal ageing rules are assumed in the chapters below unless otherwise stated.

Nothing is more important than the geographical origin of a wine. The exemplar is the French system of *appellation d'origine contrôlée* (AOC) and *vin délimité de qualité supérieure* (VDQS). Official delimitation is also long established in Spain – for instance the Consejo Regulador for sherry was established in 1933 – and is continuing apace. New areas are being defined continually. The authority responsible is INDO: Instituto Nacional de Denominaciones de Origen. Its responsibilities are not confined to wine, but wine is the major one. As Spain is part of the EU, it conforms to European rules, but so far as geographical limitations are concerned, these are not at all precise. There are only two categories: table wines and quality wines. The latter are classified as QWPSR – Quality Wines Produced in Specific Regions – or, in Spanish, VCPRD – *Vinos de Calidad Producidos en Regiones Determinadas*. Each country is left to formulate its own laws within the rules. For instance in France QWPSR includes both AOC and VDQS. In Spain there are three subdivisions for table wines – *Vino de Mesa* (VdM), *Vino Comarcal* (VC or CV) and *Vino de la Tierra* (VdlT) – and two subdivisions for quality wines – *Denominación de Origen* (DO) and *Denominación de Origen Calificada* (DOC or DOCa).

*Vino de Mesa* simply means table wine. These are wines grown in unclassified vineyards or wines blended from two or more different regions, which automatically become table wines under EU law and which may not carry a vintage date or a geographical identification. *Vino Comarcal* means local wine. They have the additional name of their area and may carry a vintage date. They are mostly simple country wines that are unlikely to progress further up the scale, but include some very distinguished wines from growers who prefer to go their own way outside the system, such as those grown by the Marqués de Griñón in his vineyards at Malpica, which he labels Vino de Mesa de Toledo, and Yllera, matured and bottled in Rueda but outside the DO, which is labelled Vino de Mesa de Castilla-Léon. These wines are described in the relevant geographical chapters.

*Vino de la Tierra* comes from defined geographical areas which produce wines having local identities that may or may not progress to DO status. In the transition period those that are going up the

scale can be classified as *Denominación Específica (provisional)* –
DE or DEp – until they have established a sufficient standing. This
happened, for instance, to the wines of Rías Baixas, which for a
time were DE Albariño. Nowadays, though, such an area is more
likely to be given the status of *Denominación de Origen Provisional*
(DOp). This happens when one or two bodegas have reached the
required standard but others have not. The most recent transition
was in 1997 when the DOp Badajoz, in Extremadura, incorporat-
ing the VdlTs Tierra de Barros, Cañamero, Matanegra,
Montánchez, Ribera Alta de Guadiana and Ribera Baja de
Guadiana, were combined together to form the new DO Ribera del
Guadiana.

All but one of the Spanish quality wines have the status of
*Denominación de Origen* (DO). Each of these is carefully mapped
out, though it is not always easy to get a copy of the map, sometimes owing to disputes around the edges. And each is governed by
its own Consejo Regulador, which is government controlled but run
locally by a board which includes representatives of wine growers
and bodegas. Each has its own strict set of rules, which are summarized in the chapters that follow. The one exception is Rioja, which
in 1991 was promoted to *Denominación de Origen Calificada*
(DOC or DOCa), a new category created in 1988 to correspond to
the Italian DOCG. If that category does not mean much in Italy, at
present it seems to mean even less in Spain. It is based on quality,
reputation and the cost of the grapes. No one could deny that Rioja
qualifies on all counts, and further regulations are under discussion
which may give real meaning to the DOC, but at the moment it
means no more than the DO. There have been various suggestions –
such as a further classification of areas within the DOC, like in
Bordeaux or Burgundy – but so far these have come to nothing. And
one can only wonder, if Rioja is a special case, why not Jerez, Ribera
del Duero, Priorato, Rías Baixas and . . . But where is one to draw
the line? That is the trouble, so perhaps things are best left as they
are.

There is one anomaly in the DO rules: Cava. This covers Spain's
finest sparkling wines, which are made by the same method as that
used in Champagne (though the French will not let them say so) and
was originally concerned only with the details of this method. Now
it does have geographical limitations but the principal thrust is still
concerned with method rather than with geography.

In surface area Spain is the second biggest country in western Europe, ranking after France, and in terms of vineyard area it is the biggest. In 1995 it had 1,327,900 ha, of which 649,792 ha were DO. But it ranked only fourth in production, after France, Italy and the USSR (as it then was). The total production was 29,740,000 hl of which 9,600,000 hl were DO wines, giving 22.4 hl/ha overall and only 14.8 hl/ha for DO wines. These figures should be compared with over 60 hl/ha in Bordeaux in 1985, admittedly a prolific year there, but nevertheless a good vintage year in a district where yields are deliberately reduced. There are several reasons for this. Spain is very sparsely populated, so the pressure to produce large yields did not exist. After Switzerland, it has the highest average height in Europe and is very rocky and infertile so that in many places only vines and olive trees will grow. In most vineyards there is a shortage of water, especially in the summer; irrigation is not allowed except 'experimentally' and to save the lives of very young vines or the vineyards generally in the years of greatest drought. This follows from EU law, and is probably a mistake when you consider what good wines are made from carefully irrigated vineyards in Australia, but it does reduce the 'wine lake'. There is a movement to do away with the ban. Many of the vines are over forty years old, which greatly reduces yield per vine. And in the DO districts yield is generally reduced deliberately in the interests of quality. Garnacha vines, for instance, tend to produce very dim wines if the yield is high but can produce great ones in the right place if it is kept very low. Whatever the vine, in the DOs quality is protected by decrees of *rendimiento*. If grapes are pressed to yield the last drop of juice, the resulting must is of very poor quality; hence each district sets a limit to the amount that can be abstracted. This is between 65 and 70 per cent. Nowadays grapes are tested when growers deliver them to a bodega. A mechanical arm is lowered into the middle of a truckload of grapes and a sample is taken that is analysed immediately by an electrical device to measure sugar and acidity, which have to be in balance if the grower is to get the highest price.

Another feature is the remarkably wide variety of the wines grown. This comes from Spain's sheer size, stretching from the Atlantic to the Mediterranean and from the Pyrenees to Tarifa, not to mention the islands. It is also very mountainous, with several massive ranges, and ascends from the coast to the high central Meseta. The northern Atlantic coast is cool and damp. The

Mediterranean coast is agreeably warm though it can be very hot in summer as you get further south. The mountains behind are much cooler, especially at night. And the whole of the central Meseta is horribly cold in winter and very hot indeed in summer. There are as many soils as there are microclimates and an enormous choice of vines. It has everything and in terms of wine it produces practically everything.

Vineyards respect geography but not politics. Thus they can straddle from one province to another or appear as small outcrops far from their nearest neighbours. It is therefore not easy to divide the country rationally into separate areas. In some, such as the Levant (Chapter 7), there is a close resemblance between the various wines. In others, such as those grouped in the north-west (Chapter 6), the vineyards are more scattered and the differences more marked; but they are all principally influenced by Atlantic rather than Mediterranean or continental weather patterns.

The chapters that follow group the vineyards into manageable areas, but very real differences can exist within them. Each DO is described separately, together with some wines that do not enjoy DO status but which are nevertheless significant – sometimes very significant. The description for each DO is prefaced by a section giving the vital data and is followed by a list of some of the major bodegas, though the choice of these is necessarily subjective. Terms that may not be understood are explained in the Glossary at the end.

# 2

# *Cataluña*

Cataluña is the north-eastern part of Spain, stretching nearly 400 km down the Mediterranean coast. It was one of the first of the Spanish Roman possessions, forming part of Hispania Tarraconensis, but there is strong evidence that wine was grown there long before the Romans arrived. It has its own language – Catalan – which has links with old French and Castilian, easier to read than to understand. During the Franco years this was actively suppressed, with the inevitable result that it has come back with a vengeance and is used as the language of choice by everyone who speaks it, though they all speak Castilian as well. Wine is grown right up to the French border, in the DO Ampurdán–Costa Brava. Then there is a gap all the way along the Costa Brava, the once remote and beautiful coastline which even the influx of tourists and the proliferation of buildings has not wholly destroyed. Travelling south, the next DO area is Alella, hidden amongst the northern suburbs of Barcelona.

Barcelona, the capital of Cataluña, is a wonderful city, the second most important in Spain, though the Catalans would certainly put it first. It is full of good things: the great Gothic cathedral, the old city, the bizarre architectural works of Gaudí and the slightly less bizarre but equally wonderful works of his contemporaries, the art galleries, which include the earlier works in the Thyssen collection (the later ones are in Madrid), the maritime museum, the seafront ... and not least a wealth of excellent restaurants where the local wines can be enjoyed to the full. Anyone exploring the vineyards should pause here for as long as they can.

As a vineyard, Cataluña has re-created itself, beginning in the 1950s, accelerating in the 1960s, and continuing to this day. The process is reflected in the histories of the bodegas that follow. The

Cavas were the mainstay of the trade, after they were invented at the end of the nineteenth century, while the table wines used to be poor things: oxidized *rancios* and nondescript *rosados* predominated. How different things are today!

The major DO, Penedés, lies to the south and west of Barcelona; apart from table wines this is also the home of some of Spain's best Cavas and brandies. Behind it to the west lies the DO Conca de Barberá and beyond that the DO Costers del Segre. Travelling further down the coast one comes to the DO Tarragona.

Tarragona, like Barcelona, is well worth visiting, though for less time. It has a wonderful cathedral and museum as well as compelling Roman remains, but the restaurants do not compare. One should not be put off by the 'concrete jungle' of the coastline: just hasten through it.

The DO Priorato is an enclave within Tarragona. It is one of the most beautiful of all wine-growing districts and produces some of the finest wines in the world. Alas, they are also amongst the most expensive; people are finding out about them. Then inland, and to the west of Tarragona, there is the DO Terra Alta.

These Catalan vineyards provide a wonderful range of wines of every conceivable kind, several appearing within a single DO. Sometimes one wonders why the boundaries are drawn at all, but they do divide the vast area into manageable units, and happily they are not pedantically enforced. After all, a Catalan wine is a Catalan wine, and one cannot conceivably object when Penedés, for example, takes in wines grown technically within the boundaries of Tarragona, Conca de Barbera or Costers del Segre; and it does. The Catalans are individualists and although there are some very great names, no one predominates. There can be a huge estate, and next to it an abundance of small growers, just as there can be a great winery and, just down the road, a boutique winery producing wine on the smallest possible scale. It is a fascinating place to visit.

## PENEDÉS

### Geography
The nearest great city is Barcelona. The capital of the area, though, is Villafranca del Penedés, inland to the north-north-west of the coastal town Sitges. There are three distinct vineyard areas:

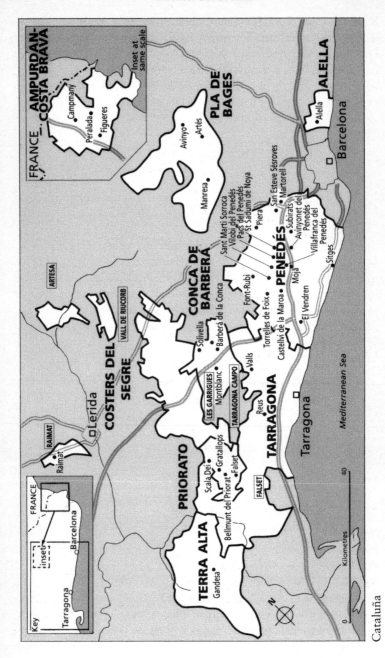

Cataluña

Baix- (or Baja-) Penedés (Low Penedés), Medio (or Mitja-) Penedés (Middle Penedés), and Penedés Superior (or Alt-Penedés) (High Penedés). The first is low lying, from sea level to 250 m; the second is on rolling hills from 250 to 500 m above sea level; and the third runs into the foothills of the mountains lying behind the coast and extends up to 800 m.

## Climate
The hottest area is Baix-Penedés, though the heat is moderated by the proximity of the Mediterranean. Temperatures vary between 2.6°C and 27.8°C with a mean of 14.4°C. Rainfall is 500–600 mm, with 2,548 hours of sunshine. The other areas, although cooler on average, are more continental, with higher peaks and lower troughs of temperature as the height rises, but as they are hilly there are many significant microclimates. This is discussed further below.

## Soils
Throughout all three areas the soil is deep and provides good drainage. All have about 20 per cent calcium carbonate, as limestone in the lower ground and chalk in the higher. The lower vineyards tend to be sandy while the higher ones have more clay.

## Grapes
There are 121 identified varieties, most of them not even of academic interest, but some may well be revived.

Recommended red varieties: Tempranillo (here called Ull de Llebre), Garnacha Tinta (Lladoner, Aragonés), Monastrell (Alcayata), Cariñena (Mazuelo), Cabernet Sauvignon and Samsó.

Permitted red varieties: Cabernet Franc, Merlot and Pinot Noir.

Recommended white varieties: Parellada, Xarel.lo (Pansá Blanca), Macabeo (Viura) and Subirat-Parent (Malvasía Riojana).

Permitted white varieties: Gewürztztraminer, Riesling, Muscat d'Alsace, Chenin Blanc, Chardonnay and Sauvignon Blanc.

Experimental white variety: Albariño.

## Planting
Old vineyards used to be densely planted with up to 7,000 vines per ha. New thinking reduced that figure to less than half, but the experimental work of Miguel Torres has shown that best quality is achieved with 4,500 to 5,000. This density is generally adopted in new vineyards, but experiments still go on and it has been found

that these unusually high densities are good for quality. Tradition-ally the vines were grown *en vaso* but newer vineyards, particularly those growing foreign varieties, use wires or trellises and are pruned *en cordon*, Guyot or Royat.

### Vineyard area
2,700 ha.

### Authorized yield
55 hl/ha for red and *rosado* wines, 65 hl/ha for white wines.

### Wines
All colours are grown: red, *rosado* and white, including some sweet whites, a little of the old style *rancio* and some sparkling wines classified as *espumoso* (which are not the same thing as Cavas, though most of the best Cavas are grown in Penedés). The usual regulations for ageing apply: *vino joven* (*vi novell*) is young wine for immediate drinking; *vino de crianza* requires two years' ageing, of which at least six months must be in oak; red *reservas* require three years' ageing, of which at least one must be in oak, while for white and *rosado reservas* the times are two years with six months in oak. *Gran reservas* must have at least two years in oak and three in bottle.

### Production
(1989 vintage) 1,709,000 hl.

### Vintages
1980 5, 1981 5, 1982 6, 1983 4, 1984 6, 1985 7, 1986 4, 1987 3, 1988 6, 1989 5, 1990 5, 1991 6, 1992 4, 1993 6, 1994 5, 1995 5, 1996 5, 1997 6.

But bearing in mind that there are three zones and many micro-climates, and that sometimes reds do better than whites, or vice versa, these figures are indicative rather than definitive.

Penedés (in Catalán Penedès) lies on the coast about 30 km south of Barcelona and extends along it for 45 km to a point about 16 km east of Tarragona; Sitges is about half-way. It stretches inland for 35 km. All these distances are necessarily approximate, as wine districts cannot be arranged to be neatly rectangular. Its shape and position are shown on the map.

Barcelona is one of the greatest cities in Europe. Much frequented by tourists, it is described in all the guide books. Sitges is still a charming little place, despite modern development and much building; it was a favourite resort of the late G.K. Chesterton and they have erected a monument to him. Well worth a visit, Sitges has some delightful museums, one of which contains a couple of El Grecos. The wine capital, however, is Villafranca del Penedés. At first sight this is a rather nondescript place, but in its centre there are the remains of an old town, with a maze of narrow streets and some fine houses. Above all it contains an excellent wine museum, which is not devoted entirely to wine but includes a fine display of plates and tiles, a fourteenth-century primitive, and some good modern paintings. For the wine lover, however, its most interesting exhibits are the amphorae, which date back to Roman times, used for transporting and exporting wine, and which prove its historical importance as a wine-growing district.

As in so many parts of Spain, wine has been grown in Penedés from time immemorial. Recent excavations suggest that it dates back to pre-Phoenician days. A beautiful piece of countryside with old farms, pinewoods, olive groves, cypress trees, orchards of nuts, and of course vines, it has a most agreeable climate. The mountains of Montserrat shelter it from the cold northern winds. It is not surprising that it was favoured by the Romans. Rich Romans had their villas here and the many remains of amphorae indicate that wine was exported as well as drunk locally. The sweet *rancio* wines that are still made in small quantities are said to date from Roman times. But after the departure of the Romans wine growing vanished into obscurity for hundreds of years. Wine was still grown, of course, but it was drunk locally and nothing is heard of it. As late as the eighteenth century there were virtually no roads to link inland areas with the coast and hence no carts, so everything had to be transported on pack animals, and such wine as was grown inland for sale was usually distilled. In the seventeenth century, wine began to appear in the export statistics. It went to most parts of Europe but the main market was Latin America. These wines came from the Baix-Penedés and were generally fortified for export, even the strongest of them. The most famous was the Moscatel from Sitges.

In the nineteenth century, bulk wines were exported to France following the devastation wrought by phylloxera there, but most of these came from other Catalán areas rather than from Penedés. Phylloxera duly arrived in Penedés in 1887. It reached its peak of

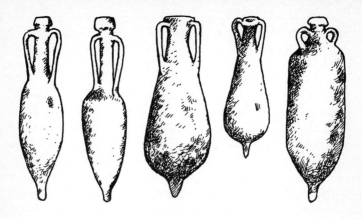

Amphorae

destruction three years later and its inexorable progress continued until 1910, by which time it had got everywhere and vineyards that were not replanted vanished. After the phylloxera, many of those that were replanted were planted with hybrid vines that gave atrocious wines. From the 1870s until the 1960s, the history of wine growing is largely that of Cava, and this is covered in a separate chapter. No nationally or internationally recognized table wines were grown until the Torres family began a revolution in wine growing that was to give the region a completely new dimension. Trained in France, Miguel Torres had an international outlook and he judged wines by absolute standards. He planted the classic vine varieties from France and Germany as well as the best of the Spanish ones. Before growing anything he meticulously investigated the soil and the microclimate, to see that each variety was grown in a place where it could give of its best. And not least he brought back with him the latest and best techniques in wine making. In the nineteenth century, wines had generally been fermented in underground pits where the temperatures could rise alarmingly and all the aromas were lost. Others were soon to climb on his bandwagon. The variety and quality of the wines available were totally transformed. Penedés is now a leading area for table wines, judged by world standards.

The significance of imported varieties must not, however, be exaggerated. They still form only a very small part of the total, though an important one. Most of the vineyards are planted with the traditional varieties originally grown to make Cavas. But the new varieties have had a profound effect on the development of the Spanish wine trade and have spread to many other areas.

Like so many of the places where fine wine is grown in Spain, Penedés is a beautiful place. Of the three parts, Baix-Penedés is the least beautiful. It lies on the coastal plain and, like nearly the whole of the Spanish Mediterranean coastline, it has been 'developed': built over with hideous modern buildings, many of them high-rise. Most of the vineyards have disappeared beneath the concrete. There are still some left, though, and a good way to see where they begin is to take the train from Barcelona to Villafranca del Penedés; they are seen much more easily from the train than from the road. The Medio-Penedés lies in a great broad valley behind a range of hills. To describe it as a valley is rather misleading, though, for it is itself an area of small hills, streams and gorges. In such a place there are inevitably many microclimates and some are much better for wine growing than others. There is mixed farming and many other crops as well, notably delightful orchards of nut trees with their beautiful blossom in spring. Penedés Superior lies high in the foothills of the mountains, though most of the vineyards are on relatively flat pieces of land, and there is the same variety of microclimates. All are delightful places to be in.

Baix-Penedés is the hottest and also the wettest. Despite the moderating influence of the sea, the summer temperature at Barcelona can rise to 31°C, though it seldom goes much above 27°C. In winter it can freeze, but this is not common. The average temperature is 14–16°C. The average hours of sunshine are 2,340 and the rainfall 450–550 mm. In most of the Baix-Penedés, however, the figures are rather different, with a mean of 14.4°C, 500–600 mm of rainfall, and 2,550 hours of sunshine. It illustrates how important microclimates can be. Storms are few and all in all it is an easy climate to grow vines in. Historically it was an area of Malvasía and Moscatel vines and its most famous wine was the Moscatel of Sitges; but sweet fortified wines have fallen out of favour and these vines are no longer widely grown. Recently many vineyards have been replanted with red wine grapes, usually with Garnacha, Cariñena, Monastrell and Tempranillo.

Medio-Penedés is in the hills 250–500 m above sea level, so that the moderating influence of the sea is less apparent, making it warmer in summer and cooler in winter – quite a lot cooler, with snow from time to time. The average summer temperature is 27.78°C and the average for the year 14.43°C. Figures for sunshine are 2,550 hours and rainfall is 500–600 mm. For most vine varieties it is the best area. All the recommended and permitted red wine grapes are grown: Tempranillo, Garnacha, Monastrell, Cariñena, Cabernet Sauvignon, Samsó, Cabernet Franc, Merlot and Pinot Noir. The recommended white wine grapes are also grown here: Parellada, Xarel.lo, Macabeo and Subirat-Parent. On the whole, though, the imported white varieties tend to do better higher up, though there are vineyards of Chardonnay and of Chenin Blanc.

Penedés Superior, being higher still at 500–800 metres, is colder in winter and snow is commonplace, but it can be hot in summer and there is plenty of sunshine to ripen the grapes. At the present time climatic statistics are not available and in the mountains they are likely to be unreliable in any case. It is here that the permitted imported varieties for white wine come into their own: Gewürztraminer, Riesling, Muscat d'Alsace, Chenin Blanc, Chardonnay and Sauvignon. Of the native varieties the most important here is Parellada. It is too cool for Cabernet Sauvignon. At the height of summer, when the temperature on the coast is 30°C by day and falls to only 25°C by night, in Penedés Superior it may rise to 40°C by day and fall to 15°C by night.

The above figures and lists of vines are only indicative. In Penedés more than in most areas, the emphasis should be on the wide range of microclimates, so that growers can plant any grape variety in the right place in any of the districts – and they do.

Statistics for the number of vines planted are largely meaningless in the context of Penedés wines, as the figures vary annually, with Malvasía, for example, at present declining and Cabernet Sauvignon (together with most of the other imported varieties) rapidly increasing. It must also be remembered that the principal product is not table wine but Cava and that large numbers of grapes are also grown for another important product: brandy. The big Cava makers and some of the larger wine growers (notably Torres) have huge vineyards, but the average holding is small at 2.5 ha, with the growers selling to the houses or to cooperatives, which are both long-established and important.

Above all it should be remembered that the rules are very flexible. Grapes can come from anywhere in Cataluña, and that includes

Tarragona, provided that they are vinified in Penedés. In particular, grapes for Penedés wines often come from Conca de Barberá. Some growers, notably Codorníu and Torres, have large vineyards there.

If a hundred years ago Penedés produced bulk wines that were very southern in style, flabby, short on acid, and lacking in aroma owing to the hot fermentation that had driven all the volatile elements off, the position today is the very opposite in every respect. The revolution is complete. There is still a very small production of old-style wines in the form of Moscatel de Sitges (which is good when you can find it) and some *rancios* which have their *aficionados*, but temperature-controlled vinification is now the order of the day and highly trained enologists create table wines to the best international standards. Full use is made of the native grapes, but supplementing them with the imported varieties has created a whole range of new wines and has added new dimensions to the old ones. The first to be recognized internationally were the whites, as one might expect from an area well versed in growing good base wines for the Cavas. These are now amongst Spain's best, but so are the *rosados* and the reds. The *rosados* are often vinified from Garnacha but there are also excellent ones from the imported varieties, notably Merlot. The reds fully realize the potential of the native varieties but these are often enhanced by blending with the imported ones, which can add backbone and complexity; Tempranillo, for instance, blends very well with Cabernet Sauvignon. And many growers produce excellent reds vinified from the imported varieties alone, notably Cabernet Sauvignon and Merlot or combinations of them. Since the 1970s Penedés has been a most exciting region and many of the wines of all descriptions produced today are world class.

## Some leading bodegas

### Albet i Noya
This family-owned bodega in Subirats, now in its fourth generation, was founded in 1903. Originally noted for its Cavas, since 1980 its 26.3 ha vineyard Can Vendrell de la Codina, 300 metres above sea level on the western slopes of the Ordal mountain range, has been cultivated on 'ecological' (semi-organic) principles with Royat pruning. White varieties planted include Chardonnay, Macabeo, Xarel.lo, Parellada and Moscatel de Alexandría; black varieties include Cabernet Sauvignon and Tempranillo. It goes in for varietal

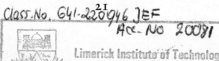

wines, including a Xarel.lo. Some of its Tempranillo is vinified by carbonic maceration to produce an appealing and very quaffable wine for early consumption. Its top range of very good wines, which include a varietal Cabernet Sauvignon, is sold under the Col.lecció label. The excellent Reserva Marti is made from 60 per cent Tempranillo, 30 per cent Cabernet Sauvignon and 10 per cent Syrah. These develop well with a year or two in bottle.

### René Barbier

This large bodega at San Sadurní de Noya was founded by a Frenchman, Léon Barbier, in 1880 but is now owned by the great Cava house Freixenet. It has large vineyard holdings of 250 ha, which include 30 ha of Cabernet Sauvignon. Good quality wines are made in a great many styles. These include a varietal Cabernet Sauvignon but most are blended from several varieties; for instance, the red Family Reserve, Reserva 1993 was 90 per cent Tempranillo and 10 per cent Cabernet Sauvignon, while the *rosado* 1996 was from Tempranillo, Garnacha and Monastrell. One of its best known wines is the well-made white Kraliner, made from the native Macabeo, Xarel.lo and Parellada grapes. There is no connection (other than through membership of the founding family) with the Priorato bodega of René Barbier Fill.

### Can Feixes

This great domaine at Cabrera D'Anoia has a history dating back to the fourteenth century and has been growing wine since 1690, though its present owners do not claim to trace their history further back than 1768. It owns 120 ha of vines that are high in the hills, up to 400 m above sea level, where there is a considerable difference between day and night temperatures. Some of the grapes are sold to other bodegas but most are used to make red and white wines of good quality as well as Cavas. The wines are blended from several varieties; the white Can Feixes 1994 consisted of 48 per cent Parellada, 28 per cent Macabeo and 24 per cent Chardonnay, while the red *crianza* 1991 was 70 per cent Tempranillo and 30 per cent Cabernet Sauvignon. The Negre Selecció 1994, made from Tempranillo and Cabernet Sauvignon, showed excellent ageing potential.

### Can Ráfols dels Caus

Founded in 1980 in an old *masía* at Avinyonet del Penedés, it has a substantial vineyard of 33 ha. The wines are excellent. Most are sold as Petit Caus and Gran Caus. Imported grape varieties predominate and these are combined much in the Bordeaux manner; for instance, Gran Caus 1988 was made from 41 per cent Cabernet Sauvignon, 34 per cent Merlot and 25 per cent Cabernet Franc, while Gran Caus Crianza 1989 was made from 53 per cent Cabernet Franc, 32 per cent Cabernet Sauvignon and 15 per cent Merlot. In some of the wines Tempranillo forms part of the blend whereas others, Caus Lubis and its highly regarded *rosado*, are varietal Merlot.

## Cavas Gramona

This family-owned bodega in San Sadurní de Noya was founded in 1881. Principally known for its Cavas, it specializes in the three classic Cava varieties: Macabeo, Xarel.lo and Parellada, but also grows Chardonnay and Pinot Noir. In addition to its Cavas it produces some noteworthy table wines, including a varietal Chardonnay, a slightly sweet white called Gessami, made from equal parts of Moscatel, Chardonnay and Sauvignon Blanc, and the only Pinot Noir *rosado*.

## Cavas Hill

This is justifiably one of the most highly regarded bodegas, producing an extraordinarily wide range of wines, red, *rosado* and white in addition to Cavas. The original Joseph Hill came from England to settle in Cataluña in 1660, but the present bodega was founded in 1887. It owns 50 ha of vineyards in the village of Mojá, 50 km south of Barcelona at a height of 200 m, and opened a new cellar complex in 1990. There is a varietal Cabernet Sauvignon with considerable ageing potential, a barrel-fermented Chardonnay, and a Tempranillo. Most of the blended wines rely on native varieties which here show their full potential. Blanc Bruc 1996 was 60 per cent Xarel.lo, 30 per cent Macabeo and 10 per cent Parellada, while the massive red Gran Civet 1994 was 60 per cent Garnacha and 40 per cent Cariñena. Its most distinctive wine is the red Gran Toc, unusually big-bodied and sold (as is the white Blanc Bruc) in extraordinary dumpy bottles with very long necks. The *reservas* are typically 60 per cent Tempranillo, 25 per cent Merlot and 15 per cent Cabernet Sauvignon. Slightly sparkling wines (*vinos de aguja*) are sold under the name Timon.

## Cavas Josep Masachs
Founded in 1940 and originally known for its Cavas, this bodega at Torrelles de Foix now produces red, *rosado* and white wines of good quality. It was rebuilt in 1987 and owns 55 ha of vineyards, with grapes also being bought in. Most of the whites are made from the traditional native varieties but the *rosados* and reds are made from Tempranillo/Cabernet Sauvignon blends and there are varietal Chardonnays and Cabernet Sauvignons. The name Painous is used as well as Josep Masachs.

## Cavas Pares Balta
This family-owned Cava house at Pacs del Penedés, founded in 1934, has the backing of an unusually big vineyard holding of 600 ha. It makes a wide range of wines. The whites include varietal Chardonnay and Sauvignon Blanc, while the Blanc de Pacs is from the classic varieties: Macabeo, Parellada and Xarel.lo. The *rosado* is a varietal Cabernet Sauvignon. The red Cabernet Sauvignons have additions of 10 per cent Merlot and 5 per cent Cabernet Franc.

## Cellers Grimau-Gol
Founded in 1986, this bodega at Villafranca del Penedés produces consistently good wines from bought-in grapes and sells them under the Duart de Sio label. The white wines are made from the traditional native vine varieties, the *rosados* from Cabernet Sauvignon and the reds from Tempranillo and Cabernet Sauvignon.

## Cellers Mas Comtal
A small bodega founded as recently as 1993 at Avinyonet del Penedés by the Mila family, one of whom, Joan Mila, is a well-known enologist. It has 34.5 ha of vineyards growing Cabernet Sauvignon, Cabernet Franc, Merlot, Chardonnay, Macabeo, Xarel.lo, Parellada and Müller-Thurgau. The aim is to keep a balance between the Spanish and foreign varieties. Allier oak is used for ageing. It has already established a reputation as a producer of quality wines.

## Cellers Puig & Roca
Although this is one of the youngest bodegas and also one of the smallest, established in 1991 at El Vendrell, it is already becoming well known and respected. Here the emphasis is on the imported grape varieties; the 9.5 ha of vineyards are planted with Chardonnay, Cabernet Sauvignon, Cabernet Franc and Merlot. The wines

are sold under the trade name Augustus. The whites include a particularly good barrel-fermented Chardonnay. The reds include varietals and blends.

### Cellers Robert
This is the last remaining producer of the once famous Malvasía de Sitges. It also produces a sweet Moscatel. The grapes are left to shrivel on the vines and are picked rich with sugar.

### Cooperativa L'Arboç 'Caycra'
The cooperative movement has played a big part in the history of Penedés and this is one of the most respected of them, founded in 1919 at L'Arboç. As one would expect of a cooperative, it has a wide choice of vine varieties. It makes Cava but also white, *rosado* and red wines under the Castell Gornal, D'Arcyac and Pupitre brands, which include varietals from Chardonnay, Cabernet Sauvignon and, more unusually, Xarel.lo. The wines sold under the Pupitre brand are well worth looking for.

### Cooperativa Vinícola del Penedés/Covides
As well as Cavas, this cooperative at San Sadurní de Noya produces good white, *rosado* and red table wines under the brands Duc de Foix, Moli de Foc and Gran Castellflorit. Some use combinations of native vine varieties; for instance, Moli de Foc *rosado* 1994 was made from 50 per cent Tempranillo and 50 per cent Cariñena, but the Duc de Foix *rosado* 1993 was 100 per cent Cabernet Sauvignon, while the 1996 was 85 per cent Cabernet Sauvignon and 15 per cent Merlot. Of the reds the Duc de Foix 1993 *reserva* was 70 per cent Cabernet Sauvignon and 30 per cent Tempranillo. A wide range of wines is made and they are well worth looking for.

### Heretat Mont-Rubí
As well as Cavas, this bodega at Font-Rubí produces good white and *rosado* wines from the traditional grape varieties, growing Macabeo and Parellada in its 110 ha vineyard at Esplugues de Llobregat.

### Juvé y Camps
Best known for its excellent Cavas, this bodega at San Sadurní de Noya also produces very good table wines. Sr Juvé and Srita Camps fell in love, married, and founded the business in 1921. Both marriage and business flourished. Still family run, it is one of the major vineyard owners, with 425 ha planted mostly with Parellada,

Macabeo and Xerel.lo, but with some Chardonnay, Cabernet Sauvignon, Pinot Noir and Gewürztraminer. As one might expect from a Cava house, its whites are notable. It uses the trade mark d'Espiells, the name of one of its properties towards the edge of the area, by Montserrat. The 1995 Ermita d'Espiells was made from 40 per cent Macabeo, 40 per cent Parellada and 20 per cent Xarel.lo, while the 1995 La Miranda d'Espiells was 100 per cent Chardonnay.

### Jean León

This bodega, along with Torres, led the way with imported vines. Jean León was a highly successful restaurateur, owning La Scala Restaurant in Beverly Hills. On holiday in Penedés in 1963 he saw a vineyard for sale at Torrelavid and bought it. He wanted his own wines to serve in his restaurant – wines that would please his American clientele – and he set about it with remarkable diligence, beginning by taking a course at the renowned wine school at Davis, California. French vines were (and are) all the rage in America and he set out to get the best. His Chardonnay came from Corton, his Cabernet Sauvignon from Château Lafite, and his Cabernet Franc from Château La Lagune. His first vintage was in 1969 and his vineyard a large one, now about 160 ha. The wines were spectacularly successful and became legendary. If the Chardonnays tended to be rather over-oaked and New Worldy, the Cabernet Sauvignons were excellent. Complexity was sometimes enhanced by a small addition of Cabernet Franc: for instance, the Cabernet Sauvignon 1990 included 15 per cent Cabernet Franc and was matured for twenty-four months in American oak. In 1995 the bodega was bought by Torres, and it remains to be seen how they will develop it, but their own standards are so high that it is safe to say the quality will be maintained, and they have left it alone to make its own wines.

### Marqués de Monistrol

This traditional Cava house in San Sadurní de Noya, founded in 1882, is one of the biggest in the region, with 500 ha of vineyard. White wines include a varietal Chardonnay and others vinified from the local varieties. One of the most highly regarded (in a fancy bottle) is the Vin Nature Blanc en Noirs; the 1994 was vinified from Xarel.lo and Parellada. The reds are generally made from combinations of Tempranillo and Cabernet Sauvignon, but one of the best is its varietal Merlot. They are very good.

**Mascaró**

This admirable bodega at Villafranca del Penedés was founded in
1945 by Narciso Mascaró Marsé as a distillery and is now owned
by his son Antonio Mascaró Carbonell, who is ably assisted by the
third generation, his daughter Montserrat. It is still perhaps principally known as a distillery, for its pot-still brandies are amongst
Spain's best. It then branched out into making good Cavas. The
family owns two estates with 60 ha of vineyards. But Don Antonio
is an enthusiastic wine man, with a great love of Bordeaux. Others
set the example of growing Bordeaux varieties and he decided to
grow his own. He planted Cabernet Sauvignon in the 35 ha vineyard at his Mas Miquel estate in 1980. The first wine was released
in 1991. There is now a white, Viña Franca, vinified from Parellada
and Macabeo, a *rosado*, Gran Reinado, which is a varietal Merlot,
and a red *reserva*, Sello Real, which is a varietal Cabernet Sauvignon from the El Castell vineyard, but the top of the range is a *gran
reserva*, Anima, also a varietal Cabernet Sauvignon; it is only made
in the best years and is aged for three years in Tronçais casks, initially in new ones but racked into old wood.

**Masía Bach**

The Bach family fortune came from selling cotton to the French
army in the First World War. The profits were ploughed into building a large mansion (illustrated on the wine labels) in the middle of
a 350 ha estate at Sant Esteve Sesrovires. In 1975 it was bought by
the great Cava maker Codorníu and, like all the properties of that
illustrious concern, it is immaculately kept up, but only 60 ha of
vineyard were retained. White wines are fermented at 18°C, reds at
28 to 30°C. The reds are aged for one year in large Limousin oak
vats and then for one or two years in small American oak casks. The
wines are first rate and there is an enormous range of them. The
leading white is Extrisimo Seco, which in 1996 was made from 55
per cent Xarel.lo, 20 per cent Macabeo, 20 per cent Chardonnay
and 5 per cent Sauvignon Blanc. Another very good white is called
Magnificat; in 1996 it was made from 60 per cent Chardonnay,
(improbably, for this vine is usually associated with northern
Atlantic wines) 30 per cent Albariño and 10 per cent Sauvignon
Blanc. There are also some good semi-sweet and sweet whites and a
very good *rosado*. The red Cabernet Sauvignon *crianza* 1991 contained 15 per cent Tempranillo. There are also excellent blended

reds sold under the name Viña Extrísima. This is a bodega which knows how to gain interest, balance and complexity by blending combinations of grape varieties and which does it very well, a wide variety of grapes being used. The combinations necessarily change from year to year, so look at the label.

## Masía Vallformosa

This is a family-owned bodega in Vilobí del Penedés, with a substantial vineyard of 307 ha, that is well known for its Cavas but also provides good table wines: whites (including some sweet ones), *rosados* and reds. The 1996 whites included a Viña Blanca from 35 per cent Macabeo, 35 per cent Parellada and 30 per cent Xarel.lo, and a slightly lightweight 100 per cent Chardonnay. The *rosado* was 70 per cent Garnacha and 25 per cent Tempranillo. The red Vall Fort Crianza 1994 was 75 per cent Tempranillo and 25 per cent Garnacha. The red Vall Reserva 1990 and Vallformosa Gran Reserva 1989 were both made from combinations of 85 per cent Tempranillo and 15 per cent Cabernet Sauvignon. The Cabernet Sauvignon Reserva 1990 included 15 per cent Merlot.

## Josep María Raventós i Blanc

This bodega was founded at San Sadurní de Noya by a rebellious member of the Raventós family that owns Codorníu, who went off to do his own thing. He followed the family tradition, however, in putting up some striking and beautiful buildings in 1986 and in making good Cavas. There are 130 ha of vineyard. The table wines are whites and are good. El Preludio is made from Macabeo, Xarel.lo, Parellada and Chardonnay. There is also a varietal Chardonnay.

## Joan Raventós Rosell

Another offshoot of the Raventós family, this bodega at Masquefa was founded in 1895 and has 60 ha of vineyard at Heretat Val-Ventos, 6 km from San Sadurní de Noya, where it grows Parellada, Macabeo, Xarel.lo, Chardonnay, Sauvignon Blanc, Cabernet Sauvignon, Merlot and Pinot Noir. Apart from its Cavas, it is well known for its varietal table wines, sold under the Heretat Val-Ventos name: Chardonnay, Sauvignon Blanc, Pinot Noir and a *rosado* from Merlot. Its blended wines include Blanc Primer, made from equal parts of Chardonnay and Macabeo, and the *rosado* Rosat Primer, made from 75 per cent Pinot Noir and 25 per cent Merlot.

## Olivella Sadurní

Although the Olivella family is an old one in Penedés, the bodega at Subirats is new, dating only from 1986, but housed in old premises. There is a 100 ha vineyard. The wines are the white Prima Lux, vinified in 1996 from Xarel.lo and Chardonnay, the *rosado* Prima Juventa, from 85 per cent Merlot and 15 per cent Cabernet Sauvignon, and the red Prima Vesper, from 85 per cent Cabernet Sauvignon and 15 per cent Merlot. The Prima Nox 1993 is a varietal Cabernet Sauvignon *crianza*.

## Sadeve/Vinos y Cavas Naveran

This bodega at Torrelavit is said to have old origins but it only really got going in 1984. There are 120 ha of vineyard. It is a Cava house which also produces good table wines. Manuela de Naveran is a cask-fermented Chardonnay. The red *crianza* and *gran reservas* are varietal Cabernet Sauvignons, as is the *rosado*. The rather affected labels are distracting.

## Manuel Sancho e Hijas

This bodega was founded at Castellví de la Marca in 1977 and took the first vintage off its 48 ha in 1981. It makes Cavas and also sells white, *rosado* and red table wines under the Mont-Marçal trade mark. The whites include a semi-sweet, but the most noteworthy wines are the Chardonnay and the Cabernet Sauvignon varietals.

## Segura Viudas/Conde de Caralt

Founded in 1954, this bodega at San Sadurní de Noya is now, like René Barbier, owned by Freixenet and is most famous for its Cavas, but it also produces good table wines under the Conde de Caralt trade mark. The whites are made from combinations of Xarel.lo, Macabeo and Parellada. There is also a varietal Chardonnay. The *rosado* is vinified from Garnacha, Tempranillo and Cariñena. The 1992 red *reserva* was made from 85 per cent Tempranillo and 15 per cent Cabernet Sauvignon and there is also a varietal Cabernet Sauvignon.

## Jaume Serra

While the origins of this bodega date back to 1943, in its present form at Vilanova i La Geltrú it started in 1985. It makes Cavas but also a very wide and interesting range of table wines, selling the cheaper ones under the Albatos trade mark and the more expensive ones as Jaume Serra. They include a number of varietals, of which the most unusual is a semi-sweet Xarel.lo. The white Opera Prima 1994 was made from 40 per cent Macabeo, 30 per cent Parellada and 30 per cent Chardonnay, the red *crianzas* and *reservas* from 60 per cent Cabernet Sauvignon and 40 per cent Tempranillo. The red varietal wines include a Merlot and a Tempranillo.

## Miguel Torres

Old-established companies seldom lead revolutions but this one did, thanks to the inspiration and energy of a member of the fifth generation of the family, Miguel Torres Jr, who had a fine foundation on which to build. Today Torres is the most famous table-wine bodega in Spain, its wine exported to eighty-five countries and found on the lists of two-thirds of the Michelin two star restaurants in France – no one can be more insular than the French, but even they have been convinced. The fame is bolstered by high-class family-run wineries in California and in Chile, so the operation is truly international.

Old documents suggest that the family have been wine growers in Penedés since 1628, but no such date is claimed for the company. Jaime Torres emigrated to Cuba in 1855. After a distinctly shaky start he made it, in the newly burgeoning petroleum industry and in shipping. In 1870 he came home a rich man and joined with his brother, a viticulturalist, in founding the company. He had big ideas and he realized one of them when he commissioned the largest wine vat in the world: 600,000 litres, a good deal bigger than the famous Heidelberg tun. In 1904 King Alfonso of Spain visited the bodega and put this monstrous vessel to bizarre use by having lunch inside it. Jaime Torres died in the same year, unmarried, and left his wine company to his brother Miguel, who himself died two years later. It has been handed on from father to son ever since. The fourth-generation Miguel took over the company in 1932 at the age of twenty-three, following the early death of his father. Four years later the Spanish Civil War broke out and the bodega, which stood next to the railway station at Villafranca del Penedés, was taken over by the Republican Workers' committee. In January 1939 it was accidentally bombed, the bomb having been intended for the station. All was ruin. Everything, including the great vat, was destroyed. Miguel Torres, however, was undaunted. In 1940, with the war ended, he set about rebuilding the bodega and re-establishing the business. He also made one very important decision: to cease selling wine in bulk and to sell it in labelled bottles. A new opportunity then arose. In 1940 Hitler invaded France and French wines were no longer available in the United States. Miguel and his wife crossed the Atlantic (a highly dangerous undertaking at that time) and set about selling their wines. They did no advertising but hawked the bottles around restaurants, insisting that the restaurateurs should try them. Stories are told of having three dinners in an evening and of Sra Torres always carrying a bottle in her handbag. A trade was established and has never been lost. Miguel lived until 1991.

Miguel Torres of the fifth generation was born in 1941. After reading chemistry at Barcelona University he went to the University of Dijon to study viticulture and enology. Meanwhile, in 1956 his father had introduced the brands Sangre de Toro, Viña Sol and Coronas. Miguel Jr came into the company in 1962, full of ideas and well equipped to carry them out. Fortunately he was allowed to do so. In 1966 he started to plant imported vines, at first Chardonnay and Cabernet Sauvignon, to be followed by Merlot, Pinot Noir, Gewürztraminer and Riesling. Since 1975 they have been practising 'ecological viticulture' and instead of using insecticides they have attacked pests by introducing their natural predators. Who knows what will be next? He also started to use stainless steel for fermentation. All sorts of combinations of grapes were used experimentally and it is rather confusing to try to look back. But the great breakthrough came in 1979 when Torres Black Label 1970 (now called Gran Coronas Mas la Plana), in a blind tasting, won the Cabernet section in the French Gault Millau Wine Olympics, beating Château Latour 1970 into second place and leaving other illustrious names well behind. Torres wines had to be taken very seriously and Penedés, as a wine-growing area, was firmly put on the map. This wine is only made in good years; there was no 1986 or 1992, for example.

Miguel Torres took a new look at everything, and not least at the relationship between the vine and the site, matching one to the other after studying the composition of the soil and the microclimate. He also studied planting density and training the vines. Torres at the moment have thirteen vineyards making a total of 930 ha. Of these, 500 ha are trained on wires and are suitable for mechanical harvesting. The debate between those who favour hand-picking and those who move to machinery is a heated one that shows no sign of abating and does not admit of a neat resolution. In climates like that of Penedés, though, where the weather can be very hot at the time of the vintage, machinery has the real advantage that it can be used at night, when the grapes are relatively cool. This avoids premature fermentation, which can ruin quality. These vineyards provide half their requirements. The other half (entirely native varieties) is bought in. Each variety is vinified separately and there is no carbonic maceration.

In enology Torres made two particularly important changes: the use of controlled-temperature fermentation and maturing the wine in small oak casks for a carefully limited period, as has long been the practice in Bordeaux. Cultivated yeasts are used and they make some of these themselves.

In 1967 Miguel Torres married an accomplished German artist, Waltraud Maczassek. She helps with the sale of Torres wines in Germany and the Riesling is named in her honour.

The range of Torres wines is so extensive as to be rather bewildering, made all the more so by the fact that both names and grape mixes have changed from time to time over the years. All the wines are good and most are very good indeed. At present the list is as follows:

**REDS**

| | |
|---|---|
| Sangre de Toro | Garnacha and Cariñena |
| Coronas | Tempranillo and Cabernet Sauvignon |
| Viña Magdala | Pinot Noir and Tempranillo |
| Gran Sangre de Toro | Garnacha and Cariñena |
| Gran Coronas | Cabernet Sauvignon and Tempranillo |
| Viña las Torres | Merlot |
| Mas Borras | Pinot Noir |
| Gran Coronas Mas la Plana | Cabernet Sauvignon |
| (formerly Gran Coronas Black Label) | |
| Grandes Murallas | Catalan varieties. At present Garnacha, Monastrell, Garrut and Samsó |

**ROSADO**

| | |
|---|---|
| De Casta | Garnacha and Cariñena |

**WHITES**

| | |
|---|---|
| Viña Sol | Parellada |
| San Valentín (semi-sweet) | Parellada |
| Gran Viña Sol | Chardonnay and Parellada |
| Viña Esmeralda | Muscat and Gewürztraminer |

| | |
|---|---|
| Waltraud | Riesling |
| Milmanda | Chardonnay |
| Fransola | Sauvignon Blanc and Parellada |
| (formerly Gran Viña Sol Green Label) | |

Torres now claim to be the biggest wine exporters in Spain.

## Jané Ventura
This family-owned Cava house at El Vendrell, which dates from 1914, used to rely on bought-in grapes but recently planted a 15 ha vineyard with foreign varieties, mostly Cabernet Sauvignon, and has branched out to make good table wines, which now account for most of its sales. Whites and *rosados* predominate but there is a modest production of a varietal Cabernet Sauvignon.

## Pere Ventura
The bodega was founded in 1898 at San Sadurní de Noya by Pere J. Ventura Perecaula. It is at present run by eight brothers, nephews of the founder. Although principally a Cava house it markets a full range of table wines, including varietals of Chardonnay, Cabernet Sauvignon Tempranillo and a Merlot *rosado*. The two companies bearing the Ventura name are not connected.


# ALELLA

## Geography
The vineyards are only about 15 km north of the centre of Barcelona, which is one of the most densely populated cities in Europe and expanding rapidly. The result is that many of the traditional vineyards have been built over, mostly with the agreeable houses of rich Barcelona businessmen. Surprisingly in such a small DO, there are really three districts: the coastal area up to 90 m, the traditional area from 90 to 150 m, and now new sites that have been opened up, higher in the foothills of the Cordillera Catalana, though they only go up to 260 m. The style of the wine so far does not seem to have altered perceptibly.

## Climate
The traditional slopes, going up to 150 m, are typically Mediterranean: mild winters and hot summers. The average temperature is 15.8°C, the rainfall 500–600 mm, and the sunshine 2,500 hours. The

new and higher vineyards are generally rather cooler but, especially when sheltered from the sea breezes, rather more continental. It is protected from cold winds by the Sierra de Parpers. There is, however, a serious frost risk, especially in the new, higher vineyards.

## Soils
The topsoil is light and sandy – the old vineyards being over granite and the new ones over limestone – and very suitable for wine growing.

## Grapes
Authorized white varieties: Pansá Blanca (meaning white grape, a clone of Xarel.lo), Garnacha Blanca, Chardonnay, Pansá Rosada, Chenin and Macabeo. Of these, the first two are the most widely planted.

Authorized red varieties: Tempranillo (Ull de Llebre), Garnacha Tinta and Garnacha Peluda. Again, the first two are the most widely planted.

Experimental red varieties: Cabernet Sauvignon and Pinot Noir.

## Planting
Garnacha Blanca is mostly planted in the lower vineyards; Pansá Blanca is planted in the intermediate heights, from 90 to 160 m, together with the red varieties; the new, higher vineyards are planted with Pansá Blanca. Old vineyards grow bush vines trained *en vaso* but newer ones are double cordon (particularly Chardonnay) on wires.

## Vineyard area
In 1956 there were 1,500 ha, but owing to the spread of the city this was reduced to 560 ha by 1990, even including the new areas, and has now fallen even further, to 380 ha, making it one of the smallest DOs.

## Authorized yield
45.5 hl/ha.

## Wines
Red, *rosado* and white (11.5° to 13.5°) but most of the production is whites. The traditional Alella was a white vinified from 100 per cent Pansá.

## Production
4,720 hl (1990).

**Vintages**
1990 6, 1991 7, 1992 4, 1993 7, 1994 6, 1995 6, 1996 3 (but some good Chardonnay) , 1997 7.

Although wine growing in this beautiful hilly countryside goes back for many centuries, traditionally making sweet white wines, the vineyards were wiped out by phylloxera at the end of the nineteenth century and, although they continued as smallholdings, they were not recreated commercially until after the end of the Spanish Civil War, so as vineyards go they are comparatively modern. They got off to a good start. In the days when most Spanish white wines were heavy, flabby and oxidized, these (together with some in the north-west) were the conspicuous exceptions: light, fresh, delicious and usually with just a touch of sweetness. They are still undoubtedly amongst Spain's best and need a year in bottle before they show to full advantage. Some have a trace of carbon dioxide, but no more than a *spritz*. The *rosados* and reds are good without being exciting. Unfortunately, many of the vineyards were, and are, small – just a couple of hectares or so, cultivated as a hobby by people who work in Barcelona. This, coupled with the great demand for building land from the 1960s onwards, has led to their tragic reduction. As would be expected of an area so close to Barcelona, where much of the modern bodega equipment is made, vinification is completely up to date.

*Bodegas*

**Alella Vinícola, S. Coop. Ltda.**
This cooperative, founded in 1906, used once to be beyond doubt the leading wine maker; and, unlike most cooperatives, it is housed in a very beautiful building. Recently it has been facing serious competition from private bodegas and its troubles have been compounded by the fact that many of its traditional growers have disappeared. Nevertheless it continues to make good wines and to sell them under the trade mark Marfil.

**Parxet**
This privately owned bodega is housed in a beautiful farmhouse dating from the sixteenth century and beneath it there is a maze of fascinating tunnels, many of which are used to mature its excellent

Cellars in Alella

Cavas – but these belong to another chapter. It first bottled its wines
in 1920 and created its leading brand, Marqués de Alella, in 1981.
It owns 40 ha of vineyards, planted mostly with Pansá but also with
some Chardonnay and a little Chenin. In addition it buys from some
eighty growers whose average holdings are less than 2 ha, but this
puts it in control of about half the DO's wine. Most of its table wine
is white, with a little *rosado*. The Pansá Blanca is fermented very
slowly, at 15°C, and some of the wine is matured in lightly toasted
Allier oak. The Marqués de Alella wines of the 1995 vintage
included a Classico, made of 100 per cent Pansá Blanca, an unoaked
Chardonnay, and Seco, a blend of Pansá Blanca with 20 per cent
Macabeo and 20 per cent Chenin, vinified without a malolactic

fermentation and almost astringent. Nineteen ninety-six was cold and wet but they made a good Chardonnay, matured in new Allier oak and given a malolactic fermentation. These are very good wines.

## Roura

Founded as recently as 1987, this bodega has already made a name for itself by planting its 35 ha of vineyard with Sauvignon, Chardonnay, Cabernet Sauvignon, Merlot and Tempranillo, and also buys from twenty small growers. It eschews tradition in favour of experiment. It matures its Chardonnays and reds in American and Allier oak, producing such wines as Memory, from equal parts of Tempranillo and Cabernet Sauvignon, a varietal Merlot, a Pansá that has 15 per cent Sauvignon in it and a good Sauvignon Blanc that has 20 per cent Pansá in it. It also makes Cava. Its wines are very good.

## AMPURDÁN-COSTA BRAVA

The name of this DO in Catalan is Empordà-Costa Brava.

### Geography
This is where the Pyrenees meet the Mediterranean, and the vineyards stretch inland practically from the coast to a height of about 200 m. They adjoin the French wine areas of Banyuls and Côtes du Roussillon, which Catalans protest are parts of their country.

### Climate
Mediterranean, ranging from 1.5°C in winter to 29°C in summer, but the average is 16°C, though slightly less in the higher vineyards. The rainfall is 600–700 mm and there are 2,400 hours of sunshine, but it is windy and the cold northern *Tramontana* can reach gale force 12.

### Soil
Light brown with some limestone, especially in the foothills of the Pyrenees.

### Grapes
Authorized red varieties: Cariñena, Garnacha Tempranillo (Ull de Llebre), Cabernet Sauvignon and Merlot.
  Experimental red variety: Syrah.

Authorized white varieties: Macabeo, Garnacha Blanca and Chardonnay.

Experimental white varieties: Chenin Blanc, Riesling, Gewürztraminer, Parellada and Xarel.lo.

## Planting
Most of the vines are grown traditionally as bushes but absolutely everything is being tried in the experimental vineyards. However they are grown, though, they need strong support against the gales.

## Vineyard area
2,640 ha.

## Authorized yield
49 hl/ha.

## Wines
Reds and *rosados* (11.5 to 13.5°) and whites (11 to 13°), but there is also an unusual traditional wine, the orange-red, sweet, long-lived Garnatxa d'Empordà, made by drying Garnacha grapes in the sun before pressing, to give a strength of 15° with a sugar content of 5° Baumé. These may be compared with those grown across the border in France. Most of the table wines are made to be drunk young but there are some *crianzas* and above. There have also been experiments with Vino Novel del Ampurdán (in Catalan, Vi Novell del'Empordà), made in the style of Beaujolais Nouveau, but these have been received with modified rapture.

## Production
62,017 hl (1994).

## Vintages
1990 4, 1991 7, 1992 4, 1993 7, 1994 7, 1995 7, 1996 7 , 1997 3.

The Pyrenees, snowcapped through all the cooler months, make a wonderful backcloth to the agreeable, rather flat countryside that lies behind the populous beaches. It is here that the vines grow, with the greatest concentration in the north and stretching into the valleys of the foothills. Most of the vineyards are small, some of them beautifully tended but others dire. With so many small growers it is not surprising that most of the wine making is in the hands of cooperatives, and although these are showing signs of entering the modern world, lethargy prevails; the mediocre local *rosados* can be sold so easily to the holiday-makers. They are made from the Cariñena grape and account for 70 per cent of the production. And as the potential of this area for growing great wines is limited, there has not been an influx of new talent and capital. Things are beginning to look up, though, with vineyards being replanted and serious experiments with new varieties. This is not a place to look for world-class wines but nevertheless there are many agreeable ones, though most of them tend to be rather clumsy and give the impression of coming from further south than they do; indeed they remain the sort of wines made in Spain thirty or forty years ago. One grower that is up to date is Castillo Perelada, whose fine castle is one of the principal architectural landmarks of the district. Known mainly for its Cavas (most of which are made in a separate establishment at Villafranca del Penedés), it also makes a very complete range of table wines.

## Some leading bodegas

### Cavas Castillo de Perelada/Cavas del Ampurdán
Both names are used but they share the same address. This is a family-owned company, now in its third generation, and is equipped with the latest technology, using American and French oak for maturing its best wines. These include good French varietals: Chardonnay and Cabernet Sauvignon, the latter made as a *rosado* as well as a red. Its showpiece, however, is Perelada Tinto Gran Claustro; the 1993 *crianza* was made from 40 per cent Cabernet Sauvignon, 35 per cent Cariñena and 25 per cent Merlot, but the grape mix varies from vintage to vintage and in the past has included Garnacha. It has ageing qualities.

### Cellers Santa María
Although the family set up this company as recently as 1955, it has a history stretching much further back and is proud of a medal won in 1877. The present proprietor's grandfather found phylloxera locally with the aid of a magnifying glass and wrote a paper about it in 1889. The family tree goes back to 1767. The bodega has 10 ha of vines, including Garnacha, Cariñena, Macabeo and Cabernet Sauvignon. Although it operates on a small scale and everything is done by hand, it does have a modern stainless-steel electronic press and an ample supply of American oak barrels. The little cellar is said to be at least 370 years old and is one of the most beautiful it is

possible to imagine, with Gothic and Romanesque vaults – the latter probably being a good deal older than claimed. It makes *rosados* but its reds are *crianzas* and *reservas*, made from 80 per cent Cariñena and 20 per cent Garnacha. They are sold under the trade mark Gran Recosind.

## CONCA DE BARBERÁ

### Geography
The vineyards are planted in an undulating valley some 200 to 500 m above sea level, making it about equal to the Middle Penedés. Most of them are planted around the town of Montblanc in the valleys of the rivers Francolí and Auguera, which provide excellent drainage, and are sheltered by the mountain ranges of Tallat to the north, Prades to the east, and Montsant to the south. They are also planted in *concas*: basin-shaped valleys that provide shelter and, at the same time, exposure to the sun.

### Climate
Mediterranean, but away from the moderating influence of the sea, so summers go up to 35°C and in winter there are frosts. The average is 14°C, with 2,500 hours of sunshine and 450 to 550 mm rainfall. The humidity tends to be relatively high. At night it is cooled by winds from the sea.

### Soil
Light with some chalk over limestone.

### Grapes
Recommended red varieties: Trepat (Garnacha Trepat), Tempranillo (Ull de Llebre) and Garnacha.
Permitted red varieties: Cabernet Sauvignon and Merlot.
Experimental red variety: Pinot Noir.
Recommended white varieties: Macabeo and Parellada.
Experimental white variety: Chardonnay.
Other varieties are being tried and it remains to see which will succeed.

### Planting
Old vineyards (the vast majority) are planted in a rectangular pattern with 1.2 m between vines and 3.4 m between rows, trained *en*

*vaso*, but new vineyards are on wires with a possibility of mechanical harvesting in the future. There are 2,000 to 4,500 vines per ha.

**Vineyard area**
About 10,000 ha, of which 8,562 ha are in production.

**Authorized yield**
49 hl/ha.

**Wines**
Red (10.5–13°), *rosado* (10–12°), white (10–12°) and white Parellada (10–11°) are entitled to the DO. The whites and *rosados* are made as *jóvenes* and a maloactic fermentation is avoided so as to preserve their fresh acidity. Some of the reds are also made as *jóvenes*, but others are fermented in oak to provide *crianzas* and above.

**Production**
1990: red 18,160 hl, *rosado* 42,160 hl and white 126,330 hl, making a total of 186,650 hl. These are for the DO wines and the total is now probably higher, but this includes a substantial amount of Chardonnay, see below.

**Vintages**
1990 5, 1991 5, 1992 4, 1993 7, 1994 5, 1995 6, 1996 6, 1997 5.

Barberá de la Conca, after which the district is named, is a very odd and rather undistinguished little hill town with many narrow alleyways, its different levels linked by flights of stone steps; it has a rather sinister atmosphere and is full of cats and dogs. On the other hand Montblanc, the capital, is a really delightful little place, full of things worth looking at. And any visitor to the area simply must take some time off and see the Monasterio de Santa María de Poblet. *Conca* means a basin, and this is the impression one gets in the vineyards, surrounded as they are by distant mountains. They are very well tended. One of them, Castillo de Riudabella, is exceptionally beautiful and has a castle in the middle, which is a family house with holiday accommodation. The surrounding vineyards are run by Codorníu, of Penedés, who grow some of their best Chardonnay there. Torres also grow some of their best Chardonnay here in the vineyard of Milmanda.

The existence of this Chardonnay, and its current importance, shows how hard it is to understand this area. The youngest Catalan

DO, bordered by the DOs of Tarragona and Costers del Segre, it got its classification in 1989 after protracted negotiations, but already the DO seems to be shrinking in importance and it has been suggested that it should go in with Penedés as a subdistrict, which would make good sense, though local loyalty may prevent it from happening. About half of the vineyards are owned by Penedés houses and most of the rest of the wine is made by a number of cooperatives. The DO whites tend to be lightweight but are most agreeable. The DO reds are not generally of the first class but some excellent Cabernet Sauvignons are made that have ageing potential. The wine making is good and all modern facilities, such as controlled temperature fermentation, are available. But already the DO wines are getting rather hard to find, and there are two reasons for this. The first is the booming market for Cavas. The Cava makers have found that the grapes here are excellent for their wines, so several have acquired vineyards and take their wines away. The second is the phenomenon of Chardonnay and 'double vintaging'. Chardonnay grapes are grown on sites where they ripen early, are picked while they have lots of fresh acidity, and are vinified by flying wine makers (notably by Hugh Ryman) using cold fermentation to give very accessible wines that can be sold young at very competitive prices. This is good for cash flow and also means that the plant can be used twice over, with obvious economic advantages, the local classic vines coming in after it has already been used for the Chardonnay. It is hard to say where it will all lead, though.

## Some leading bodegas

### Cavas Sanstrave
A family bodega founded in 1985. It has 14 ha of vineyard growing Chardonnay, Tempranillo, Merlot and Cabernet Sauvignon, and its wines reflect these mainly French varieties. They are sold under the name Sanstrave Gasset.

### Concavins
This is a large, well-equipped bodega that was originally a cooperative but is now privately owned. It sells most of its wines under the trade marks Xipella, Santara and Castillo de Montblanc. Hugh Ryman has been the visiting wine maker since 1993 and has a stake in it. His Castillo de Montblanc Dry White Wine, made mostly from

Macabeo, is an excellent wine with plenty of fruit and good length, but the Chardonnays are at present less impressive. Good reds include varietal Merlots and Cabernet Sauvignons.

### Coop Vinícola Sarral
A larger cooperative which bottles a proportion of its wines under the trade mark Prat de Medea but also sells in bulk.

## COSTERS DEL SEGRE

### Geography
The meaning of the name is 'the banks of the Segre', a river that rises in the Pyrenees and flows through Lérida (Lleida in Catalan). Although there may be some poetry in the name there is little reality, as the vineyards are separated into four parts. The most important, though smallest, is Raimat, to the north-west of Lérida and near the border of the province of Huesca. Artesa lies to the north-east of Lérida, actually by the river. The other two subzones – Vall de Riu Corb and Las Garrigas – are to the south-east, next to each other and within the Province of Tarragona. The height above sea level is 200 to 350 m.

### Climate
Continental, rising to 35°C in summer and falling to zero or below in winter, with an average of 14–15°C. There is a big drop at night: at Raimat in summer it falls from 32–35°C to 17–18°C. The climate is harshest in Artesa, which has a long, cold winter. Rainfall is 300–440 mm but is unusually unpredictable; in 1995 the total at Raimat was only 160 mm but in January 1996 180 mm fell in one month. There are 2,800 hours of sunshine.

### Soil
Very alkaline. Sandy topsoil over limestone.

### Grapes
Authorized red varieties: Garnacha, Tempranillo (Ull de Llebre or Gotim Bru), Cabernet Sauvignon, Merlot, Monastrell, Trepat, Mazuelo (Cariñena) and Pinot Noir.

Authorized white varieties: Macabeo, Parellada, Xarel.lo, Chardonnay and Garnacha Blanca.

Experimental white varieties: Sauvignon Blanc and Albariño.

## Planting

There are still old vineyards planted *en vaso* but modern ones are planted on wires for mechanical harvesting, the height of the trellises varying with the vine variety. The density is 2,000 per ha. At Raimat the Chardonnay, on trellises 1.1 m high, has 3.2 m between rows and 1.7 m between vines, whereas with the Cabernet Sauvignon the trellises are 90 cm high and there are 2.1 m between rows.

## Vineyard area

4,080 ha, of which 3,700 ha are actually planted.

## Authorized yield

65 hl/ha for whites and 52 hl/ha for reds.

## Wines

Reds, *rosados* and whites, all between 9.5° and 13.5°. Most whites and *rosados* are sold as *jóvenes* but reds can go as high as *gran reserva*. Many of the wines are sold as varietals. There are also sparkling wines from 10.8° to12.8° and *vino de aguja* from 9° to 11°.

## Production

115,000 hl.

## Vintages

1988 5, 1989 6, 1990 5, 1991 6, 1992 6, 1993 7, 1994 5, 1995 7, 1996 7 (white wines 5), 1997 5.

This DO cannot be summed up in a few words; it is too complex. Yet a great deal of it can be summed up in one word: Raimat. The other three districts usually make rather rustic wines from Spanish grape varieties. In general, the reds come from Artesa, the whites from Riu Corb and Las Garrigas. But many of the white wines are taken off to Penedés to be used as base wines for Cava, and there is also something of that free and easy movement of wines that takes place throughout Cataluña. Traditionally it was an area of small growers who took their grapes to cooperatives, and much of the wine is still made that way, but the rise of Raimat, making world-class wines and exporting a substantial part of them, changed the whole picture. Now, at one end of the scale there are still the cooperatives, at the other end Raimat, and in between a whole gamut of privately owned wineries, ranging from the boutique to the substantial, and most of them anxious to emulate Raimat's success. It will be an interesting area to watch, and wines coming from here are usually at least worth looking at.

The story of the creation of Raimat is an extraordinary one: the story of a far-sighted entrepreneur and wine lover. Don Manuel Raventós Doménech was a member of the family that owns the great Cava house of Codorníu in Sant Sadurní de Noya in Penedés. He knew the area that is now Raimat, and which in those days was just a desert – though wine had been grown there many years before – and he learned that an irrigation canal had been cut through it in 1910, bringing water from the Pyrenees. He thought that with irrigation the ground would blossom – and how right he was! But it was not so simple as that. In 1914 he bought an estate of 3,200 ha with a castle and one tree. Nothing else grew. The castle has foundations dating back to the Moors but was substantially rebuilt in the seventeenth century – a beautiful place. The tree was standing next to it. (As a sideline of history Franco took the castle over and stayed in it during the crucial battle of the Ebro.) The rest of the land was bare and 300 to 350 m above sea level. On the castle was a coat of arms with a bunch of grapes (*raïm* in Catalan) and a hand (*mat*), pointing to its ancient connection with wine growing, hence the name he gave to his new property. And he created not just an estate but a whole village, complete with houses for his workers, a school, and even a railway station. The irrigation was put in hand, but the ground was no good for vines as it was infertile and salt-laden, so his first crop was mainly lucerne, followed by pine trees. These put things right and in due time they were grubbed up. In 1918 he optimistically built the winery, and he did it magnificently. The Raventós family has always had a feeling for architecture; the buildings at Codorníu itself are described in the Cava chapter. At Raimat, Don Manuel commissioned Rubió Bellver, one of the great Gaudí's pupils and followers, to design a huge avant-garde building in reinforced concrete, the first in this material to be built in Spain. It has worn very well indeed. The fine wines that were to fill it took some time to come, though. At first the traditional Penedés varieties were planted: Macabeo, Parellada and Monastrell, for Cava. But the family had noticed what was going on in the rest of the world and took advice from the University of California, Davis, and Fresno, which advised that they should experiment with Cabernet Sauvignon and Chardonnay. They did, but these were not successful until, with continuing advice from California, they found the right rootstocks and methods of planting. Cabernet Sauvignon and Chardonnay were being grown successfully by 1975 and Merlot and Tempranillo by 1980. In 1988 the vineyards were planted as follows: white grapes, Chardonnay 300 ha, Parellada 93 ha, Macabeo 90 ha, Xarel.lo 59 ha; red grapes, Cabernet Sauvignon 400 ha, Tempranillo 95 ha, Merlot 55 ha, Pinot Noir 15 ha and some Monastrell. Since then, the vineyard area has expanded to 1,200 ha and experiments with other varieties continue, including Albariño. They are now also being advised by the Australian wine maker Richard Smart. The rest of the land is planted with fruit trees and cereal crops. Driving from Lérida, you know at once by the vast and perfectly tended vineyards when you have reached the edge of the Raimat estate. Then suddenly there is a large vineyard that looks totally chaotic and you assume it belongs to someone else. But no! It is an experiment with minimal pruning, which is being tried in Jerez, too. Experiments are continuous on this estate. Most of the vineyards are designed for mechanical harvesting which can be done at night – a good thing here in view of the heat during the day at vintage time – and it only takes an average of eighteen minutes to get the grapes to the press. Cultivation is almost entirely organic. There is a certain amount of irrigation, however, in hot weather, from eighteen reservoirs. Vintaging usually starts in mid-August, beginning with Chardonnay picked at 8°C for Cava followed by Chardonnay picked at 13°C for table wine.

Raimat is by no means the only bodega in the DO of Costers del Segre but it is by far and away the largest and most important; without it there would be no DO. Now that it has shown the way, others are following and are beginning to compete, but most of the wines produced by the small growers still go into Cava.

### Some leading bodegas

### Castell del Remei

The bodega, south-west of the town of La Fuliola, was founded in 1871, but it has only really taken off since it was bought by the Cusiné family in 1982. It has a 40 ha vineyard. It is a beautiful place with a castle and chapel in addition to its bodega and restaurant. Its wines include a white made from 50 per cent each of Chardonnay and Sauvignon, a *rosado* made from 60 per cent Cabernet

46

Sauvignon and 40 per cent Merlot, and red *crianzas*, one (Gotim Bru) made from 85 per cent Tempranillo and 15 per cent Cabernet Sauvignon, and others from Merlot and from Cabernet Sauvignon. All the wines used only to be sold in Cataluña but they are being launched on the export markets and are worth looking for.

### L'Olivera
This small cooperative dates from 1975 and sells a number of interesting white wines, including varietals such as Macabeo and Chardonnay, both barrel-fermented. The Parellada has 30 per cent Chardonnay added.

### Raimat
Much has been written above because the whole story of the DO is so closely bound up with Raimat. As the vineyards expanded, the original winery, large though it is, proved inadequate and a new one was added. Architecturally this fully maintained the aesthetic traditions of the Raventós family. Designed by Domingo Triay and built in 1988, it is as ultra-modern as the old winery was in 1918 and will wear as well. To build it, a hill was excavated to 90 m and much is below ground, but what one sees is a glass structure in the shape of a pyramid with the top cut off, or a Mexican pyramid; on the flat top there is a vineyard of Cabernet Sauvignon. It is original to the point of eccentricity, but none the worse for that, and it is extremely efficient.

For making red wines Raimat uses an Australian Potter gravity fermenter, in which the grapes are pressed gently by their own weight, only extracting half the juice. The white grapes are lightly pressed by a modern belt press which produces a similarly light extraction. All the grapes are destalked. Red wines are fermented at 26 to 28°C, and whites at 18°C. Most unusually, a malolactic fermentation is effected in the white wines before the main fermentation. Of the whites only the Chardonnays see oak, but the reds are generally oak-aged. The casks are 300 litres rather than the usual 225, so as to limit the oakiness imparted. Regardless of where the oak comes from, they are all coopered in Spain and are kept for a maximum of six years. American oak is used for Cabernet Sauvignon and Tempranillo, French for Pinot Noir, and both French and American for Chardonnay, while Merlot starts in American and finishes in French.

There is an exceptional range of high-quality table wines, and also good Cavas, which will be considered separately. The white wines include a straight Chardonnay without oak and an oak-fermented Chardonnay Selección Especial. The most widely distributed of the reds is Abadia, a blend of 65 per cent Cabernet Sauvignon, 25 per cent Tempranillo and 10 per cent Merlot (though the exact blend varies from year to year), fermented separately, producing a well-balanced wine, with some complexity and good length, that ages well and is sold at a very competitive price. The top range includes excellent varietals of Merlot, Pinot Noir, Tempranillo and (exceptionally good) Cabernet Sauvignon, which has 10 to 15 per cent Merlot blended in, and a *rosado* made from 100 per cent Cabernet Sauvignon. They also make good-value wines sold under the Gran Calesa trade mark by Marks & Spencer.

**Vall de Baldomar**
Founded as recently as 1989, this bodega has already established a reputation. Its trade marks include Baldomá.

## PLA DE BAGES

### Geography
Before this DO came into being in 1995 the wines were sold under local names, notably Artés. The principal town is now Manresa, towards the south of the DO area and in its narrowest part. It lies to the north-west of Barcelona, in fairly mountainous country, isolated from the other Catalan DO areas. The vineyards are planted at heights of 200 to 500 m, averaging 400.

### Climate
Mediterranean, with limited rainfall. But owing to the mountainous terrain there are wide variations and significant microclimates. It is driest in the north-east and wettest in the south-east. The average temperature is 13°C and the average rainfall 500 to 600 mm.

### Soils
These again vary significantly from place to place, but are generally loam with clay or sand and some chalk.

### Grapes
Authorized red varieties: Garnacha, Tempranillo (Ull de Llebre), Merlot and Cabernet Sauvignon.

Experimental red variety: Syrah.

Authorized white varieties: Macabeo, Parellada, Picapoll and Chardonnay.

Sumoll is also grown locally but this is not suitable for quality wines and is used for non-DO reds.

## Planting
2,000 to 4,500 per ha on a pattern of 1.4 by 2.8 m with cordon pruning.

## Vineyard area
500 ha.

## Authorized yield
Of grapes, 5,000 kg/ha for reds and 7,500 kg/ha for whites.

## Wines
Reds of 12.5°, rosados of 12° and whites of 11.5 to 12°, with a small production of sparkling wines.

## Production
4,425 hl (1995/6).

## Vintages
1996 6, 1997 6.

Wine growing throughout Cataluña has an ancient history, and no doubt this area has one like the rest, but little seems to be known about it. The name Bages is derived from the ancient Roman city of Bacassis, which in turn was said to have been named after Bacchus, the Roman god of wine, but it would be unwise to build any theories on this. What is more certain is that in the more recent past, much of the wine was destined for Cavas. More recently still the growers have decided to develop a market for table wines, and there is no doubt that the potential is there, notably for red wines. Recent plantings have largely been of French varieties. How this new DO will develop remains to be seen, and the wines have certainly not yet reached the top flight, but it is certainly worth watching.

### Some leading bodegas

### Cellers Cooperativa d'Artés
Founded in 1908, this is the biggest as well as the oldest established

bodega, a cooperative with 250 members having 3,000 ha of vines between them – six times the area of the DO. Naturally, most of its wines are therefore no more than table wines, but the DO wines are sold under the name Artium. They include a varietal white Picapoll, a varietal Cabernet Sauvignon *crianza* and a red *crianza* sold as Artium Rocas-Albas, made from 70 per cent Tempranillo, 20 per cent Merlot and 10 per cent Sumoll.

### SAT Masies D'Avinyo
A small, modern bodega founded in 1983. Its wines include a white 'Chardonnay' made from 85 per cent Chardonnay and 15 per cent Picapoll, a *rosado* made from 85 per cent Cabernet Sauvignon and 15 per cent Garnacha, varietals from Cabernet Sauvignon and from Merlot, a red *joven* called Bacasis, made from 50 per cent Tempranillo with 25 per cent each of Cabernet Sauvignon and Merlot, and a red *reserva* made from 70 per cent Cabernet Sauvignon, 20 per cent Merlot and 10 per cent Syrah.

### Ramón Roqueta
A small, modern bodega making good wines that include white varietals from Macabeo and from Chardonnay, a *rosado* from Garnacha, and red varietals from Tempranillo and from Cabernet Sauvignon. The labels are modern and the Catalan or French names are used for the grape varieties.


## PRIORATO (PRIORAT in Catalan)

### Geography
The vineyards are in the mountains, ranging from 100 to 700 m. above sea level with an average height of 450 m. Although there is a little flat land in the valley of the river Siurana, most of the vineyards are on terraces carved out of 15 per cent or even 30 per cent slopes and terribly hard to work.

### Climate
The climate is unique and helps to distinguish this *comarca* from all the others in Catalonia. It is sufficiently inland to be continental, but high in the mountains, so that it can freeze in winter to about −6°C, with a maximum of 35°C in summer but sometimes rising to no more than 26°C. The mean annual temperature is 15°C and the mean summer temperature is 24 to 26°C. It is affected by cold north

winds and warm, moist winds from the Mediterranean. The rainfall averages 600 mm but the rain falls only in limited periods: October–November and March–April. There are 2,600 hours of sunshine.

## Soil
The area is of volcanic origin and the topsoil, of quartzite and slate, looks grey, sometimes almost black. Underneath there is a base of *llicorella*, a reddish slate with particles of quartzite (mica), through which the roots of the vines penetrate deeply. Bits of quartzite sparkle in the sun. In the higher vineyards there is a subsoil of schist, which passes in a stratum beneath central Spain to re-emerge in the best port vineyards of the Douro.

## Grapes
Recommended red variety: Garnacha Tinta.

Permitted red varieties: Garnacha Peluda, Cariñena and Cabernet Sauvignon.

Experimental red varieties: Syrah and Pinot Noir.

Permitted white varieties: Garnacha Blanca, Macabeo and Pedro Ximénez.

Experimental white varieties: Chenin Blanc and Parellada.

## Planting
*En vaso*, with some on espalier double cordon Royat.

## Vineyard area
17,018 ha, of which 1,756 ha are planted with vineyards but only 800 ha are at present yielding wine. These figures, however, are out of date and should be revised upwards.

## Authorized yield
42 hl/ha, but in practice this is never even approached in the most serious vineyards, where the vines are often very old and the yield is minuscule: 5–6 hl/ha.

## Wines
Practically the whole of the production is red wines, which range from *joven* to *gran reserva*, and the regulations are rather different from the normal ones. *Crianzas* must have a minimum of twelve months in oak and twelve months in bottle, *reservas* twelve and twenty-four, *gran reservas* twenty-four and forty-eight. All are unusually strong (13.75° to 18°). American and French oak are used. The whites and *rosados*, which are no more than 10 per cent

of the total, are all *jóvenes*. But in addition to these there are two kinds of traditional wines: *generosos*, mostly from Pedro Ximénez (14° to 18°) and *rancios*, which must be aged for at least four years (14° to 20°).

**Production**
10,546 hl (1993), but 66,000 hl may in future be expected in a good year.

**Vintages**
1980 6, 1981 5, 1982 6, 1983 5, 1984 5, 1985 6, 1986 5, 1987 5, 1988 5, 1989 5, 1990 5, 1991 5 (quantity reduced by hail), 1992 6, 1993 7, 1994 7, 1995 7, 1996 7, 1997 4.

Priorato is a very special place. Up in the mountains the scenery is indescribably beautiful, and the wines are some of the finest grown anywhere in the world. It is an exciting place to be in, too. The wine makers are young, doing the work themselves vigorously, aiming for the heights and scaling them. Their work has been well recognized, and in one respect this is unfortunate, for their wines are not only amongst the best anywhere, they are also amongst the most expensive. As with all great wines, their potential lies in the soil and the microclimate. It is the work and dedication of the wine growers and enologists that enables this to be realized.

There is a long tradition of wine growing stretching back, as it so often does, to a monastery. There is a story that a shepherd tending his flocks in the valley of the river Siurana had a vision of angels rising as if up a staircase to the heavens. He told a travelling order of Carthusian monks who established a monastery on the spot in 1162, and of course made wine. Another version ascribes the vision to a monk. In the landscape and atmosphere of Priorato one can believe it. The monastery was called Priorat de Scala Dei – the Priory of the Staircase of God. Today it is a beautiful ruin but the old monastic cellars are still in use.

It is here that the Garnacha shows what it can do if the yield is kept low enough and the wine well made. Far from oxidizing easily and having a short life, the best Priorato wines need to be kept until they are twelve to fifteen years old before they begin to show their best and will clearly last much longer, though they can be drunk with pleasure when they are five or six years old, especially if they are given time to breathe, and they are best decanted. In the past

The landscape of Priorato

they had the reputation of being practically black, enormously strong, heady and unsubtle. They were used for blending and in Bordeaux made a cheaper substitute for Hermitage; nevertheless there were some good ones which were sought out by people who knew about them, and some are still being made in the old-fashioned way, mostly by the cooperative, which was formed by amalgamating several small ones, and is well equipped; it still produces about 70 per cent of the wine.

The revolution came with an influx of young wine makers, which began in the 1970s in the high country at Gratallops. They appreciated the area's enormous potential at a time when it looked as if it would be abandoned. Vines were dying and not being replaced, while the countryside was becoming depopulated. They had their first success with the creation of the DO in 1975. Then they realized the potential by a number of steps. In the first place they were content with very low yields from very old vines pruned short. Tasting the wine from seventy-year-old Garnacha vines one can see at once how much better and more concentrated it is than wines made by the same wine maker from fifteen year old vines. They were at pains to keep the yield down rather than to increase it. Most of the growers do not irrigate at all, despite the climate; the exception is Clos Martinet, which uses a sophisticated and unusual system producing a fine spray on the surface. The vines reach down for water by growing roots down 12 or even 20 m – but some of them die. The newcomers harvested the grapes earlier, while they still had enough acidity to secure a good balance in the wine. They saw, too, that the addition of small proportions of foreign varieties would add new dimensions of complexity. The Syrah, for instance, is hard to grow here, where it is planted towards the top of the slopes, but is well worth while. A small proportion of Cabernet Sauvignon also helps, and is grown on the cooler sites, sometimes on north-facing slopes. But the major grape is still the Garnacha. Cariñena gives a much higher yield and good colour but less intensity, and is very little used by the new wine makers, though very old vines can give good results. Picking the grapes at perfect maturity sometimes involves as many as twelve passes through the vineyard.

The whites and *rosados* are mostly cold-fermented in stainless-steel tanks, though some are fermented in Limousin casks; they do not have a malolactic fermentation. Some of the reds are also made in stainless steel, others, particularly the old-fashioned sort, in epoxy-lined cement tanks, and they are all put through a malolactic fermentation before cask ageing. In the boutique wineries of Gratallops, where the exquisite new-style wines are made, everything is of the latest, though some growers have fibreglass as well as stainless steel. The old-fashioned wines are then matured in American oak, but for the new ones there is also French oak. René Barbier uses only French oak. The strength of the new wines is generally kept down to a modest 13.75° but does sometimes go up to 16°.

## Some leading bodegas

### René Barbier Fill/Clos Mogador

Run by René Barbier with his wife and son in an old grange, this is a real family concern: a perfect example of a small, dedicated winery. Sr Barbier is Spanish but of French descent and is a member of the family that owned the eponymous bodega in Penedés, which is now part of the Freixenet group, but there is no connection. There is a beautiful little bodega surrounded by 18 ha of vineyards on a superb mountain site: a little bit of paradise, but very hard work. It is practically a one-wine bodega, producing a superb red wine called Clos Mogador from Garnacha, Cabernet Sauvignon and Syrah, matured in French oak. It has no fining or filtration but precipitates naturally when the door is opened in winter to let the cool air in. It also makes 200 cases of wine a year from a friend's vineyard, Clos Erasmus, which is sold entirely in the USA.

### Cellers de Scala Dei
This is one of the largest and oldest-established of the privately owned bodegas, founded in 1973 by Manuel Peyra de Ameller, who still runs it, in the delightful village of Scala Dei, and housed in old monastery buildings. The date 1692 appears above the cellar door. The monks used to control the fermentation temperature by circulating water round the fermentation tanks in the cellar. It took centuries to reinvent that process, but now everything is up to date and thermostatically controlled. It has 70 ha of vineyards, which are unusual in including Chenin, and even more unusual here in being trained on wires. It makes a very full range of wines: white, *rosado* and red up to *gran reserva*. The whites include a Garnacha Blanca which is matured on its lees in Allier casks. Called Blanc Prior, it is a wine to look for, though the oak is distinctly prominent. The red Cartoixa D'Scala Dei is 100 per cent Garnacha and is a really excellent *reserva*. The new, young wine makers have taken the glamour, and their wines, with their tiny productions and the complexity introduced by infusions of foreign grapes, may have the edge, but this bodega helped to lead the way and its wines are good, even though they got left behind for a time; however, a new wine maker has been appointed and may well bring them to the fore again.

### Costers del Siurana
Privately owned by Carles Pastrana and Mariona Jarque, who bought the property in 1984–5 and got going in 1987, this bodega produces superb wines from four vineyards, amounting to 100.5 ha, which are vinified separately and supply all their needs. An enormous amount of trouble is taken in planting, fitting each variety into the most appropriate aspect and microclimate. They introduced Cabernet Sauvignon, Merlot and Syrah, while retaining the indigenous varieties and restoring a vineyard of fifty-year-old

Cariñena to health. The flagship wine is Clos de L'Obac, first made in 1989 from 35 per cent each of Garnacha and Cabernet Sauvignon and 10 per cent each of Syrah, Merlot and Cariñena, fermented at 22 to 26°C in 100 hl containers and matured in 100 per cent new French oak. Miserere, first created in 1990, comes not far behind it, from one of the old vineyards of the Priory, Mas d'en Bruno. This is made from 27 per cent each Garnacha and Cabernet Sauvignon, 26 per cent Tempranillo, 10 per cent Merlot and 10 per cent Cariñena. The wine is matured in 50 per cent new oak, the remainder being of the second year. Only 60 to 70 per cent of the grapes picked are used for these wines after a careful selection; the rest are used to make *cupadas*. After the grapes have been selected, they are all fermented together. There are only about 1,000 cases of each. The *cupada*, which contains Garnacha, Cabernet Sauvignon, Cariñena, Tempranillo, Merlot and Syrah, is matured in three-year-old French oak and is sold as Usatges, a wine that does not pretend to be great but that nevertheless is very good. There is also a white wine which is made in very small quantities for friends and restaurants and which came about rather by chance as the grapes – Garnacha Blanca, Viura, Moscatel de Alejandría and Parellada – happened to be there. Fermented in Limousin oak, it is dry and very good but, at any rate when young, is very oaky. Finally there is a very small production of delicious sweet red wine – Dolç de L'Obac – first made in 1991 from very ripe grapes from the Clos de L'Obac vineyard, 80 per cent Garnacha, 10 per cent Syrah and 10 per cent Cabernet Sauvignon. It is really what might be described as a *beerenauslese*. It is fermented in new French oak and the skins are taken out through a large hole in the top after the fermentation and maceration: a unique method. The fermentation is blocked with 1° alcohol and cooling. It is strong stuff at 16°.

### Mas Martinet Viticultors
The Pérez i Ovejero family had a wine-growing tradition but founded this bodega as recently as 1982, with 7 ha of terraced vineyard. Unlike most of the younger generation of growers, they do not avoid irrigation but are proud of their own system, which produces a very fine spray and does not appear to dilute the wines, which taste anything but diluted. They make only reds. The best grapes – about 40 per cent – are used for Clos Martinet; the second wine is Martinet Bru. Both are matured in Allier oak, the latter in

three-year-old casks. While the Martinet Bru is a good wine, the Clos Martinet is very good indeed; and as the vineyard is still young one can only suppose that it will get better and better. The grape mix for both is 70 per cent Garnacha and Cabernet Sauvignon with 15 per cent each of Merlot and Syrah.

## Masía Barril

Hermanos Barril is one of the old brigade of bodegas, established in 1931. It started to bottle its wines in 1981 and produces a complete range of reds with various alcoholic strengths: Extra (13.5°), Tipico (15°), Classico (16.6°) and Especial (17.75°). The Tipico is the wine most easily found; made from 75 per cent Garnacha and 25 per cent Cariñena, it is massive. There are also whites and a *rancio*. Wood is not used.

## Alvaro Palacios

Alvaro Palacios, a scion of the famous Rioja family, is one of the best and most dynamic of the new wave of young wine makers. His unusually wide knowledge and experience includes a stint in the Napa Valley and another at Château Pétrus, so his sights are aimed high. Instead of taking the easy course and going into the family bodegas, he wanted to do his own thing, and looked for a vineyard not in Rioja where he could grow world-class wine. He found it in Priorato. For his bodega he acquired a little old disused theatre where the proscenium arch rises mysteriously behind the fermentation tanks. Arriving in 1989, he in fact found and bought two vineyards: L'Ermita and Finca Dofí. L'Ermita, 550 m above sea level, was planted with very old Garnacha vines. It slopes north-east, so it does not get a very great exposure to the sun and this results in unusually fragrant wines. He is now establishing new vineyards on terraces prepared with an enormous amount of work. Most of the oak used is French but there is a small proportion of American, which adds an element of creaminess. The various vine varieties are fermented separately. L'Ermita 1995 was made from 80 per cent Garnacha, 15 per cent Cabernet Sauvignon and 5 per cent Cariñena. The Finca Dofí 1994 was made from 64 per cent Garnacha, 25 per cent Cabernet Sauvignon, and the rest a blend of Syrah and Merlot. Las Terrasses 1995 was made from 50 per cent Garnacha Peluda, 40 per cent Cariñena and 10 per cent Cabernet Sauvignon. L'Ermita is already one of the most expensive wines in the world, and it is not overpriced. Production is very small. In 1994 there were about 5,875 bottles of L'Ermita and 13,250 bottles of Finca Dofí.

## TARRAGONA

### Geography
The largest area in Cataluña, it is divided into two parts. Tarragona Campo surrounds the ancient city in an arc of approximately 30 km and in height ranges from sea level (though the lowest vineyards are at about 40 m) to about 200 m, where the mountains begin and the vineyards end. The other part is Falset, which is itself divided into two. The comarca Falset is just beyond Reus in the direction of Zaragoza, in a mountain valley some 360 m high and rising to 450 m, with the Serra de Montalt to the south and the Serra de Montsant (leading to Priorato – but that is a different story) to the north. The other part of Falset is Falset/Ribera de Ebro which, as its name suggests, goes down into the valley of the River Ebro in the direction of Mora de Ebro, where the vineyards are at a height of about 100 m.

### Climate
In the Campo the climate is pure Mediterranean, but as you go inland towards Falset it becomes slightly more continental: hotter in summer and colder in winter. Tarragona has a most agreeable climate to live in: the average temperature is 16°C, falling to 3°C in winter and rising to 35°C in summer, though there are colder, frosty days in Falset during the winter. Rain falls mainly in September and October and averages 500 mm in El Campo, 500 to 600 mm in Falset, and 305 mm in Ribera de Ebro. There are 2,600 hours of sunshine.

### Soils
In El Campo these are generally dark brown with some limestone, in Falset they are loam and limestone over granite, and in Ribera de Ebro they are more fertile and alluvial along the river.

### Grapes
Authorized red varieties: Garnacha, Cariñena and Tempranillo (Ull de Llebre), the last being only 'permitted' in El Campo.

Experimental red varieties: Cabernet Sauvignon, Merlot and Syrah.

Authorized white varieties: Macabeo, Xarel.lo, Parellada and Garnacha Blanca.

Experimental white varieties: Chardonnay and Moscatel.

Additional varieties, however, are certainly grown.

## Planting

The grapes are grown *en vaso* in the older vineyards and on wires in the newer ones, but there is a unique, local rectangular pattern: fourteen vines by seven, with 1.4 m between the vines and 2.8 m between the rows.

## Vineyard area

18,422 ha (1994).

## Authorized yield

El Campo: white 70 hl/ha, red 59.5 hl/ha. Falset: 52.5 hl/ha.

## Wines

There is a bewildering variety. Tarragona Campo white, *rosado* and red, all with 11 to 13°. Falset red, with the same strength. Tarragona Clásico Licoroso, with a minimum of 13.5° (it can go up to 23°) which must be aged in oak vats of less than 2,000 litres for a minimum of twelve years. All can be sweet, medium or dry, but most are dry. And there are *rancio* wines, which must have a minimum of 14°. But there are many versions of each category. All the white and *rosado* wines are sold as *jóvenes*. Some of the red wines and *vinos de licor* are aged according to a unique local system. There are no *crianzas*. *Reservas* must spend a minimum of twelve months in oak and twenty-four in bottle, while for *gran reservas* these periods are respectively increased to twenty-four and thirty-six, but many are in practice aged for longer, especially *vinos de licor*. Traditional *rancios* are still made in demijohns and are fully oxidized.

## Production

439,404 hl (1993).

## Vintages

Some are said to be better than others but really there is little variation.

Tarragona is easily the biggest and easily the least distinguished Catalan DO. A journey through it shows that most of the land does not look promising for growing fine wines. Yet until the rise of Penedés and Cava in the 1960s it was the only Catalan wine that drinkers in the United Kingdom had ever heard of. And it had a terrible reputation. In the nineteenth century it used to be sold as 'Tarragona port' and was known as 'poor man's port' or, more commonly, 'red biddy'. These were the red *vinos de licor*, imported to be sold very cheaply. They are still made, but not much, though the best have a certain quality about them and some are matured on the *solera* system. It also has a remarkable and very long tradition of making wines for the church, which lays down a very strict specification. Some of its wines are sold in bulk to France to form the base wines for proprietary aperitifs and for strengthening weak wines: a very ancient trade. It is an area that can, and does, grow practically everything but so far has achieved no identity with quality wines. Indeed, some of the best of them, in the Catalan tradition, are taken into other districts for blending, including some of the best of the whites, which are used for Cava. Most are made by cooperatives but some of these are passing into private hands. Tarragona *clásico* is generally 100 per cent Garnacha, which can ripen so as to achieve 17° alcohol unaided and still leave sugar in the wine, which is certainly remarkable. Of the table wines, the Campo reds tend to be fairly light, while those from Falset are more massive. I have yet to find an amateur of Tarragona wines, yet the potential is there. It would have needed a very far-sighted person visiting the Penedés in the 1950s to predict where they are today. The same could happen to parts of Tarragona, especially Falset.

## Some leading bodegas

### José Anguera Beyme

A family bodega founded in 1830 and now in its fourth generation, with 30 ha of vineyard at Damós, planted 50 per cent with Syrah, the rest being Garnacha, Cabernet Sauvignon and a little Cariñena. The Syrah shows through strongly in the good red wines. Joan d'Anguera is a *joven* and Finca L'Argata has ten months in American oak and shows considerable ageing potential.

### Cooperativa Agrícola i Caixa Agraria

Some highly praised reds.

## Cooperativa Agrícola Capçanes
It produces a full range, with the Flor de Maig trade mark used for the best, and is now busy moving up-market.

## Cooperativa Agrícola Falsetenca
A wide range which includes *rosados* and reds that are well thought of. The Castell de Falset 1993 *reserva* was made from 40 per cent Cabernet Sauvignon, 30 per cent Tempranillo, 20 per cent Garnacha and 10 per cent Cariñena and was given sixteen months in wood.

## Cooperativa de Masroig
Some good reds.

## de Muller
Established in 1851, this family-owned bodega is perhaps the largest in the DO, with its business founded on wines for the church, which it makes in four styles, and noted for its *vinos de licor*. Moscatel Oro is unoaked, while Moscatel Añejo has several months in small American oak casks. Both are excellent. It has a range of table wines: dry and semi-sweet white, *rosado* and red. It has 100 ha of vineyards and a new, modern winery at Reus. It is also active in Priorato and Terra Alta.

## Emilio Miro Salvat
A small bodega producing, amongst other things, *rancio* and *vino de licor* as well as some non-DO wines.

## TERRA ALTA

### Geography
Remote in the mountains in the southernmost part of the province of Tarragona, it borders with Zaragoza and Teruel, with vineyards on rolling hills at an average height of 400 m and rising to 960 m.

### Climate
Continental, with very hot summers and very cold winters, moderated only slightly by the influence of the Mediterranean. The average temperature is 16.4°C, with rainfall of 400 to 600 mm and 2,700 hours of sunshine.

## Soils
Deep and well drained with some limestone and variable amounts of clay.

## Grapes
Authorized red varieties: Cariñena (Mazuelo), Garnacha Peluda, Garnacha Tinta, Cabernet Sauvignon, Merlot and Tempranillo.
  Experimental red varieties: Pinot Noir and Pinot Meunier.
  Authorized white varieties: Garnacha Blanca, Macabeo, Parellada and Moscatel.
  Experimental white varieties: Chardonnay and Colombard.

## Planting
Generally *en vaso* but with trellises taking over; 2,500 to 3,000 per ha.

## Vineyard area
10,800 ha with 9,800 ha in full production.

## Authorized yield
56 hl/ha but in practice a good deal less.

## Wines
Reds (12–25°), *rosados* (12–16°), whites (12.5–16°), *rancios* and *mistelas* at least 15°.

## Production
150,000 hl (1995), though in a good year 400,000 hl are expected.

## Vintages
Most vintages have been good but 1991 was very good, while 1988 and 1996 were exceptional.

This area is almost as beautiful as Priorato, and before the roads came it must have been just as remote. It is high in the mountains, and on the horizon there are misty mountain ranges with more mountain ranges rising behind them. Some of the vineyards, as in Priorato, are on terraces fashioned by massive work and others, more manageable, occupy plateaux. This used to be, and to some extent still is, a backwoods area, with very old, low-yielding vineyards, producing fortified *rancios* and clumsy table wines of staggering strength. These have clearly had their day. Some are still made that way and the startling strengths permitted by the DO allow for this. But the Consejo Regulador saw that the future lay in making lighter wines and encouraged the replanting of vineyards to increase the yield, which had fallen to 11 hl/ha, and the trial of new varieties. Many of the wines are made by cooperatives, and it is worth making the journey just to see the wonderful art nouveau buildings of the cooperatives in El Pinell de Brai and Gandesa, designed by Cèsar Martinell, a pupil of Gaudí. Many of their wines are sold in bulk to the Cava houses. This is clearly an area with real potential. Some very agreeable modern, light wines are already being made and boutique wineries are moving in. Leading bodegas include Pedro Rovira, which is also very big in Tarragona, and Vinos Piñol. They both make ranges of modern wines and Rovira makes some fortified ones. The cooperatives are actively bringing themselves up to date and boutique wineries are beginning to emerge. This is a DO to watch.

The cooperative at Gandesa

## OTHER WINES

There are three Catalan CVs: Anoia in the province of Barcelona, Bajo Ebro-Montesiá in the province of Tarragona, and Conca de

Tremp in the province of Lérida. The first-named grows wines for Cava, but apart from that they produce nothing of interest.

There is, however, the young bodega of Mas Gil with a 12 ha vineyard growing Cabernet Sauvignon, Merlot, Syrah and Monastrell for red wines and Viognier, Marsanne and Rousanne for whites. Nestling in the delightful hills near Calonge, behind the Costa Brava, the bodega was bought by Englishman Reggie Williams and his wife Phoebe, who was an enthusiastic wine maker and who started to produce quality wines. By 1958, Mas Gil's wines were fetching twice as much as any of the others grown near by. Now, under local ownership, it produces a complete range of excellent wines up to red *reservas*, which it sells under the name Clos d'Agon.

# 3
# *Aragón*

The Romans liked Aragón so much that when the legions left Spain many of the citizens remained. One can see why. It is a beautiful place, dominated in the north by the Pyrenees, and well watered. As you go south, though, the landscape changes and becomes practically a desert. The scenery is extremely varied, and so, of course, are the wines. It is steeped in history. Indeed, the history of modern Spain really began here, in 1469, when Ferdinand married Isabella, Queen of Castile. In 1479 he succeeded to the throne of Aragón and the two kingdoms were united under the Catholic Kings. The Moors were expelled and America was discovered. Their daughter Caterina, known to history as Catherine of Aragon, married Prince Arthur, heir to the English throne, and when he died she married his brother King Henry VIII. So a great deal of English as well as Spanish history had its roots here.

Its political importance gave Aragón a ready market for its wines, and they were counted amongst the best in Spain right into the nineteenth century. The leading vineyard then was Cariñena, and its vine spread over the border into France, where it became known as Carignan, and is still widely grown. If one looks at Aragón today, however, although it shares the prosperity that has come to the whole of Spain, its vineyards, and many of the little towns where wine is made, somehow got left behind. But all that is beginning to change, and in the vanguard is Somontano, which has risen from being practically nothing to being world class. But the other areas are exciting, too. Calatayud is producing wines of notable balance that are well worth seeking out; in Campo de Borja the wines are bigger-bodied and perhaps somewhat more rustic so far; Cariñena is set to regain its old reputation, producing well-balanced wines, but there is still much to be done; Somontano is the modern success story.

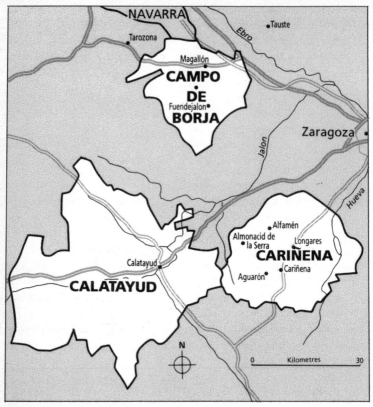

Calatayud, Campo de Borja and Cariñena

## CALATAYUD

### Geography

Calatayud is in the province of Zaragoza, south of Navarra and Campo de Borja and west of Cariñena, which it joins. It is a hilly area with several small rivers, and the motorway from Barcelona to Madrid passes through the middle. The vineyards are high, at 500 to 900 m above sea level, and there are high winds alleviated by wind breaks.

### Climate

Although this is continental, with cold winters and a high frost risk, the summer heat is kept down by the winds to an average of 22 to 24°C, and the average in winter is 2 to 6°C. Although not large, the area has many microclimates and the rainfall varies from 300 to 550 mm, depending on where you are. There are 2,800 hours of sunshine.

## Soils
Brown, loose and stony over gypsum, with marl in the north and slate in the south.

## Grapes
Recommended red varieties: Garnacha, Tempranillo and Mazuelo.
Authorized red variety: Monastrell.
Recommended white varieties: Viura (Macabeo) and Malvasía.
Authorized white varieties: Garnacha Blanca and Moscatel Romano.
There are also old vineyards of Juan Ibáñez (also called Miguel de Arco) and Robal, with recent experimental plantings of Chardonnay, Cabernet Sauvignon and Syrah. None of these is officially permitted but the last two named are certainly used.
Garnacha is the most widespread, with 65 per cent of the vineyard, while Viura has 15 per cent. Growers are being encouraged to plant Tempranillo.

## Planting
Traditionally in *marco real* with 2.2 m spacing, but some of the more recent vineyards are *en espaldera* with a 3 by 1.5 m spacing. The *espaldera* method has been a great success, producing very healthy grapes, and irrigation is installed in 40 per cent of these vineyards. The vine density is 1,500 to 2,400 per ha.

## Vineyard area
9,529 ha, of which 7,300 ha are actually planted. This is one of the few areas in Spain where the vineyard area may be going down rather than up.

## Authorized yield
Whites 56 hl/ha, reds 49 hl/ha.

## Wines
All three colours are made with strengths from 12.5° to 18°, but the modern tendency is to make wines intended for bottling on the

spot towards the lower limit. Most are sold as *jóvenes*, but whites are authorized up to *reserva* and reds up to *gran reserva*.

**Production**
170,000 hl.

**Vintages**
The years are pretty even and, as most wines are sold as *jóvenes*, are irrelevant.

The name Calatayud is a corruption of *Qualat Ayub* – the castle of Ayub, or Job, a Moorish governor. The agreeable countryside is widely planted with fruit trees and is particularly famous for its peaches, but the rather ruinous town of Calatayud, despite some good Mudéjar church towers, is not one for the traveller to seek out. The Roman poet Martial, whose vinous epigrams are often quoted, was born and died near by but spent most of his life in Rome. Most of the bodegas are rather ramshackle and hard to find, losing them-selves in a very Spanish anonymity, but most of the wine making is done in the cooperatives, which are trying hard to bring themselves up to date with stainless steel, but generally lack capital. Tradition-ally the wines are hefty and short-lived, most of them sold in bulk and exported to France or drunk in bars. They are reminders of Spain's vinous past. Even the bottled wines tend to be distinctly rustic and are often slightly sweet, but not excessively so. With Garnacha predominating for the reds, they are usually short-lived and fall apart if kept. But since the establishment of the DO in 1990, things have been gradually changing, and the best whites and *reserva* reds are delicious; they show that there is real potential here which will probably eventually be realized. In particular, blending Cabernet Sauvignon or Syrah gives the reds the backbone they need, and in some of the more modern wines Cabernet Sauvignon predominates.

*Some leading bodegas*

**Bodegas San Alejandro**
Otherwise known as Cooperativa San Alejandro, this is a coopera-tive with 600 members, having between them 1,400 ha of vineyard, some of which are 800 m above sea level. At present it produces mostly *jóvenes*, and the *rosados* bubble away in underground tanks,

but it is also equipped with stainless steel. The whites and *rosados* are fermented at 17 to 18°, the reds at 25 to 26°. It makes modern, fresh wines under the marks Marqués de Nombrevilla and Viñas de Miedes. The good Marqués de Nombrevilla 1994 red *crianza* was made from 80 per cent Tempranillo and 20 per cent Garnacha, fermented at 28°C and given eight months in small oak. The Viñas de Miedes white *joven* 1995, from Viura, was fresh with plenty of acidity and the red, mostly Garnacha, was just as good. These show the way the wines are moving and promise well for the future.

### Cooperativa del Campo San Isidro
Situated in the village of Maluenda, just south of Calatayud, it now trades under the name Bodegas Maluenda, using the marks Castillo de Maluenda, Viña Alarba and Marqués de Aragón. It is the largest producer in the DO and is also probably the most progressive, having invested heavily in recent years. It now has a substantial export market. The 500 members have 2,000 ha, about 75 per cent Garnacha, 10 per cent Tempranillo, 3 per cent Viura and 7 per cent Robal, but they also have a young experimental vineyard of 10 ha of Syrah, which is very promising. The wines include a very concentrated Old Vine Garnacha made from vines 40 to 60 years old. It also makes a *rancio*.

### Cooperativa San Gregorio
Another big cooperative, with 480 members and 1,100 ha of vineyard. Its *jóvenes*, sold under the Monte Armantes brand, are well regarded and it makes a red *gran reserva*.

### Gabriel Ibarra
A small, rather dilapidated and hidden away bodega with no vineyards of its own that produces good *jóvenes* under the brand Marqués de Sandañon.

### Langa Hermanos
Founded in 1982, this privately owned bodega has 16 ha of vineyard, which include 2 ha of Chardonnay and 4 ha of Cabernet Sauvignon, but also buys from growers. Most of its wines are sold in bottle under the marks Castillo de Ayud, Portalet and Viña Ribota. Fermentation is in stainless steel. The wines include a varietal Cabernet Sauvignon. It also makes a very good Cava.

# CAMPO DE BORJA

## Geography

Campo de Borja is contiguous with Navarra to the south-east but is separated historically, lying within the province of Zaragoza, and climatically. The vineyards are at altitudes of 300 to 700 m. The beautiful Sierra de Moncayo lies to the west and the vineyards reach into the foothills of the Cordillera Ibérica. To the east there are rolling hills. The twelfth-century Monasterio de Verula lies at the edge of the area. No longer a monastery but used for promotional purposes and concerts, it includes a wine museum and is well worth a visit; it is a beautiful building that contains a memorable tomb.

## Climate

This is continental, with extremes of temperature. In 1990, for example, the highest temperature was 40°C and the lowest −7°C. In winter there is a dry north wind and severe frosts which can extend into the spring. The average temperature, however, is 14.3°C and there is plenty of sunshine: 2,800 hours. But the nights, even in summer, are cool, which makes all the difference. The average rainfall is 434 mm.

## Soils

Mostly sandy over limestone; stony and well drained.

## Grapes

Authorized red varieties: Garnacha and Tempranillo.

Experimental red varieties: Mazuelo, Cabernet Sauvignon, Merlot and Syrah.

Authorized white variety: Macabeo.

White variety grown for non-DO wines: Moscatel.

The traditional variety for the area is Garnacha and this still fills 74.55 per cent of the vineyard, but Tempranillo is encouraged and is being more widely planted for the higher-quality wines, at present accounting for 11.15 per cent. Macabeo, however, is the second most widely planted with 13.49 per cent. The areas of the experimental varieties are likely to increase, as these have been successful, particularly Cabernet Sauvignon.

## Planting

Traditionally *en vaso*, *marco real* with 2.2 m spacing; growing the vines low in this way is essential on the windier sites, but some new vineyards are being planted in espalier, spaced 3 by 1.5 m *en espaldera*. The density of planting is 1,600 to 2,500 vines per ha.

**Vineyard area**
6,847 ha.

**Authorized yield**
49 hl/ha for reds and 56 hl/ha for whites.

**Wines**
Reds, *rosados* and whites with minimum strengths of 12°, 11° and 10.5° respectively. The regulations allow for *crianzas*, *reservas* and *grandes reservas*, but all the whites and *rosados* are sold as *jóvenes*. There are a number of red *crianzas* and *reservas*, and *grandes reservas* are on the way. In a DO red at least 50 per cent must be Garnacha. In addition to these DO wines some sweet *mistelas* with a strength of 17.5° are made from the Moscatel grapes.

**Production**
148,000 hl.

**Vintages**
Most recent vintages have been classed as good or very good, but as most of the wines are sold as *jóvenes* and intended for early consumption, and a *reserva* would not be made in a poor year, there is no point in listing them.

Campo de Borja means the field, or territory, of Borja, named after the noble family that owned it. One member of the family, Alfonso de Borja, became pope as Calixtus III and, moving to Rome with his notorious family, Italianized his name to Borgia. His nephew, Rodrigo de Borja, became Pope Alexander VI in 1492, and apportioned the New World between Spain and Portugal; he was the father of Cesare and Lucrezia. Happily their exploits are irrelevant to this book. The great family castle can still be seen in ruins above the eponymous town.

Although wine has been grown here from time immemorial, it was heady plonk from the traditional Garnacha, easily rising to 14° thanks to the hot summers, and sold in bulk for drinking in bars and for blending and bottling elsewhere. Vineyards are small (there are 2,584 growers) and nearly all the wine is produced by six cooperatives, with only four private bodegas, but the leaders have recently taken a leap forward, experimenting and setting out to make quality wines. They have succeeded. The DO was established in 1980 and since then progress has been rapid. The best wines today are bottled in the bodegas. They are very good and, not surprisingly, resemble those from neighbouring Navarra. They are gradually establishing a reputation and a following, but these are comparatively early days and they still represent very good value.

Generally speaking, the lower vineyards are planted with Garnacha, those on the higher slopes with Tempranillo and the experimental varieties. There is no irrigation nor is there ever likely to be, owing to shortage of water. Some old wooden and epoxy vats remain but these are steadily being replaced by the most modern stainless steel, in which all the best wines are already being made. Some of the red *jóvenes* are made by carbonic maceration. Some of the whites are barrel-fermented but so far these tend to be over-oaked; however, an experimental barrel-fermented red shows enormous promise and could turn into a world-class wine.

## Some leading bodegas

### Bodegas Aragonesas

The company was founded in 1984 to sell the wines of the Cooperativa San Juan Bautista (founded in 1955), which is at Fuendejalón, and in the same year was joined by the Cooperativa Santo Cristo at Magallon. The members have 7,000 ha of vineyard, most of which is Garnacha, but there is 12 per cent Tempranillo and experimental plantings of the other varieties, including 25 ha of Cabernet Sauvignon. It is now the largest producer in the DO, accounting for about 65 per cent of the whole, selling all over Spain and exporting to twenty-two countries. Since 1995 all its wines have been fermented in stainless steel. Red wines account for 80 per cent, *rosados* for 15 per cent and whites for 5 per cent. It has six brands: Crucillón, Viña Tito, Don Ramón, Mosen Cleto, Coto de Hayas and Duque de Sevilla. There are three *jóvenes* sold under the Viña Tito brand: a white Macabeo, which is slightly sparkling and semi-dry; a Garnacha *rosado*; and a red from Garnacha and a little Tempranillo. Its most popular wines are in the middle Don Ramón range, made from the same varieties. Mosen Cleto is a *crianza* with nine months in American oak, also made from Garnacha and Tempranillo. The top Duque de Sevilla, from the same varieties, is a *reserva* which is given twelve months in wood and two years in bottle before sale. The Crucillón red is a varietal Garnacha. The white Coto de Hayas is a Macabeo, part cask-fermented; for the future they are considering adding a little Chardonnay. The red Coto de Hayas is 75 per cent Garnacha and 25 per cent Tempranillo with seven to nine months' oak ageing, fermented at 24°C, giving lots of fruit, some tannin, and a good acid balance.

### Bodegas Borsao

This is the trading name of the Sociedad Cooperativa Ltda. Agrícola de Borja, dating from 1954, though the bodega itself was founded four years later. Although wine is its particular interest, it is a general cooperative for the local farmers and has extensive interests in olive oil, together with almonds, tomatoes, asparagus and other crops. The members have 1,200 ha of Garnacha, 100 ha Tempranillo, 25 ha Cabernet Sauvignon, 10 ha Mazuelo and 25 ha Macabeo. Most of the wines are therefore necessarily reds. There are three brands: Borsao for *jóvenes*, Gran Campellas and Señor Atares for *crianzas* and *reservas*. Some of the fermentation is still done in epoxy-lined tanks but there is a substantial installation of stainless steel, the whites being fermented at 18°C, the young reds at 25°C and the *crianzas* at 30°C, with each variety separately fermented. The *jóvenes* come from the lower vineyards, the grapes from the higher ones being used for *crianzas* and *reservas*. Although some French oak is being tried experimentally, American oak is almost entirely used for ageing, 15 per cent replaced each year. The wines are very well made and are excellent examples of each category. The 1995 Borsao *joven* was made from 50 per cent Garnacha, 25 per cent Tempranillo and 25 per cent Cabernet Sauvignon. The 1990 Gran Campellas *reserva* was 50 per cent Garnacha and 50 per cent Tempranillo. The 1987 Gran Campellas *reserva* (the first *reserva* they made) was 100 per cent Garnacha. Proportions vary from vintage to vintage and the Gran Campellas now contains 10 per cent Cabernet Sauvignon. They also make a *dulce* and a *mistela*.

### Bodegas Santo Cristo Sociedad Cooperativa

Apart from DO wines, this cooperative makes a Cava, Reinante, and a well-liked Moscatel under the Ainzon mark. Its most notable wine, however, is Viña Ainzon Reserva. The excellent 1988 was made from 80 per cent Tempranillo and 20 per cent Garnacha, a complex wine of great length. Other brands include Berramon, Santo Cristo and Viña Collado.

## CARIÑENA

### Geography
Cariñena lies to the south-west of Zaragoza and to the east of the Calatayud DO, which it adjoins. The vineyards lie in an attractive countryside of high plains and small hills – in the foothills of the Sierra de Algairén, which forms part of the Cordillera Ibérica – and range in height from 400 to 800 m.

### Climate
Continental, with hot summers up to 38°C, but it cools down at night, in cold winters going down to −8°C; the yearly average is 15°C. It is relatively dry, with a rainfall of 300 to 350 mm and averages 2,800 hours of sunshine. Drought and hail are hazards.

### Soils
Ochre-coloured limestone with slate in places and some alluvial soil.

### Grapes
Recommended red varieties: Garnacha, Tempranillo and Cariñena.
   Permitted red varieties: Juan Ibáñez, Monastrell and Cabernet Sauvignon.
   Experimental red variety: Merlot.
   Recommended white variety: Viura (Macabeo).
   Permitted white varieties: Garnacha Blanca, Parellada, Moscatel Romano.
   Experimental white variety: Chardonnay.
   Garnacha occupies 55 per cent of the vineyard, followed by Viura with 20 per cent and Tempranillo with 15 per cent. It is ironic that the local Cariñena grape, which is widely grown in France under the name Carignan, and is known elsewhere in Spain as the Mazuelo, is now down to 6 per cent.

### Planting
*Marco real* with 2.2 m spacing and *en espaldera* with 3 by 1.5 m spacing. The latter is being encouraged in new or replanted vineyards as those on the high plains are very suitable for mechanical harvesting. The density is 2,000 to 2,500 vines per ha.

**Vineyard area**
44,300 ha, of which 19,675 ha are within the DO.

**Authorized yield**
Whites 52 hl/ha, reds 45.5 hl/ha.

**Wines**
Whites and *rosados* of at least 11.5°, reds of at least 12°, *rancios* of at least 15° and with three years in oak, and *vinos de licor* of at least 17.5°. The latter two are only produced in very small quantities. Most of the wines are *jóvenes*, with reds predominating, but about 30 per cent are made as *crianzas*, *reservas* and *grandes reservas*, the last only being produced in the best years.

**Production**
400,000 hl average, but often less owing to drought or hail.

**Vintages**
1985 7, 1986 3, 1987 6, 1988 6, 1989 5, 1990 6, 1991 6, 1992 6, 1993 6, 1994 5, 1995 5, 1996 7, 1997 4.

The countryside of high plains and small hills is most agreeable, but the town of Cariñena gives an impression of poverty and its old buildings are so dilapidated that some have fallen down, and one fears that the rest well might. The Mudéjar belfry is one of the most beautiful and one can only hope that its church will be restored.

In the world of wine things are much healthier. This has never been regarded as a fine wine district but always as a reliable one, though in 1824 Al Henderson wrote of Spanish wines in general: 'That which is obtained from the species called *garnache* ... is in highest repute; and the growth of Cariñena are preferred to all others.' Traditionally it made sweet wines of enormous alcoholic strength and colour by picking the grapes very late. Happily the bodegas have been brought up to date with stainless steel and the wines are very well made, so that the lusty and unsubtle wines of the past have disappeared and new, lighter wines have taken their place. The red wines are the best. Most are sold as very agreeable *jóvenes*. The *reservas* and *grandes reservas* are well worth looking for. A good export trade has been developed but mostly in cheap, good-value wines.

The Consejo Regulador has an admirable little museum which is well worth a visit. Amongst other things it shows the work of Jules

Lichenstein, who had a bodega here (as did several French wine merchants at the end of the last century). He died in 1886, but before his death he had described the life cycle of phylloxera so that when it arrived in 1901 everyone knew what to do.

## Some leading bodegas

### Covinca Sociedad Cooperativa

This young cooperative at Longares, founded in 1988, whose members have 3,000 ha of vineyard, bottles about half its wine, including a small quantity of *crianzas*, and has a small export trade. Its brands include Marqués de Ballestar, Torrelongares, Viña Oria and Vivadillo.

### Cooperativa San José

This leading cooperative, in the village of Aguarón just west of the town of Cariñena, was founded in 1955 and has 500 members with 1,500 ha of vineyard. Its bodega is completely modern and very well run. All the fermentation is done in stainless steel, at 25° to 28°C for the reds and 17° to 20°C for the whites. There is a strong export market, including leading UK supermarkets, and they go in for ageing Tempranillo and Cabernet Sauvignon in new American oak casks, the *grandes reservas* being given a minimum of eighteen months, with twelve months for the *reservas* and eight months for the *crianzas*. It sells under a number of brands. Top of the range comes Monasterio de las Viñas. The 1985 *gran reserva* was 50 per cent Garnacha, 30 per cent Tempranillo and 20 per cent Mazuelo, a wine with bottle ageing potential. The *reserva* had a similar grape mix but with 5 per cent less Tempranillo and 5 per cent more Mazuelo. The 1992 *crianza* was 60 per cent Garnacha with 20 per cent of each of the others. There is also a red varietal Tempranillo. The *rosado* is a varietal Garnacha and the white a varietal Viura. Other brands include Valdeflor, Valdemadera, Viña Rotura and Campo Rojo.

### Bodegas San Valero

A large cooperative with 700 members having 5,500 ha of vineyard. It makes well-regarded wines under the brands Don Mendo, Monte Ducay and Marqués de los Tosos. In the 1996 vintage the white Marqués de los Tosos was barrel-fermented and made from 80 per cent Viura with 20 per cent Moscatel, the *rosado* was made from 90 per cent Garnacha and 10 per cent Cabernet Sauvignon, and the red from 80 per cent Garnacha, 15 per cent Tempranillo and 5 per cent Cabernet Sauvignon.

## Bodega Ignacio Marín

One of the few substantial private bodegas, this family concern was founded in 1903 and has 49 ha of vineyard. It uses both French and American oak for ageing its wines, which are sold under the marks Barón de Lajoyosa and Castillo de Viñaral. They include a varietal Tempranillo as well as a Moscatel and a sweet *rancio*.

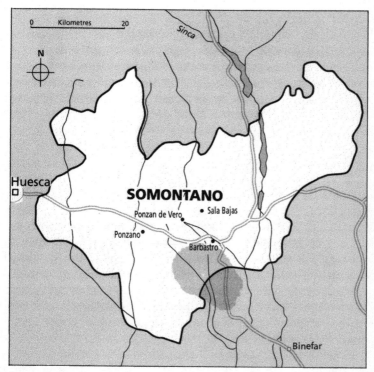

Somontano

# SOMONTANO

## Geography

Somontano means 'under the mountains', and the mountains are the Pyrenees. The principal town is Barbastro, about 80 km south of the French border; the vineyards surround it, but principally lie to the west, towards Huesca, and to the north, in the Pyrenean foothills, at altitudes of between 350 and 650 m. Unlike most of the Spanish vineyards, these are in a lusciously green, hilly landscape. It lies within the province of Huesca, which is itself within the old kingdom of Aragón.

## Climate

Far from the moderating influence of the sea, this is continental, with temperatures up to 40°C in the summer and falling to –10°C in the winter, but nevertheless is more moderate than most, sheltered from the cold north winds by the Pyrenees; there is a modest yearly average of 11°C, 550 mm rainfall and 2,700 hours of sunshine, but the summers are dry and arid. Hail can be a big problem.

## Soils

Thanks to a high proportion of sandstone and clay, these are red-brown to look at but contain a good deal of calcium, which makes them good for wine growing.

## Grapes

Although this is a long-established wine-growing area, relying historically on the local red Moristel and white Alcañón grapes, its renaissance is very new and, untrammelled by tradition, all sorts of varieties are being tried, most of them successfully. Others will undoubtedly be tried in the future, and it may well be many years before a set pattern emerges. At present the position is:

Authorized red varieties: Moristel, Garnacha, Tempranillo, Parelleta and Cabernet Sauvignon.

Experimental red varieties: Merlot, Pinot Noir and others.

Authorized white varieties: Macabeo, Alcañón, Garnacha Blanca and Chardonnay.

Experimental white varieties: Chenin Blanc, Gewürztraminer and others. Riesling was tried but appears to have gone, and the same fate probably awaits Chenin Blanc, which has already been cut out from those allowed for DO wines.

## Planting
Various patterns are used depending on the highly irregular sites and the grape variety, but typically they are planted in a rectangular pattern and trained *en vaso* or single or double cordon. The more modern vineyards have water-spraying equipment to counter the risks of frost in March and April. The density is 1,500 to 3,000 per ha.

## Vineyard area
1828 ha but expanding.

## Authorized yield
Reds 56 hl/ha, whites 70 hl/ha.

## Wines
Whites from 10 to 13.5° with, exceptionally, late-gathered Macabeo varietals up to 16°. Light reds and *rosados* from 11 to 13.5° and reds from 11.5 to 14°. The whites come as *jóvenes* and *crianzas*, the *rosados* as *jóvenes*, and the reds as *jóvenes*, *crianzas* and *reservas*, though *grandes reservas* are on their way.

## Production
45,000 hl, though this is likely to increase, and 70,000 hl at least is possible.

## Vintages
1985 7, 1986 5, 1987 6, 1988 6, 1989 6, 1990 5, 1991 6, 1992 6, 1993 7, 1994 7, 1995 7, 1996 6, 1997 7.

Somontano is a most beautiful place, with the peaks of the Pyrenees, snowcapped for much of the year, making the perfect distant backcloth to the vineyards. The ancient city of Barbastro, unlike most Spanish towns, has agreeably resisted development and has a good, small, sixteenth-century cathedral; and Alquézar is a most beautiful hilltop village, very well worth a visit, in the north of the DO area. As a wine-growing region it is one of the most exciting in Spain. A few years ago no one had ever heard of it. It made light, rustic wines which travelled into and over the Pyrenees. Then, in 1984, it was given DO status. (The regulations were revised in 1993.) It took off. For all practical purposes, it was virgin territory in wine terms. Young wine makers with ample capital and all the latest equipment poured in, transforming old cooperatives and creating superb modern bodegas. They also brought with them foreign vines. This can be dangerous, as a prejudice is building up against yet more Chardonnay and Cabernet Sauvignon, but in this instance there was nothing to worry about. The French vines took on a different personality in their new environment; Spanish varieties that had been little grown, such as Tempranillo, flourished, and new blends were created, such as Tempranillo/Cabernet, Chardonnay/Macabeo and Macabeo/Alcañón. The wines spoke for themselves: they were and are well balanced and delicious, some of the best in Spain. The bodegas are full of energy and enthusiasm, and as they are untrammelled by the traditions of an established market, they can experiment as they like, which they have done to very good effect.

## Some leading bodegas

### Bodegas Borruel
A small family-owned bodega in Ponzano which was the first to bottle the wines of the region. It owns 14 ha of vineyard and buys from other growers. It produces a well-regarded range under the brands Barón de Eroles, Castillo de L'Ainsa, Villa de Ainsa, Viña Osca and Villa Benasque. The Viña Osca *rosado* and red are varietal Tempranillo. The Castillo de L'Ainsa *crianza* is a varietal Merlot, given fifteen months in wood.

### Viñedos y Crianzas del Alto Aragón
No bodega could be more up to date than this. Visiting some Spanish bodegas is like stepping back into the nineteenth century. Here one seems to be stepping forward well into the twenty-first. Everything is spacious, clean and, above all, computer-controlled. From the very start the aim was to produce top-quality wines, and they have done it. It is a family-owned company founded in 1991, but the bodega was not started until 1992 and was opened in 1993. It acquired 40 ha of vineyard and has planted more to bring the total to 250 ha, on chalky clay soil with large stones, in the hills 500 m up. The views are wonderful. Irrigation is provided by a large reservoir, with the water pumped up by a solar pump. The principal red vines are Moristel, Cabernet Sauvignon, Tempranillo and Merlot; the whites are Macabeo, Chardonnay and a little Gewürztraminer; but there is also an experimental vineyard that includes Italian

varieties. Neither herbicides nor insecticides are used and the grapes are hand-harvested. About three quarters of the production is reds. All the wines are sold under the brand Enate and the bottles have striking modern labels. The whites include a barrel-fermented Chardonnay, fermented in Nevers oak of 225 litres, medium-plus toasted and new every year – the casks later being used for the maturation of red wines. The wine is left on the lees, which are stirred every two weeks, and undergoes a malolactic fermentation. The alcohol content is a lusty 13.5° but thanks to its big flavour it is in perfect balance and does not taste over-oaked. It benefits from three to four years bottle age. Enate Blanco is an interesting and excellent blend of 35 per cent Macabeo and 65 per cent Chardonnay. The varietal Gewürtztraminer is also impressive and avoids the problem that this grape can have of becoming over-intense. The very good *rosado* is a varietal Cabernet Sauvignon. Enate Tinto is also a blend, but this time of 15 per cent Moristel and 85 per cent Tempranillo (the 1996, however, is a Merlot/Cabernet Sauvignon blend). Enate Crianza is a blend of 70 per cent Tempranillo with 30 per cent Cabernet Sauvignon, fermented separately at 28°C and then aged for nine months in one- and two-year-old casks. It is worth keeping for a year or two to give extra bottle age. A varietal Cabernet Sauvignon Reserva has plenty of tannin and will benefit from at least ten years' bottle age. Although the bodega especially prides itself on its white wines, the reds are every bit as good. One needs to remember that most of the vineyards are still young. The wines can only get better still.

### Compañia Vitivinícola Aragonesa (COVISA) – Viñas del Vero

This bodega is also a producer of top-quality wines. It was founded in 1986 with that object by the local Aragón development agency, owned by the savings banks, the Government of Aragón and a private company. A building, which has been admirably restored and extended, was bought from the old-established company of Lalanne and large areas of vineyards were acquired, together with planting rights. It is now the biggest vineyard owner in Somontano, with close on 600 ha. These are semi-organic: they generally manage to avoid diseases but will spray if they have to. Some grapes are machine-picked. The yield is deliberately kept down to 36 hl/ha. The vineyards are divided into three separate sites which were developed with the aid of advice from the University of Madrid and the University of California, Davis. One of them surrounds the bodega while another is in a beautiful position on the top of a hill. It planted all the traditional local varieties and a number of imported ones, all of which have now been approved for the DO with the exception of Riesling and Chenin Blanc, which have been abandoned, while Sauvignon and Syrah proved to be mistakes and came to nothing. Again, it must be remembered that most of the vineyards are still young and that their full potential for quality has yet to come. Although the bodega buildings are old, everything inside is state of the art and computer-controlled. They are tall, which gives the advantage that the wine can be moved by gravity. American oak is used for maturing Tempranillo and Moristel, but French Allier oak is used for Merlot, Cabernet Sauvignon, Pinot Noir and Chardonnay. A complete range of wines is produced, all of which are of the highest quality, and include several varietals, perhaps the most unusual of which is from that extremely difficult variety, Pinot Noir, which is given eight months in French oak and is of world standard. It tastes like a rather spicy Burgundy. The white varietals include a very good and agreeably restrained Gewürztraminer and two Chardonnays, one of which is barrel-fermented. The *rosados* include one made from Tempranillo and Monastrel and one that is a varietal Cabernet Sauvignon. The red varietals are Tempranillo, Pinot Noir, Merlot and Cabernet Sauvignon. The straightforward Tinto is 60 per cent Tempranillo and 40 per cent Moristel, and the same mix is used for the Duque de Azara *crianza*. The Gran Vos Reserva, however, which is particularly good, is made entirely from French varietals: 65 per cent Merlot, 30 per cent Cabernet Sauvignon and 5 per cent Pinot Noir. There is also a sparkling wine, made from Pinot Noir and Chardonnay, which cannot call itself a Cava owing to the Pinot Noir.

**Bodegas Pirineos**
Starting life as the Bodega Cooperativa de Somontano in the 1960s, this was totally transformed in 1993. It became a company, and an enormous investment was made to bring it into line with the latest technology. The change was visionary. It pioneered the development of Somontano as a fine wine area selling bottled wines, and is one of the three bodegas producing first-class wines on a large scale today. Further capital was raised for improvements in 1994. It still relies on the original 200 wine growers for its grapes, and between

them they own about half the vineyard area in the DO, with the following holdings: Tempranillo 323.54 ha; Moristel 283.19 ha; Macabeo 139.38 ha; Cabernet Sauvignon 77.71 ha; Alcañón 55.29 ha; Garnacha 33.74 ha; Chardonnay 9.28 ha; Parelleta 4.46 ha; and 77.13 ha of other varieties. Four qualified viticulturalists are employed full time to supervise the vineyards. All the wines, apart from some barrel-fermented Chardonnay, are fermented in stainless steel, the reds at 25 to 28°C, the whites and *rosados* at 16°C. It sells under a number of brands. Villa de Alquézar is used for the *jóvenes*, the white being a varietal Macabeo, the *rosado* made from Moristel, Macabeo and Garnacha and the red from equal quantities of Moristel and Tempranillo. The brand Montesierra is used for a varietal Macabeo white, a *rosado* made from 50 per cent Tempranillo, 25 per cent Macabeo, 13 per cent Moristel and 12 per cent Garnacha, a red made from 50 per cent Tempranillo, 25 per cent Cabernet Sauvignon and 25 per cent Moristel, and a red *crianza* from equal quantities of Tempranillo and Moristel. The brand Monasterio del Pueyo is used for a red *crianza* made from equal quantities of Tempranillo and Cabernet Sauvignon, which are given ten months in American oak. Señorío de Lazan is used for the top of the range red *reserva* made from 60 per cent Tempranillo, 15 per cent Cabernet Sauvignon and 25 per cent Monastrel, given at least twelve months' ageing using both American and French oak. Its most unusual reds are a varietal Moristel, a unique wine which is mostly sold to the United States, and a wonderfully fragrant varietal Parelleta. Its most unusual, and excellent, white is Montesierra Vendímia Tardia (late vintage) varietal Macabeo.

## Bodegas Lalanne
This family bodega, founded in 1842, is the oldest in the DO and has 32 ha of vineyard. It has rather got left behind by the march of events, though, and it remains to be seen whether it will move forward. It sells a range of agreeable wines under the brands Laura Lalanne and Viña San Marcos.

## OTHER WINES

The ancient kingdom of Aragón extended further than the present Autonomy, which comprises the provinces of Huesca, Teruel and

Zaragoza. The DO wines of Calatayud, Campo de Borja, Cariñena and Somontano have already been described, but apart from these, as in the whole of Spain, wine is grown all over the place. For the most part the wines are strong, lusty and rustic, made from the Garnacha Tinta, but the new knowledge and enthusiasm that has transformed the DO wines in recent years is not confined to them and serious wine growers may emerge elsewhere before long. There are five CVs, briefly described below.

### Alto-Jiloca-Daroca

Most of the rather massive wines from the 10,000 ha of this area are sold in bulk. The two main centres are Daroca and Calamocha, on the road between Zaragoza and Teruel. The two main grapes are the red Garnacha and the white Macabeo, but others are grown, including Monastrell, Bobal and the rare Provechón.

### Bajo Aragón

This also consists of 10,000 ha in the north-west of the province of Teruel and is divided into three parts: Oriental, which is the biggest producer, Medio, which is the largest area but where the vineyards are more scattered, and Occidental, which is the smallest. The principal grapes are the two Garnachas, Tinta and Blanca, and wines of all three colours are produced, with two versions of red: one strong and dark, the other lighter and sometimes with some white grapes included. The tendency nowadays is to pick the grapes earlier and to make the wines lighter. There is an enological station in the Oriental, or eastern part, at the principal town, Valderrobes, which also has the best-known grower, Cooperativa Santa María la Mayor, selling wines under the brands Valderrobes and Peña Lagaya. If the enological station is able to bring pressure on the growers, things could look up.

### Muniesa

With 2,200 ha of vineyard in the north of the province of Teruel, most of the wines are strong, rustic reds from the Garnacha grape but a number of white varieties are also grown.

### Valdejalón

This CV, with 15,000 ha of vineyard, more or less fills in the area between Campo de Borja, Calatayud and Cariñena. There seems to be no good reason why it should not emulate the examples of its more illustrious neighbours, but it does not, and is content to produce massive bulk wines from the Garnacha, with a few wines of other colours; and if the business is profitable, why should it change?

# 4
## *The Centre-North*

———

Sheltered by the Pyrenees, and far enough north for the sun not to be too hot, this part of Spain is very well placed for growing top-quality table wines, and it grows them. The two great areas of Rioja and Navarra, although next to one another, are very different in history and culture, not least in their vinous history. Rioja was the first to get off the mark with world-class wines and is not resting on its laurels; its great bodegas look forwards, not backwards. Navarra, however, is catching up fast. Uninhibited by tradition, its wine makers have been free to experiment, particularly in the use of French grapes, while by no means neglecting the potential of the Spanish native varieties. Their wines have earned a place amongst the very best and continue to develop; if they do not yet enjoy the international recognition of Rioja, they are getting there fast.


## RIOJA

**Geography**
The Rioja wine district is in the centre-north of Spain and should not be confused with the autonomy La Rioja, the capital of which is Logroño. The total area is 44,000 ha, stretching 120 km along the Ebro valley, never more than 50 km wide, sheltered in the north by the Sierra de Cantabria and in the south by the Sierra de la Demanda. The greater part of the vineyards are within La Rioja, but 7,000 ha lie within the Province of Alava and 4,000 ha within the Province of Navarra. It is divided into three parts: Rioja Alta, Rioja Alavesa (the part that lies within Alava) and Rioja Baja, as the map shows.

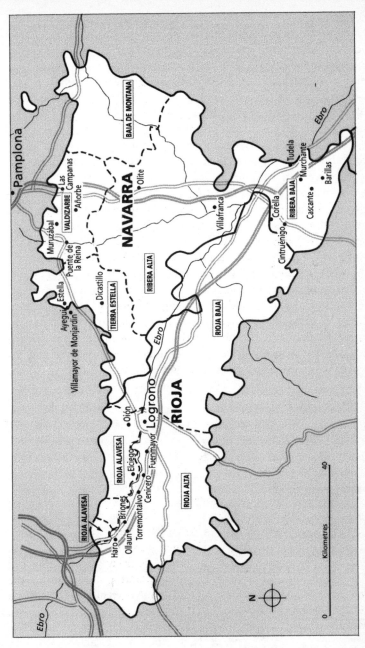

Rioja and Navarra

## Climate

Alta and Alavesa are in the highlands 400–500 m above sea level, where the height and a certain Atlantic influence give an average temperature of 12.8°C and an average rainfall of 450 mm. Hot spells in summer do not usually last long. The Baja subdistrict is lower, at about 300 m, and has a more Mediterranean climate, with an average temperature of 13.9°C and 370 mm rainfall, though at its southern extremity it reaches into the foothills of the mountains and there are some vineyards with a more continental climate. In all three subdistricts, sheltered from north winds by the mountains, the summers are hot, autumns long and mild, but winters cold with a considerable frost risk in the Alta and Alavesa that extends into the flowering and can seriously reduce yield. Snow is apt to fall there between the middle of January and the second half of February. There is little frost and snow, however, in the more Mediterranean climate of the Baja. In the summer the wine districts look arid, and crossing the mountains reveals a greener, cooler world that is quite different and generally unsuitable for wine growing. The average hours of sunshine are 2,750, though higher figures of over 3,000 are sometimes given, as are lower ones, down to 2,000. It undoubtedly varies considerably from place to place. About 43 per cent of the vineyards are in the Rioja Alta, 20 per cent in the Alavesa and 37 per cent in the geographically much larger Baja.

## Soils

In both Alta and Alavesa they are calcareous clay, though there are some ferruginous and alluvial soils in the former. In the Alavesa in particular there is a problem with rocks, which have to be removed laboriously if a new vineyard is to be planted; there are piles of them all around. In the Baja, on the other hand, the land is flat, with mainly ferruginous clay and alluvial soils. The light-coloured calcareous clay, which may contain as much as 45 per cent calcium carbonate, is the best, certainly for red wines. A map showing exactly where each kind of soil is to be found is so complicated that it looks like a jigsaw puzzle.

## Grapes

The forty or so varieties that were grown in the eighteenth century have been reduced to seven.

Recommended red varieties: Tempranillo (60 per cent of the vineyard), Garnacha (19 per cent), Mazuelo and Graciano.

Experimental variety: Cabernet Sauvignon. This French grape led the drive for quality in the nineteenth century but now forms only 1 per cent of the vineyard and is not mentioned on back labels.

There have been moves to add Cabernet Sauvignon to the official varieties and to introduce Merlot, Syrah and Pinot Noir, but although the door has been left open, this has not happened yet and the general feeling is for developing the local varieties.

Recommended white: Viura (15 per cent), Malvasía Riojana and Garnacha Blanca.

A number of other white varieties are being grown experimentally and probably illegally. These include Rousanne, Marsanne, Sauvignon Blanc, Viognier and Chardonnay.

### Planting
*En vaso*, with 2,850 to 4,000 vines per ha. Some recent vineyards are, however, being trained on wires and pruned by the Guyot method. There is no mechanical harvesting.

### Vineyard area
50,635 ha, of which 47,357 ha are currently in production. Although some major shippers have large vineyard holdings, the average size of a vineyard is still only 4.4 ha.

### Authorized yield
Red 45.5 hl/ha, white 63 hl/ha. But as is so often the case in Spain, the actual figures realized for both are less, for instance 33.2 hl/ha average in 1994 and 43.04 hl/ha in 1995.

### Wines
Red, *rosado* and white. Rioja *joven* (formerly known as *sin crianza*, a term still often used) has seen at most three or four months of oak and may not have seen any at all; these are released in their first or second year. Rioja *de crianza* can be released in its third year (which is not necessarily three full years after the vintage) and must have spent at least six months in 225 litre oak *barricas* if white, and twelve months if red. These wines, particularly in Spain, used to be labelled simply 'third year' but nowadays are sold with their vintage and have to be labelled with it if they are for export. At least 85 per cent of the wine must come from the vintage specified; this has been so since 1981. Rioja *de reserva* must have the same minimum oak ageing but cannot be released until its fourth year. The highest category is Rioja *de gran reserva*, made only in exceptional

years. Whites and *rosados* must spend at least six months in oak but wines of these colours are very rarely made as *grandes reservas*. Reds must spend at least twenty-four months in oak and thirty-six months in bottle. They can be released in their sixth year. Many bodegas, though, especially the old-established ones, mature the wines in wood for much longer than the minimum period. The minimum strength allowed depends on where the wine is grown. For white wines it is 11° in Alta and Alavesa, 11.5° in Baja. *Rosados* can be 0.5° less but reds must be 0.5° more. A Garnacha grown in Baja can attain an awesome 16°C but most wines are shipped at about 13°.

**Production**
Average 1991–95: 1,711,920 hl.

**Vintages**
Despite being not so very far from Bordeaux, the vineyards are on the other side of the Pyrenees and the vintage years are very different.

1945 2, 1946 3, 1947 6, 1948 7, 1949 6, 1950 3, 1951 3, 1952 7, 1953 2, 1954 5, 1955 6, 1956 5, 1957 3, 1958 7, 1959 6, 1960 5, 1961 5, 1962 6, 1963 3, 1964 7, 1965 2, 1966 3, 1967 3, 1968 6, 1969 3, 1970 6, 1971 1, 1972 2, 1973 5, 1974 4, 1975 6, 1976 5, 1977 1, 1978 6, 1979 3, 1980 5, 1981 6, 1982 7, 1983 5, 1984 3, 1985 6, 1986 5, 1987 6, 1988 4, 1989 6, 1990 6, 1991 6, 1992 4, 1993 4, 1994 7, 1995 6, 1996 4, 1997 3.

With such a large area and several varieties of vine, there are always exceptions to the rule and the above classification can only be taken as indicative. The best recent vintage was 1994, which was exceptional, with 1995 not far behind it.

La Rioja is a very beautiful place that does not reveal itself immediately. The town of Haro at first seems nondescript, but the oldest part, in the centre, has some fine stone houses bearing proud escutcheons, though most are tumbledown and there are far fewer than there were thirty or forty years ago. Logroño is bigger and is rapidly, like so many other Spanish towns, becoming a concrete jungle; but it has some good things, such as the eighteenth-century church of Santa María de la Redonda. Many of the small towns and villages, though, remain unspoiled. Laguardia, in the Rioja Alta, succeeds in keeping cars out and is exquisitely preserved, with a wonderful view to the mountains. It is worth going to the Rioja just to look at the hilltop villages such as Briones. The countryside in the Alta and Alavesa is beautiful, too, packed with vineyards and revealing unexpected vistas as you drive through the hills. The mountains are all around, still snowcapped at the beginning of May. And in the autumn, after the vintage, the leaves on the Tempranillo, Graciano and Mazuelo turn into wonderful shades of red and brown. The Rioja Baja, however, is not beautiful, nor is it so densely planted with vines. On leaving a vineyard you often have to travel quite a way to find the next. And the rather dull countryside is reflected in many of the wines that grow there.

Like most of the major Spanish vineyards, Rioja has a long and complex history, but the early years are rather obscure and the wines we know today only really go back to the beginning of the nineteenth century. The first known written use of the word Rioja was in 1092, and it is said to be derived from the Rio Oja, a small tributary of the Ebro; probably it originally referred only to a limited area, but it came to cover the whole. There are records of wine being exported in the sixteenth century. At that time the wines grown there were almost entirely white and these were the most expensive; the reds were the cheapest and in between were some *vinos claretes*. Wine growing increased considerably during the seventeenth century but there was little hope of building up a significant export market as the roads were terrible and the area isolated. Two of the best vines currently used for making red wine – the Tempranillo and the Mazuelo – became prominent in the eighteenth century, and with them the *claretes*, but the Spanish economy was in a dreadful state at that time and by the end of the century so much bad wine was being produced that there was a problem selling it.

The change came in the nineteenth century and was brought about by a number of factors, some of them far-sighted improvements and others fortuitous. The first of the pioneers was a local priest, Manuel Quintano y Quintano, who was born in Labastida, where he was to become the incumbent and a canon of Burgos cathedral. At the end of the eighteenth century he visited Bordeaux and saw how wine was made in the leading châteaux. He and his brother began to experiment with the French method and made some of the best wines so far seen, but he did not persuade the growers to change their ways. In 1795 he successfully sent his new wine to Cuba, but the local growers would have none of it and rebelled against the innovative. The far-reaching change that led to international success was finally brought about by the two great marquises, Murrieta and Riscal, whose wines have made them immortal. Luciano de Murrieta y García Lemoine was born in Peru in 1822. Of small stature but great spirit, he unfortunately embraced the revolutionary Carlist cause and was exiled to London, where he lived from 1843 to 1848, with his friend the Duque de la Victoria. While there, he took a liking to French wine and went to study it in Bordeaux, returning to Logroño by 1850, when he produced his first wine. Initially he made it in the duke's bodegas and his fame spread abroad, for the London *Times* of 9 April 1850 reported:

THE WINES OF SPAIN – The following appears in the *Clamour Publico* of Madrid of the 28th of March: 'The Duke de la Victoria has for many years past, entertained the patriotic idea of applying himself, whenever he should be able to reside on his property in Logroño, to improve the condition of the Rioja, a province as fertile as it is deficient in capital for cultivating its products, especially as to its wines, which, although the principal wealth of the district, from want of proper treatment have not hitherto been exported. The Duke, during his emigration in London, made arrangements with his friends, Messrs. Ysasi & Co., for exporting the wines of the Rioja, and immediately on his arrival at Logroño he proceeded to carry his plans of amelioration into effect by putting in practice all the modern operations for the more perfect preparation of the wines, which are now fit for exportation, to any country. The Duke has not spared any expense in completing his project and making known to all the other wine proprietors the improved method of preparation for export. To the public exhibition of the productions of the country, now open in Madrid, the Duke has sent a few bottles as a competitor for the principal prize. The wine is beginning to be known abroad under the title of "Ebro claret", and there are already large orders for it . . . The district of Logroño and all the Rioja is likely to become one of the richest in Spain, and the farmers will reap an advantage hitherto unknown to them, since, for want of a market, they have been often obliged to sacrifice the vintage of a whole year. We have tasted the wine and it has the qualities of a pleasant sort of Bordeaux.'

Ysasi & Co were a famous firm of Sherry shippers. The prophecy came true, but not until after a number of ups and downs. Murrieta evidently lived down his involvement in the Carlist rebellion and was created Marqués. In 1872 he brought a fine estate at Ygay and from then onwards traded under his own name, which remains one of the most honoured in Rioja.

The authorities evidently approved of the new wines, for in 1862 the provincial government employed a Bordelais wine grower, Jean Cadiche Pineau from Château Lanessan, to teach the new methods of wine making, but the peasants again would have none of it – indeed, some of them still make their wine today as they made it then. Although Pineau made some excellent wines, various things militated against him: his methods called for the ageing of wines in casks and that in turn called for capital, which was not available; the wines were relatively expensive and therefore difficult to sell; there were no merchants to buy young wine and to age it, as there were in Bordeaux; and not least there were local politics. His contract was not renewed. After six years he gave up and decided to go home, but fortunately his work was not entirely ignored and Don Camilo Hurtado de Amégaza, Marqués de Riscal, a great landowner who lived in Bordeaux as a liberal exile, persuaded him to stay on and engaged him as enologist. Riscal's bodega was the first to be built on the Bordeaux model. He also imported French vines including Cabernet Sauvignon, which are still used by his successors today to supplement the Spanish varieties, adding an element of individuality and complexity to the wines.

The French wine making was a great advance but it was events in France itself that completely changed the history of Rioja. In 1852 the fungus oidium, originating in the United States, struck the French vineyards and ruined the crops. French wine merchants sought new supplies in Spain and naturally tried the north first. Rioja had obvious potential and it was not far over the Pyrenees, so then, and for the rest of the century, it received a large part of their attention. Oidium was not long confined to France, though. It arrived in Rioja via Portugal and wrought havoc between 1855 and 1862, sometimes reducing the yields almost to zero before it was eventually conquered by the use of sulphur on the vines. France had worse to come. Phylloxera, a destructive aphid also originating in the United States, struck the vineyards in 1867, and although it reached Portugal only a year later, some at least of the French growers held the extraordinary belief that it would be unable to cross the Pyrenees. They, together with *négociants*, came in droves, establishing vineyards and bodegas in which they actually matured the wine before shipping it. This in itself was a revolutionary change, as the peasant growers had been wont to throw away any wine left from the previous vintage when a new one came along. They did not have the capital to invest in casks for maturation even if they were aware of the technique. Phylloxera did eventually reach the Rioja in 1899 but in the meantime the French led the way to establish a new world-class vineyard.

The decade 1870–80 was dynamic. Rioja took off. One of the old problems that has already been mentioned was inaccessibility. In 1790 there had been a movement to make a new road to the coast, but nothing came of it, thanks to the Napoleonic invasion, the Carlist wars, and the devastation brought by a visitation of cholera. The nineteenth century, however, was predominantly the era of railways. They spread throughout the world, revolutionizing life and industry. In Rioja the Madrid–Irun railway, constructed in 1862, passed through Miranda de Ebro, but 1880 brought the vital link in the form of a railway linking Haro with Bilbao. Many of the grand new bodegas were built near the railway station, where they still are. And the trade with France was reinforced in 1882, when a Franco-Spanish treaty reduced duties on wine imported from Spain into France. Another problem was that the wine was not well made, was too weak, and would not travel. Valuable improvements in the making and ageing of wine followed from the advice of the *Estación de Enología*, established by royal decree in 1888. It is still there. The trade fluctuated, peaking at more than 9 million litres in 1891 but down to 2 million in 1894. Many of the great bodegas that still flourish today date from this time: Marqués de Riscal, 1860; Faustino Martínez, 1861; Rioja Santiago, 1870; Luis Gurpegui and Marqués de Murrieta, 1872; Montecillo, 1874; Berberana and López de Heredia, 1877; CVNE, 1879; AGE, 1881; Martínez Lacuesta and Lagunilla, 1885; Gómez Cruzado, 1886; Berceo, 1888; Campo Burgo, 1889; Franco Españolas, Riojanas and Rioja Alta, 1890; Palacio, 1894; Carlos Serres and Paternina, 1896; and Bilbainas, 1901.

Trade was good in Spain, too. Rioja was the wine to serve on special occasions. But in Spain's *belle époque* the fashion was for things French, and Rioja came to be labelled Cepa Chablis (for dry white wines), Cepa Sauternes (for sweet wines), Cepa Borgoña (for the fleshier reds) and Cepa Burdeos (for the lighter reds). The word *cepa* was itself misleading, though, for it means vine, and others used the more descriptive *tipo*, or style. Another name used for this new style of wine was Médoc Alavésa. Not surprisingly, this unfortunate usage was carried forward into the export markets and until Spain's entry into the EU it was only too common to find wines labelled Rioja Chablis, Rioja Burgundy and so on. The growers also had to face fraud, as it was only too easy for a restaurateur to refill a Rioja bottle with cheaper wine from elsewhere. To counter this, they started to put wire cages, or *alambrados*, round the bottles, so that drinkers could see if they had been tampered with. However, it is said that some of the growers themselves were not above fraud, watering the wine and bringing the strength back up with industrial alcohol imported from Germany. From the beginning the embryo Consejo Regulador addressed its mind to this.

Then everything went wrong. By 1890 many of the French vineyards had been reconstructed and this major export market was lost, a position exacerbated when in 1892 France doubled the duties on imported wines in retaliation for Spain's protectionist policy initiated by Canovas. Other valuable export markets went when Spain lost Cuba and the Philippines in 1898. Between 1901 and 1905 the phylloxera spread and ravaged the vineyards. Of the 50,000 ha, 36,000 ha had been destroyed by 1909 and much of the land was returned to cereals. In this year the vineyards began to be reconstructed, with advice from an agronomist, Francisco Pascual de Quinto, appointed by the provincial government; but the lowest trough of production was not reached until 1912, just as the reconstructed vineyards were beginning to yield fruit. The growers got a chance to rebuild their fortunes two years later when the outbreak of the First World War cut off supplies of wine from France to the United States and opened new markets. By 1935 there were 35,000 ha of vineyard, but the following year the Spanish Civil War started and as soon as that was over the Second World War came. The only substantial exports were to neutral Switzerland.

Every wine-growing district in Europe has found the need for some degree of official regulation, and this applied to Rioja as much as to the others. A Consejo Regulador was set up in 1926, the first in Spain, and at about this time cooperatives were established which have played a very important part in the trade ever since. The Consejo Regulador was not a success and a second was set up in 1944, but this did not work either. Then a third was established in 1953 and was given teeth: effective legal sanctions to enforce its regulations. It needed them, for in the good years of 1964, 1968 and 1970 more young wines were sold than were grown. This is unlikely ever to happen again, for in 1976 everything was tightened up and there is now a close control over every aspect of wine making.

By the 1970s trade was flourishing, helped by a surge in French wine prices, which caused drinkers to expand their horizons, and this brought a second spate of new bodegas. The list that follows does not pretend to be complete and includes establishments of every possible size: Campo Viejo, 1963; Remelluri, 1967; Dinastia Vivanco, 1968; Luis Casado Fuertes and Real Divisa, 1969; El Coto, Marqués de Caceres and Ostata, 1970; Castillo de Cuzcurrita, 1971; Alavesas, 1972; Beronia, Domecq, Hurtado, Lan, Olarra and Viña Salceda, 1973; Contino, 1976; Faustino Rivero Ulecia, 1979; La Plana, El Santuario and Real Junta, 1980; David Moreno Peña and Julio Merino Royo, 1981; Propiedad Grial, 1982; Bodega de Luis, 1983; Marín Palacios, 1984; Breton, Ontañón, Primicia and Viña Artuke, 1985; Amezola de la Mora, Araco, Carlos Serres Luis Pérez Foncea, Roda Moraza and Muriel, 1986; Abel Mendoza, Torres-Librada, Varal, Viña Villabuena and Virgel del Valle, 1987; Afersa, Estraunza, Marqués de Vitoria, Monteleiva and Valcor, 1988; Antigua Usanza, Luberrí, Rubí, Salabal and Viña Valoria, 1989; Alta, Luis Angel and Casado Manzanos, 1990; Marqués de Vargas, 1991; Sayalva, 1992; and Cardema, 1993. Most of these are admittedly obscure, but they do include some that are already amongst the very greatest names, and those most recently founded are still finding their feet. The number of bodegas licensed to age wine went up from fifty-two in 1982 to 148 in 1996. And there was money enough for all the latest equipment their enologists needed.

By the 1970s eighty countries were importing Rioja, and by 1996 the number had risen to eighty-eight, with Germany in the lead, importing 132,234 hl, followed by the United Kingdom with 101,193 hl – but in terms of money these positions were reversed, as the average price of the German imports was 397.47 ptas per litre while that of the United Kingdom was 519.84. Sweden came third with 94,582 litres, at an average price of 499.31 ptas per litre. Total exports were 588,474 hl.

In the old days the small growers used to make their wines in the way practised all over the north of Spain, in *lagos*. Spanish-English dictionaries translate *lago* as 'lake', which indeed is right: that is the usual meaning. On a visit to Spain I was once surprised when an English-speaking wine grower told me that in the old days every house had its own lake. But in the context of wine the meaning is different. A *lago* is a tank, usually underneath the house, made of stone or plastered brick. Everything was tipped in: grapes, stalks and all. Then they were lightly pressed by foot and a violent fermentation – known as the tumultuous fermentation – soon started. There was no way of controlling the temperature, which could rise to heights that today would be regarded as alarming. After a week, the first wine – *vino de lágrima* – was run off into a smaller tank. Most of the grapes were still intact, though, and these were turned over. Then there was another fermentation, producing *vino de corazón* (the heart wine), which was considered the best. Then the contents of the *lago* were pressed and the wine of the first, light pressing added to the heart wine. The must was run into large oak casks where it completed its fermentation over a period of months. This method of wine making is still used by a few small growers who supply wines to the local bars and is really a primitive form of carbonic maceration (*maceración carbónica* or, in France, where it is widely used, *maceration carbonique*). In a more advanced form the grapes are destalked first.

So far as the major shippers are concerned, the Bordeaux method took over in the last century and has remained in use ever since. The wines are made in the same way as they are made all over Europe. There have been developments, however. Until the 1960s the wines were matured in old oak casks, many of them very big, where they remained for a long time; eight years was not at all unusual. This resulted in wines that tasted strongly of vanilla and were oxidized. In those days *reservas* had to have at least six years' maturation and *gran reservas* at least eight. It is not surprising that they had their detractors. The red wines stood up to this surprisingly well but the whites came as a shock to those used to the light wines from more northerly vineyards. They were deeply coloured, did not have much fragrance (what survived was largely oak), and lacked acidity. A revolution began in the 1970s. Nowadays nearly all the bodegas are completely up to date, with stainless-steel tanks where the fermentations are carried out under controlled temperatures, and 225 litre oak barrels, either American or French, many of them new, are used for maturation, though the lighter white wines, and some of the red *joven* wines, do not see oak at all. Here, as in most of the Spanish fine wine districts, there is argument as to which kind of oak to use, but Spanish oak is very rarely used, as it adds nothing to the wine, and the use of oak chips is strictly forbidden.

In 1991 Rioja became the first DOCa – Denominación de Origen Calificada – and as such subject to very tight control throughout the wine-making and ageing process. The promotion could have prompted a radical revision of the rules, and several suggestions have been made, for instance the creation of smaller geographical areas, the exclusion of jóvenes from the DOCa, and the demotion from DOCa to DO of wines that do not pass a specially stringent tasting test. But these options were eliminated on the grounds of practicality and the politics of the wine trade. It is doubtful if they would have added much in any case. In reality, little has changed and one relies on the reputations of the individual bodegas.

As in Bordeaux, the complexity of the wines reflects the combination of a number of different grape varieties but, in the Rioja, it also reflects the blending of wines from different vineyards and areas. The old practice used to be to plant together in one vineyard all the varieties that the grower needed for his wines. These were usually picked and vinified together. Nowadays each variety is kept separate, picked at the right time, and vinified separately. Each has its own characteristics of flavour. For the red wines, the leading vine is the Tempranillo, a native vine that is undoubtedly one of the greatest in the world, and that forms the basis of the finest Riojas. It gives powerful yet well-balanced, subtle, fruity wines of great fragrance and ageing potential. The amount planted is going up, mostly at the expense of the Garnacha. The Garnacha, though, is a very fine vine, as the French have discovered. Too often trained to produce excessive yields, it tends to be underrated, but trained to produce a moderate yield it gives strong, full-bodied, fruity wines of great charm. It is particularly good for making *rosados*. The Mazuelo gives rather tannic, though not very alcoholic, wines that keep their colour well and can be important in a blend intended for long ageing. The Graciano gives wines that are rather weak in alcohol but high in tannin, colour (though the colour tends to turn brown rather quickly) and acid, with floral overtones, ageing very well and particularly useful for including in *grandes reservas*. There is at present a government subsidy for planting Mazuelo and Graciano. Cabernet Sauvignon forms only 1 per cent of the total, but is important in some vineyards and is notable for its characteristic aroma and backbone; it has long formed part of the tradition of Marqués de Riscal, though that bodega is now relying largely on Tempranillo. Of the white grapes, the leader is undoubtedly the Viura (the same as the Macabeo), which is productive yet of high quality, giving white wines that do not oxidize easily and hence are ideal for cask-ageing. Although it ripens rather late, it can become overripe and the wines are then dull, but picked at the right time they are fresh and fruity. It is sometimes blended into red wines to give lightness and freshness. The Malvasía Riojana (which is the same as the Subirat-Parent of Penedés) is not very widely grown but has a fragrance all of its own, though the wines tend not to age very well. The Garnacha Blanca gives strong wines, not very high in acidity, which used to be regarded as rather dull, but it has been transformed by modern low-temperature fermentation and now produces fresher and more aromatic wines. A typical combination for red wines in the Rioja Alta is traditionally 60 per cent Tempranillo, 25 per cent Garnacha, 15 per cent Graziano and Mazuelo. In the Rioja Alavesa it is 90 per cent Tempranillo and may include a little Viura. In the Rioja Baja the Garnacha predominates and may be 100 per cent. But in practice a wide variety of combinations is used, as set out in the descriptions of the individual bodegas that follow.

The fact that there are three distinct subdistricts and eight different vine varieties gives some idea of the large choice of wines. As in all major wine-growing areas throughout the world, much depends on the precise site in which the grapes are grown. Each subdistrict, however, has its own general style. Rioja Alta produces wines of good acidity that require ageing. Rioja Alavesa provides softer wines that mature more quickly and sometimes have a slightly earthy taste. Rioja Baja, where the Garnacha predominates, gives big fruity wines that do not need much age, and some are sold straight off for early consumption in the bars. But there are many exceptions. For instance, Rioja Alavesa has some firm wines age very well and the best vineyards in Rioja Baja produce wines of considerable character and quality.

The types of wine made are listed at the beginning of this chapter, and specific wines are described below under the names of individual shippers, but there are some generalizations that should be made first. Although some wines are the products of specific estates, such as those of Domecq, Contino and Remelluri, the majority are blended from wines originating in various districts to give the house styles of the individual shippers. There are two basic styles of red:

*clarete*, generally lighter in style and bottled in Bordeaux-shaped bottles, and *tinto*, bigger bodied and softer, bottled in Burgundy-shaped bottles. But there is no rigid distinction between them. It all depends on the practice of the individual shipper and the shape of the bottle is not a sure guide.

There is a heated debate going on between the traditionalists and those who think of themselves as international. The traditionalists want Rioja to taste like Rioja and not to produce yet another Cabernet Sauvignon or Chardonnay. One does see the point. But the younger generation of wine makers points out that the combination of grapes is not writ in stone. In Bordeaux, for instance, it has changed notably over the years. And in Rioja a little Cabernet Sauvignon adds backbone and structure to a red wine, while Chardonnay can add grace to a white wine and make it more acceptable in world markets. The traditionalists say that the same or better results can be achieved by making wiser use of local grapes, for instance by using more Graciano rather than Cabernet Sauvignon. There is strength in both points of view.

In the 1980s, in the new wave of prosperity, it must be admitted that some bodegas lost their way, even one or two of the great names, and at the bottom end things were made worse by price cutting. Up till then the wines had certainly tended to be very woody, and one of the early Masters of Wine told me thirty years ago, 'I don't like Rioja. I like wine, not wood.' He could not make that generalization today, but at the time it was justified. At the bottom end the wines were cheap and cheerful, at the top they were often superb, but in the middle there were some disasters: sweet with overripe grapes, flabby with lack of acid, dumb from hot fermentations and too long in large casks, and sometimes frankly rather unclean. At the same time the bodegas were faced with the competition of burgeoning quality vineyards from all over Spain and, not least, from the New World. The wines made in Rioja were different, of course, but people were worried. New prosperity enabled both the old and new generations of wine makers to change all that, and they succeeded abundantly. One solution was to produce young, *joven*, wines without ageing, sometimes made by carbonic maceration, and lacking any vanilla oakiness. This was certainly good for cash flow, but time has shown that greater ageing is generally more popular, and the majority of the red wines still are *crianzas*, with smaller quantities of the older *reservas* and *grandes reservas*. Nevertheless, there are clearly two styles: the old, big wines and the new, vinified to be generally lighter. The only fault that still occasionally shows up (and it is a very minor one) is a tendency for some of the less exciting reds to be slightly too sweet.

Of the whites, the older, traditional style still has a large connoisseur following. Exemplified by such wines as the excellent whites of Marqués de Murrieta and López Heredia, they are dry but very full-bodied, deep with vanilla overtones; almost unique in the world of white wines, the only ones they can be compared with are the white Rhônes from Châteauneuf-du-Pape and Hermitage. They go very well with highly flavoured foods. The new-style whites, pioneered by Faustino Martínez and Marqués de Cáceres, are now made by practically everyone and are totally different: fresh, light and crisp. The Cáceres wines now include an oak-fermented white, though. And the *rosados*, too, should be looked at. In the past they were not worth taking seriously, but are now very well made and delicious.

Red Riojas are amongst the longest lived of wines and most are drunk before they reach their peak, which is apt to happen ten, twenty or even thirty years after the vintage. In the past, vintage years used not to be taken very seriously and one of my Spanish friends joked that a shipper had registered 'Vintage 1929' as a trade mark, but this is certainly no longer so, nor was it ever so with the leading shippers, and they can be relied on. The oldest red that I have tasted so far was Marqués de Murrieta 1925. Drunk in England in 1982, it was still full of fruit and had a magnificent, lingering flavour, with no signs of decay. The same shipper's 1931, bottled in 1934 and drunk in Spain in 1996, was still wonderfully young, packed with fruit, and marvellously complex: one of the best wines I have ever tasted. I have no doubt that the best of the wines being made today will last every bit as well.

It is now almost impossible to buy a bad Rioja. To mention every Rioja shipper would be impossible; the number is vast and it is increasing. Those listed below have been chosen because of their historical or commercial importance, or for the sheer quality of their wines, or often for a combination of all these things. Some that deserve a mention have undoubtedly been left out. They are listed in alphabetical order of what is likely to appear to an English reader the most significant part of their name.

## Some leading bodegas

### Bodegas AGE

This is a large bodega in Fuenmayor dating from 1881, when Félix Azpilicueta y Martínez founded a company which in 1967 merged with two others: Cruz García and Entrena. Its name is taken from the initials of the three companies. It uses a number of trade marks, including Azpilicueta, for its best *gran reserva* and Marqués de Romeral for its second best, but its most popular wines are sold under the name Siglo and include Siglo Saco, which is sold in a Burgundy-shaped bottle covered with sacking. The wines tend to be thoroughly sound and reliable rather than exciting. It has been a member of the big Bodegas y Bebidas group since 1995. It was the first bodega in Spain to receive the Certificate of Quality from the European Unión.

### Bodegas Alavesas

As its name would suggest, this bodega, founded in 1972, is in Rioja Alavesa at Laguardia. It makes good red wines in the light Alavesa style, including an excellent *joven*. For *crianza*, *reserva* and *gran reserva* it uses the name Solar de Samaniego, named in honour of an eighteenth-century local poet. The reds are usually varietal Tempranillo.

### Alejos

Founded as recently as 1988 in Argoncillo, it sells good-value wine under the name Alabanza.

### Bodegas Amezola de la Mora

This is another recent foundation, dating from 1987, in Torremontalbo. It has 80 ha of vineyards planted mostly with Tempranillo but with 10 per cent Mazuelo. Its red wines (*crianzas* and *reservas* only) are very good indeed.

### Bodegas Ramón Ayala Lete

A small family-owned bodega in Briñas making good wines up to an excellent *gran reserva* under the name Viña Santurnia (Santurnia is a small mountain).

### Baron de Ley

A very up-to-date bodega, founded in 1985 (though its bottling plant is in an old Benedictine monastery) at Mendavia, in the province of Navarra. It has 90 ha of vineyards, 70 ha of Tempranillo and

20 ha of Cabernet Sauvignon. It uses a small proportion of Cabernet Sauvignon in its red wines, which are matured in new or nearly new oak, 80 per cent American and 20 per cent French, and also produces whites. It is in the same group as El Coto de Rioja. Its wines deserve their good reputation.

## Arco Bodegas Unidas/Bodegas Berberana

This important bodega was founded in 1877 at Ollauri by the Martínez Berberana family and the beautiful old building there is still retained, housing some of the finest wines, but the main bodega is now at Cenicero. After various vicissitudes of ownership, including a period in the Rumasa group – which was expropriated by the state – it is once again in private ownership, with seven cooperatives having a 30 per cent share, and is associated with some other famous names: Marqués de Griñón, Bodegas Lagunilla, Viñedos y Bodegas de Malpica (Castilla y León), and Marqués de Monistrol (Penedés). The 50 ha of vineyard that it owns is only enough for a small part of its needs, but it also buys in grapes and has first call on its shareholder cooperatives, who are free to sell off anything it does not want. The beautiful old cellars were carved out of the living rock by Galician and Portuguese stonemasons in the seventeenth century, and they are perfect for maturing wine, with a temperature of between 12 and 14°C throughout the year and a humidity of 90 per cent, giving a slow evolution. The wines are matured for a good deal longer than the regulations require: the *reservas* for five to six years and the *gran reservas* for seven to eight years. The company owns Lagunilla, which it brought from IDV in 1994, and the joint venture with Carlos Falcó, Marqués de Griñón, also dates from that year. All the wines are now made and bottled in Cenicero, the old Lagunilla bodegas now being used for country wines which, by law, are not allowed to enter Rioja bodegas. Everything is as clean and as up to date as it is possible to be, with controlled-temperature fermentation, though as the fermentation bodega faces north and the red wines are fermented at 26 to 28°C, cooling is not often necessary. *Remontaje* is computer-controlled with interior levers moving the caps: one of the few such installations in Spain. The casks are nearly all American oak, though some French is used, principally for Marqués de Griñón wines. Some reds are varietal Tempranillo but most are blended with 20 per cent Garnacha. The wines from this bodega can be relied on as being consistently good and good value. They are long-lasting, including some excellent *grandes reservas*. The white Carta de Oro is a fine example of an old-style oaky Rioja. Its associated company Berberana Vinícola in Fuenmayor produces good non-DO wines, including a white from the unusual Pardina grape variety, which is not authorized for Rioja.

## Bodegas Berceo

This is one of the oldest bodegas in every sense, founded by the French in 1872 and named after Gonzalo de Berceo, a monk who was the first person known to write Spanish. It is now privately owned by the Gurpegui family, who run it and have other wine interests in Navarra. Situated in the old part of Haro, where the ground rises to the castle, the bodega has two secret passages, one to the castle and the other to the main square. Because it is against a hillside, the old stone buildings are constructed in five levels with the top and bottom levels in different roads; it is quite a long journey to go from one to the other outside the building. It has the advantage, though, that everything can be done by gravity: grapes in at the top and bottles out at the bottom. There is the enchanting eccentricity that it has an experimental vineyard on top in its roof garden; apart from this the family owns 300 ha of vineyard with part in each of the three subdivisions of the Rioja, so that it is self-sufficient in grapes, over which it has full control. This is not a bodega where you look for stainless steel. Instead there are massive and ancient vats made of Limousin oak. Fermentation is in concrete but temperature is controlled by pumping the must through a cooler. The wine for the *reservas* and *grandes reservas* is then matured in French oak, but American oak is used for the *crianzas*. The *grandes reservas* can be as much as twenty years old when they are put on the market. There are two versions of the white Viña Berceo, one completely modern, fresh and ultra-cooled, the other cask-fermented and given five months in oak; it is not ultra-cooled and is wonderfully complex. There is a *joven*, made from 75 per cent Tempranillo and 25 per cent Garnacha, sold as Viñadrián. The Viña Berceo mark is used for the *crianzas* and *reservas* and for the *rosado*, but the *grandes reservas*, only made in the best years, such as 1970 and 1978 (the next will be 1991) are sold as Gonzalo de Berceo. The Viña Berceo Crianza 1993 was 75 per cent Tempranillo and 25 per cent Garnacha, while the Gonzalo de Berceo Gran Reserva 1978 was 75 per cent Tempranillo, 15 per cent Graciano and 10 per cent Mazuelo, but other vintages also include some Graciano. They are all very good wines.

## Bodegas Berónia

With this bodega one gets straight back into the twentieth century. Founded in Ollauri in 1970, it first operated on a very small scale, expanded in 1974, and in 1982 became associated with González Byass of Jerez, who invested heavily and built a new, up-to-date bodega complex outside the town on the road to Nájera. The substantial vineyards next to the bodega, at a height of 540 metres, are not enough to provide all the grapes they need, but the rest are all bought from growers within 10 km, as they like the soil and microclimate, and it also enables them to supervise the growing carefully. The white wines are made almost entirely from Viura while Tempranillo predominates for the reds, but there are very small experimental plantings of Cabernet Sauvignon, Merlot and Chardonnay. They ferment in an unusual way. As wild yeasts do not function at above 4° of alcohol, they put some wine of a previous year into the tanks so that they start at this level and a very slow fermentation, lasting about 120 days, is then induced with cultured yeasts, the temperature being kept below 30° for the reds and below 18° for the white. The wines are matured in American oak from Ohio and Missouri, but the casks are made in France and may soon be made in Logroño. Some new casks are bought each year but the average age is five to six years and none is kept after fifteen. *Crianzas* have sixteen to eighteen months in the wood, *reservas* twenty-four to thirty, and *grandes reservas* (only made in the very best years) have four years. As examples of blends, the Reserva 1987 was 86 per cent Tempranillo, 12 per cent Garnacha, 1.5 per cent Mazuelo and 0.5 per cent Graciano, while the Crianza 1993 was 80 per cent Tempranillo, 12 per cent Garnacha, 4 per cent Mazuelo and 4 per cent Viura. The whites include new-style wines and some that are barrel-fermented and then left on the lees to give great complexity of flavour. All the reds age very well and one, a *reserva* of 1991, is a varietal Mazuelo aged for two and a half years in American oak: powerful, rather astringent and very long. All the wines are very good.

## Bodegas Bilbaínas

This is one of the largest bodegas in Haro, high on the hill behind the railway station, with a beautiful garden. It was founded in 1901 by a Bilbao wine merchant, Santiago Ugarte, who took over some of the assets of a French company, Sauvignon Frères, which had been founded in 1850 but which went out of business in the changes that took place at the beginning of the century. Some of their oak vats are still in use. More versatile than the other Rioja houses, the bodega also makes a notable Cava and brandy. The phylloxera that was rampant at the time did not prevent Sr Ugarte from investing heavily in vineyards, and it now owns no fewer than 278 ha, mostly on the slopes immediately behind the bodega buildings, but these are not enough to supply all the needs and 30 per cent of the grapes are bought in. The vineyard names have now become famous as the names of wines produced from them: Viña Pomal, Viña Zaco and Viña Paceta. Viña Pomal, which is the most famous of the wines, is produced as a *reserva* and, in the best years, as a *gran reserva*. In 1982 the grape mix for the *gran reserva* was 70 per cent Tempranillo, 10 per cent Garnacha and a total of 20 per cent Graciano and Mazuelo; it spent its first year in a 30,000 litre oak vat then five years in American oak casks of various ages before bottling. La Vicalanda is a 7.5 ha plot within Viña Pomal which gives its name to a *reserva* made exclusively from Tempranillo grapes grown there and introduced for the first time as a *reserva* of the 1981 vintage. Viña Zaco is a rather softer style with 60 per cent Tempranillo, 15 per cent Garnacha and 12.5 per cent each of Graciano and Mazuelo. The 1988 *reserva* spent twenty months in large casks and forty-two in small before bottling. A white wine, Viña Paceta, is unusual in being made exclusively from Malvasía. Some years ago this well-established house appeared to be in decline, but it is now clearly on the up again and the wines deserve their good reputation. A controlling interest has recently been acquired by the major Cava house Codorníu, which intends to invest a very large sum of money and may well rapidly return it to the forefront.

### Bodegas Bretón

This bodega was founded in 1985 at Logroño by an old wine-growing family and some friends. They engaged the services of a first-class manager, Miguel Angel de Gregorio, who is also the technical director and was able to design the bodega from scratch to meet his very exacting requirements. His first wine was made in 1985 and sold in 1988. The bodega is now in the very top flight, producing superb wines, headed by the single vineyard Dominio de

Conte, which is only made in the best years (there was none in 1992 or 1993), and closely followed by the complete Loriñón range. It owns 106 ha of vineyard and began planting in 1985, but these supply only 70 per cent of its needs, the rest being bought in, including grapes from eighty-year-old vines. Aimed only at the top end of the market, the wines are made with enormous enthusiasm and meticulous care. This is illustrated by the way in which the bodega gets its casks. Initial experiments were with French oak and with American oak from Missouri, Ohio, Lousiana and Virginia. The last was eventually chosen as giving the best results, but instead of buying the casks, they buy wood which is kept for three years before it is made up by a local cooper, who also supplies Alejandro Fernández of Ribera del Duero fame. They are careful not to overdo the oak, though, aiming at fruit and fragrance. They are one of the few bodegas producing a barrel-fermented Viura, which is given about one day's skin contact (the amount depending on the year) and is fermented with selected yeasts, but there is no *bâtonnage* as the lees from Viura are described as 'very hard in the mouth'. An unusual feature is that the casks of white wine are left out in the winter. It also produces steel-fermented whites. *Crianzas* are given fourteen to eighteen months in cask, *reservas* twenty-four to thirty and *gran reservas* forty. The authorized grape varieties are used. As examples, the Dominio de Conte 1991 was made from 85 per cent Tempranillo, 10 per cent Mazuelo and 5 per cent Graciano, while the Loriñon Crianza 1994 consisted of 75 per cent Tempranillo, 10 per cent Garnacha, 10 per cent Mazuelo and 5 per cent Graciano. These are fine wines which age well and repay laying down.

## Bodegas Campillo
Part of the Faustino Martinez group, this bodega at Laguardia was started from scratch in 1987 and officially inaugurated in 1990. Its grapes come from 50 ha of fifteen-year-old Tempranillo vines which are owned by Faustino Martínez, but it leads a totally separate life. Although the bodega does have a white wine, most of its wines are upmarket reds of very good quality and generally 100 per cent Tempranillo, but the 1990 *reserva* also contains Cabernet Sauvignon.

## Campo Burgo
A large bodega founded in 1898 in Alfaro, it was acquired by Don Julián Cantarero in 1969 and forms part of a group that also

includes Viñedos de Calidad and the Navarre bodega Vinos Catalán Bozal. It expanded greatly and in 1995 further capital was subscribed by NatWest Ventures and by the insurance group Axis. The bodega has 28 ha of vineyard and the rest is bought in. In 1996 it was Rioja's biggest exporter, with a range of very good-value wines, including a varietal Tempranillo. Its *nuevo* 1996 beat Beaujolais on to the shelves in Germany. Its flagship is Alex Reserva Familiar, made by Viñedos de Calidad from a 19 ha vineyard surrounding the bodega. The 1990 vintage had the unusual grape mix of 80 per cent Tempranillo and 20 per cent Merlot, aged for ten months in French Limousin casks followed by eight in American oak. It also uses the name Viña Hermosa.

## Campo Viejo
Founded in Logroño in 1963, this is part of the big Bodegas y Bebidas group and has expanded to be one of the largest in Rioja. Its 502 ha of vineyards can only supply 25 per cent of its requirements. It uses a positively bewildering number of names: Campo Viejo, Viña Alcorta, Marqués de Villamagna, Almenar, Albor, Tres Ducados, Marqués de Mudela, Foncalada, Montés de Ciria, Selección José Bezares, Dominio de Montalvó and Castillo de San Ascensio. And it goes without saying that it produces a very complete range of wines: new-style and barrel-fermented whites, *rosados* and every category of red. All are good, commercial wines, and the barrel-fermented white is excellent, but three of its marks, Viña Alcorta, Marqués de Villamagna and Dominio de Montalvó, are reserved for its best, which are very good. The first contains a proportion of Cabernet Sauvignon. Albor is made by a unique vinification of their own which bears some resemblance to carbonic maceration. There is also a range of varietal wines.

## Bodegas Luis Cañas
This is a family-owned bodega of modest size at Villabuena, with 24 ha of vineyards. It produces a range of wines of sound quality and value.

## Luis Angel Casado Manzanos
A small bodega established at La Puebla de Labarca with 15 ha of vineyard, producing wines under the mark Jilabá that are well regarded. In addition to Riojas there is a Cava.

## Viñedos del Contino

Hidden away beyond the village of Laserna in the Rioja Alavesa, Contino must be one of the most difficult bodegas to find, but its wines are amongst those most worth finding. Vines have been grown on the site since medieval times, which is not surprising, as it has a perfect microclimate, the vineyards sloping down to a curve in the River Ebro, and the bodega itself is housed in a fine old stone building. It is amongst the most beautiful estates in the Rioja. Contino was founded in 1974 and the great house of CVNE has a half share, but the bodega is allowed to go its own way and makes its wines exclusively from its own vineyards – 47 ha of Tempranillo, 2.5 ha of Mazuelo and 3 ha of Graciano – so it makes only reds, and it only makes them in the good years; in 1993, for instance, it sold its grapes. For maturing it used to have equal numbers of French and American oak casks, but the American gave rather better results and now account for 60 per cent. A typical grape mix is 85 per cent Tempranillo, 6 per cent Graciano and 9 per cent Mazuelo, but it was also the first bodega to produce a varietal Graciano, an excellent wine. These wines are unusual in the Alavesa in that they mature only very slowly – and very well. In the best years they certainly repay keeping until they are twenty years old and benefit from breathing for a while before being drunk. They are definitely in the top flight.

## Compañía Vinícola del Norte de España/Cune

Known generally by its initials CVNE, or more usually still by their corruption into Cune, which it uses as one of its principal brand names, this is one of the biggest and most traditional of Rioja establishments. Founded in 1879 at Haro, one of several bodegas conveniently near the station, by two brothers, Eusebio and Raimundo Real de Asúa, it is still run by Eusebio's descendants, now in the fourth generation. Its wines have long been amongst the most popular in Spain and in many export markets, but they can be sold for a higher price in Spain than, for example, in England, so it is not surprising that it concentrates on the Spanish market. Its vineyard holdings are amongst the largest: five vineyards with a total area of 600 ha, planted with the authorized varieties together with minute experimental plots of 1 ha Chardonnay and 0.1 ha Cabernet Sauvignon. It would have more Chardonnay if it could, but if this is allowed it lies in the future. Nevertheless, these large holdings are only enough for 60 per cent of its needs, and the rest are bought in. Although amongst the oldest established bodegas, it has kept completely up to date. Everything is immaculate and stainless steel abounds. One of its great pioneering efforts was the dry white Monopole, the first of the new generation of light modern wines. If this no longer occupies the pre-eminent position it once did, it is not because it has gone off but because everyone else has gone into competition: a brilliant idea has caught on. It has now been joined by a barrel-fermented version. The standard version, which is given a year in oak, has the grape mix of 70 per cent Viura, 15 per cent Malvasía, 10 per cent Garnacha Blanca and a rather mysterious 5 per cent 'other varieties'. For the barrel-fermented version the first-picked grapes are used, mostly Viura and Malvasía. There is also a good semi-sweet white, Corona, and an excellent *rosado* made from Garnacha. Its most important wines, though, are the reds, which account for 80 per cent of the production. All are given wood age-ing, using 85 per cent American oak, which is preferred, and 15 per cent French, varying in age from new to twenty-five years. The very popular basic red Cune has a grape mix of 70 per cent Tempranillo, 20 per cent Garnacha and the rest made up from Mazuelo, Graciano, Viura and Garnacha Blanca. At the top of the range there are two fine reds. The Viña Real, which comes as a *crianza*, a *reserva* and, in the best years, a *gran reserva*, contains a substantial proportion of grapes from the Alavesa and is of a soft and accessible style. The 1989 Reserva was made from 80 per cent Tempranillo, 15 per cent Garnacha and 5 per cent Mazuelo. In some years a little Viura is added in the Alavesa tradition. The bench-mark wine, though, is Imperial (named after the imperial pint in which wine used to be exported from Bilbao to England), which comes only as a *reserva* and as a *gran reserva*. It is one of the best and most highly respected of all red Riojas, made typically from 80 per cent Tempranillo, 10 per cent Graciano and 5 per cent each of Mazuelo and Garnacha, grown entirely in the Rioja Alta and mostly from the Villalba vineyard, which is protected by the mountains and has a special microclimate. These wines mature well in bottle and are worth laying down.

## Cosecheros Alaveses

Founded in 1985 as a cooperative at Laguardia, in 1992 it turned itself into a company, with grapes coming from nine growers. It is modern, well equipped and is producing wines of very good quality and value under the marks Artadi and Viñas de Gain. The Viñas de Gain barrel-fermented whites are very good but the red Artadis are quite exceptionally good, the top wine being Artadi Pagos Viejos Reserva, made from 90 per cent Tempranillo and 5 per cent each of Garnacha and Mazuelo. Viñas de Gain 1994 *crianza* was a varietal Tempranillo, while the 1992 *reserva* contained 5 per cent Graciano.

## Bodegas Domecq

In 1970 the great sherry and brandy house Pedro Domecq decided to branch out into table wine and, as would be expected, went about it in a very scientific way. After a brief partnership with the international House of Seagram in Bodegas Palacio, it set about exploring various possibilities in the Rioja. The choice fell on the Rioja Alavesa where, in 1973, it bought a large tract of land and built a magnificent new bodega in Elciego. In 1984 Domecq was taken over by Allied Lyons to become Allied Domecq, with world-wide ramifications. Domecq had already gone into wine growing in Mexico, and in Spain the group now includes Harveys and Terry. Nothing was wanting either in expertise or in capital, and the results are impressive. The vineyards had to be cleared of rock, much of it beneath the surface, and planted. The 600 ha or so are all on the best chalky soil, but this holding, the largest in Rioja Alavesa, provides only half the grapes required. Fermentation is temperature-controlled with the whites fermented at 16 to 17°C and the reds at 29 to 32°C. American oak is used. The cheaper wines are sold under the mark Viña Eguia and they are excellent value, but at present are sold only in Spain. The top end of the range is sold internationally under the mark Marqués de Arienzo (the Marqués is actually a real person) and the wines are very good indeed, particularly the *reservas* and *gran reservas*. The usual grape mix for the reds is 95 per cent Tempranillo and 2.5 per cent each of Mazuelo and Graciano, but the Gran Reserva 1987 was a varietal Tempranillo. There is also a modern-style white made as a varietal Viura.

## Faustino Martínez

Founded in 1861 at Oyon in the Rioja Alavesa by Eleuterio Martínez Arzoc, who already owned vineyards, it is still run by the family, now in its fourth generation. His son, Faustino Martínez Pérez de Albéniz, started to bottle wine in 1930. It specializes in *reservas* and *grandes reservas*, which it exports all over the world, with a 25 per cent share in these classes. It has 500 ha of vineyard in some of the best soils of the district, which makes it self-sufficient for *reserva* and *gran reserva* wines, but which can supply only 40 per cent of its total needs. Everything is very clean and up to date, the old epoxy fermentation tanks having been abandoned in favour of stainless steel, which is found to give closer temperature control, and those for reds have built-in systems for *remontaje*. The fermentation temperature for the reds is between 26 and 28°C, always below 30°C. For the whites it is 16°C. *Rosados* are made by bleeding must from the tanks after twelve to sixteen hours. They have experimented with various kinds of oak and have found that wine in American oak oxidizes more slowly than in French (which gives more chocolate and caramel flavours), and that, of the French oaks, wine oxidizes faster in Limousin than in Allier (which gives finer tannins). As a result American oak is used to age most of the wines but with 20 to 25 per cent medium toast French for the *grandes reservas*. Some of the difference may come about through the way the oak is treated, the French splitting it with a wedge and the Americans using saws. New casks are bought each year but are never used for the *reservas* or *grandes reservas* until they are two years old. They are kept for a maximum of fourteen years and an average of seven. The *grandes reservas* are given thirty to thirty-six months in cask and a minimum of four years in bottle before sale. The bodega sells all its wines under the mark Faustino but with numbers. Faustino I is used for *grandes reservas*. The grape mix varies from year to year: for example, in 1982 it was 85 per cent Tempranillo and 15 per cent Graciano while in 1987 it was 85 per cent Tempranillo, 12 per cent Graciano and 3 per cent Mazuelo. These excellent wines age particularly well. Faustino V is used for *reservas* and again the grape mix varies from year to year; in 1991 it was 85 per cent Tempranillo, 12 per cent Graciano and 3 per cent Mazuelo, while in 1993 it was 90 per cent Tempranillo and 10 per cent Mazuelo. The same mark is also used for reds, for *rosados* (a typical grape mix being 80 per cent Tempranillo and 20 per cent Garnacha) and for whites, some of which are *crianzas* and are barrel-fermented, made from 100 per cent Viura. The emphasis on Tempranillo in the *rosados* perhaps accounts for their being unusually good. Faustino VII is used for reds and whites of the second quality, mostly intended for the home market, and for *rosados* made from Garnacha. It also makes Cavas. This bodega is undoubtedly one of the finest producers of Rioja and its wines are consistently good. Apart from Campillo, which has already been mentioned, the group also includes Marqués de Vitoria (see below) and a non-DO bodega producing the popular range of Don Darius wines.

## Bodegas Franco-Españolas

Now part of the Paternina group, Bodegas Franco-Españolas in Logroño traces its history back to the French connection in the nineteenth century. In 1890 Frédéric Anglade, a Bordeaux wine merchant, started growing wine in the Rioja and formed a company with French and Spanish capital and with directors of both nationalities. Despite phylloxera the company flourished, but the French interest waned; more Spanish capital was subscribed and by 1922 it was Spanish-owned. In 1973 it was bought by Rumasa. This group was dispossessed by the state, which ran it for a while before selling it on to Don Marcos Eguizabal Ramírez. The bodega has 100 ha of vineyard. It is kept separate from Paternina and has its own range of well-known, sound, commercial wines. It makes a dry, fruity white wine, an excellent example of the modern style, but also a white *crianza* and a white *gran reserva*, all sold under the mark Viña Soledad, and a semi-sweet white sold under the mark Diamante. Its Rosado de Lujo, made from 70 per cent Garnacha and 30 per cent Viura, is well worth seeking out. Its red Royal contains 25 per cent wine made by carbonic maceration, to provide lots of fruit and early drinking. Its red *crianzas*, *reservas* and *gran reservas* are sold under the mark Royal and Royal Bordón. Royal Bordón Reserva is made from 80 per cent Tempranillo and 20 per cent Garnacha. Top of the range is the *gran reserva* Excelso; the 1964 was made from 70 per cent Tempranillo and 15 per cent each of Mazuelo and Graciano, aged for two years in tanks and four in oak before bottling.

## Grandes Vinos

This is a merchant, not a bodega. It buys very high-quality wines from Rioja, Rueda and Toro, selling them under its own trade marks. Its Rioja is sold under the mark Meridiano.

## Herencia Lasanta

Founded in 1935, this bodega at Logroño has 120 ha of vineyards and produces a complete and well-regarded range under the company name, together with a red Tempranillo made by carbonic maceration and sold under the mark Iuvene.

## Bodegas Lan

Founded in 1973 in Fuenmayor, this is one of the new generation of large and very up-to-date commercial enterprises. For a time it formed part of the Rumasa empire, but is now privately owned again and is part of the Santiago Ruiz group from Rías Baixas. It has 70 ha of vineyards, which are used for the top-of-the-range Viña Lanciano, supplemented with grapes from other growers for the rest of the wines. It produces a complete range of good wines, mostly under the name Lan, but also Lander, Viña Lanciano and Señorio de Ulia. The Viña Lanciano reservas are particularly good. From the 1994 vintage onwards it has taken a firm step towards the 'new style', with long maceration to give deep colour, limiting the barrel ageing to avoid oakiness, and using new barrels. The *jóvenes* and *crianzas* are made from 85 per cent Tempranillo, 10 per cent Garnacha and 5 per cent Mazuelo. The Reserva 1994 was made from 80 per cent Tempranillo, 10 per cent Garnacha and 10 per cent Mazuelo, while the Viña Lanciano 1994 was made from 85 per cent Tempranillo and 15 per cent Mazuelo, matured for a year in 60 per cent American and 40 per cent French oak.

## Bodegas R. López de Heredia Viña Tondonia

Founded in 1877, this is one of the grand old bodegas down by the station in Haro. One cannot miss it, with its large nineteenth-century buildings and enchanting tower, all in a Swiss style. Unlike most of its rivals, it has resolutely refused to move with the times, but it seems none the worse for it, as its wines are unquestionably in the very first flight. It is still family-owned, run by descendants of the founder, Rafael López de Heredia, who at first had a French partner. They are very individualistic, though, and make wines in the old style of Rioja: a law unto themselves. To cross the threshold is to walk into the past. While the new-generation wine makers worship cleanliness and have bodegas that would satisfy the most fastidious housewife, here they could not care less. There are cobwebs all over the place and they are encouraged; spiders do not get into the wine and they eat insects, including the flies that produce cork weevils, so they have their own, odd cleansing function. Viña Tondonia is its best vineyard: over 100 ha on the right bank of the River Ebro. There are three other vineyards – Viña Cubillo, Viña Bosconia and

Viña Zaconia – a total of 170 ha, providing all the grapes for its top wines, and very little is bought in. In the early days some French grapes such as Cabernet Sauvignon and Merlot were tried but were rejected, and the vineyards are now planted entirely with the authorized Spanish varieties, some of the vines being seventy years old. There is no stainless steel here. The emphasis is entirely on oak. They buy their own American oak from the Appalachians, Ohio and Michigan, season it, and make all the barrels by hand in their own cooperage. The emphasis is on ageing in the enormous, deep cellars, and mercifully the accountants have not got at them, so stocks are enormous. All the wines are made to last for ever, and they do, with sufficient acidity to balance their oakiness, which gives a slightly musty aroma, much enjoyed by lovers of old-fashioned Rioja. The lightest of all the wines is the white Viña Gravonia, which is not a single vineyard wine but derives its name from the old 'Rioja Graves'; made from the Viura grape, even this is oak-aged and sold at four years old. A white wine that is really in the old tradition is Viña Tondonia Blanco, which has at least four years in cask. The *rosado*, too, is given cask-ageing. The youngest red wine, Viña Cubillo, is given three years' ageing with at least two in oak, while Viña Tondonia Tinto is given four years in oak and is made from 75 per cent Tempranillo, 15 per cent Garnacha, 5 per cent Mazuelo and 5 per cent Graciano; but the Garnacha comes entirely from the Rioja Alta, which gives wines from this vine good ageing capabilities. The red *reservas* and *grandes reservas*, which are the pride of the bodega, are sold in two styles. Viña Bosconia is the fuller in flavour and sold in Burgundy-shaped bottles; it is given at least three years in cask and is made from 80 per cent Tempranillo, 15 per cent Garnacha and the rest Mazuelo and Graciano. Viña Tondonia spends at least four years in oak and is made from 75 per cent Tempranillo, 15 per cent Garnacha and 5 per cent each of Mazuelo and Graciano. *Grandes reservas* are not usually sold until they are at least twenty-eight years old!

## Bodegas Luberri
Although this small establishment was founded in Baños de Ebro, in the Alavesa, as recently as 1989, its Luberri and Altun wines have already been highly praised. It has 50 ha of vineyard.

## Unión Vitivinícola, Marqués de Cáceres
This bodega was founded as recently as 1970 by Enrique Forner,

whose training was in Bordeaux, where he owns Châteaux Camensac and runs Château Larose-Trintaudon, which he formerly owned. He was advised by the great Bordeaux enologist Professor Peynaud. The Marqués does exist (indeed he is a grandee of Spain) but his part in the bodega is that of a benevolent bystander. The wines, though, do not attempt to imitate Bordeaux and have gained an international reputation as amongst the most serious in Rioja. They are consistently good. The bodega has practically no vineyards of its own – 2.2 ha! – but is able to buy from excellent nearby vineyards, including those that have very old vines. The premises and equipment are first rate and perfectly maintained; indeed they are exemplary. It produces a complete range of wines. There are four whites: a young one in the modern style, an oak-aged *crianza* in the traditional style, both from 100 per cent Viura; Antea, mostly from Viura but with 10 per cent Malvasía grapes, which is barrel-fermented in Allier oak; and Satinela, a delicious sweet wine with an aroma of apricots, which is vinified from very ripe grapes, 85 per cent Viura and 15 per cent Malvasía. There is a very fresh *rosado* from 80 per cent Tempranillo and 20 per cent Garnacha, and a complete range of reds, made from 85 to 90 per cent Tempranillo and the rest Graciano and Garnacha; it includes all levels up to *gran reserva*. The *crianzas* spend fifteen to eighteen months in oak, the *reservas* thirty-six and the *grandes reservas* forty-eight. Maturation is in American and French oak with a little Spanish, but French oak exclusively is used for the *reservas* and *grandes reservas*. The young whites and *rosados* have a very long, cool fermentation in iso-thermal stainless-steel tanks; the reds are fermented at 26 to 28°C.

## Marqués de Griñón

Don Carlos Falcó y Fernández de Códova, Marqués de Griñón, is one of the best wine growers in Spain, who also has interests in Argentina. But apart from making wine, he markets wine chosen by himself, made and matured by others according to his requirements. This is how he produces his Riojas. They are actually made by Bodegas Berberana (see above) in their beautiful old cellars at Ollauri. His range is a modest one in size but far from modest in quality. There are only reds: a *crianza*, the Reserva Especial and the Reserva Colección Personal, all nearly 100 per cent Tempranillo, given six months in new French and American oak. They are very good.

## Bodegas Marqués de Murrieta

The origins and early history of this great bodega have already been given, for it is tied in intimately with the origins of the Rioja that we know today. It was founded in 1872 by Luciano de Murrieta y García-Lemoine, who was born in 1822 to a father who had emigrated to Peru and a Creole mother whose father owned a silver mine. His upbringing, however, was influenced by his uncle Cristóbal Pascual de Murrieta who, amongst other interests, was a banker in London, where he learned what good wine tasted like. After some military adventures, in 1872 Luciano bought his fine estate at Ygay, just outside Logroño on the road to Zaragoza, near the border of the Rioja Alta and the Rioja Baja. By this time he knew all that was to be known at the time about wine making. He died a bachelor in Logroño aged 89. The estate remained in the family until it was bought in 1983 by Vicente Cabrián, Conde de Creixel, who moved to live there. Soon afterwards he restored his beautiful estate at Pontevedra, the Pazo de Barrantes, where he makes fine Rías Baixas wines. Two more different wine styles are hard to imagine. Following his tragically early death, it is now owned by his son Vicente. The estate includes 300 ha of vineyards, notable for their enormous number of big, reddish stones. It is planted with the red varieties Tempranillo (75 per cent), Mazuelo (12 per cent), Garnacha (10 per cent) and Graciano (3 per cent), and the white varieties Viura, Malvasía and (a rare choice) Garnacha Blanca. The white wines are pressed in vertical presses and fermented at 18°C. The red wines are tank fermented for eighteen to twenty-five days at a temperature of 30°C. The tanks are equipped with French *pigeage* machines (most unusual in Rioja), which work like stirring a vast stewpot very slowly. The caps (of grape skins) are pressed very gently in large old cage presses and 20 per cent of the press wine is added. The wines, both red and white, are cask aged in 13,200 casks, all of which are American with the exception of 700 French; 500 are replaced every year. This is the place for oak-aged whites and no one produces anything remotely like them save for López de Heredia. Only a couple of decades ago Spanish white wines in general, and those from the Rioja in particular, tended to be demonstrably over-oaked, flabby and oxidized. This was never so with those from the Marqués de Murrieta, and the present range of full-bodied whites balances oakiness with an ample acidity, remarkable complexity of flavour and great length. They are also unusual amongst whites in that not only do they last well but they actually repay laying down, particularly the top of the range. Even the youngest is a *reserva*, made from 87 per cent Viura, 3 per cent Malvasía and 10 per cent Garnacha Blanca, with two years in oak. The Misela, made from 79 per cent Viura, 6 per cent Malvasía and 15 per cent Garnacha Blanca, is at least three years old when sold and should be kept for another three. Top of the range is Castillo Ygay Gran Reserva Especial, made from 95 per cent Viura and 5 per cent Malvasía only in the best years and sold at ten years old. The unusual inclusion in most of these wines is the Garnacha Blanca, which is used in France to make the best white wines of Châteauneuf-du-Pape, and one can see the resemblance. The red wines are equally remarkable. The first thing one notices is their intense colour. The second, with experience, is their remarkable longevity: they seem to go on for ever and actually to improve into extreme old age. The 1931, which has already been mentioned, was made from 56 per cent Tempranillo, 17 per cent Garnacha, 17 per cent Mazuelo and 10 per cent Graciano; it spent five months in tanks and then twenty-nine months in fairly new oak before bottling. Drunk in 1996, it was a superb old wine. But it was by no means the oldest in the cellar, which has every vintage back to 1877. These are recorked as necessary, the 1931 in 1957 and 1987. The bottle store is under a large pond fed by a spring, which is very good for temperature control. Even the bottom of the range is a *reserva*. The 1992 was made from 75 per cent Tempranillo, 10 per cent Garnacha, 12 per cent Mazuelo and 3 per cent Graciano and was bottled in March 1995. The Reserva Especial 1989 was made from 78 per cent Tempranillo, 7 per cent Garnacha, 12 per cent Mazuelo and 3 per cent Graciano; it was matured for six months in tank and forty-two months in American oak before bottling. Top of the range Castillo Ygay Gran Reserva Especial 1987 was made from 74 per cent Tempranillo, 10 per cent Garnacha, 13 per cent Mazuelo and 3 per cent Graciano and spent three months in tank and thirty-nine in American oak before bottling. These special reserves are only made in the best years: 1959, 1964, 1970, 1975, 1978, 1981, 1982 and (probably) 1994 and 1995. The 1959 was still for sale in 1996, but it will be many years before we see the youngest. One could lay them down for one's grandchildren. In 1997, however, there came a new venture: two *jóvenes*, a white and a red, sold as Colección 2100, the white made from 90 per cent Viura, 5 per cent Malvasía and 5 per cent

Garnacha Blanca, the red from 75 per cent Tempranillo, 12 per cent Mazuelo, 10 per cent Garnacha and 3 per cent Graciano. Compared with the traditional wines of this bodega they come as a shock, but they are undoubtedly amongst the very best of their kind.

## Herederos del Marqués de Riscal

The importance of this bodega in the early history of Rioja has already been related. In 1860, having personally decided to engage the services of Jean Pineau, Don Camilo Hurtado de Amézaga, Marqués de Riscal, set about establishing a model bodega on French lines at Elciego in the Rioja Alavesa. He engaged an architect, Ricardo Bellsola, and sent him to study the *chais* in Bordeaux. When he came back he built the fine stone bodega that we see today, though it has since been extended. The most modern wine-making equipment was installed with *barricas* for maturing the wine, the first to be used on a commercial scale in Rioja or indeed in Spain. Within five years medals were being won at exhibitions all over the world. Ever since then the red Riscal wines have provided a standard by which others have been judged. But it must be admitted that there was a hitch. From the mid 1970s to the early 1980s the wines failed to live up to their high reputation. This was mainly due to trouble with casks; they were old and some had become tainted. There was also perhaps an element of resting on laurels. In 1985 there was a big shake-up and 80 per cent of the barrels were scrapped. Now the bodega is completely back to its old, great form. In the earliest days the emphasis was on Cabernet Sauvignon, producing wines sold as 'Médoc Alavesa', but for many years now the emphasis has been on Tempranillo. Of the 202 ha of vineyard, there are 25 ha Cabernet Sauvignon (some of which date back to 1898), 28 ha Graciano (perhaps the largest holding of this variety), 10 ha Mazuelo and all the rest are Tempranillo. In addition, grapes are bought from 250 ha of vineyards owned by local growers, who are meticulously supervised and who are paid more for grapes from old vines. Some Viura is used for the *rosado* but any white wine left over is sold to other bodegas. There is no white Riscal Rioja. There are indeed white Riscals of excellent quality, but these are all grown in Rueda, and that is another story. The red grapes are divided by age of vines: under fifteen years, used principally for *rosado*, fifteen to thirty years, and over thirty years old, which are used for making wines at the top of the range. The bunches of grapes are examined to eliminate by hand any below standard. The red wines are fermented in epoxy-lined cement tanks which are temperature-controlled to between 28 and 30°C by immersed stainless-steel coolers; but a stainless-steel installation is on the way. The *rosado* is fermented at between 13 and 17°C. Various kinds of oak have been tried for maturation, including American, Canadian, French Nevers and even Bosnian, but American has been found to be the best; it is bought as wood, seasoned, and made up into casks by the bodega's own coopers. There are no *jóvenes* or *crianzas*, only *reservas*, *grandes reservas* and the superb Barón de Chirel. *Grandes reservas* are made every year but only after a careful selection of grapes and wine. Barón de Chirel is only made when everything is exactly right. The Reserva 1993 was made from 90 per cent Tempranillo and 10 per cent Mazuelo and aged in oak for twenty-five months. The Gran Reserva 1986 was made from 65 per cent Tempranillo, 10 per cent Graciano, 5 per cent Mazuelo and 20 per cent 'other varieties', which may be taken as meaning principally Cabernet Sauvignon, and aged in oak for thirty-six months, while the Gran Reserva 1987 was made from 45 per cent Tempranillo, 20 per cent Graciano and 35 per cent 'other varieties', aged in oak for thirty-two months. The 1991 Barón de Chirel Reserva was made from grapes picked before rain wrecked the latter part of the vintage, 45 per cent Tempranillo and 55 per cent 'other varieties'. The 1994, with a high proportion of Graciano from old vines, is superb and should age wonderfully. The *rosado* 1996 was made from 90 per cent Tempranillo and 10 per cent Viura. The reds have excellent ageing potential, especially the Barón de Chirel, which can age for decades. Indeed, the 1871 was still excellent in 1997. The bodega is fully back on form.

### Marqués de Vargas
A small bodega in Logroño with 60 ha of vineyards which are enough to make it self-sufficient. It produces only one wine, a red *reserva*, which is very good. The 1993 was made from 75 per cent Tempranillo, 10 per cent Mazuelo, 10 per cent Garnacha and 5 per cent Graciano.

### Bodegas Marqués de Vitoria
This bodega at Oyón in the Rioja Alavesa began life in 1988 as a cooperative but has since been acquired by the old-established firm of Faustino Martínez. It retains its independence and is in fact being expanded, producing a complete range of good-quality wines. Some

are organic. It goes in for varietals, the white from Viura and the reds from Tempranillo.

## Bodegas Martínez Bujanda

Joaquín Martínez Bujanda was a wine grower on a very modest scale with 10 ha of vines in the Rioja Alavesa. In 1889 he set up a small winery built into a cave near Oyón. Those were modest beginnings, but the business expanded, steadily buying more vineyards. The wine, however, was sold in bulk to other bodegas and it was not until 1966 that the name appeared on a label. It is still a family-owned company, now in the fourth generation, and amongst the largest. A new, completely modern winery was opened in 1984 and the old one has since become a fascinating museum of old vineyard and bodega tools and equipment. It is now run by Jesús Martínez Bujanda, whose father, also called Jesús, had a philosophy for making good wine: 'A clean cellar, a clean cellar, a clean cellar!' And how he has followed his father's precept! It is almost a fetish. He even goes to the length of softening the water to make cleaning easier and the whole place is immaculate. Another unusual feature is that it is entirely self-sufficient for grapes, owning four vineyards in the Rioja Alta with a total area of 105 ha, one of 120 ha in the Rioja Baja, and twenty-three in the Rioja Alavesa with a total area of 88 ha, making 313 ha in all. The Rioja Baja vineyard, Finca La Esperilla, has a rare microclimate on a relatively cool hillside, producing lighter wines with more finesse than is usual in the region. Finca Valpiedra is on a stretch of land by the river. Another unusual aspect is that Cabernet Sauvignon is grown, together with an unusually high proportion of Mazuelo. All the fermentation is done in temperature-controlled stainless-steel tanks (with the exception of a barrel-fermented white), the whites being fermented at 16 to 17°C over a two-month period, the *rosados* at 17 to 18°C and the cask-aged reds at 25 to 28°C. There is also a young red, using 100 per cent Tempranillo, made by carbonic maceration for early drinking. American oak is used for maturation save for the Cabernet Sauvignon, which spends the first year in American oak and is then put into French; and the casks are kept in carefully temperature and humidity-controlled conditions. There is a complete range of wines, the young sold under the name Valdemar and those with ageing under the name Conde de Valdemar. All of them, save for the *joven* made by carbonic maceration, which is disappointing, are exceptionally good. The Conde himself is a benevolent bystander and takes no part in the business. The barrel-fermented white avoids being over-oaked and is notably successful. The *rosado* is a varietal Garnacha. Of the red wines, the Crianza 1993 was made from 87 per cent Tempranillo and 13 per cent Mazuelo, the Reserva 1992 from 80 per cent Tempranillo and 20 per cent Mazuelo, and the Gran Reserva 1987 from 80 per cent Tempranillo and 20 per cent Mazuelo; it spent ten months in stainless steel followed by thirty-two months in oak. The very elegant Reserva 1990 is the beginning of a new departure, being made of equal parts Tempranillo and Cabernet Sauvignon, and a wine will shortly be released made from 75 per cent Cabernet Sauvignon and 25 per cent Tempranillo. There is also a varietal Garnacha Reserva, which shows how well a balanced and carefully made Garnacha can age. All the mature reds are notable for their ageing potential, helped perhaps by the unusually generous use of Mazuelo or Cabernet Sauvignon, which blend very well with the softer, fruity Tempranillo. Finca Valpiedra is now being sold as an excellent single vineyard wine, the 1994 *reserva* being made from 95 per cent Tempranillo and 5 per cent Cabernet Sauvignon.

### Bodegas Martínez Lacuesta
Established in 1895, this family-run bodega operates from the middle of Haro. It has no vineyards of its own and relies on cooperatives to supply the wine for a complete, reliable range. The grape mix is varied considerably in the different wines. The Reserva Especial of 1980 was 80 per cent Tempranillo, 15 per cent Mazuelo and 5 per cent Graciano, the Campeador Reserva of 1985 was 60 per cent Garnacha and 40 per cent Tempranillo, while in the 1989 the proportions were the other way round. The Reserva 1989 was 80 per cent Tempranillo, 10 per cent Mazuelo, 5 per cent Graciano and 5 per cent Viura.

### Bodegas Montecillo
With a history going back to 1874, this was originally called Hijos de Celestino Navajas and was one of the bodegas established in the first boom, by two brothers, one of whom had studied in Bordeaux. It changed its name and was bought in 1973 by the great sherry and brandy house Osborne of Puerto de Santa María. The resulting influx of capital and knowledge enabled it to move into the big league. Located at Fuenmayor, it has a complete range of good,

reliable wines, offering good value and sold under the marks Montecillo, Viña Cumbrero and Viña Monty. They tend to be varietal – Viura or Tempranillo as the case may be – and use is made of French oak. The Viña Monty *grandes reservas* are excellent.

## David Moreno Peña

David Moreno Peña, originally an automobile engineer with Seat, came back home to the Rioja and founded his bodega at Badaran in 1981, selling his first wine in 1989, mostly from his own 1 ha vineyard and from grapes bought from members of his family, who are long-established growers. He uses both French and American oak and some of his reds are made by carbonic maceration. He produces a complete range of attractive and attractively priced wines in the modern, light style under his own name and under the mark Monasterio de Yuso. His first *reserva*, made from 90 per cent Tempranillo, the remainder being Graciano and Garnacha, was the 1991.

## Bodegas Muga

It is impossible not to be enthusiastic about Muga wines. The bodega was founded by Isaac Muga Martínez in 1932, right between the two boom periods, at a time of consolidation rather than enterprise. Originally it was in the middle of Haro, but Sr Muga was planning a move to premises near the station when he died in 1969. It was inherited by his three children, who made the move in 1971, subsequently digging cellars and most recently building a tower. At the moment they have only 35 ha of vineyards but are expanding in this area; the rest of the grapes needed are bought in, some from growers who have been supplying the family for over forty years. The bodega prides itself on being 'artisanal', or in other words completely traditional. Here there is no stainless steel but plenty of oak. Some of the white wines are barrel-fermented but all the reds are fermented in the old way, using 18,000 litre oak *tinas* for eight days at 30 to 32°C. This does not mean that it is unwilling to experiment, though. For maturation it has tried oak from Kentucky, Ohio, Rouvre, Limousin, Allier and Spain, maturing the same wine in different barrels, side by side. It buys the wood and makes all the barrels in its own cooperage. The result so far is that there is slightly more French oak than American. New barrels are used for fermenting white wine and are then used for maturing red, being kept until they are eight to ten years old. There is a full range of wines and only traditional Spanish grape varieties are used. Any wine that does not come up to standard is immediately sold on. Muga Blanco is made from 90 per cent Viura and 10 per cent Malvasía; it is barrel-fermented, using both American and French oak, is bone dry and beautifully balanced, avoiding being over-oaked. The *rosado* is very pale in colour, made from 60 per cent Garnacha, 30 per cent Viura and 10 per cent Tempranillo. The emphasis, though, is on red wines, which account for 90 per cent of the production. The classic Reserva 1991 was made from 70 per cent Tempranillo, 20 per cent Garnacha and 10 per cent of Mazuelo and Graciano. The excellent Prado Enea 1987 Gran Reserva was made from 80 per cent Tempranillo with 20 per cent of the other varieties and spent twelve months in wooden vats, thirty-six months in oak barrels and a minimum of thirty-six months in bottle before being released. A new wine, Torre Muga, has recently been introduced, the 1991 being made from 75 per cent Tempranillo, 15 per cent Mazuelo and 10 per cent Graciano. It also makes a Cava, Conde de Haro. The red wines need some age to give of their best, and their best is very good indeed.

### Bodegas Olarra
Housed in a large, elegant building on the edge of Logroño, this bodega was founded in 1972 by Don Luis Olarra, a steel magnate from Bilbao, and some of his friends. It is part of a group that includes Bodegas Ondarre and Antina Vins in Penedés. Owning no vineyards of its own, it buys from all three regions and produces a complete range of wines sold under the marks Otoñal, Añares and Cerro Añon. The Cerro Añon wines are very good indeed.

### Bodegas Ondarre
This bodega, at Viana in the province of Navarra, is part of the group that includes Bodegas Olarra and Antina Vins in Penedés. It prides itself on being technically advanced and produces a complete range of good wines with notable *reservas*. The 1993 was made from 75 per cent Tempranillo, 10 per cent Garnacha, 7.5 per cent Mazuelo and 7.5 per cent Graciano.

### Bodegas Palacio
Founded in 1894 by Don Cosme Palacio, this bodega at Laguardia has had a very complicated recent history. In 1972 the Palacio family sold it to Domecq, the great sherry and brandy firm in Jerez. Then Seagram, the Canadian international group, moved into an

equal partnership with Domecq. In 1977 Seagram bought Domecq out. However, Seagram decided to reduce its wine interests and in 1987 Bodegas Palacio was bought out by the management, headed by M. Jean Gervais, a Frenchman who had been manager of Barton & Guestier in Bordeaux and a vice-president of Seagram Europe. In 1998 it was bought by the Spanish group Hijos de Antonio Barcelo, but the management was left in place. M Gervais's consultant is the flying wine maker Michel Rolland, who owns five châteaux in Bordeaux, advises many more, and has consultancies that take him all over the world. The philosophy is therefore French but without any intention to produce a French style of wine; indeed, it is to produce the best style of Rioja using only the traditional Tempranillo and Viura grapes. It does use French oak, though: 5,800 out of the 6,000 casks. It took a few years to get its act together but recent vintages have been very well made. It offers a complete range. Glorioso is the mark used for its very good standard wines, matured in French oak, then El Portico, aged in new American oak, and there is a top range of Cosme Palacio wines, aged partly in new French oak. It is planning to introduce two new wines, a white *reserva* from Viura grapes, to be called Regio, and a red Reserva Especial.

## Bodegas Palacios Remondo

A bodega of modest size in Logroño, with 120 ha of vineyard (of which 75 are currently in production), it is owned and entirely run by the Palacios family. Its wines are well regarded and are sold under the name Herencia Remondo. Merlot is used in some of them.

## Bodegas Federico Paternina

Paternina is perhaps the most famous bodega in the Rioja. It has a complicated history. It was founded in 1896 by Federico de Paternina y Josué, the fifth son of an aristocratic wine maker, Eduardo de Paternina, Marqués de Terán, who decided to go it alone and established his bodega at Ollauri, with wonderful cellars dating from the late sixteenth century carved out of the living rock, where the *reservas* and *gran reservas* are still matured. In 1919, however, something went wrong and the bodega was bought by Joaquín Herrero de la Riva, a banker from Logroño, with the backing of four Spanish families. Three years later they brought in a French wine maker, Etienne Labatut, who took the bodega to new heights. At the same time they acquired the premises of the Cooperativa de Sindicatos Católicos in Haro, where the headquarters still are. In

1972 it was bought by the large group Rumasa, and after their dispossession it was run by the state for a short time before being sold to a rich businessman, Marcos Eguizábal Ramírez, who also bought some of the Rumasa interests in Jerez, but most of these have been sold on. At the time of the Rumasa take-over, Paternina had acquired a special position as the supplier of the most popular Rioja in Spain: the red Banda Azul. When a Spanish family wanted a treat, it was Banda Azul that they bought. Then a catastrophe happened: 1972 was one of the worst vintages on record and orders were given that the young wine from this vintage, which had not yet finished its malolactic fermentation, was to be blended in with the wine being bottled for sale. The wine duly completed its malolactic fermentation – but in bottle. Bubbles rose up. There was a current joke that people who asked for Banda Azul were asked whether they wanted it *con* or *sin gaz*, like mineral water. Unfortunately, to many unsophisticated drinkers Banda Azul *was* Rioja, and the whole district passed beneath a cloud. All of this is now ancient history. Rioja has recovered its image, and Banda Azul has long since recovered its quality and its place as a very good buy. But it was a bad time. Things are very different today. The bodega is thoroughly up to date and fascinating in its automation: one massive control panel organizes the movement of wine throughout the vast building. White wines are fermented at 18 to 20°C and reds at 23 to 26°C. All the wood is American. The range of wines is very comprehensive. The basic white wine is Banda Dorada, which is a varietal Viura. Monte Haro is a semi-sweet white made from Viura with a little Malvasía. The white *reserva* is made from Viura, Malvasía and Garnacha Blanca before ageing in cask and bottle: a good example of a traditional white Rioja. The very aromatic and classic Banda Oro is made from a similar grape mix but is one-half cask-fermented, a good compromise which others might emulate. Graciela is the top semi-sweet white, made in limited quantities and only in very good years, from very ripe Viura and Malvasía grapes grown in a vineyard governed by the phases of the moon; it was planted in the first lunar quarter, pruned during the waning of the moon and so on. The fresh and fragrant *rosado*, Banda Rosa, is made from 60 per cent Tempranillo, 20 per cent Garnacha and 20 per cent Viura grapes, and there is a superior version which is also called Banda Oro. The ubiquitous and very agreeable red is Banda Azul, a *crianza* made from 75 per cent Tempranillo, 20 per cent

Garnacha and 5 per cent Mazuelo grapes and given twenty-four months in the wood. Viña Vial is a red *reserva* with 80 per cent Tempranillo, 10 per cent Garnacha and 10 per cent Mazuelo, given thirty months in oak followed by three years in bottle. A further step up in the reds is Banda Oro, again from a similar grape mix. The Gran Reserva red is made 90 per cent by the usual red wine fermentation but the other 10 per cent by carbonic maceration using a grape mix of 65 per cent Tempranillo, 15 per cent Garnacha, 10 per cent Mazuelo and 10 per cent Graciano; it spends thirty-two months in wood and then at least four years in bottle before it is sold. The renowned, elegant *gran reserva* Conde de los Andes is made from 80 per cent Tempranillo, 10 per cent Graciano and 10 per cent Mazuelo grapes with thirty-six months wood-ageing. Finally there is the newly introduced Clos Paternina, made only in very small quantities and matured in new French oak casks.

### Granja Nuestra Señora de Remelluri

It is impossible to imagine a more beautiful estate than this, and the wines it grows are just as beautiful. It is up in the hills above Labastida, on the edge of the Sierra Toloño, 600 to 800 m high, in the Rioja Alavesa but bordering on the Rioja Alta. Originally belonging to the monastery of Toloño, by the fourteenth century it was independent and growing wine. At the end of the eighteenth century some of the vineyards were in the hands of Manuel Quintano, whose part in the history of Rioja has already been described. In the 1960s it was bought by Jaime and Amaya Rodríguez Salis; he is Spanish and she is French. He went to a local wine maker, who asked him whether he wanted to produce Bordeaux or Burgundy. He went to another wine maker. His first vintage was in 1971. Nowadays the estate is run by their daughter, also Amaya, and the wine maker is their son, the dynamic Telmo, who studied at the University of Bordeaux and later in the Rhône with the great Auguste Clape, and who has become one of Spain's flying wine makers, making wine in Rueda and Navarra as well as here. Another son, Diego, sells the wine. The whole estate is 90 ha, with 70 ha of vineyards planted on chalky clay soils in all the right places, with some at the very top, and they supply all the grapes for the wine apart from some bought from a 1 ha vineyard owned by the cook. The red grapes are 80 per cent Tempranillo, with some Garnacha and Graciano, which grows very well here. Some white grapes are also grown – Garnacha

Blanca and Moscatel del País, with other varieties being grown experimentally – but no white wines are made for sale. They do not wish to jump on the bandwagon of 'organic viticulture' but use no herbicides, systemic products or chemical fertilizers, just organic compost and manure applied once in four years. Owing to its height, the estate is very cold at night and can catch the frost; in the spring of 1997 half the crop was destroyed. For the same reason the vintage is unusually late, with picking generally at the end of October. The yield is about half the average for Rioja, which is itself low by world standards. And they face another rather unusual hazard: wild boar. To keep them from eating the grapes, they play wirelesses in the vineyards, and the boars think that men are there. The fact that the press house is in the middle of the vineyard enables the grapes to be crushed quickly without risk of oxidation. After the malolactic fermentation the wine is aged for two years in oak, but any that does not reach the standard set is sold off: about a quarter. Of the 3,300 *barricas*, 1,000 are American oak, the rest French. One-year-old casks are bought from Château Latour. The wines are neither filtered nor fined. In a good vintage they are second to none and age well. Of recent vintages, the 1991 is excellent; the 1992 was frankly disappointing but was not sold in England; the 1994 and 1995 are again excellent.

## La Rioja Alta

If any one bodega were to be singled out as the exemplar of the classic style of Rioja, this would have to be it, producing year after year wines of the highest quality and only the highest quality, without a single hitch. They are remarkable. The company was founded in 1890, when Don Daniel-Alfredo Ardanza y Sánchez got together with some friends: Doña Saturnina García Cid y Gárete, Don Dionisio del Prado y Lablanca, Don Felipe Puig de la Bellacasa y Herrán and Don Maríano Lacorte Tapia. They raised the necessary and very modest capital, which has been increased several times since. Their trade mark, the Río Oja flowing by four oak trees, was registered in 1902. After over a hundred years the company now has many shareholders but remains essentially a family concern, managed by the fifth-generation descendants of the founders, and has now expanded to form a group that includes Torre de Oña, in Rioja, Lagar de Fornelos in Rías Baixas, and vineyards in Ribera del Duero. It is one of the great bodegas by the railway station in Haro.

Over the years it has accumulated 350 ha of vineyard but has to buy additional grapes from a number of growers. It has kept up with the times and is immaculate, with controlled-temperature fermentations in stainless steel. All the wood is American. It concentrates on red wines from *crianza* upwards (though it ages its *crianzas* so long that they could officially be offered as *reservas*), and these account for 99 per cent of the production, but there is one white wine: Viña Ardanza, made from 95 per cent Viura and 5 per cent Malvasía, aged for nine months in large wooden vats and then for twenty-four in barrel. Of the red wines, the *crianza* is sold as Viña Alberdi; the 1992 was made from 85 per cent Tempranillo and 5 per cent each of Mazuelo, Graciano and Viura, with two years in barrel. There are two *reservas*. Viña Arana is the lighter style and in 1988 was made from 90 per cent Tempranillo with 5 per cent each of Mazuelo and Graciano; after six to eight months in large oak vats it had three years in barrel. The red Viña Ardanza is a big, robust and beautifully smooth wine, slightly more alcoholic (13° as compared to 12.5°), complex, with perfect balance and great length. In 1989 it was made from 70 per cent Tempranillo, 25 per cent Garnacha and the rest Mazuelo and Graciano. There are two extremely fine *grandes reservas*. Gran Reserva 904 was in the past called Gran Reserva 1904, not to indicate a vintage but the year when the bodega merged with one owned by one of its directors. However, the possibility of confusion was obvious and the name was changed. It is a big wine and one of the best of the *grandes reservas*. The 1985 was made from 85 per cent Tempranillo and 7.5 per cent each of Mazuelo and Graciano, aged for four months in large oak vats and then five years in barrels, giving an elegant wine of perfect structure and exquisite complexity. Top of the range comes Gran Reserva 890. Again its name was originally 1890, the year of the bodega's foundation, but it was changed for the same reason. If the 904 is a big wine, the 890 is bigger still, with a magnificence that does not hide its subtlety. The 1981 was 90 per cent Tempranillo with 5 per cent each of Graciano and Mazuelo, aged for six months in wooden vats and then for no less than seven years in oak barrels.

## Bodegas Riojanas

This notable bodega, which has a charming little fantasy castle, was founded in Cenicero at the height of the French influence in 1890. It produces a remarkably wide range of wines that rise from good to excellent quality, and is still a family-owned company. It has 200 ha of local vineyards which supply 60 per cent of its needs and buys from a number of growers. All the oak used is American. Its two best-known trademarks are Monte Real and Viña Albina, the former used for the more commercial wines and the latter, which is the name of one of the founders, for the more expensive ones. About 85 per cent of its wines are reds and most are *reservas*, the whites fermented at 18°C and the reds at 28 to 30°C. The Monte Real 1993 and the Viña Albina Gran Reserva 1983 whites were both made from 90 per cent Viura and 10 per cent Malvasía, but the former was given twelve months in tanks and another twelve in barrel, while the latter was given eight months in tanks and twenty-four in barrel. There is also a barrel-fermented white Viña Albina. The *rosados* include a Monte Real 1993 Crianza made from 40 per cent Tempranillo, 40 per cent Viura and 20 per cent Garnacha with twelve months' wood ageing. The grape mix for the reds is generally 80 per cent Tempranillo, 15 per cent Mazuela and 5 per cent Graciano and the Viña Albana *grandes reservas* are very good. The Monte Real wines are found all over Spain and can be relied on. They can age well.

## Bodegas Roda

This new boutique bodega, hidden away and strangely anonymous on the hill above the station at Haro, is fantastic. It was set up in 1986 by the Rotllant-Daurella family, who are wine merchants in Barcelona, where the commercial headquarters are. It has vineyards of its own, densely planted to give a small yield, and organically cultivated, but the grapes from these are not used, nor will they be until the vines are at least fifteen years old. At the moment grapes are bought from a number of growers and have to be from vines that are at least thirty years old. When the bunches are delivered they are individually selected by hand so that only perfect ones are used. The site on the hill is a remarkable one, with the deep maturation cellars carved out of the living rock, and at the end one emerges on to a balcony, hidden away on the hillside, with a glorious view over the River Ebro. Vinification is in large vats of French oak equipped with temperature control, and after the malolactic fermentation the wine is matured in French oak barrels, one-third of which are renewed each year. Owing to the peculiarity of the site, everything can be done by gravity. The grapes are introduced through a door high up in the bodega wall and it all follows from there. They make only two wines, both red: Roda I and Roda II, the first and second quality. Anything that is not good enough for the second is sold on. Nineteen ninety-two was generally a poor year in Rioja, but in that place of many sites and microclimates some first-rate grapes were nevertheless grown. Roda I was a varietal Tempranillo: a superb wine which will benefit from long ageing. Roda II contained 5 per cent Garnacha. It is softer and already drinks well, but although it does not match up to Roda I, by any normal standards it is very good indeed. In 1993 it contained 19 per cent Garnacha.

## Cooperativa San Isidro/Viñedos de Aldeanueva

The 850 growers who are members of this cooperative at Aldeanueva del Ebro have between them 2,500 ha vineyards growing 80 per cent Tempranillo and 20 per cent Garnacha. They have recently introduced an unusual wine in the form of a 1995 barrel-fermented red, Viña Azabache, which has been highly praised.

## Viña Salceda

Vines have been grown here for a very long time by the family of the Conde de la Salceda, and in 1969 a group of friends decided to establish a bodega, but it took some years to reach fruition. The company was founded in 1973 and the bodega built in a delightful position just above the River Ebro, near Elciego, in 1974. It produces only red wines and only *crianzas* and above. It has 90 ha of vineyards, growing mostly Tempranillo and some Mazuelo, with additional grapes and wines being bought in. Most of the vineyards used are over fifteen years old. The bodega, as would be expected, is completely up to date with a stainless-steel fermentation plant operating at 32 to 33°C. American oak is preferred for the maturation and the barrels are thrown away after ten years. The Viña Salceda Crianza of the rather dim year 1993 was made after a careful selection of grapes and is elegant. The Reserva 1989 was classic but the top wine is the Conde de Salceda Gran Reserva and the 1987 was excellent. The grape mix is 85 to 90 per cent Tempranillo with Graciano and Mazuelo. These wines mature well.

## Bodegas Carlos Serres

Founded in 1986, this bodega in Haro produces a complete range. It is noted for its Carlos Serres Grandes Reservas and its *reserva* and *gran reserva* sold under the mark Onomástica. The Onomástica Reserva 1991 was mainly Tempranillo and Garnacha but with a little Macabeo. The wines are very good.

## Sierra Cantabria

Situated in San Vicente de la Sonsierra, this bodega was founded in 1870 and has been in the hands of the Eguren family ever since. It has 100 ha of vineyard and supplies a complete range of wines. Its good red *joven*, sold under the name Murmuron, is made from 90 per cent Tempranillo and 10 per cent Viura. Its best wines are the reds from *crianza* upwards. The *crianza* is a varietal Tempranillo, while the *reserva* and *gran reserva* have 10 per cent Garnacha.

## Bodegas de Crianza SMS

This bodega in Villanueva, Alava, produces good white and red wines under the mark Valserrano.

## Bodegas Sonsierra Sociedad Cooperativa

Situated in San Vicente, this is one of the best of the cooperatives. Having sold wine to many of the leading houses, it decided to bottle its own, and has done so with notable success. The red wines are varietal Tempranillos, the *reservas* and *grandes reservas* being sold under the name Viña Mindiarte.

## Torre de Oña

There could be no bodega more up to date than this, founded in 1987 at Páganos-Laguardia; it is full of stainless steel and is even air-conditioned. But the founders decided to sell it, and in January 1995 it was bought by La Rioja Alta. It is surrounded by its 50 ha of vines all trained *en espaldera*, mostly Tempranillo with some Mazuelo and a little Cabernet Sauvignon, but these last are under threat. When it changed hands it was using entirely French oak, some of it from Château Margaux, but now there is 50 per cent American. Until recently it only made one wine, a red *reserva*, but now there are two. Both are sold under the mark Barón de Oña. The white is cask-fermented and made from 90 per cent Viura and 10 per cent Malvasía. Unlike so many cask-fermented wines, it is fresh, crisp and not over-oaked. The red *reserva* is made from 80 per cent

Tempranillo, 3 per cent Cabernet Sauvignon, Mazuelo and a very small amount of Graciano. It is a very different style from the wines of Rioja Alta and very good indeed, in a totally separate way. It needs bottle ageing and the 1990, after two years in wood and four in bottle, still needed to be kept for a year or two. The 1994 is exceptional and will certainly age well.

### Bodega Torres-Librada
Founded as recently as 1987, this family bodega has 20 ha of vines which supply all its needs. It sells red wines made from 95 per cent Tempranillo under the mark Torrescudo.

### Bodegas Viña Ijalba
The story starts in 1975, when Don Dionisio Ruiz Ijalba planted his first vineyard near Logroño. He is a local businessman who is involved in gravel extraction, and the vineyard was planted on land that was a near desert after the gravel had been extracted, unsuitable for any other crop. Further vineyards were subsequently planted and there are now 70 ha of them, all cultivated on ecological lines and low-yielding. They include one of the largest plantings of Graciano in Rioja: 16 ha of a grape which at present accounts for only 0.4 per cent of the total. The very modernistic bodega was built in 1991. It produces a complete range of wines under a number of names. Genolí is a modern-style white made from Viura. Aloque is a *rosado* made from equal amounts of Garnacha and Tempranillo. Livor is a red *joven* made from Tempranillo. Solferino is also a red joven but made by carbonic maceration. Ijalba Graciano is a unique varietal *joven*. Múrice is a red *crianza* made from 90 per cent Tempranillo and 5 per cent each of Mazuelo and Graciano. Ijalba Reserva is made from 90 per cent Tempranillo and 10 per cent Graciano. Ijalba Reserva Especial is made from equal quantities of Tempranillo and Graciano. This bodega already makes excellent wines and is likely to go from strength to strength.

### Viña Valoria
This small bodega in Logroño, founded in 1989, has 25 ha of vineyard. It makes a complete range of wines. The red *reservas* are unusually subtle.

# NAVARRA

## Geography

Navarra is a single autonomous province stretching up into the Pyrenees and adjoining Rioja. Its capital is Pamplona, which lies to the north of the main wine-growing areas. A small part of Navarra is included within the Rioja DO. Apart from that, wine is grown in five areas: Tierra de Estella, the most westerly subzone with 15 per cent of the DO vineyards; Valdizarbe, in the middle, which has 10 per cent of the vineyards; Baja Montaña, to the north-east, with 15 per cent of the vineyards; Ribera Alta, adjoining Valdizarbe to the south, with 30 per cent of the vineyards; and Ribera Baja, at the south around Tudela, with 30 per cent of the vineyards.

## Climate

There is not much difference between the first three subzones. All are described as dry sub-humid, far enough from the sea to be essentially continental yet far enough north to avoid being too hot in the summer. The variable rainfall is of the order of 600 mm, though in the Baja Montaña it tends to be a little higher. The average temperature is 12°C but a little cooler in the Baja Montaña. The summer high is 28°C and the winter low is −2°C. The northern part of Ribera Alta is drier and warmer, with an average temperature of 13°C and a rainfall of 525 mm, but the southern part is drier still, to the point of being classed as semi-arid, with a rainfall of 435 mm and a mean temperature of 13.6°C. Ribera Baja is yet hotter and drier, with a rainfall of 350 mm and a mean temperature of 14°C. The vineyards in the pleasant, undramatic rolling countryside vary between 250 and 560 m in height. Throughout most of the area there are 2,200 hours of sunshine but as many as 2,500 in the Ebro valley.

## Soils

Generally rather light brown with plenty of calcium and fairly fertile; beneath is gravel subsoil above chalk.

## Grapes

Recommended red varieties: Tempranillo, Mazuelo, Graciano, Garnacha Tinta, Cabernet Sauvignon.

Authorized red variety: Merlot.

Experimental red varieties: Ruby Cabernet, Cinsaut, Bolicaire, Alicante, Gamay, Royalty, Tinta de Toro, Cabernet Franc, Pinot Noir, Sangiovese Syrah, Barbera.

Recommended white varieties: Macabeo, Moscatel de Grano Menudo.

Authorized white varieties: Malvasía, Chardonnay, Garnacha Blanca.

Experimental white varieties: Xarel.lo, Parellada, Colombard, Sémillon, Chenin Blanc, Airén, Verdejo, Palomino, Syrah Blanc, Pinot Blanc, Riesling, Gewürtztraminer, Thomson Seedless.

**Planting**
Traditionally, vineyards were planted in the square *marco real* pattern with 1.6 m spacing but some were on a wider pattern known as *ancho*, with up to 3 m between rows. The vines were pruned *en vaso*, but recently there has been a lot of experimenting, using Guyot in the cooler regions, Geneva Double Curtain in the warmer ones and Gobelet for the hottest sites. Growers are being encouraged to use wires, and about 40 per cent of the vineyards are already being harvested mechanically, which has the advantage, particularly for white wines, that it can be done in the cool of the night.

**Vineyard area**
30,000 ha of which 12,833 ha are currently in production.

**Authorized yield**
Ribera Baja: white 56 hl/ha, red 42 ha/ha. Other zones: white 42 hl/ha, red 35 hl/ha. In practice the average production is 35 to 40 hl/ha.

**Wines**
Traditionally Navarra is noted for its *rosados*, which may be between 10 and 13.5°, but the demand for these is static, and there is an increasing production of whites, which may be between 10 and 12.5°, though barrel-fermented Chardonnays may be 1° higher, and more especially of reds, which may be between 10 and 14°. There are also some white *vinos de licor* Moscatel, which may be from 15 to 18° and which must contain not less than 4 per cent unfermented sugar. In the past the emphasis was on *jóvenes*, but is now moving more and more to *crianzas*, *reservas* and *grandes reservas*. *Crianzas* must be aged for at least two years, of which at

least one year (for reds) or six months (for the others) must be in oak. Red *reservas* must be aged for a minimum of three years of which at least one must be in oak, while white and *rosado reservas* must be aged for a minimum of two years with at least six months in oak, as for *crianzas*, but the best wines are usually labelled *reserva*. Red *grandes reservas* must spend at least two years in oak followed by three in bottle, while whites and *rosados* must be aged for at least four years with a minimum of six months in oak. The oak casks used may be up to 350 litres but most shippers use 225 litre *barricas*, which give the right balance of oak in contact with the wine. Some enologists think that two years is too much, as the wine can get over-oaked, but this period is at present stipulated by the regulations. Moscatel *vino de licor* must be aged for at least two years with at least eighteen months in oak but for these there is no limit on the size of casks.

## Production
500,000 hl.

## Vintages
1980 3, 1981 7, 1982 7, 1983 5, 1984 5, 1985 4, 1986 4, 1987 5, 1988 5, 1989 5, 1990 4, 1991 4, 1992 5, 1993 4, 1994 6, 1995 7, 1996 6, 1997 5.

With so many zones and microclimates, however, these figures act only as a rough guide.

As Navarra lies next to Rioja (a substantial part of which lies within the province of Navarra), it might be assumed to have had the same history, but this is not so. Wine growing is inevitably traced back to the Romans, and the Moors did not put an end to it. In the Middle Ages, like Rioja, it benefited from the steady passage of pilgrims along the route to Santiago de Compostela. As Navarre it was one of the most powerful kingdoms, stretching right into what is now France. It became part of the new kingdom of Spain when Ferdinand the Catholic seized all the land south of the Pyrenees in 1512. It was not until 1791 that Louis XVI renounced his title as King of France and Navarre to become King of the French. But the more recent history is what matters. Traditionally the leading grape of the area was the Garnacha, which can produce very good wines, especially *rosados*, but which tends to give short-lived wines and is not by itself generally favoured for fine wines, save in a few areas where the results are exceptional, as in parts of Rioja and Priorato. Nevertheless the wines were historically held in high regard. Samuel Pepys in his diary for 10 February 1669 recorded: 'And then he [the Duke of York] did now mightily comend some new sort of wine lately found out, called Navarr wine; which I tasted, and is I think good wine.' The editor's footnote suggests that it may have been Jurançon, but this is manifest nonsense. The Spanish ambassador had recently given the Duke a recipe for a sauce and probably gave him the wine as well. The wines of Navarra were highly esteemed in Spain. They were also exported to England from San Sebastián. The trade was described in a book published in London in 1700 and entitled *A Description of San Sebastián by one who has been there*. The author described how 'The late war with France, from which we received those excellent Graves Medoc and wines from Pontacq, was the reason for which our Parliament placed such high custom taxes on French wines and other liquors from that nation so that the merchants, in order to pay fewer taxes, looked for a way to supply themselves elsewhere ... fortunately they found within Spain a region called Navarra ... which supply us with wine as good as any which comes from France ... ' But although they were exported to England and to Ireland at the end of the seventeenth century, and continued to be exported until the end of the eighteenth century, the wines of Navarra made little mark here until recent years. Production was large. At the beginning of the nineteenth century there were 30,000 ha of vineyards, a good deal more than there are today, though they were probably less productive, and by the time of the phylloxera the figure had increased to 49,213 ha. The French arrived and traded in the wines, as they had in Rioja, but with less impact and they left no permanent legacy. Navarra was overshadowed by its neighbour, and things remained that way until quite recently. The relatively greater difficulties of transport and communication no doubt played their part, and also the predominance of the Garnacha grape.

The phylloxera arrived in 1892 and, as has been seen, the French vineyards were re-established and France went protectionist. The phylloxera wiped out nearly all the vineyards in Navarra but these were gradually replanted, rising from practically nothing to 11,350 ha in 1906 and to 26,330 in 1920. The growers were mostly smallholders and the history of this time is very much that of the cooperative movement, largely thanks to the leadership of the Catholic Agrarian Cooperative Movement with its motto *Unos por Otros, Dios por Todos*. Ninety per cent of all the wine produced came from the co-ops and it was not very good: massive 'jug' wines for immediate drinking. The regular creation and occasional failure of these co-ops makes a fascinating story, but it falls within the sphere of economic history rather than that of a book about wines. The area under vines steadily increased until in 1935 it was 30,000 ha, though this includes the vineyards within the province of Navarra that were, and still are, included in the Rioja DO. But although there were eventually some sixty-nine cooperatives (and there are still about fifty), the area never quite got back to what it had been before phylloxera, and eventually started to decline, so that in 1980 there were 28,000 ha and no new cooperatives were being founded. At that time the cooperatives were producing 93 per cent of the wine.

The great increase in the quality and prestige of Navarra wines was led by the merchant houses, which are described below and some of which are of considerable age. The first moves to create a DO date as far back as 1933, but everything got stifled by the Civil War and then by the economic consequences of the Second World War, so that the regulations for the new DO were not finally approved until 1975. Soon afterwards there was a very important development: the establishment of a viticulture and enology centre, at first a company called EVENSA and subsequently EVENA (Estación de Viticultura y Enología de Navarra), with the aid of funds provided by the provincial government and enthusiastically supported by the wine growers. It is an extremely impressive place, with vine nurseries to produce virus-free plants of many varieties, experimental vineyards in all the subzones, and microvinifications to test grape varieties and techniques: 250 a year. On a larger scale, experiments are now being carried out by maturing wines in different kinds of oak, and comparing wines from hand-picked vineyards with those that are machine-picked. The great thing achieved initially, though, was simply to clean the bodegas up: old casks that harboured all manner of false flavours were burnt and stainless steel started to come in. Bodegas that had been producing filthy wines began to make clean, good ones that showed the immense potential of the district. Now everyone has stainless steel and temperature control. While Rioja chose to stick to its very successful traditions, Navarra could and did branch out, moving away from the production of Rioja lookalikes to create new, highly attractive wines. In this they were helped by the very liberal attitude taken by the authorities to the introduction of foreign grape varieties. There is a strong school of thought that favours sticking to Spanish varieties and developing them, but while this is perfectly understandable in areas that have been producing very successful wines for many years, Navarra was effectively starting in the quality wine markets from scratch, and some of the new varieties, notably Chardonnay, Merlot and Cabernet Sauvignon, have proved very successful. Viura is still substantially used for making white wines, but it has been joined and enhanced by Chardonnay; some excellent wines are being produced from each and often from blends of the two, sometimes barrel-fermented. The traditional Graciano is now little grown. Garnacha is still used on a large scale for the excellent *rosados* and *jóvenes*, but has been joined by the French varieties. New vineyards have been planted and others replanted, so that the proportion made by cooperatives has declined to 80 per cent. And the proportion of wine bottled has gone up from 15 per cent in 1970 to almost 100 per cent today. Some of the most impressive of all wines are the new, fine reds intended for ageing. A typical grape mix in the past had been 82 per cent Garnacha, 7.5 per cent Tempranillo, 5 per cent Viura and 5.5 per cent other varieties, which include Mazuelo, Graciano and Moscatel. The authorities recommend a change to 35 per cent Garnacha, 31 per cent Tempranillo, 16 per cent Cabernet Sauvignon, 11 per cent Viura and 7 per cent of the other varieties, but this is a mix that no one at present seems to use. Some remarkably fine wines have been produced from blends, but growers go their own way to achieve their aims, and varietal wines are being made as well. Specific blends for some of the wines are given below. The days when the trade was dominated by *rosados* and *claretes* have gone. Navarra is no longer lurking beneath the shadow of Rioja but has emerged as a grower of world-class wines which, although they may contain varying quantities of foreign varieties, are proudly Spanish and do not attempt to be anything else, even though critics occasionally say that Navarra is an outpost of the New World. Things really started to take off in the 1970s and 1980s, with the foundation of new bodegas, as was happening in Rioja, and the use of the latest stainless-steel technology. With the aid of EVENA, Navarra is still developing and it is an exciting place to be in.

## Some leading bodegas

### Bodegas Beamonte

This bodega in Cascante was founded in 1938, began exporting in 1985, and was completely modernized in 1986. It produces traditional wines of good quality, the white being Chardonnay and Viura, the *rosado* 100 per cent Garnacha and a red *joven* likewise 100 per cent Garnacha, but other varieties are also used for the *crianzas* and *reservas*. The red *crianza* 1993 was made from 60 per cent Tempranillo and 40 per cent Garnacha, while the 1991 *reserva* was 85 per cent Tempranillo and 15 per cent Garnacha.

### Bodegas Beremendi

José-Antonio Janices, who founded this bodega in 1990, had been head of the local cooperative. The 50 ha of high altitude vineyards are planted with Tempranillo, Garnacha, Cabernet Sauvignon and Merlot. The red *jóvenes* are very good.

### Castillo de Monjardín

This family-owned bodega in Villamayor de Monjardín is right at the forefront of modern Navarra. The family has owned land on the Pilgrims Way since the twelfth century and the castle is a thousand years old, but the bodega is much more recent. It has extensive vineyards planted with French varieties: 52 ha Chardonnay (the first Chardonnay vineyards in Navarra), 36 ha Merlot, 32 ha Cabernet Sauvignon and 10 ha Pinot Noir. The Pinot Noir is classified as experimental and cannot as yet officially be mentioned on the labels, but that may soon change. The vineyards were planted in 1986 and 1987, before the company itself was formed in 1988. Initially the grapes were all sold but in 1992 the vines were considered old enough to make good wine and vinification started. The bodega began to export in 1995. The whole winery is semi-underground, built into the side of a hill, and is completely modern. The Chardonnay grapes are picked by machine in the cool of the night. Those from the best vineyard, which is 345 metres above sea level, are barrel-fermented in new Allier oak, the rest in stainless steel at 18°C, but only the free-run juice is used, the pressings being sold on. The whites are not put through a malolactic fermentation.

The reds are fermented at 23°C and are matured half in Allier and half in American oak. The excellent barrel-fermented Chardonnays are matured to be sold as *reservas*, the first, a 1992, being released in 1995. The red *joven* 1995 was made from 80 per cent Pinot Noir and 20 per cent Tempranillo. The Merlot *crianza* 1995 was outstanding. The excellent *crianza* 1995 was 40 per cent Merlot, 38 per cent Cabernet Sauvingon and 22 per cent Tempranillo. There are also varietals from Pinot Noir and Cabernet Sauvignon. The El Cerezo 1996, a Pinot Noir, was excellent; it is a triumph to grow this difficult grape so successfully in Spain. It is still young days but the wines are already amongst the best and one can eagerly anticipate the future.

## Bodegas Julián Chivite

The date given for the foundation is 1860, when Claudio Chivite started taking his wines into France, but the Chivite family has been growing wine in Navarra for much longer than that. There is documentary evidence going back to 1633, but although there is no continuous record, the members of the family who now run the bodega credibly claim to be the eleventh generation of wine growers. And not only was their ancestor the first named person known to have exported wine, but they have been doing it ever since, and are usually the largest exporters from Navarra. Their success has been based on quality, but far from resting on their laurels they have kept completely up to date and their wines are firmly positioned amongst those that are taking Navarra into a new prosperity. The enologist member of the family, Fernando Chivite, got his training at the University of Bordeaux and at Geisenheim, which gives him a truly international outlook. The bodega is in Cintruénigo. As an example of its modernity, the bottle-ageing area is temperature and humidity-controlled by computer. They have been investing heavily in vineyards and now own 400 ha backed up by long term contracts with growers, who are paid 30 to 40 per cent more than the average price to produce fruit of the quality required. All grapes are picked by hand. They use rather higher fermentation temperatures than most and increased that for whites from 16°C to 18–20°C and 2° higher for *rosados*. The *joven* is fermented at 23–25°C and the reds intended for ageing at 28–30°C. *Grandes reservas* are only made in the very best years. Three names are used: Viña Marcos for the *joven*, Gran Feudo for the more popular wines (but these include very good *crianzas* and *reservas*) and the Colección 125 Aniversario range at the top, named in 1985 to celebrate 125 years from the official foundation; the first vintage to be sold under this name was 1981. The Gran Feudo white is made from Chardonnay, the *rosado* from Garnacha and the reds principally from Tempranillo with some Garnacha, but the *reserva* is enhanced with some Cabernet Sauvignon and is aged in equal parts of Allier and American oak. The Colección 125 reds are based on Tempranillo and include a varietal Tempranillo that ages very well, but most contain proportions of the French varieties: the 1992 *reserva* contained 12 per cent Cabernet Sauvignon and 8 per cent Merlot, the 1993 *reserva* was 78 per cent Tempranillo, 16 per cent Cabernet Sauvignon and 6 per cent Merlot, the 1994 *reserva* was 80 per cent Tempranillo and 20 per cent Merlot, and the 1995 *reserva* was 74 per cent Tempranillo, 14 per cent Cabernet Sauvignon and 12 per cent Merlot. The white Colección 125 was barrel-fermented Chardonnay with ten months on the lees, which were stirred weekly, and had a malolactic fermentation in the wood, producing a wine of notable complexity. There is also a very good Moscatel.

### Cooperativa Vinícola Murchantina
A relatively young cooperative, founded in 1958, it joined forces in 1970 with another cooperative in Murchante to form the present company. Its members have 720 ha of vineyard. It produces a reliable range (including a Cabernet Sauvignon) under the trade mark Remonte.

### Cooperativa Virgen Blanca
The members of this cooperative in Lerín have 395 ha of vineyard. It also produces a reliable range using the trade marks Viña Sardasol and Viña Ezkibel.

### Bodegas Guelbenzu
Dating from 1851 or thereabouts, this family-run bodega in Cascante is beyond doubt one of the best for sheer quality. The ancient bodegas are next to the enchantingly pretty, pink nineteenth-century family house, standing high on a hillside above its garden. But although the bodega buildings are ancient, their contents are right up with the times. There was a period of eclipse when the grapes were sold to the cooperative, but things really got going again in 1980. All the grapes come from their own small, scattered

vineyards, adding up to 36 ha and planted with 50 per cent Cabernet Sauvignon, 30 per cent Tempranillo, and 20 per cent Merlot, but they also have access to some Garnacha from vines over thirty years old, which is used only for the *joven*. All the vineyards are near by in the Queiles valley, which enjoys a continental microclimate. There is sometimes a little winter watering but none in summer. They are between 360 and 480 metres above sea level, on chalk and gravel, and enjoy an average of 2,700 hours of sunshine. They are planted and pruned for very low yields. They make mostly red wines, which are fermented at 25 to 30°C, usually at 28°C, and which are aged exclusively in French oak of an average age of two to three years. The *joven*, which is sold under the name Jardín, is of course not oak-aged and is quite remarkable: it shows what a mouth-filling opulence the Garnacha can achieve in Navarra if the vines are old and the yield low. A white Jardín has just been introduced. The excellent Guelbenzu 1995 was made from 50 per cent Cabernet Sauvignon, 30 per cent Tempranillo and 20 per cent Merlot, and was given twelve months in oak. The very top wines are sold under the mark Guelbenzu Evo. The 1995 was made from 75 per cent Cabernet Sauvignon, 13 per cent Tempranillo and 12 per cent Merlot, and was given twelve months in oak and another twelve in tank before being bottled. Excellent at the end of 1996, it would benefit from at least five years in bottle.

### Luis Gurpegui Muga

This large bodega in Villafranca, founded in 1921, was acquired by the present owners in the 1970s. The family has a wine-growing history in Rioja extending back to 1872. It is a family business, and although it has moved with the times in installing stainless-steel fermentation tanks, some of the wine is still fermented in large casks with effective temperature control through heat exchangers. It produces a complete range of wines, mostly sold under the trade mark Monte Ory, that are very good value. The white is 100 per cent Viura, the *rosado* 100 per cent Garnacha. The red 1995 was 50 per cent each of Tempranillo and Cabernet Sauvignon, the 1995 *crianza* was 75 per cent Tempranillo and 25 per cent Garnacha, while other blends include Tempranillo/Cabernet Sauvignon and Tempranillo/Merlot.

### Bodegas Irache

Established in 1891, this old bodega in Ayegui was taken over in

1960. Run now as a family business, it has been brought up to date and has been considerably expanded. It uses the names Viña Irache, Castillo Irache, Gran Irache and Real Irache in ascending order of quality. The Castillo Irache *rosado* is made from 90 per cent Garnacha with 10 per cent Tempranillo. Its best wines, though, are the *reservas* and *gran reservas*. The very good 1982 Real Irache *gran reserva* was made from 70 per cent Tempranillo and 10 per cent each of Garnacha, Mazuelo and Graciano. Other varieties are being experimented with and this is a bodega to watch.

## Bodegas Magaña

Situated in the remote little town of Barillas and not all that easy to find, this small bodega is something quite apart, and makes wines of the very highest class, all of which are red. It was founded in 1968 by three brothers, who modelled themselves on a Bordeaux château and pioneered the growing of French vines, which they rear themselves in their own nurseries and train on wires, pruning them to give a low yield of 40hl/ha. It is self-sufficient in vines with, at the moment, 120 ha of vineyard planted almost entirely with French varieties (there is a little Tempranillo), including a very large planting of Merlot, with Cabernet Sauvignon coming second, but only the best of the grapes are used, the rest being sold on. In 1995 there was some barrel fermentation but most of the wines are fermented in stainless steel at 20 to 25°C and all are put through a malolactic fermentation. Each variety is fermented separately, with a *coupage* when their styles are developed. Maturation is in small oak casks, at present 80 per cent French (Allier tends to give the best result of the French oaks) and 20 per cent American, but the proportion of American is likely to increase. The fact that several kinds of oak are used gives another area of choice in making the *coupage*. There may in the future be a *joven*, which has been given the provisional name Dignus, but at the moment all the wines are *crianza* and above, which are capable of fine ageing. The *crianza* Eventum, which is given one year in the oak, was made in 1992 from Merlot and Tempranillo (between them amounting to 60 per cent), Cabernet Sauvignon, Cabernet Franc and Syrah (30 per cent) and Malbec and Mazuelo (10 per cent). The *reservas* are sold under the mark Viña Magaña. There is a varietal Merlot *reserva*, which is exceptionally good, as are the *reservas* and *grandes reservas*. The *gran reserva* 1982 was made from 70 per cent Merlot, 15 per cent

Cabernet Sauvignon, 10 per cent Cabernet Franc and 5 per cent Malbec. The Gran Reserva Selección Especial 1985 was made from 65 per cent Merlot, 25 per cent Cabernet Sauvignon and 10 per cent Malbec. It cannot be overemphasized, though, that these are not Bordeaux lookalikes: of course they reflect the vines, but they have characters of their own that are unique to Navarra and to this bodega.

## Bodegas Vicente Malumbres
This family-owned bodega in Corella was founded in 1940 and considerably expanded in 1987. It produces wines of consistently good quality including varietals from Chardonnay and from Garnacha, the latter both as a red and as a *rosado*. The white *joven* 1997 was made from 75 per cent Chardonnay and 25 per cent Viura, while the red was from 75 per cent Garnacha and 25 per cent Tempranillo. The 1995 *crianza* was made from 60 per cent Tempranillo and 40 per cent Cabernet Sauvignon.

## Bodegas Marco Real
Founded as a company in 1988 but not in production until 1991, this modern bodega in Olite has already established a good reputation for its wines, sold under the mark Homenaje. In 1995 it launched a varietal Chardonnay and two *crianza* varietals: Tempranillo and Garnacha. The red Homenaje 1996 was made from 40 per cent Tempranillo, 40 per cent Garnacha and 20 per cent Cabernet Sauvignon. The 1994 *reserva* was made from 40 per cent each of Tempranillo and Cabernet Sauvignon with 10 per cent each of Mazuelo and Garnacha.

## Bodega A. & B. Marino
Another young bodega, established in 1991 in the north at Muruzábal, it is surrounded by vineyards but only uses 30 per cent of the grapes for its own wines, the rest being sold on. Its barrel-fermented Chardonnay, Palacio de Muruzábal, is one of the best, and it makes excellent red *crianzas*.

## Bodegas Nekeas
Founded in Añorbe as recently as 1987 as a joint venture by six families, it is a sort of cooperative. It has extensive vineyards: 71 ha Tempranillo, 42 ha Cabernet Sauvignon, 20 ha Chardonnay, 15 ha Viura and 15 ha Merlot. Most of its vineyards are still fairly young, planted around 1989–90, but are already producing good wines

and their potential must be enormous. It sells wines under the marks Nekeas and Vega Sindoa. The 1995 Vega Sindoa Tempranillo Cabernet and the 1995 Merlot were in Parker's 90+ class and the 1997 barrel-fermented Garnacha, from 100-year-old vines, was extraordinarily good. Amongst the whites the Vega Sindoa Chardonnay Cuvée Allier is outstanding. This is one to watch.

**Bodegas Nuestra Sra. del Romero S. Coop.**

The Cascante cooperative bodega, founded in 1951 and since enlarged by amalgamation, is now the biggest in Navarra, and one of the best, with a well-established export trade. If its wines do not rise to the heights, they are reliable and good value. They are sold under a bewildering number of names: Malon de Echaide, Torrecilla, Plandenas, Señor de Cascante, Señorío de Yaniz, Juan de Merry and Viña Parot. The Señor de Cascante 1989 *gran reserva* was made from 90 per cent Tempranillo and 10 per cent Garnacha. The Viña Parot 1990 *reserva* was made from 85 per cent Cabernet Sauvignon and 15 per cent Tempranillo.

**Bodegas Ochoa**

This family bodega in the beautiful old town of Olite was established in 1845, though the family can trace its wine-growing history back as far as the fourteenth century. Today it is one of the leaders for quality; indeed, the head of the family, Javier Ochoa, led Navarra into quality wines and did much to establish EVENA. It has extensive vineyards 450 m above sea level, and is increasing them: 16 ha were planted in 1995. But it also buys in from trusted local growers. It goes without saying that the wines are immaculately made. The whites are fermented at 18 to 20°C, the rosados at 20 to 22°C and the reds at 25 to 30°C. The oak used for ageing is 70 per cent American and 30 per cent French. Viura is used for the white. The 1996 Lágrima *rosado* was made from equal parts of Tempranillo and Cabernet Sauvignon and is remarkably aromatic. There is also a good, simpler *rosado* made from Garnacha. The 1995 *joven tinto* was two-thirds Tempranillo and one-third Garnacha. The 1990 Reserva was made from 70 per cent Tempranillo and 30 per cent Cabernet Sauvignon with one year in new oak and two in old before bottling, to give a delicious wine of impressive length. The excellent *grandes reservas* are made from the same grape mix. But apart from the blends, there are very good varietal wines matured as *crianzas*, which the bodega pioneered: Tempranillo, Cabernet

Sauvignon and Merlot. All of these reds have real ageing potential. Finally, there is a delicious, light, sweet Moscatel, not made, like most are, as a *mistela* by adding alcohol, but by late harvesting, chilling to cut off the fermentation, and then microfiltering.

## Bodegas Orvalaiz

Founded as recently as 1993, this young cooperative bodega in Obanos has already acquired a good reputation. Its sixty-four members have 300 ha of vineyard. Its wines include a *rosado* made from Cabernet Sauvignon and varietal reds of Cabernet Sauvignon and of Tempranillo. This is clearly another bodega to watch.

## Palacio de la Vega

Palacio de la Vega at Dicastillo, set up in 1991, really is in a palace, albeit a nineteenth-century one. Having no vineyards of its own, it buys its grapes from local growers and vinifies them well, so that its wines have already established a good reputation. The wines include varietals: Chardonnay, Cabernet Sauvignon, Tempranillo and Merlot. The 1994 Merlot *crianza*, matured in Allier oak, was excellent, as was the *reserva* Cabernet Sauvignon of the same year. The 1995 *rosado* was made from 65 per cent Garnacha and 35 per cent Cabernet Sauvignon, while the 1995 red *crianza* was 70 per cent Cabernet Sauvignon and 30 per cent Tempranillo. Also a bodega to watch.

## Alvaro Marino Pérez de Rada

Also founded in 1991, but in Muruzábal, this bodega produces Chardonnays that have been highly praised.

## Bodegas Piedemonte, S. Coop.

One of the most recent and most modern of the cooperatives, founded in Olite in 1992, it bottles rather more than half of its production from 380 ha of vineyard. Its best wines are sold under the marks Agnes de Cleves and Oligitum, and they are well regarded. The former mark is used for the whites and *rosados*, the latter for the reds. The 1995 white was a varietal Viura, while the *rosado* was made from 85 per cent Garnacha and 15 per cent Cabernet Sauvignon. Its reds include varietals: Cabernet Sauvignon, Merlot and Tempranillo. The 1995 red *crianza* was made from 40 per cent Cabernet Sauvignon, 30 per cent Tempranillo and 30 per cent Merlot.

## Bodegas Príncipe de Viana

This large concern in Murchante was established in 1983 with the assistance of some funding from the provincial government, originally under the name Cenalsa (Comercializadora Exportadora Navarra de Alimentación, SA), to improve the marketing of agrarian products and particularly the wine produced by the cooperatives. At first it was not successful but one of its shareholders, the Caja Rural de Navarra (cooperative bank), stepped in and it turned the corner. The concern changed its name in 1992. It buys the wine from cooperatives, which make it under the guidance of its enologist, and of recent years it has clearly been getting what it wants, backed by 700 ha of vineyards. It took in hand the processes of selection, ageing and blending, and did them so well that it steamed ahead to become principal exporter in 1996. For ageing, 90 per cent American oak is used, and this is likely to increase, the remainder being French. It produces a complete range of wines under three trade marks: Campo Nuevo for the cheapest, Agramont for the middle range, and Príncipe de Viana for the best. All are very good value and one gets the impression that a degree of inspiration has come from the wines of the New World. Indeed, they claim to have been the first to use barrel fermentation in Navarra, guided by the Australian wine maker Nick Butler. The wines of the Agramont range are consistently good and those of the Príncipe de Viana range are very good. The white barrel-fermented Agramont 1995 was made from 40 per cent Viura and 60 per cent Chardonnay, fermented separately. There is also an excellent varietal Garnacha 1995 made from old vines, and a varietal Tempranillo. The Agramont *crianza* 1993 was made from 70 per cent Cabernet Sauvignon and 30 per cent Tempranillo. The Principe de Viana wines include an excellent Chardonnay barrel-fermented in French oak, a *rosado* made from Cabernet Sauvignon, varietal Garnachas – including an impressive Garnacha de Viñas Viejas made from sixty-year-old vines – and a varietal Cabernet Sauvignon *crianza*. The very good Príncipe de Viana Reserva 1991 was made from 35 per cent Tempranillo, 35 per cent Cabernet Sauvignon and 30 per cent Merlot.

## Bodega de Sarria

Founded in 1954, this bodega owed its origin to an industrialist who bought 1,100 ha of land – which included vineyards but was mostly forests, orchards and farmland – and whose aim was to produce top-quality wine. In 1981 it was bought by a savings bank, La Caja de Ahorros de Navarra, which greatly expanded it. There are now nearly 200 ha of vineyard. The wines are always thoroughly sound, reliable and good without, perhaps, hitting the peaks. They are sold under the mark Señorío de Sarria. The basic white is made from Viura with some Malvasía, but there is also a wine rather unusual in Navarra: a *semi-dulce* made from 60 per cent Viura and 40 per cent Malvasía. The *rosados* are made from 100 per cent Garnacha. The reds include a good varietal Cabernet Sauvignon. The *reservas* and *grandes reservas* are the most impressive. The Reserva 1986 was made from 70 per cent Tempranillo and 10 per cent each of Garnacha, Graciano and Mazuelo. The Gran Reserva 1985 was made from 80 per cent Tempranillo, 7.5 per cent each of Graciano and Mazuelo and 5 per cent Garnacha. The wines also include varietal *crianza* and varietal *reserva* Cabernet Sauvignons.

## Vinícola Navarra

This magnificent bodega at Campanas is one of the oldest in Navarra, dating back to 1864, and claims to have been the first to bottle the wine of the district. In 1982 it became part of the big Bodegas y Bebidas group and suddenly became modern, producing good and reliable wines under a surprising number of names: Las Campanas, Castillo de Javier, Castillo de Olite, Castillo de Tiebas, Castillo de Ebro, Bandeo, Viña del Recuerdo and Viña Alaiz. It has 25 ha of vineyard, planted with Cabernet Sauvignon and Tempranillo, and buys the rest in. It produces a complete range of wines, including a good varietal Cabernet Sauvignon, and they are usually very good value.

# 5
## Castilla and León

Castilla – or Old Castile – is the cradle of Spanish culture. The Spanish language is properly called Castillian and it is here spoken in its purest form. Castilla is rightly thought of as a country of castles, for the citizens were armed to the teeth and needed their castles. The Moorish occupation of Spain got as far as the Cordillera Cantábrica. On the other side the Christians were in the little Kingdom of the Asturias. But they were to reconquer Spain and to drive the Moors out. This was where it all began, and beneath the towns there were mazes of secret passages for defence and escape. Later they came in useful for the wine makers and many of them are still there. It was here, too, that you find the great medieval university of Salamanca and some of Spain's most wonderful cathedrals, such as those of Burgos and Léon.

In terms of wine, though, the past was not very illustrious until Vega Sicilia was established in the nineteenth century – the first Spanish table wine to be acknowledged as great by world standards. Today, like so much of Spain, its wines are exciting. It is impossible to write of, though, in terms of generalities. Its four major districts have very different histories, are separate, and do not have a common culture. There is a fifth – El Bierzo – that is so much apart that, although it is part of Castilla, will be included in the next chapter. You may pick up a glass of wine and say 'This comes from Ribera del Duero' or 'from Rueda', but two more different styles of wine are impossible to imagine; and you could not possibly say 'This is Castillian.' It can only be considered in its parts.

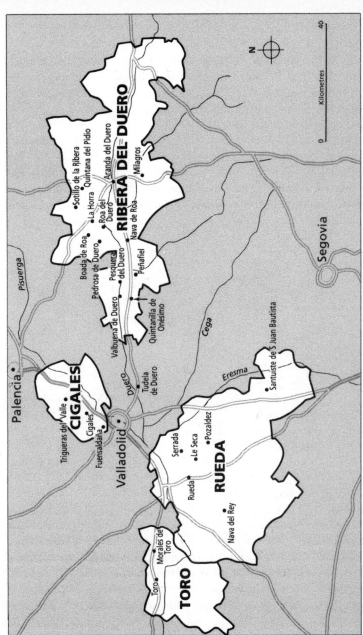

Vineyards of the River Duero

# CIGALES

## Geography

Cigales lies to the north of Valladolid and to the west of Ribera del Duero, in a fairly flat, infertile piece of countryside drained by the river Pisuerga, which flows into the Duero just south-west of Valladolid. The town of Cigales itself is a sleepy little place with a rather disproportionate Renaissance church; but the striking feature for a vinous visitor is the array of *luceras* (chimneys) rising from the earth and each showing the presence of an ancient cellar. The villages are even sleepier. Finding the bodegas is difficult, as they revel in anonymity and can only be identified by diligent enquiry. Cigales is high up in the central plain with the vineyards 800 metres above sea level.

Luceras in Cigales

## Climate

The climate is said to be moderated by Atlantic influences, but if so, goodness only knows what it would be like without them. It is continental, with summer temperatures rising to 40°C and with very cold winters. There is frequent frost damage. The average temperature is 12°C and there are 350 to 400 mm rainfall, mostly in spring and autumn. There are 2,500 hours of sunshine.

## Soil
This looks typical of the rather infertile soil that is usual in good vineyards: light brown, sometimes with a touch of red, containing some limestone and lots of large stones.

## Grapes
Authorized red varieties: Tempranillo (here called Tinto del País), Garnacha Tinta, Garnacha Roja.

Experimental red varieties: Cabernet Sauvignon and Merlot.

Authorized white varieties: Verdejo, Viura, Palomino and Albillo.

Experimental white variety: Sauvignon.

The red varieties occupy 80 per cent of the vineyard.

## Planting
Traditionally this was in a square *marco real* pattern with 3 m spacing; some recent vineyards are trained on wires, but these may require irrigation.

## Vineyard area
2,655 ha.

## Authorized yields
49 hl/ha for reds and 42 hl/ha for whites.

## Wines
Rosado Cigales Nuevo. Jóvenes which must be labelled with the vintage year. Alcoholic strength 10.5 to 13°. Must contain at least 60 per cent Tempranillo and at least 20 per cent of the white varieties.

Rosado Cigales. These may not be sold until after 31 December of the year after the vintage. The minimum strength is 11°, but otherwise the regulations are the same.

Rosado Cigales Crianza. The regulations are the same as for Rosado Cigales, but these wines must spend at least six months in oak and be aged for at least two years before sale.

Tinto. Alcoholic strength 12 to 14°. They must be made from at least 85 per cent of the red varieties.

The reds are comparative newcomers and look like having a good future. There are already *reservas*. There are no white wines within the DO, the grapes being used in the *rosados* or for making table wines.

## Production
About 26,000 hl, but 35,000 hl are expected.

## Vintages
There does not appear to be a great deal of variation from year to year and as most of the wines are intended to be drunk young, individual years matter little. It is early days to assess the reds yet.

Cigales makes unusually good *rosado* wines, which have been traditional here for centuries. There has always been a great demand for them in the north of Spain, but they are practically unknown on the export markets thanks to their colour. Despite the versatility of *rosados*, they have never become universally popular; perhaps people think that they fall between two stools, and they are so easy to drink that there is a snob reaction against them. At their best on a hot summer's day, this does not help them in the frozen north; and while they can give great pleasure, no *rosado* can possibly be regarded as a great wine, and these would certainly make no such claim. They come in various colours: *rosado*, shading into *clarete*, and *clarete* into red. The deeper *claretes* have always approximated to reds but the real reds are new things, dating from the 1990s when bright young wine makers came in, planting vineyards and bringing their inevitable, and admirable, stainless steel. They also wanted a return on their capital and saw it in red wines. These are very promising and they may well be right. But their stainless steel has effected less of a revolution in quality here than it has in some other places. It enables good wines to be made above ground in bright new bodegas, but the local growers, thanks to the temperature control of their deep, cool cellars, have been making good *rosados* without it for years. The creation of the DO in 1991 encouraged new wine makers but did not make a great deal of difference to the old.

### Some leading bodegas

### Bodega Cooperativa de Cigales
Founded in 1956, this cooperative makes wine for 183 growers, whose grapes are mostly Tempranillo. It has recently brought itself up to date, with stainless-steel fermentation tanks controlling the fermentation temperature at 18 to 20°C for *rosados*, which account for 80 per cent of the production, the rest being reds. It

is willing to experiment and its wines are good. It sells them under the name Torondos.

## Bodegas Frutos Villar

This family-owned bodega sells its wines on the export markets, including the United Kingdom, and is active throughout Castilla y León, in Ribera del Duero, Rueda and Toro as well as in Cigales, where it has 100 ha of vineyard that is just coming into production. At present, most of its grapes are bought in from local growers. Fermentation is in fibreglass with temperature control: 12 to 13°C for *rosados* and 18°C for reds. It has an old, deep, cool cellar where it matures its wines in American and some French oak (but it prefers American). It produces table wines, including a white Don Frutos, made from 80 per cent Verdejo and 20 per cent Sauvignon in the manner of Rueda, as well as a complete range of DO wines. Its *rosados* are sold under the names Calderona and Cansina, its reds under the names Ansurez, Conde de Ansurez, Barbaldos and Don Frutos, the first being 100 per cent Tempranillo and the second containing 10 per cent Cabernet Sauvignon. Barbaldos is made by carbonic maceration.

## González Lara

Although the property was bought by the present proprietor's father, a Madrid restaurateur, in 1978, it did not really get going until 1990, when it was completely modernized with stainless steel. It has 33 ha of vineyard planted with Tempranillo, the other varieties being bought in. The *rosados* are fermented at 15°C. It is a very impressive little set-up, making mostly *rosados* but with some reds. The *rosados* are sold under the names Fuente del Conde and Viña Zapata, the red under the name San Antón.

## Lezcano Bodegas y Viñedos

This young family-owned bodega, founded in 1991, has a lot going for it and will be worth watching. It has a 12 ha vineyard, planted *en vaso* on one of the highest sites, principally with Tempranillo but with a small proportion of Cabernet Sauvignon and Merlot. Some of the vines were there when the vineyard was bought and are very old. Fermentation is in stainless steel, 16 to 17°C for the *rosados* and 24°C for the reds. The red wine bodega is very old and is dug into the hill, maintaining a temperature of 14°C. The wines are matured here in American oak imported from Ohio but coopered in

Logroño. Production is equally of *rosados* and reds, the latter already including a very impressive *reserva*. The *rosados* are sold under the name Docetañidos, the reds (which contain minor proportions of the French varieties) under the names Lezcano and Tinto del Carcavo. The reds go up to a *reserva*, the 1991 being made from 85 per cent Tempranillo, 10 per cent Merlot and 5 per cent Cabernet Sauvignon.

### Bodega Rosados de Castilla y León

This very modern little family bodega was founded in 1991, but its proprietor had been in the wine trade in Valladolid since 1971 and has interests in Rueda and in Ribera del Duero as well as in Cigales. The grapes are bought from local growers and are fermented in stainless steel at no higher than 17°C. Nearly all the production is of *rosados*, sold under the names Alarde, Carrosantos, Valdechozas and Solar de Laguna. A red is sold under the name Grand'on.

### Bodega Remigio de Salas

This very old-established family bodega in Dueñas is something entirely apart. One gets used to the anonymity of bodegas in Cigales, but finding this one sets a challenge. Its entrance is a hole in a hillside protected by rows of hanging beads, and nothing to suggest that it is a bodega at all. Inside there are groups of locals talking with animation while they drink glasses of wine, each with a vessel to be filled up before they go home. That is the way the wine is sold. None is bottled, unless you ask for a bottle, when one is filled up and corked on the spot; there is no label. It has 100 ha of vineyard and no grapes are bought in. The cellars are remarkable: a rabbit warren of tunnels, some very small and a thousand years old, one made only a few years ago by hand, chipped out of the hillside, with the stone carried out in a barrow. The temperature changes not more than 1°C throughout the year. Here there is indeed no stainless steel. Apart from some resin-lined cement vats, it looks as if nothing has changed for 150 years, not even the presses. It makes only one style of wine, a dark *rosado* or *clarete*, which is sold with varying degrees of ageing. A sample was taken in a most unusual way. A ladder was placed by the side of an enormous barrel, a piece of rather dirty old carpet was removed from the top, a trap door opened, a jug lowered in and then everything was put back into place. One might have expected the wine to be acetic or at least slightly tainted. Not a bit of it! The wine was clean and utterly delicious. But would it travel? It did! Several bottles were jogged all the way back to England in the far from ideal conditions of the boot of a car. Tasted several months later, they were even more delicious. It goes to show that a good wine maker can produce fine results using very old methods. It was well worth seeking out.

## Hijos de Félix Salas

This really is a family bodega, with members of the family doing absolutely everything. It has 40 ha of vineyard, and everything is completely up to date, fermenting the *rosados* at 18°C and the reds at 22 to 24°C. American oak is used for ageing. The wines are 80 per cent *rosados*, sold under the names Viña Perrote and Viña Picota, and the rest reds. The *rosados* are made predominantly from Tempranillo but with minor quantities of Garnacha, Albillo and Verdejo. The reds include 10 per cent Cabernet Sauvignon.

# RIBERA DEL DUERO

## Geography

The River Duero rises near Soria, makes its way past Valladolid, and crosses the Portuguese frontier, where it changes its name to the Douro and flows through a dramatic valley before reaching Oporto and the sea. It is unique amongst river valleys in growing two of the greatest wines in the world in two different countries: Ribera del Duero in Spain and Port in Portugal. The wines could hardly be more different. And on the way it passes through Rueda and Toro, too. What a river! The wine-growing area of Ribera del Duero is centred around Roa de Duero, though the larger town of Aranda de Duero is more of a commercial capital. The vineyards occupy parts of four provinces: Burgos, Valladolid, Soria and Segovia. The name means the bank of the river Duero but very few of the vineyards are actually on the banks. Some of the best are high above it, with a cliff descending to the river, and although many are within 3 km of the river, others are far away. The delimited area is 113 km long, about 50 km at its broadest width, and 10 km at its narrowest. It is high and hilly, with the vineyards at 700 to 1,000 metres above sea level. Most of the land is taken up with mixed farming and the vineyards are scattered. The highest areas are generally too bleak, and right down by the river they are too damp.

## Climate

Winters are cold, with many frosts, but although the temperature has been known to fall to as low as −20°C, temperatures below −5°C are fortunately rare. There are fewer than 140 days in a year that are entirely free from frost, and frosts are the main problem; in one year out of three they halve the crop. Preventative measures are being experimented with, and the most promising at the moment appears to be a spray of warm water. Summers are warm with temperatures of 25 to 32°C, though occasionally going as high as 42°C. However, owing to the height, nights are cool. The median temperature is around 11°C. Rainfall is from 430 to 580 mm but there is little or none in summer, so that irrigation has recently been legalized but is not widely used; and there are 2,200 hours of sunshine.

## Soils

In so large an area, and a hilly one at that, there are many kinds of soil, depending on height and whether one is east or west of Roa de Duero. The lower soils, down by the river bank, are alluvial with sand and clay. The gentle slopes on which the vineyards are generally planted are of clay, marl and limestone to the east and limestone, marl and gypsum to the west. The important factor is the limestone, which makes up a third of the soil to the west and half to the east.

## Grapes

Recommended red variety: Tinto Fino, also known as Tinto del País, which is a clone of Tempranillo. This is now said to occupy about 85 per cent of the vineyard but the figure may be somewhat overstated. A minimum of 75 per cent has to be used in the DO wines; and a minimum of 95 per cent of Tinto Fino, Cabernet Sauvignon, Merlot and Malbec combined.

Authorized red varieties: Cabernet Sauvignon, Merlot, Malbec and Garnacha (also known as Tinto Aragonés).

Authorized white variety: Albillo.

The French varieties are long-established, having been brought in during the nineteenth century, but may only be replanted in the villages where they already grow. There are no DO white wines; the Albillo is used for lightening *rosados*, is sometimes found (to the extent of about 5 per cent) in reds, and is occasionally used for non-DO wines. The Garnacha does not ripen reliably here; it is only used for making *rosados* and may well be eliminated.

## Planting

Traditionally in a rectangular pattern of 1.75 by 2 m or a square pattern with 2.25 m spacing, but new vineyards are planted with 1.3–1.8 m between vines and 3.1 m between rows, to make mechanical harvesting possible. The permitted density is not less than 2,000 or more than 4,000 per ha. Traditional pruning was *en vaso* with a maximum of twelve buds per vine, but there is now a move towards *espaldera* trained in double cordon with a maximum of sixteen buds per vine. In either case there is a maximum of 40,000 buds per ha.

## Vineyard area

11,300 ha.

## Authorized yield

49 hl/ha. The amount produced by individual growers is carefully regulated by the Consejo Regulador. Each has a 'smart card' which records his planting and yield, and this is processed when he delivers grapes to a bodega.

## Wines

There are only reds and *rosados*, which must have a minimum strength of 11°, though a few white wines (not part of the DO) are made. The regulations for the aged wines are the normal ones save that *crianzas* must have a minimum of one year in oak. Most of the *rosados* are sold as *jóvenes* though there are some *crianzas*. Some of the reds are also sold as *jóvenes*, and they can be delicious, but as the price of grapes continues to rise, it becomes less and less economic to make them, and some growers are phasing them out. The great wines of this area are the *crianzas* and above. Some of the *crianzas* would be entitled to be sold as *reservas* but growers keep the categories of *reserva* and *gran reserva* for their finest wines; and the ageing potential of these is enormous. A *gran reserva* must spend at least two years in oak.

## Production

The production in 1994 was 166,500 hl but in a good year 261,000 hl is the quantity to be expected.

## Vintages

1976 5, 1977 2, 1978 4, 1979 4, 1980 5, 1981 7, 1982 5, 1983 4, 1984 3, 1985 5, 1986 7, 1987 5, 1988 5, 1989 6, 1990 5, 1991 5, 1992 4, 1993 3, 1994 6, 1995 7, 1996 6, 1997 4.

Although easily accessible from Madrid and from the ancient cities of Burgos and Valladolid, the area of Ribera del Duero is off the beaten track. Tourists are refreshingly few; indeed, no one in their right mind would go to winter there; and in summer they are drawn to the beaches, to the mountains, and to those many areas of Spain that are replete with ancient monuments. Nevertheless, it is an enchanting countryside. In June the verges are red with poppies and with wild flowers that would delight a botanist, and all around there are hills remarkable for their striations, many of them flat-topped, like miniature Table Mountains. The river Duero flows through it from end to end and is joined by a network of tributaries, but the land is not very fertile even when irrigated. And although the towns do not entice tourists, there are delightful places to visit and many good things to be seen: castles (notably at Peñafiel), cloisters, unspoiled villages . . . It is a place that one always wants to go back to. For wine drinkers it is something else. For many years there was only one wine grower of note – Vega Sicilia – and that was very notable indeed, producing one of the rarest, most sought after and most expensive wines in the world. Now the whole area has sprung into life, growing great, world-class wines. It is a very exciting place to be in.

Inevitably wine growing goes back to Roman times, but there is a difference: Roman cellars are often still in use. Around the towns and villages in this and neighbouring areas, notably Cigales, small towers or chimneys mysteriously rise from the ground, sometimes a profusion of them. They are the air vents and light shafts of cellars. Each house had its own vineyard and its own *lago* (see Rioja, pp. 96–7). In the days when the Duero lay at the border of the Spanish and Moorish kingdoms these cellars, some dating from Roman times but most from the fourteenth and fifteenth centuries, were also used as hide-outs and many are linked up, making subterranean networks and escape routes. There were 304 of them in 1752 and there are still 120. The history of wine making here can be divided into three parts, of very different durations: the old traditions, the time of the cooperatives, and the present day. The peasant vineyards were very small – and most of them are still under 1 ha. Families grew a profusion of red and white grapes such as Tinto Fino, Garnacha, Mollar, Albillo, Jaén, Viura and Bobal, to produce rustic wines of the pale red colour known as *clarete*. They were drunk locally and never bottled, and were described as tannic, acid and not more than 11°. In the nineteenth century the French influence was only indirect. Wine was taken into Rioja for blending and then sold on. Inevitably, phylloxera arrived towards the end of the century and had its usual effect. The local authorities started to distribute American rootstocks in 1908 but growers found that the Tinto Fino did not do well on them, giving a much reduced yield, and this great variety largely gave way to the inferior ones. Apart from Vega Sicilia, no wine had any but a local reputation.

Although the first cooperative, the Cooperativa Ribera del Duero founded at Peñafiel by fifteen wine growers, made its first wine in 1927, using the modern techniques of that time, the movement took

The Parish Church at Gumiel de Izán

a long time to catch on. This cooperative and Vega Sicilia were the only two producers in the district to bottle their wines. Things might have got going sooner had it not been for the Civil War, but the disruption this caused and the aftermath of starvation, which moved resources into food growing, caused the wine trade to stagnate. In the 1950s and 1960s, though, the rapid expansion of industry in the towns brought an exodus from the countryside which made the old methods of wine making practically unworkable. New cooperatives were founded. By 1976 there were thirty-two. At first the wines were little different from those that had been made before, with the cooperatives paying by weight, so that what mattered was a high yield. Initially the *rosados*, or *claretes*, were more highly prized than the reds, and only a few of the cooperatives made reds, but gradually good reds came into being.

The next change was the great one. The DO was created in 1982, and with it came the concept of Ribera del Duero wines. At first the change this brought about was gradual: the DO got off to a rather sticky start, with problems in marketing the wines, and some growers gave up. But with the superb quality and high price of Vega Sicilia as the exemplar, it is not surprising that other growers, notably Alejandro Fernández, began to see that the future lay in quality. A new era of planting began in about 1984. The first thing was to plant more Tinto Fino. This happened and escalated. In 1987 90.71 ha were planted but in 1988 the figure was 500.31 ha and it has gone on at the same pace ever since. But by 1990 about 76 per cent of the holdings were less than 1 ha and only about 4 per cent were more than 25 ha. Many large vineyards have been planted since, but there is clearly scope for a good deal of consolidation.

In the 1980s money started to pour in. Spain had become prosperous; restaurateurs and rich men wanted to boast of the quality of their own wines. Some of the cooperatives were bought up and others were rented, but most of the newcomers started from scratch, with impressive buildings, state-of-the-art equipment, and newly planted vineyards. And not all were newcomers. The message had been received by some families that had been making wine for generations and they suddenly brought themselves up to date. So despite the Roman cellars and the pioneering efforts of Vega Sicilia, the Ribera del Duero wines that we know today are amongst the most recent to be created in Spain. The story emerges from the histories of the individual houses, which follow.

There is nothing unusual about the wine making, which follows the modern trend with lots of stainless steel and controlled-temperature fermentations. The wine is aged in oak and various cask sizes are used, up to 580 litres, but the traditional Bordelaise barrel of 225 litres is rapidly becoming universal, both American and French oak being used. It is the results that are staggering. The *jóvenes* are fruity, fresh, delicious and intended for early drinking. The *crianzas* are excellent and can go on improving for years in bottle. But the *reservas* and *grandes reservas* are superb. Vega Sicilia can last and improve for decades, and some of its closest rivals may well match up to it; indeed, their growers claim that their *grandes reservas* are Spain's most long-lived wines, and they may well be right. These are still early days. Some of the old bodegas are setting their sights higher and many of the new ones have been founded with the avowed intention of producing the very best. And the best wines are big, dark, fruity, long and impressively complex.

## Some leading bodegas

### Bodegas y Viñedos Alion
Alion is going to be a name to conjure with. It is owned by the great Vega Sicilia (see below) and is next door at Peñafiel, with its own 110 ha of vineyard, but is run quite separately. This has avoided the problems that could have arisen if Vega Sicilia had expanded, but has created a serious rival. Some of the vineyard originally belonged to Vega Sicilia and some has been added. The wine is fermented at 30 to 32°C in stainless steel and then remains in stainless steel for three months before being given fourteen to sixteen months in Nevers oak. The ultimate aim is to produce 30,000 cases of top-quality wine. The first vintage was 1991 but the first to be exported was the 1992, a wine of great concentration, still dumb in 1998, which will certainly not reach its peak until it is at least twelve years old and which looks as if it will last for ever. And 1992 was not generally a very good vintage. If this bodega goes on the way it has started, it will produce some of the world's greatest wines.

### Bodegas Arzuega-Navarro
Founded in 1993 by the two families whose names it bears, but its

impressive building at Quintanilla de Onésimo was not ready until 1995. It owns 64 ha of vineyard, which provides it with nearly all its needs and is principally planted with Tinto Fino, but has small quantities of Cabernet Sauvignon and Merlot. Its good red wines are made from 85 per cent Tinto Fino, 10 per cent Cabernet Sauvignon and 5 per cent Merlot.

### Bodegas Balbás

The Balbás family can trace its history as wine growers as far back as 1777 but was reborn as a producer of fine bottled wines when the brothers Juan José and Víctor founded the present bodega at La Horra in 1981. Its 60 ha of vineyard provides it with 60 per cent of its requirements and it buys the rest from local growers. Its very good red wines used to be varietal Tinto Fino but more recent vintages include 10 per cent Cabernet Sauvignon. There is also a Tinto Fino *rosado*.

### Bodegas del Campo

Founded in Quintana del Pidio in 1989, it has 10 ha of old vines which provide 20 per cent of its needs, 60 per cent coming from local growers and another 20 per cent from bought wines. It makes highly regarded red wines entirely from Tinto Fino and markets them under the brand Pagos de Quintana.

### Condado de Haza

The bodega was founded in 1993 by Alejandro Fernández, of Pesquera fame (see below). It is, however, run as an entirely separate enterprise. He has bought land and in 1986 planted 166 ha of Tinto Fino in wonderful vineyards 950 m above sea level near the river Duero. These supply 70 per cent of the grapes required. The new bodega buildings, between Roa and La Horra, were only completed in 1997. Although not yet up to the exceptionally high standards of Pesquera, the wines are already very good. There is a parallel between Alejandro Fernández creating Condado de Haza and Vega Sicilia creating Alión: they have produced rivals to themselves.

### Bodega Dehesa de los Canónigos

This bodega in Pesquera de Duero was founded in 1988 and has 62 ha of vineyard, formerly the property of the church, which gives rise to its name: the canons' meadow. These are enough for its needs and are planted with 85 per cent Tinto Fino but also with Cabernet Sauvignon and a small amount of Albillo, which is blended into the red wines. The usual blend is 85 per cent Tinto Fino, 12 per cent Cabernet Sauvignon and 3 per cent Albillo. Both Limousin and American oak are used. Its red *crianzas* and *reservas* are very good.

### Dominio de Pingus

This bodega was founded only recently but it draws its grapes from a 4.5 ha organic vineyard of sixty-year-old vines. It is owned by Peter Sisseck, the Danish wine maker and minority shareholder in Hacienda Monasterio. Yields are minuscule and the wine very concentrated and first rate. The excellent second wine is called Flor de Pingus.

### Bodegas Durón

In 1983 one of the leading bodegas in Rioja, Bodegas Alavesas, decided to branch out into Ribera del Duero and bought land. The result was Bodegas Durón, which has 135 ha of vineyard, planted mostly with Tinto Fino but also 5 per cent Cabernet Sauvignon, which supply all its needs. Its red wines, aged in American oak, are already highly regarded. This is one to watch.

### Bodegas Félix Callejo

Although founded as recently as 1989, this family bodega in Sotillo de la Ribera has already acquired a well-deserved reputation for quality. It has 30 ha of vineyard, which provides about 20 per cent of its requirements, and buys the rest from local growers. Most of its wines are varietal Tinto Fino, including the *rosado*, sold under the brand Viña Pilar. The reds are all sold under the Callejo and Buena Cepa brands, the *reservas* and *grandes reservas* containing 5 to 10 per cent Cabernet Sauvignon.

### Alejandro Fernández, Tinto Pesquera

If Vega Sicilia is the most prestigious bodega in Ribera del Duero, Alejandro Fernández certainly comes second. He was put on the map when the American wine writer Robert Parker described his wine as Spain's Château Pétrus, and he was not exaggerating. But before he received this accolade, his wines were already being sought out by those looking for something rare and superb. Subsequently they have had to pay a great deal more for them but have willingly gone on paying. Before he founded his bodega in 1972 at Pesquera de Duero, Alejandro Fernández was an engineer and inventor. Those who would disparage him have been known to call him a peasant. But what a peasant! It would be more just to describe him as a genius. His background has contributed greatly to his success; all his equipment is immaculate and he knows about welding stainless steel, so there is not a crevice where bacteria can collect. He lives simply and works hard. He has 220 ha of superbly kept vineyards, 800 metres above sea level, planted entirely with Tinto Fino, and is busy planting more on very good sites. In addition, a small quantity of grapes is bought in some years. The wine is fermented in stainless steel at not more than 25°C, but owing to the climate it is not always necessary to refrigerate. The wines are matured in oak, mostly American but with a small amount of Limousin, and 10 per cent is renewed every year. Only *crianzas*, *reservas* and *grandes reservas* are made, given respectively eighteen months, two years and two and a half to three years in the wood, and six months, one year and two and a half to three years in bottle before sale. All the wines are first rate and the *grandes reservas* are magnificent. In the very best years there is a special *gran reserva*, Janus, which is superb. These are the wines that others seek to emulate.

### Bodegas Fuentespina

In 1994 this company bought the Santísima Trinidad cooperative at Fuentespina, which had been founded in the 1960s. A large amount of money was poured in and the whole enterprise was modernized. It has 400 ha of vineyard and its reds, sold under the Fuentespina brand, rapidly became established. Its other brands include Viña Carpio, Vega de Castilla, Arco Viejo, Don Matías, Duque Cándido, Montes de Oca and Mayor de Castilla.

### Grandes Bodegas

Founded in Roa in 1987, this young bodega has 280 ha of vineyard planted with 85 per cent Tinto Fino, 10 per cent Cabernet Sauvignon and 5 per cent Merlot, with land suitable for further planting. It uses a number of brands: Cañal for a *rosado* and Roero for a *joven*, but its principal brands are Conde de Mirasol and Marqués de Velilla. The *rosados* and the reds, matured in French oak, are well regarded.

### Hacienda Monasterio

A modern bodega founded in Pesquera de Duero in 1991, it has 68 ha of vineyard planted with Tinto Fino, Cabernet Sauvignon,

Merlot and Malbec and buys in a few grapes from local growers. Its reds, matured in French oak and sold under the bodega name, are very good, with great ageing potential. The second wine, La Granja de Monasterio, is almost as good. See also Dominio de Pingus above.

## Bodegas Ismael Arroyo

This family-owned bodega in Sotillo de la Ribera is as beautiful as it is possible to imagine. The isolated village is a remarkable place, built on a hill that is a hive of cellars: eighty of them in all, with their chimneys sticking up all over the place, but some are very small. Wine growing used to flourish here but practically collapsed in the economic depression following the Civil War. Now it is increasing again. The company was founded in 1979, but this is misleading, as the family has been growing wine for generations. In that year it decided to set up as a shipper and to do its own bottling. To descend the rather frightening steps into the sixteenth-century tunnels that are the cellar is to enter a dream world. There are 400 metres of them and they are 30 metres down, maintaining a constant temperature of 11°C. It is here that the wines are matured, mostly in American oak but with a little French. It has 7 ha of its own, planted with Tinto Fino and cultivated entirely without chemicals. The rest of the grapes are bought in from the village's 230 ha. But if the cellars are ancient, the wine-making plant is completely modern, producing 80 per cent reds and 20 per cent *rosados*. The reds are made entirely from Tinto Fino and the *rosados* from Tinto Fino with 20 per cent Albillo. The wines are sold under two brands: Mesoneros de Castilla for the *rosado*, the red *joven* and the red *crianza*, and ValSotillo for the red *reserva* and *gran reserva*. The *crianza* has at least one year in oak and six months in bottle, the *reserva* two years and one year, and the *gran reserva* two years and three years. The wines are excellent and have great ageing potential.

## Bodegas Montevannos

In 1987 a group of Swedish businessmen bought a lease of the local cooperative in Baños de Valdearados but did not make a go of it. In 1992 it was reconstituted with 85 per cent Spanish and 15 per cent Swedish capital. It has one vineyard of 50 ha leased from the town hall, of which at present 33 ha are in production with Tinto Fino, Merlot and Cabernet Sauvignon. The vineyard used to contain some Pinot Noir but this was not a success and has been grafted over. It is one of the highest in the district at 1,000 m. Most of the grapes used, however, are those that used to go to the cooperative. It does not go in for new oak, and the casks are 90 per cent American and 10 per cent Limousin. The grape mix used for the 1994 red was 90 per cent Tinto Fino, 5 per cent Merlot and 5 per cent Garnacha, for the 1990 reserva it was 85 per cent Tinto Fino and 15 per cent Garnacha. It also makes a non-DO white, Barón de Vannos, from 90 per cent Albillo and 10 per cent Verdejo. The wines used not to be impressive but recent vintages have been much better and there may be good things to come.

### Emilio Moro
A family-owned bodega founded in 1989 in Pesquera del Duero, it has 35 ha of vineyard, planted almost entirely with Tinto Fino but with a small planting of Albillo. It makes very good, well-balanced red wines, the *joven* being sold under the brand Finca Resalso, while the name of the bodega is used for the *crianza* and *reserva*.

### Pago de Carraovejas
Founded in 1988, this small bodega in Peñafiel gets all its grapes from its own 60 ha vineyard, formerly a joint enterprise by the local doctor and the pharmacist. It is now owned by a syndicate of restaurateurs and wine men, and is planted with 70 per cent Tinto Fino and 30 per cent Cabernet Sauvignon, though the proportions used in its red wines are somewhat different, with 5 per cent more of Tinto Fino and less of Cabernet Sauvignon. At present it produces *joven*, *crianza* and *reserva* reds of excellent quality.

### Bodegas Peñalba López
The old property of Torremilanos, 3 km from Aranda de Duero, has a wine-growing history going back to 1903, but it took a completely new turn when it was bought by the Peñalba family in 1975. They increased the size of the property from 60 to 170 ha of vineyard, built a fine new bodega, and installed modern equipment. The results have justified the effort and they sell a range of good quality wines. The brand Torre Albéniz is used for a *reserva* made from 85 per cent Tinto Fino, 8 per cent Cabernet Sauvignon and 7 per cent Merlot. The principal range is sold under the brand Torremilanos, reds made entirely from Tinto Fino and extending up to a *gran reserva*. These are given ample ageing, for instance the 1989 *gran*

*reserva* had twelve months in tanks and two years in casks before bottling. A cheaper range of wines, including a *rosado*, is sold under the brand Monte Castrillo.

## Bodegas Hermanos Pérez Pascuas

This is undoubtedly one of the most serious quality bodegas. It was founded in 1980 by the three Pérez Pascuas brothers but the date is misleading as the family had been established as wine growers for a very long time, and some of the vines they use today were planted by their great-grandfather. They gutted the local cooperative and started their own business. With 70 ha of vineyard 840 metres above sea level, planted in loose, friable soil with no clay, they are completely self-sufficient for grapes: 90 per cent Tinto Fino and 10 per cent Cabernet Sauvignon. They limit themselves to 4,000 kilos per ha. But there is also an experimental vineyard where twenty-five varieties are grown and microvinifications are carried out to study their behaviour in this climate and soil. The grapes are fermented in stainless steel at 29 to 30°C and are then aged in American oak from Virginia and Ohio, one-third of which is new each year. The *crianzas* are given eighteen months in wood and nine months in bottle, the *reservas* are given twenty-four months in wood and fourteen months in bottle, and the *grandes reservas* are given twenty-four months in wood and three years in bottle before sale. They are made from 90 per cent Tinto Fino and 10 per cent Cabernet Sauvignon. The wines are generally sold under the brand Viña Pedrosa, but the very special Pérez Pascuas 1990 was made from eighty-year-old vines, entirely Tinto Fino, and given twenty-six months in the wood. It is truly outstanding and is due for a very long life, but unfortunately there were only 4,600 numbered bottles, reserved for very good customers of the bodega.

## Bodegas Protos

The pioneering cooperative, Cooperativa Ribera Duero, was founded in 1927, as has been mentioned above. Its wines were the first to bear the name of what is now the DO and Protos SA is its descendant. It is situated just beneath the magnificent castle at Peñafiel and its wines are matured in a medieval tunnel, 2,000 m long, in the castle mound. Today there are 280 members who between them have 500 ha of vineyard, growing almost entirely Tinto Fino. It was the great pioneer, the first to go in for the high quality bottled wines that are now produced by everyone, and it invented the brand Protos to help with the marketing. Apart from Vega Sicilia, which was a unique enterprise, they were the first wines from Ribera del Duero to become known outside Spain. Nowadays everything is completely up to date, with stainless-steel equipment and both American and French oak for maturation. The quality of the wines is very good, 15 per cent *rosados* and 85 per cent reds, which go up to a *gran reserva*.

### Bodegas Reyes
The owner of this recently established bodega at Peñafiel is Teófilo Reyes, formerly wine maker at Pesquera. He was astonishingly old when he set up the bodega, encouraged by his sons, who work with him. His first vintage was the 1994 and he is now an octogenarian. The wines are very good indeed, with great ageing potential.

### Bodegas Riberalta
This is one of the youngest companies, founded in 1988, and it started from scratch. At the beginning it had a small warehouse and rented tanks from a cooperative. In 1991 it started building and in 1992 the new facilities were used for the first time. Building was still in progress in 1995. Gumiel de Izán, where it is located, is one of the main centres of viticulture, though it never fully recovered after the phylloxera; it is a prime place for growing grapes. At present Riberalta has only 18 ha of vineyards and is anxious to plant more, but in the meantime one of the eight shareholders has a 10 ha vineyard of his own and supplies his grapes, together with those of a number of local growers under long-term contracts, from vines over thirty years old – and many of them even older – whose viticulture is carefully supervised. One local vineyard, which escaped the phylloxera, is said to be 300 years old; it is a remarkable if rather unproductive sight. It goes without saying that everything is of the latest, spick and span. American oak is used for the ageing, high and medium toast, French oak having been tried and rejected. A *rosado* is made but effort is concentrated on the very good reds, sold under the brand Vega Izán; the top of the range at the moment is a *reserva*, but it is highly likely that *grandes reservas* will follow. This is one to watch.

### Bodegas Rodero
The date 1990 given for the foundation of this bodega, although right, is totally misleading, as the Rodero family has been growing

vines in Pedrosa de Duero for many generations. They used to sell their grapes to Vega Sicilia but in 1991 decided to start making wines themselves. It is a very small operation, almost a one-man band, and one gets the impression that Carmelo Rodero regularly works a twenty-five hour day. At present he has 39 ha of vines but would like to build it up to 100 ha and has planted an impressive vineyard of 10 ha on crumbly, sandy soil with lots of stones at the top of a cliff 30–40 m above the river. His philosophy is that good wine begins in the vineyard: you should talk to it, and at vintage time select the bunches of grapes with great care. Fermentation is in stainless steel at 27 to 28°C and is never allowed to go up to 30°C. No press wine is used. The wine is aged in 25 to 30 per cent French oak, both Nevers and Allier, and the rest in American with very little toasting. The *joven* wines are varietal Tinto Fino but 5 to 10 per cent Cabernet Sauvignon is included in the *crianzas* and above, which extend to *grandes reservas* and which are made with grapes from the oldest vines. The wines are very good and are sold under the marks Ribeño and Val Ribeño.

## Bodegas Hermanos Sastre

The Sastre family has been growing grapes at La Horra, in a 35 ha vineyard of Tinto Fino, for three generations, and 70 per cent of its vines are over fifty years old. It used to sell its grapes but in 1992 it decided to make the wine itself and installed a modern plant. The wines are sold as Viña Sastre and go up to a well-respected *reserva*.

## Señorío de Nava

A small and primitive cooperative, founded in 1956, the Bodega Cooperativa de San Antolín was bought by the Señorío de Nava company in 1986 and totally transformed. Impressive buildings were erected and all the new technology was installed. It has 140 ha of vineyards planted with Tinto Fino, Cabernet Sauvignon and Merlot. It produces *rosado* and red wines under a number of brands: Don Alvaro, Vega Cubillas and, for its best wines, Señorío de Nava. The new company brought with it a philosophy of quality, and although it took longer than some to get its act together, its wines, already good, are becoming increasingly regarded.

## Bodegas Valduero

The bodega was founded in Gumiel de Mercado in 1984 by buying the local cooperative, Santa María la Mayor, and was added to four years later by the purchase of another cooperative, Nuestra Señora del Río, in Gumiel de Izán. It is now a family concern where everyone gives a hand at doing everything. The cellar is a deep dungeon, 500 years old, which was enlarged in 1989 and leads into a maze of underground passages, 670 metres long, keeping at a constant 12°C and 80 per cent humidity. At one point it is 36 metres down, under a hill, and there are four chimneys. At present the bodega has 72 ha of vineyard and the rest of the grapes needed are bought from growers around the two Gumiels, but it is looking for more vineyards and plans to reach 150 ha. It tried French oak but did not like the results and uses American, with 10 per cent replaced each year. An unusual wine is a very agreeable non-DO white made from Albillo grapes, some of which is made as a *crianza*. The bodega also makes a *rosado* from Tinto Fino with 20 per cent Albillo, fermented at 16 to 17°C, but it is mostly known for its very reliable reds, which include 5 per cent Albillo. The white is sold under the brand Viadero, the reds under the brands Valduero and Viña Valduero.

## Bodegas Vega Sicilia
This bodega led the way, and has long been acknowledged as producing one of the world's best (and most expensive) wines, a wine that is almost mythical. It was not all plain sailing, though. The date of foundation of the bodega is given as 1864 but the story begins in 1859, when Don Eloy Lecanda Chaves was given an estate by his rich father. This included two adjacent parcels of land, Vega Sicilia and Carrascal at Valbuena de Duero, following the course of the River Duero. In 1864 he went to Bordeaux and bought 18,000 vine shoots: Cabernet Sauvignon, Carmenère, Malbec, Merlot and Pinot Noir, which he planted. The Carmenère and Pinot Noir have vanished, but descendants of the others still flourish and have adapted themselves to the alien soil and climate. The wine did not, however, achieve instant renown. Antonio Herrero was the next owner, acquiring a controlling interest in 1888 and ownership in 1903. From 1890 to 1903 the bodega was known as Bodegas de Lacanda, and then as Hijos de Antonio Herrero before becoming Vega Sicilia. Until 1915 much of its wine was sold in bulk to Laguardia, to be sold on as Rioja. Then, under the management of Domingo Garramiola, known as Txomin, who died in 1933, the

great age began, and many prizes were won in the 1920s. The legend had been born. The bodega changed hands again in 1952 and in 1966 before falling into the safe hands of the Alvarez family in 1982. Unfortunately, under the previous ownership the wine making had become suspect, and quite a lot of the bottles suffered from volatile acidity. When they were good they were very, very good but when they were bad they were horrid. A bottle of the 1945 drunk in England in 1988 tasted like the wreckage of a great wine. Of two bottles of the 1948, drunk in 1977 and 1980, the first was superb but the second, though obviously great, was spoilt by volatility. Happily those perils have passed. The bodega had failed to keep up with the improvements in vinification that were taking place all over Spain, but the Alvarez family immediately changed all that, pressing on with renovation inside and out, and carefully tending the vineyards, which they were able to extend. Anyone visiting the bodega today cannot fail to be impressed by the total dedication to excellence of the wine maker, Maríano García Fernández, who is an artist to his fingertips. But it is not a bodega to call on casually. It is the only one in Spain where a security guard demanded to see my passport – and I had an appointment.

There are 200 ha of vines and although a very small number of grapes are bought in, for all practical purposes the bodega is self-sufficient. The care with the wine begins with a very careful selection of grapes. They are selected according to variety, climatic zone and age of vine. The vines are picked over four to six times and each lot is fermented separately. The aim is to bring out the individuality of each wine. The yield is not more than 32 hl/ha. The grapes are moved into the fermentation vessels by gravity, without the use of any pumps. For fermentation there is a choice of stainless-steel or epoxy-lined cement vats. They find the former are better if the weather is hot and cooling may be called for, but the latter produce more interesting wines when the weather is cool. Both American and French oak is used for ageing but is bought as planks, matured on the premises (Allier oak is dried for five years) and made up into barrels by the bodega's own coopers. They choose the casks to use according to the wine's personality. As used to be the practice in Rioja, the wine spends a very long time in the wood. It begins in new oak for four to eight months and then moves step by step into older and older wood. The Vega Sicilia 'Unico' spends a minimum of four years in cask and three in bottle before sale. Sometimes the maturation period can be very long indeed; for instance a 1970 tasted in 1995 had spent sixteen years in the wood. The finest wines are made into 'Unico', which is never less than a *gran reserva*, and unless the year is very good indeed, none is made at all; for instance there was none in 1993. Vega Sicilia 'Unico Reserva Especial' is blended from several years and sold without a vintage. The second wine is Valbuena, a very fine *reserva*, which again is not made unless the wine is good. In two years, 1963 and 1971, neither was made, with an enormous loss to the bodega. When this happens the wine is not sold on the market but is sent for distillation, as is any cask that falls below standard. The 'Unico' is typically made from 70 per cent Tinto Fino, 20 per cent Cabernet Sauvignon and 5 per cent each of Merlot and Malbec, the Valbuena from 80 to 85 per cent Tinto Fino and the rest Merlot, sometimes with a little Malbec. It is impossible to describe Vega Sicilia: one just has to taste it. It is on a Wagnerian scale, with all that master's subtlety and complexity.

### Bodegas Viña Mayor

To give it its full title, this is Hijos de Antonio Barceló, Bodegas y Viñedos Viña Mayor. The old firm of Hijos de Antonio Barceló was founded in 1876 but took a leap into modernity with Bodegas Viña Mayor in 1987, and everything now is as modern as it could possibly be. The bodega at Quintanilla de Onésimo, to the west of the DO, has a modest vineyard of 9 ha, buying in the rest of the grapes it needs and a little wine. American oak for the most part is used for ageing but there is a little French. It is a very efficient commercial operation with a wide distribution network producing a very full range of wines, including, apart from Ribera del Duero, table wines and Rueda. Its Ribera wines offer very good value.

### Viñedos y Bodegas de Valbuena

This young bodega was founded in 1988 at Valbuena by a group of enthusiasts that include a member of an old-established grape-growing family. Everything in this elegant new bodega is as up to date as can be and supported by 30 ha of vineyard, mostly Tinto Fino but with 0.5 ha each of Cabernet Sauvignon and Merlot; 5.5 ha surround the bodega. The first vintage was in 1994. The avowed intention is to produce wines of the very highest quality, but it will be some years yet before the bodega can attain a *gran reserva*. It will, though, and its first offerings, under the brand Matarromera, have been very good. This is another one to watch.

## Winner Wines
Although this bodega was not established until 1986, it is supplied by 400 ha of vineyard and has already established an excellent reputation. Its wines are sold under the name Ibernoble. The 1995 crianza was made from vines with an average age of thirty-seven years – 90 per cent Tempranillo and 10 per cent Cabernet Sauvignon – and given a year in oak.


# RUEDA

## Geography
This is the most southerly DO in Old Castile. The countryside is flat and there is little of interest here except for the wines, which are very interesting indeed; however, there are some pleasant towns, including Medina del Campo and Tordesillas. Although flat, the area is high, with the vineyards at 600–780 metres above sea level, mostly in the province of Valladolid but some in Avila and Segovia. They are scattered amongst cornfields, centred on the town of Medina del Campo and bordered to the north by the River Duero.

## Climate
Like the whole of the centre of Spain, this is continental, temperatures falling to −7°C in winter and rising to 35.7°C in summer, with an average of 12°C. There are 2,700 hours of sunshine. The average rainfall is 407 mm, but this is highly irregular. Sometimes there are showers throughout the year, which produces the best conditions for a good vintage; but in other years there is little or no rainfall in the growing season. It is therefore not surprising that the most modern vineyards have provision for irrigation, but this is used to secure quality and not to increase yield.

## Soils
There are some alluvial soils, with limestone and clay, near the river, but most are sandy and stony, made up of sandstone and clay.

## Grapes
Authorized white varieties: Verdejo, Sauvignon Blanc, Palomino Fino and Viura.

Experimental white variety: Chardonnay.

Experimental red varieties: Tempranillo and Cabernet Sauvignon.

Of these, by far the most important today is the Verdejo, which gives the wines their unique character and which is on the increase. Palomino Fino used to be the most important variety, but it is not recommended for replanting and is in a steady decline. Viura is traditional here and is widely planted, but Sauvignon Blanc is a newcomer which is proving very successful and, although not widely planted at present, is likely to increase. It is the vine that everyone talks about. The position and future of Chardonnay is uncertain; it has been experimented with but so far rather unsuccessfully. As there is as yet no DO for red wines, the red varieties are necessarily experimental, but some good wines have been made from them and their future looks interesting.

### Planting
The traditional method of planting was the square *marco real* with 2.8 m spacing and pruned in an unusual way: *en rastra*, which is similar to *en vaso* but with five buds instead of three, as buds tend to be killed off by frosts. Traditionally, the Verdejo vines used to trail along the ground to benefit from the heat of the soil. More modern vineyards are planted on *espaldera* wires, with 1.5 m between the vines and 3 m between the rows, or Guyot. The vine density is from 1,100 to 1,700 per ha.

### Vineyard area
6,253 ha in 1996.

### Authorized yield
Verdejo and Sauvignon trained *en rastra*: 49 hl/ha. Verdejo and Sauvignon trained *en espaldera*, together with Viura and Palomino: 56 hl/ha.

### Wines
There are five kinds within the DO, all white, the red wines being at present sold only as *vinos de mesa*. These are:

Rueda, which must contain not more than 50 per cent Palomino and/or Viura. Alcoholic strength 11 to 14°.

Rueda Superior, which must contain a minimum of 85 per cent Verdejo and which must carry a vintage date. Alcoholic strength 11 to 14.5°.

Rueda Espumoso, which is a sparkling wine made like Cava but with at least 85 per cent Verdejo grapes and which must also carry a vintage date. Alcoholic strength 11.5 to 13°.

Pálido Rueda, which is a dry *vino de licor*, grown under *flor*, like Sherry, and aged for at least three years in oak. The minimum alcoholic strength is 15°.

Dorada Rueda, which is also a dry *vino de licor*, made in the old-fashioned *rancio* style, aged for at least two years in oak and four years altogether. It is fortified or concentrated to 15°.

The last two were traditional and still have a following locally and in the north of Spain, but they are clearly in decline and are not exported.

## Production
140,000 hl.

## Vintages
Generally speaking these wines are best drunk young, within two years of the vintage, but some (especially if barrel-fermented) may be kept longer.

1988 5, 1989 5, 1990 5, 1991 5, 1992 5, 1993 5, 1994 6, 1995 6, 1996 6, 1997 6.

As with almost everywhere in Spain, wine growing in Rueda has a long history – but not as long as in some places. There is no mention of the Romans and for a substantial time Rueda lay at the frontier of the Christians and the Moors; it was so often laid waste that it became known as the Tierra de Nadie – no man's land. But when the Christians finally conquered it, King Alfonso VI (1040–1109) encouraged wine growing by making freehold gifts of land to those who planted vines. As in so much of Old Castile, mazes of tunnels lie below its towns and villages, sometimes refuges and, in more peaceful times, wine cellars. So although its history as a vineyard may be short by Spanish standards, it is long by almost anyone else's. Its wines were favoured at court, which sat originally at Valladolid, León and Zamora, and remained in favour when the court moved to Madrid, as all those places were relatively close. In those days the wines were strong, direct competitors with Sherry. The wine growers were prosperous and by the middle of the eighteenth century there were 29,000 ha of vineyard. By 1909 there were 45,541 ha. But then everything went wrong. The immediate cause was the arrival of phylloxera in that year. By then, the big cities were linked up by the railway network with areas like Valdepeñas and the Sherry country, which could supply their needs, and when the vineyards were reconstituted the growers, tempted by the high yield, made the mistake of planting that negative vine (for table wine purposes), the Palomino. By 1922 there remained only 13,637 ha and much of the wine went for distillation. There was no driving force to bring about change, so there was an inevitable period of stagnation and decline during the Spanish Civil War and the Second World War. Then the growers did start to develop the district in the hope of regaining their former prosperity and they obtained their DO in 1972. But this did not come about as a result of any sudden improvement. They were still making a bewildering number of wines: *generosos*, which could not compete with Jerez or Montilla, whites largely from the Palomino, which could not hope for any-thing better than a local sale, and whites from the Verdejo, but this grape variety provided, under the old methods of vinification, wines that oxidized very easily.

It needed someone with money, knowledge and flair to create wines that could compete at the end of the twentieth century. In 1970 the great Rioja house, Marqués de Riscal, decided that it wanted a white wine that it could sell alongside its famous reds. Unlike practically all its competitors it had never made a white Rioja and decided that the wine it was looking for could not be grown there. It looked at various other areas of Spain but decided that there were already too many vineyards in Galicia and in Penedés, many of them producing first-class wine. Assisted by the great Professor Peynaud of Bordeaux, it searched around Spain and found what it was looking for in Rueda. The professor recognized the enormous potential of the Verdejo grape. Marqués de Riscal established its bodega there in 1972, coincidentally with the cre-ation of the DO. It also introduced the Sauvignon grape. At that time it was criticized by its friends in Rioja for having moved else-where and by the growers in Rueda for producing uncharacteristic wines. But time soon proved the professor to have been entirely right. Some old-established bodegas began to mend their ways and many others have jumped on the bandwagon. The story emerges from the individual histories which are set out below.

The old style *generosos*, the *vinos de licor* listed above, are still made and are fascinating to try, as they show what Spanish wines used to be like; and if there is no future for them, they nevertheless retain an informed local following. But the new-generation wines are a revelation. Verdejo is a very powerful grape that gives the wines an enormous flavour that can go on and on like a herb garden. In the past it was invariably spoiled because its wines oxidized so easily. Picked in the cool of the early hours, cold-fermented in stainless steel, and kept away from oxygen by precautions that almost seem exaggerated but that are essential, it can give big wines of ample acidity and great length. But complexity is added, and the tendency to oxidize further reduced, by blending in some Sauvignon or Viura, which adds a bite at the end of the flavour. The Sauvignon grape has proved so adaptable that it now produces excellent wines all over the world, all with varietal characteristics but no two tasting the same. The varietal Sauvignons made in Rueda are amongst the best. Some, however, of all the varieties are fermented in oak and take on so much oak flavour that their appeal is limited to those who have this particular taste; however, they are still rather experimental and their oakiness may be moderated in the future. The sparkling wines are agreeable but not, so far, very much more. All these wines should be drunk as young as possible.

## Some leading bodegas

### Agrícola Castellana
Founded in 1935, this old-established cooperative with 350 members has brought itself up to date. It still makes the old-style wines but also the new-style, which are of excellent quality, and sparklers. It sells them under a number of names: Accolado, Azumbre (a blend of 85 per cent Verdejo and 15 per cent Sauvignon), Brindis, Campo Grande, Cuatro Rayas (a varietal Verdejo), Pámpano (rather sweet and made from equal parts of Verdejo and Viura) and Veliterra (60 per cent Viura and 40 per cent Verdejo). It also works with the Marqués de Griñon, who makes his excellent Rueda here, using his own wine maker, and also uses the cooperative for his Durius non-DO wines.

### Alvarez y Diez
This bodega, in which the Cava house of Freixenet has an interest, is one of the new wave, founded in 1978. It has 75 ha of vineyard and since 1986 has been vinifying its wines organically. They are good and are sold under the name Mantel.

### Bodegas Antaño
Although this is another of the new wave of bodegas, founded only

in 1989 by a prosperous Madrid restaurateur, its cellars are very old indeed – perhaps 500 years old – and very beautiful, dug down to three levels. It has 120 ha of vineyard, trained on wires so that the grapes can be mechanically harvested in the cool of the night. They are planted with 30 per cent Verdejo, 10 per cent each of Viura and Sauvignon, 30 per cent Cabernet Sauvignon, 25 per cent Tempranillo and 5 per cent Merlot, pruned short for low yields. It follows that half the production is of very agreeable red wines which have no DO, though they think that the DO will in time be extended. Red wines in Rueda are really still experimental, though here the experiment may be deemed to have succeeded. Their best wines, though, are the excellent whites. The white wines are sold under the name Viña Mocen, the reds under the names Vega Bravía and Viña Cobranza. This young bodega is doing great things and may well do even better ones when its vineyards are older. It is determined to expand and is one to watch.

### Angel Lorenzo Cachazo
A family-owned bodega that produces good wines under the names Carmín and Martivillí. It also produces non-DO *rosados* and reds.

### Félix Lorenzo Cachazo
This family-owned bodega predated the influx of fresh talent, having been founded in 1945, but it has been brought completely up to date. It produces a wide range of wines, including the trad-itional *generosos*, which it sells under the name Delatierra, and a non-DO red sold under the name Carriles, but it is principally noted for its modern whites, sold under the names Larrua and Carrasviñas.

### Bodegas Cerrosol
A modern bodega producing some exceptionally good whites under the names Cerrosol and Doña Beatriz. They include varietals of Verdejo and of Sauvignon.

### Bodegas Con Class
Despite its seventeenth-century premises, this small bodega was not founded until 1988. Although it buys wine in, the results have been impressive. Its wines include an excellent Especial blended with a combination of Verdejo, Viura and Sauvignon and a barrel-fermented Chardonnay which is outside the DO. It is run by Marco Antonio Sanz, who cooperates with the brilliant wine maker Telmo

Rodríguez of Compañia Vinos de la Granja (see Granja Nuestra Señora de Remelluri, under Rioja) to make an excellent wine from Verdejo and Viura, with a little Sauvignon, sold as Basa.

## Bodegas de Crianza de Castilla la Vieja

Founded in 1973, this was one of the earliest of the new bodegas, but its founder, Antonio Sanz, is a fourth-generation wine grower with a fine reputation. It is now run by Ricardo Sanz. He produces a very wide range of wines: whites and sparkling wines (which he pioneered), sold under the name Bornos and Palacio de Bornos; the Palacio de Bornos Rueda Superior made from 90 per cent Verdejo and 10 per cent Viura is particularly good, and there is an excellent varietal Sauvignon. There is also a non-DO Garnacha *rosado*, sold under the name Huerta del Rey, and a non-DO red from Tempranillo, sold under the name Almirantazgo de Castilla. He goes in particularly for barrel fermentation, and the Verdejo succeeds very well, as does a non-DO Chardonnay. A steel-fermented Sauvignon is exemplary. His wines are consistently excellent.

## Grandes Vinos

This is a wine merchant rather than a bodega. Very good whites are sold under the name Mirador.

## Hijos de Alberto Gutiérrez

Although this family bodega was officially founded in 1949 it has older roots and much older cellars, 1 km long and with beautiful brickwork dating from the Moorish period. It is said that the Christians used to hide from the Moors in them – and perhaps vice versa. It makes every kind of Rueda wine, sells in bulk as well as in bottle, and even has a bag in the box. It has a large vineyard holding of 420 ha: 50 ha Tempranillo, 30 ha Cabernet Sauvignon, 80 ha Verdejo, 200 ha Viura, and 60 ha Palomino. Grapes, including Sauvignon, are also bought from other growers, including members of the family. Viña Cascarela is a good varietal Verdejo; Viña Mancera is a blend of Viura and Verdejo, and so is Tempero as sold in the United Kingdom, but it is a varietal Viura as sold in Spain; Viña Lisonja is a slightly sparkling wine produced from Verdejo; Viña Valdemoya is a *rosado* produced from Tempranillo; Valdemoya is a red varietal Tempranillo; the red Viña Valdemoya is similar but given a year in American oak; Don Alberto is also a Tempranillo but given two years in American oak and three in bottle before sale. The *rosado* and the reds do not, of course, have DO. San Martín is a *generoso* which comes in two styles, dry and medium sweet. It used to be fortified but is now concentrated by freezing and taking the water out. The result is a most agreeable wine, rather of the sherry style, with lots of oak. The *rancios* are initially matured in glass *garrafas*, left out of doors so that they are very cold in winter and very hot in summer; they are protected against hailstorms by wire screens. They are then given a further period in oak. These wines are popular in the north of Spain. The method is similar to one used by the Romans with amphoras.

## Marqués de Irún

A small bodega and one of the most recent, founded in 1990, it is part of the group controlled by the major sherry shipper Luis Caballero of Puerto de Santa María, whose other interests include Lustau in Jerez. But although the bodega is of recent date it can call on the produce of well-established vineyards. Its aim is to produce wines of very high quality, and it succeeds. The name of the bodega is used for a top-quality wine made from 70 per cent Verdejo, 20 per cent Sauvignon and 10 per cent Viura, and for a non-DO red. A simpler Rueda, made from equal parts of Verdejo and Viura, is sold under the name Viña Tejera.

## Bodegas S.A.T. Los Curros

The González family had grown wine for generations and had sold in bulk. Then, in 1973, a new generation decided to set up in Rueda. Led by Jesús González Yllera, they formed the present company and started to bottle wine. In Rueda they established Bodegas Cantosan and acquired a beautiful Mudéjar cellar dating from the fourteenth century. They have a modest holding of 27 ha of vines, planted with Verdejo and Sauvignon, which has just come into production. They also have a property – Bodegas Boada de Roa – in Ribera del Duero, which they bought in 1984. Looked at in the round, therefore, this is a combined enterprise, and it works that way. In Rueda they produce good quality DO whites and sparkling wines. The whites include excellent varietal Verdejo and Sauvignon wines sold under the name Viña Cantosan and an elegant blend of equal parts of Verdejo and Viura sold under the name Tierra Buena. The driest sparkling wine, *brut nature*, is a varietal Verdejo, the others containing about 10 per cent Viura. They also make a non-DO *rosado*, Viña del Val. But their most famous wine is the red non-DO Yllera, which is very popular in Spain. It deserves to be, as it is unusually good. But it is a complete anomaly: it comes mostly from Ribera del Duero with a little from Toro, but is matured and bottled in Rueda, so it is not entitled to any DO and is sold simply as a table wine, on its considerable merits.

## Vinos Blancos de Castilla

Alphabetical order brings this bodega almost to the bottom of the list but any other criterion would put it right at the top, for it is the Rueda arm of the Marqués de Riscal; it pioneered the development of the new style Ruedas and its wines are second to none. The earliest part of its history has already been given. In 1988 it started to plant vineyards and now has 150 ha, planted with 60 per cent Verdejo and 40 per cent Sauvignon. These supply 40 per cent of its needs, the rest being bought in, and now that they have the basis they can be very selective. After destalking, the grapes are chilled to 5°C before being lightly pressed; the harder pressings are sold off for table wines. There is then a cold maceration. After a vacuum filtration, the must is fermented in stainless steel at 13 to 15°C, which is allowed to rise at the end of the fermentation to 18 to 21°C, never more. The slow fermentation generally lasts for twenty to thirty days but can go on for as many as fifty. At the beginning the Spanish market was looking for oak and the wines were finished in barrels, but now the market seeks young, fresh, fruity wines and oak is not used save for some old Verdejo, which spends eleven to fifteen months in Limousin casks; and a small amount of wine is barrel-fermented. There is no malolactic fermentation. The delicious 1994 Riscal was made from 85 per cent Verdejo and 15 per cent Viura and there is also an excellent varietal Sauvignon and a Reserva Limousin.

## Vinos Sanz

This family bodega is one of the oldest in the area, dating from 1870. It has 100 ha of vineyard and has moved with the times, run by another member of the ubiquitous Sanz family, Juan Carlos Ayala Sanz. It produces a Rueda Superior, 90 per cent Verdejo and 10 per cent Viura, as well as a varietal Sauvignon, both of which are very good. It also has a non-DO red, Campo Sanz, which is a varietal Tempranillo.

# TORO

## Geography
The Toro vineyards adjoin those of Rueda and lie to the west of them, east of Zamora. The district takes its name from the agreeable little town of Toro, with its wonderful Romanesque Colegiata, on the river Duero, though most of the vineyards lie to its south and west. The little river Guareña passes through them and flows into the Duero just south of Toro. It is on Spain's central plateau and the vineyards are from 600 to 750 metres above sea level.

## Climate
The climate is continental with very cold winters and long, hot summers. The average temperature is 13.5°C. There is very little rain – 350 to 500 mm a year, most of which falls in the spring – and it is very sunny, with 3,000 hours of sunshine.

## Soils
The alluvial soil down by the river is not much used for vineyards, which are planted on sandy, well-drained, infertile soil, with large pebbles, at higher levels.

## Grapes
Preferred red variety: Tinta de Toro. This is a long-established clone of Tempranillo, though it has taken on a character of its own to such an extent that some authorities deny that it is Tempranillo at all.
   Authorized red variety: Garnacha.
   Experimental red variety: Cabernet Sauvignon.
   Authorized white varieties: Malvasía and Verdejo.
   Palomino used to be widely planted but was banned in 1990.

## Planting
Pruning is *en vaso* with 900 to 2,700 vines per ha. A lot of consolidation and replanting is in progress.

## Vineyard area
3,364 ha.

## Authorized yields
Tinta de Toro: 42 hl/ha. The permitted yields of the other varieties vary according to district. Garnacha and Malvasía: 49 or 63 hl/ha. Verdejo: 28 or 49 hl/ha.

CASTILLA AND LEÓN

## Wines

Reds from 12.5 to 15°. All categories up to *gran reserva* are available and the standard rules apply. They must be made from not less than 75 per cent Tinta de Toro, and while some bodegas use a little Garnacha, or even the white varieties, the best reds are 100 per cent Tinta de Toro. *Rosados* from 11 to 14°. Whites from 11 to 14°.

## Production

33,425 hl (1994/5, now probably higher).

## Vintages

1987 5, 1988 4, 1989 5, 1990 5, 1991 7, 1992 7, 1993 6, 1994 7, 1995 6, 1996 6, 1997 5.

Toro has long been known for its wines and its name has given rise to many jokes about bulls' blood, especially as its red wines used to be very dark indeed (they are still dark) and dauntingly alcoholic, sometimes rising to as much as 17°. They were aimed at the cheap end of the market and often had wines from further afield blended in to make the price right, so a very old Toro should be approached with circumspection. Non-DO table wines indeed are still made here and can be very acceptable. But a great change came in the 1980s. The better growers had long known that they could produce fine wines and in 1987 they got their DO. Now everything is very different. The DO made it worthwhile to invest and in came the latest enology with temperature-controlled fermentations and so on, for those who could afford it. Toro has a growing reputation and it is highly likely that new names and new capital will come flooding in, as has happened in other districts. The first few years were necessarily experimental and not all the wines were as good as they have subsequently become, but the best shippers are now producing very good wine indeed and are doing so at an affordable price, for unlike those of Ribera del Duero, these wines have not yet become fashionable. The whites and *rosados* are crisp and dry, with plenty of acid and good length: wines that would have been inconceivable in such a hot climate in the old days. But it is the reds that are really worth looking for. They are still splendidly strong stuff but no longer dauntingly so, the usual strength being 13.5° to 14°. They have plenty of tannin but are well balanced. The *jóvenes* are meant to be drunk young, but the *crianzas* are aimed at five to eight years old and it is likely that the *grandes reservas* will last for twenty, though all can be drunk with great pleasure a good deal younger than that.

## Some leading bodegas

### Bodegas Fariña

A family-owned bodega founded in 1941 by the present owner's father, this was the first whose wines made a real impact. It has two totally separate bodegas, a new one in Toro, built in 1987 for DO wines, and the other outside, to make their very agreeable table wines. At present they have 40 ha of vineyard and plan to plant another 100 ha. In the new bodega everything is stainless steel, from the reception of the grapes onwards. The whites are fermented at 13 to 15°C and the reds at 26 to 27°C, and two days' maceration are given for the *joven*, five to six for the *crianza*, and up to fourteen for the *reserva*. The *crianza* spends six months in wood, the *reserva* one year and the *gran reserva* three years, the casks being 80 per cent American oak and 20 per cent French, 20 per cent of which are new each year. The whites and *jóvenes* are sold under the name Colegiata, the *crianzas* and above under the name Gran Colegiata, the labels illustrated by a picture of the Colegiata in Toro. A particularly good *crianza* is sold as Vino Primero. At the cheaper end of the scale, Dama de Toro is a good wine to look for in supermarkets. There is also a very good non-DO made from equal parts of Tinta de Toro and Cabernet Sauvignon.

### Bodegas Frutos Villar

Originally established in Cigales (it is described in the context of that district), Frutos Villar has branched out into Toro, where it is making good wines, both red and white, under the name Maruve and, for the red *gran reserva*, Gran Maruve.

### Bodegas Vega Sauco

This small bodega established in 1991 makes very good wines exclusively from Tinta de Toro.

## OTHER WINES

You can find vineyards almost anywhere in Castilla and León. Some of these are within areas that have not yet reached DO status and probably never will, but that nevertheless are delineated; others are out on their own, including some of the best.

### Bodegas Alta Pavina
Isolated in a vast, dull plateau near the village of La Parrilla in the province of Valladolid, this recently planted vineyard is financed by a Valladolid businessman for his daughter, who is a qualified and very keen wine grower. There are vineyards of Cabernet Sauvignon and of Pinot Noir, both varieties for the most part, and bravely, ungrafted. The Cabernet Sauvignon, given a year in oak, is already very good and the Pinot Noir is very promising. Recent vintages, however, have been variable.

### Los Arribes del Duero-Fermoselle
There are two areas in this CV, one to the south-east of the province of Zamora and the other to the north-east of Salamanca. Red grapes: Juan García, Bobal, Rufete, Garnacha and Tempranillo (here known as Tinta Madrid). White grapes: Malvasía, Verdejo and Palomino. There is said to be great potential in developing wines from the local Juan García grapes but practically all the wine is made by cooperatives and this potential has not yet been realized.

### Benavente-Campos
This CV, in the north of the province of Zamora, is in decline and not much wine is made, mainly *rosados* and *claretes*. Red grapes: Mencía, Picudo Prieto, Garnacha and Alicante. White grapes: Palomino, Malvasía and Verdejo. The principal bodega is Bodegas Otero in Benavente.

### Cebreros
Although Cebreros, in the south-east of the province of Avila, has got as far as having DEp status it does not at the moment look as if it is likely to get much further. It produces very alcoholic wines, the reds from Garnacha and the whites from Albillo and Viura.

### Bodegas Mauro
This excellent bodega at Tudela de Duero makes non-DO wines from its 20 ha of vineyard just outside the DO area, planted with 80

per cent Tinto Fino (Tempranillo), 15 per cent Garnacha and 5 per cent Albillo. The very good red wines extend up to a *reserva*. It prefers to go its own way, operating outside the DO regulations.

### Finca Retuerta

This huge estate of 205 ha combines being very old with being very new. The vineyards at Sardón del Duero surround the ancient abbey of Santa María de Retuerta, founded in 1143. The estate is just to the west of the Ribera del Duero DO region, on the road to Valladolid. Until recently it was owned by a Spanish seed company that grubbed up all the vines. This company was acquired in 1988 by the Swiss chemical giant Sandoz, and the chairman of the Spanish subsidiary decided to replant with vines, as the rights to replant had not expired. In 1995 Pascal Delbeck, late of Château Ausone, was brought in to run it. He found the site to be an ideal one, with a variety of soils and slopes suitable for different vine varieties. The vines are planted at high density on rootstocks selected to limit the yield, and are trained on wires, with drip irrigation. The main variety planted is Tempranillo (65 per cent), the rest being Cabernet Sauvignon and Merlot with small plots of Petit Verdot and Syrah. There is a vast and superb new bodega. Both American and French oak are used, and a wider range of wines is planned. The first wines, of the 1996 vintage, have been very well received and the potential when the vineyard is mature is obvious. Abadía Retuerta Primicia was made from 60 per cent Tempranillo, 20 per cent Merlot and 20 per cent Cabernet Sauvignon, while Abadía Retuerta Rivola was made from 60 per cent Tempranillo and 40 per cent Cabernet Sauvignon, given three months in new French oak.

### Ribera del Arlanza

This small CV in the province of Burgos used to have 10,000 ha of vineyard but is now down to 1,500 ha. There are some signs of a revival. Red grapes: Tinto del País (Tempranillo), Mencía and Garnacha. White grapes: Albillo and Macabeo.

### Ribera del Cea

This slightly larger CV, in an arid plain in the north of Valladolid, has some 5,000 ha of vineyard producing mostly *rosados* and *claretes*. Red grapes: Mencía, Prieto Picudo and Aragonés (Garnacha). White grapes: Albillo, Macabeo, Palomino, Verdejo and Cañarroyo.

## Bodegas S.A.T. Los Curros

An important bodega in Rueda, S.A.T. Los Curros also produces non-DO wines of excellent quality. The Cuvi *rosado* is made from 60 per cent Tempranillo, 20 per cent Cabernet Sauvignon and 20 per cent Garnacha. The red Cuvi is made from 60 per cent Tempranillo, 25 per cent Cabernet Sauvignon and 15 per cent Garnacha. The red Yllera wines have already been mentioned on p. 182. Although these wines lack a DO, they are very well made and excellent; they are well worth seeking out.

## La Sierra de Salamanca

Producing short-lived *rosados* and *claretes* in the mountains of Peña de Francia, this small CV of 2,000 ha in the south of the province of Salamanca is unusual in that its principal grape is the Rufete, with some Garnacha and Tempranillo. White grapes: Macabeo and Pedro Ximénez.

## Tierra del Vino

The province of Zamora used once to grow large quantities of wine, but wine growing went into a decline in favour of cereals, so that there are now only 1,500 ha in this CV. However, there are now efforts to create a revival. Most of the wines are *rosados* (which include white grapes) and light reds, made from Tinto del País (Tempranillo) but a recent development has been a sweet Moscatel. Cabernet Sauvignon is being experimented with. White grapes: Malvasía and Moscatel.

## Valdevimbre-Los Oteros

Things are said to be happening in this CV in the province of León which at present has only 3,900 ha of vines; but there may be a regrouping. The wines are light reds, *rosados* and whites. It is unusual in that the most widely planted red variety is the rare Picudo Prieto, which provides little colour, but other red varieties grown include Mencía and Aragonés (Garnacha). White varieties: Malvasía and Palomino. The principal bodega is Bodegas Vinos de León-Vile in Armunia.

## Viñedos y Bodegas de Malpica

In terms of strict geography, this bodega should not be included here at all but in Castilla-La Mancha. However, although it could well be in the area of Méntrida, which is described in a later chapter, it avoids any such association and its strongest connections are with

Rueda and Ribera del Duero. As a vineyard, it is a thing entirely apart.

When Carlos Falcó, Marqués de Griñón, has a hand in anything one may be sure that the results will be good and usually outstanding. It is so with his table wines produced in Castilla. They are not merely good, they are positively exciting. The estate has been in the family for centuries and in 1982 Falcó decided to go into wine making seriously – very seriously. At first sight the *finca* Dominio de Valdepuesa does not look very promising. It is a charming eighteenth-century house with a modern air-conditioned cellar, in a flat, rather dull piece of countryside at Malpica de Tajo, between Toledo and Talavera de la Reina, with the river Tajo flowing through it. But it all goes to show that not *all* Spain's best wines are grown in its most beautiful countryside. The soil is clay on top with limestone underneath and on the way down into the cellar there is a sort of subterranean window, a sheet of glass through which you can see the striations of the land. The vineyard is beautifully kept, with 24 ha of vines and hedges of lavender; it was the first in Europe to be drip-irrigated. There are 14 ha Cabernet Sauvignon, 5 ha Syrah and 2.5 each of Petit Verdot and Chardonnay. The technique of canopy management has been successfully imported from the New World with the advice of Richard Smart.

The best wines, including all the varietals grown in the Malpica vineyard, are sold under the name Dominio de Valdepusa. The first Spanish varietal Syrah was made here in 1991 and was very good; it is clearly a vine with great potential in this vineyard. Petit Verdot is an odd and inspired choice; it yields well and attains maturity here more readily than in the Médoc, producing an excellent varietal wine which is given eighteen months in French oak. The first-rate varietal Cabernet Sauvignon is given eighteen to twenty-four months in French oak. The Chardonnay is fermented in Allier oak using yeasts from Le Montrachet. These wines have no DO, nor do they seek or need one – like the 'Super Tuscans' – though the wines themselves could hardly be more different.

Apart from these single vineyard wines, Falcó has a flourishing merchanting business, producing blends sold under the name Marqués de Griñón Durius, Durius being the Latin name for the river Duero. The white Durius 1995 was assembled in Rueda from equal parts of Verdejo (to give structure), Viura and Sauvignon Blanc; wood was not used. The red is a blend of the local clones of

Tempranillo grown in Ribera del Duero and in Toro with Garnacha grown in Toro, and given six months in American oak, one-third in new casks. There is also a varietal Tempranillo, Durius Colección Personal, made from grapes grown in Ribera del Duero.

Falcó's Rioja wines have been described earlier. None of these wines comes cheap but all of them are very well worth seeking out.

# 6
## *The North-West*

People imagine Spain as a country shimmering under the hot sun. For much of the country much of the time this is true, but it is not at all true of the north-west. Here the weather is Atlantic and there is no Gulf Stream to warm the sea. It rains a very great deal, though it is far enough south for the sun to be warm in summer. The result is a countryside as lusciously green as Ireland, full of exquisite scenery. But the map shows that much of it grows little or no wine at all. The wines that do grow there, apart from some favoured places, are white and very light. Not only are they northern in style, they are *very* northern in style.

Someone suddenly transported to the Asturias might well guess himself to be in Wales. It is a rugged countryside, with people to match, and was never conquered by the Moors. What is more, it is a principality, and the Crown Prince of Spain always has the title of Príncipe de Asturias – Prince of the Asturias. There is some wine, even red wine, but there is more cider.

Cantabria, with Santander as its capital and the wonderfully wild and beautiful Picos de Europa as its greatest scenic feature, grows hardly any wine at all.

The País Vasco, or Basque country, has its own language of obscure origin, full of xs, and its own government in Bilbao. It extends right into the Rioja DOCa, but most of the rest does not grow wine, with the notable exception of the Chacolís, which are very light and are delightful with the local seafood.

Further to the south and west there is the DO of Bierzo, which is at the edge of Castilla-León and which stands alone, well inland. To the north and north-west of El Bierzo there is little or no wine at all, and the weather can be very wet. But directly to the west and to the south-west, there are major regions in Galicia: Valdeorras, Ribera

North-west coast

Sacra, Ribeiro and Rías Baixas. In these places the weather can still be damp, though the climate is perhaps more kindly described as soft, but microclimates provide warmth and shelter, giving wines of great individuality and charm. The coastline is notable for its large inlets, or *rías* – Rías Baixas being the country of the lower, or southern *rías* – and it still retains a good deal of its beauty despite some horrible 'developments'.

## BIERZO

### Geography
Although the DO is Bierzo, the region is El Bierzo. Looking at it on the map, one might reasonably think that it should be included with

the wines of Galicia rather than with those of the north-west, but it is in fact in Castilla-León (Old Castile), though it has grave doubts as to whether it should be. An old county, it has a degree of rugged independence. And the climate puts in with Castilla, too, though that again is different. It is in a hollow surrounded by mountains. To the west and north there is the Cordillera Cantábrica, to the south the Sierra de Cabrera, and to the east the Montes de León. The principal town is Ponferrada – an agreeable old town that must once have been a gem but is now a mess, surrounded by hideous development. Villafranca del Bierzo, on the other hand, is a delightful little town.

## Climate
Sheltered by the mountains yet influenced by the sea, El Bierzo is more temperate than the other wine districts of Castilla, despite the altitude of the vineyards at between 500 and 650 m. The temperature rises to 32°C in summer and falls to −1°C in winter, with an average of 13.1°C and 2,700 hours of sunshine. The rainfall is 670 mm. Severe damage can be caused, as in 1995, by frosts after an early flowering.

## Soils
These are many and various: alluvial low down, sand and granite in the middle, and slate high up.

## Grapes
Recommended red variety: Mencía (62 per cent of the vineyard).

Permitted red variety: Garnacha Tintorera.

Red varieties also grown: Cabernet Sauvignon, Merlot, Pinot Noir and Tempranillo.

Recommended white varieties: Godello and Doña Blanca.

Permitted white varieties: Malvasía and Palomino (here often called Jerez).

White varieties also grown: Gewürztraminer and Chardonnay.

Although Palomino still occupies about 15 per cent of the vineyard, it is a relic of the past and is on its way out.

## Planting
Traditionally *marco real* with 1.6 m spacing pruned *en vaso*, but more recent vineyards are trained *en espaldera*.

## Vineyard area
6,800 ha, but only 3,400 ha have actually been planted.

## Authorized yield

Garnacha Tintorera and Palomino 84 hl/ha. All other varieties 77 hl/ha.

## Wines

Reds must contain a minimum of 70 per cent Mencía and are 11 to 14°, *joven*, *crianza* and *reserva* with occasionally a *gran reserva*.

*Rosados* are of the same strength and go up to *reservas*. The whites are all *jóvenes* and are 10 to 13° in strength.

## Production

210,000 hl.

## Vintages

1989 6, 1990 6, 1991 6, 1992 4, 1993 2, 1994 7 , 1995 4 , 1996 6, 1997 5.

The fact that this is a book about wine and not about travel makes El Bierzo rather an exasperating place to write about. It is one of the most fascinating areas even in Spain. It is a coal-mining district, but does not look like one, and also mines iron ore. The scenery on the way to Galicia is incredibly beautiful, with dramatic, verdant mountains. The Romans flourished here and, with an army of slaves, made great waterworks with the unusual object of washing away mountains by hydraulic force, for the mountains were rich in gold. The mud carried in the water was filtered and the gold extracted. If you go up to the Mirador de Orellán you can look over Las Médulas, the fantastic landscape that was left behind. And it was one of the last stops on the pilgrim route to Santiago de Com- postela. The superb monastery of San Nicolás el Real at Villafranca is one of its grandest relics and the castle at Ponferrada was the headquarters of the Knights Templar. But it is the small towns and hermitages in the mountains, like Peñalba de Santiago, that are the most enchanting places, reached by narrow roads that are exciting to navigate. It also has some of the best fruit orchards in Spain.

It does not have a long history, though, as a source of fine wines. Galicia, lacking red wines of its own, was an easy market for indif- ferent reds, from Mencía and Garnacha Tintorera grapes grown in over-fertile soils in the valleys, while even more indifferent whites from the high-yielding Palomino were apparently just as easy to sell. The decline had set in after 1882, when phylloxera arrived. After

Peñalba de Santiago

that the shy-bearing Godello grape practically disappeared, to be
replaced by the dim and high-yielding Palomino. When good wines
came to be grown all over Spain, and transport became easy, the
days of such wines as those were over. The immediate answer, as in
so many parts of Spain, was the development of a cooperative
movement. Vinos de Bierzo Sociedad Cooperativa was founded in
1963 with 600 members, and it now has 2,000. This started the rise
and brought about the establishment of the DO at the end of 1989,
which made it worth while to inject capital in the hope of creating a
fine wine region. The potential had always been there. The climate
is very similar to that of Rioja, the soils are excellent for growing
vines, and the best local vines were capable of producing highly
individual wines. Even so, it cannot at present be classed amongst
Spain's leading wine districts. The wines tend to be worthy and
agreeable but wholly unexciting. The Mencía is said to be related
to the Cabernet Franc (research is continuing) and could well

have been brought in by French monks in the high days of the pilgrimage. Its wines certainly have ageing capabilities. The Garnacha Tintorera, which has pink juice, is said by those who use it to add colour and complexity, but it does not of itself produce very good wines and is not found in the best blends. The *rosados* are unusually big in flavour but the reds and whites are more interesting. They are lusty in flavour and have some ageing potential, though perhaps lacking something of subtlety and tending to be rather short. The Godello provides white wines of real fragrance and finesse. The best examples are now made by the independent shippers. Yet perversely some of the most interesting wines grown here are non-DO and made mostly with French varieties together with Tempranillo. It will be most interesting to see what develops. There is still considerable untapped potential, and this is a district worth watching.

## Some leading bodegas

### Bodega Bernado Alvarez Fernández
A bodega in Villadecanes, founded in 1920, which sells good wines under the name Viña Migarrón. The white is made from equal parts of Godello and Doña Blanca, the *rosado* from 75 per cent Mencía, 20 per cent Palomino and 5 per cent Doña Blanca, the red from Mencía.

### Bodegas y Viñedos Luna Beberide
Founded in 1986, this small family-owned bodega in Cacabelos has 50 ha of vineyard which contain only one authorized variety, Mencía, the rest being planted with Cabernet Sauvignon, Gewürztraminer and Chardonnay, which are of course used for making non-DO wines. It is therefore willing to experiment. The Gewürztraminer and a blend of equal parts of Gewürztraminer and Chardonnay, sold under the name Viña Arella, are very good indeed.

### Pérez Carames
Although this family company in Villafranca del Bierzo was not founded until 1986, members of the family had been growing vines in the district for forty years. The 30 ha of vineyard, on remarkably stony soil near Villafranca, are cultivated organically and are exemplary. They are trained on *espalderas* – and the wires are stainless steel. They claim it to be the largest single vineyard in Bierzo. Of

the recognized grapes, they grow Mencía and Palomino but they also grow experimentally Cabernet Sauvignon, Merlot, Pinot Noir, Tempranillo and Chardonnay. The bodega is fully equipped with stainless steel for fermentation, and some reds are made by carbonic maceration. Wines intended for sale as *jóvenes* are fermented at 17°C and those intended as *crianzas* at 28 to 30°C. The oak used for ageing is entirely Allier. As may be surmised from the contents of the vineyard, they make DO and non-DO wines. Young DO wines of all three colours are sold under the name Casar de Valdaiga and the name Casar is also used for bag-in-the-box wines. The DO reds made from Mencía, especially the *crianzas*, are very good examples and well worth looking for. Some of the most interesting wines, though, are those that are not DO and are sold under the name Casar de Santa Inés. These include a white made from Chardonnay and Malvasía, a *rosado* made from Merlot, Cabernet Sauvignon and Pinot Noir, and reds that include varietal Tempranillo, Cabernet Sauvignon and Pinot Noir, and a blend of Merlot and Tempranillo. All of them are very good.

### Bodegas Prada a Tope
This bodega in Cacabelos is a most extraordinary place. *A tope* can loosely be translated as 'flat out', and that is the way the place is run. But is it a bodega at all? The answer is emphatically yes, and it is a very good one, but at first sight it is a shop, selling the most delectable foods of all kinds, including its own jams and bottled fruits, and quite different things like shoes. It is also a very good restaurant. It all began in 1975, when a cobbler started to bottle cherries in brandy. He started in wine the following year and the creation of the DO in 1989 provided the incentive for expansion. It was clearly on the way up in 1988 and it was in that year that he bought the ancient Canedo Palace to use as a bodega and planted vines; he now has 20 ha. The bodega was established with state-of-the-art equipment in 1990. He makes some of the best wines of the district, reflecting the qualities of the local grapes. The white is 90 per cent Godello; the *rosado* is 40 per cent Mencía, 40 per cent Godello and 10 per cent Doña Blanca; the red *crianza* and *reserva* are never less than 85 per cent Mencía and usually 100 per cent; and there is a young red made by carbonic maceration. Finally there is an agreeable sparkling wine called Xamprada made from 50 per cent Chardonnay, 40 per cent Godello and 10 per cent Doña Blanca.

## Sociedad Cooperativa Vinos del Bierzo

There are several cooperatives in Bierzo but this was the first and is the biggest. It was founded in 1963 at Cacabelos with 600 members and now has 2,000, with a total of 1,000 ha of vineyard. It is very well equipped and has stainless-steel fermentation tanks, where the whites and *rosados* are fermented at 18°C and the reds at 25°C. Between a quarter and a half of the production is of DO wine. Ageing is in American oak. Wines of all colours are sold under various names: Fontousal, Guerra, Señorío del Bierzo and Viña Oro. The red Viña Oro is remarkably good value and shows the ageing potential of the Mencía grape. A sparkling wine is sold under the name Don Perejón. The reds and *rosados* are made from Mencía, the whites from Doña Blanca and Palomino.

## THE CHACOLÍS

There are two Chacolís: Bizkaiako Txakolina or Chacolí de Vizcaya, and Getariako Txakolina or Chacolí de Guetaria. They have separate DOs but both come from the Basque country on the Bay of Biscay, and although separate have so much in common that they will be described together.

### Geography

The two Chacolís are grown in two different provinces: Vizcaya or Bizkaya to the west, and Guipúzkoa or Gipuzkoa to the east. The former is centred round Bilbao and stretches inland to beyond Durango, where there are three vineyards. The rest are very scattered and most are to the east of Bilbao, but all are very small. Nearly all are well inland, on sites chosen for their sheltered locations and good microclimates. The latter is centred around Guetaria, to the west of San Sebastián, and again the vineyards are small and scattered. Most are near the sea and some are on beautiful terraces with marvellous views over the Bay of Biscay.

### Climate

This is hardly propitious for grape growing. It is very damp and the summer has been described as 'five days clear, five days cloud'. The summer maximum is 35°C and the winter minimum 2°C, despite which there are frosts. The average temperature is 13.5°C. The average rainfall is no less than 1,600 mm. The sunshine is 1,800 hours. Some of the inland vineyards, however, have a more continental climate with warmer summers. The height of the vineyards varies between 10 and 100 metres above sea level.

## Soils
With such a scattering of little vineyards, these are varied. Most, though, are on alluvial clay soil beneath a sandy topsoil.

## Grapes
The most extraordinary thing about the vines is that they are on their own roots; phylloxera does not flourish here. Consequently many of them are eighty years old.

Authorized white variety: Ondarribi Zuri.

White variety also grown (Vizcaya only): Folle Blanc.

Authorized red variety: Ondarribi Beltza.

Chardonnay has been planted experimentally but has not been a success. Some growers are experimenting with Riesling and with Albariño.

The Ondarribi Beltza is said be a relation of the Cabernet Franc but this is far from certain.

Eighty-nine per cent of the vines are white. The main grapes have the alternative spelling Hondarribi.

## Planting
Traditionally the vines have been planted in the local *parral* style, which is a low pergola with the vines intertwined to provide protection against winds from the sea. The gaps are 1.8 m between vines and 2 m between rows. More modern vineyards, however, are planted *en espaldera*, with the fruiting branches 70 cm above ground level to protect them from frosts. Maximum vine density is 2,500 per ha for *parral* and 3,500 per ha for *espaldera*.

## Vineyard area
This is almost startlingly small. In Vizcaya it is 56 ha and in Guetaria it is 64 ha. These are the smallest DOs in Spain.

## Authorized yield
93.6 hl/ha, but in practice it is usually less. In 1992 it was 56.67 hl/ha.

## Wines
These are all *jóvenes* and should be drunk very young. All three

colours are made and must have a minimum alcohol level of 9.5°, but those that are bottled generally work out at about 10.5 to 11°. Almost all are white and the other colours can only be found in local bars.

## Production
No figures are available for Vizcaya. In 1992 the production of Guetaria was 2,720 hl.

## Vintages
These necessarily vary, but as the wines should be drunk at no more than a year old (though they can last a bit longer) there is no point in listing them.

That wine was grown here in the past can come as no surprise: at least since Roman times it has been grown all over Spain. But that it should still be grown commercially, albeit on a minuscule scale, is a triumph of enthusiasm over climate.

The two provinces in which the wines are grown are part of the País Vasco, or Basque country. Although everyone can speak Castillian, it also has its own Basque language and more than its share of local patriotism, combining the national culture of Wales with the violence of Ireland; as in Wales (where wine is also grown), Castillian names on signposts are often painted out and Basque ones substituted. Thanks to the heavy rainfall the country is wonderfully green and beautiful, with a fine coastline.

In the Royal Historical Archives there is a mention of the word 'Chacolín' in 1622 but the origin of the name is obscure. In the middle of the nineteenth century there were as many as 250 ha of vineyard, but wine growing went through a crisis brought on by a number of factors. Improved transport and the removal of restrictions on the movement of wine brought competition from Rioja and Navarra. Then there were the plagues from America: oidium in 1860, mildew in 1885 and then phylloxera, which attacked the bulk of the vineyards but mysteriously left some of them untouched, and these are the ones that flourish today. Mildew was a particular problem in the damp climate. The vineyards practically disappeared and the wars of the twentieth century caused them to stagnate. By the 1980s there were only 25 ha. Then there was a revival, spurred by local pride and an increasing interest in local gastronomy. The current figures are given above. They are minute but increasing, stimulated by the grant of DO status to Guetaria in 1990 and to Vizcaya in 1994, though EU regulations make it difficult or even impossible to expand the vineyard area further. All the vineyards and bodegas are privately owned: there are no cooperatives.

The wines are made in an unusual way. They are left on their lees in tightly sealed containers so that some of the carbon dioxide from the fermentation gets dissolved and gives them their characteristic prickle. In a decent year they attain about 11° without chaptalization but they are light and very acid. This can be accentuated by a tendency to pick too early to avoid some of the hazards of the climate, together with insects and birds, but conversely some fruity and especially delicious wines can be produced by careful selection of the grapes. Malolactic fermentation is not practised, though it can happen in bottle. The production, however, is minute and the prices high. The reds and *rosados* have a very small production indeed and are only found in local bars, but there are enough whites for there to be occasional exports and in the summer they are delicious to drink in the fish restaurants from Bilbao to San Sebastián. They are well worth seeking out.

## Some leading bodegas: Vizcaya

### Txakoli Aretxaga
A very modern little bodega, founded in 1978, with 3 ha of Folle Blanc and Ondarribi Zuri *en espaldera*, producing very good wines.

### Ignacio Dañobeita Gangoiti
An old-established bodega, founded in 1883, but equipped with a modern plant. It has 3 ha of vines, producing wines of all three colours from the Ondarribis with some plantings of Folle Blanc and experimental Riesling. The wines are sold under the brand Torreko Txakolina.

### Roberto Ibarretxe
A small, very modern bodega, founded in 1987, which grows a number of grape varieties experimentally in its 2 ha vineyard, but produces only white wines, and very good ones, under the brand Txakoli Uriondo.

### Bodegas Virgen de Lorea

Although old-established, with its first vintage in 1929, this bodega, recently bought by a millionaire, been totally modernized and is now a showplace. It makes a first-class white wine under the brand Señorío de Otxaran, entirely from Ondarribi Zuri.

### *Some leading bodegas: Guetaria*

### Ameztoy

A family-owned bodega, now in the third generation, producing good wine from 9.7 ha, sold under the brand Ameztoi.

### Roque Eizaguirre Aguinaga

A reliable bodega in Zarautz, founded in 1930, with 3 ha of vineyard planted *en espaldera* with 15 per cent Ondarribi Beltza and 85 per cent Ondarrabi Zuri, selling good wines under the brands Eizaguirre and Hilbera.

### Etxaniz Txakolina

A family-owned bodega with a substantial vineyard of 13 ha, producing excellent wines under the brand Txomin Etxaniz.

## GALICIA

With Monterrei we enter Galicia, which occupies the north-west corner of Spain, an autonomy of four provinces: Coruña, Lugo, Ourense and Pontevedra. In the distant past it used to be Celtic, but very few traces of that civilization remain today. Its northern and western coastlines are Atlantic, while in the south it borders Portugal. In the east it is separated from the rest of Spain by the mountains of the Cordillera Cantábrica. The Atlantic weather gives its special character. It is exceptionally green. Over most of it there is a lot of rain but in such a large area there are also many microclimates. The inhabitants of Pontevedra claim theirs to be the best climate in Europe to live in. It is also remarkably beautiful. The coastlines are notable for their huge inlets, called *rías*, which are even more remarkable to view from the air than from the land, but alas, like nearly all of the Spanish coasts, they have been all but ruined by uncontrolled development. It is a country of unspoiled villages, exquisite mountains and noble cities, the finest of which is Santiago de Compostela. Medieval pilgrims came here from all over

Europe to visit the tomb of St James, and there seem to be just as many today, a refreshing number of whom still walk. Lugo retains its Roman walls. It is a marvellous area of Spain to visit for those who seek art and beauty – but not for the sunbathers.

In such a damp and temperate area one would not expect there to be many vineyards, nor are there. Those producing quality wines are all in the southern half and most are found in the valleys of the rivers Miño and Sil, which provide a dramatic landscape of almost vertical gorges. Others are found around the smaller rivers that flow into the Atlantic.

## MONTERREI

### Geography
The Val de Monterrei borders Portugal. Monterrei is a fortified town with a castle and a thirteenth-century church. Verín, small as it is, is the commercial centre. The vineyards are 400 to 450 metres above sea level.

### Climate
Being so far inland, this is essentially continental, but no complete statistics are available. It is said to be the warmest place in Galicia, with an average temperature of 12.6°C and 680 mm rainfall.

### Soil
Reddish to look at, clay with a fertile topsoil.

### Grapes
Preferred red varieties: Mencía, Merenzao.

Other red varieties grown: Alicante, Gran Negro, Tempranillo, Cabernet Sauvignon and Mouratón.

Preferred white varieties: Treixadura, Verdello (Godello) and Doña Blanca (Dona Branca).

Other white variety grown: Palomino (Jerez).

### Planting
Not known. The density must be between 3,700 and 5,000 vines per ha.

### Vineyard area
3,000 ha with 2,600 ha actually under vine, though other figures published put it as low as 400 ha.

**Authorized yield**
56 hl/ha.

**Wines**
Red, *rosado* and white. To carry the DO they have to have at least 65 per cent of the preferred varieties, and to be labelled Monterrei Superior they have to have at least 85 per cent.

**Production**
129,900 hl.

Monterrei, or Valle de Monterrei, was granted DO status in 1995 but so far has made little use of it. It is perhaps the most obscure DO in Spain. The emphasis is on white wines, but the principal grape remains the ubiquitous and wholly undistinguished Palomino. Most of the wines are made in two cooperatives and sold in bulk. One private grower is José Luis Vilera of Adegas Ladairo. His white wine made from 50 per cent Verdello, 40 per cent Treixadura and 5 per cent each of Loureiro and Doña Blanca, and his red *joven*, made from 75 per cent Mencía and 25 per cent Tempranillo, have been praised.

## RÍAS BAIXAS

**Geography**
These Galician vineyards all lie within the province of Pontevedra. The DO has three distinct subzones: Val do Salnés (the Salnés valley) is the most northerly and is on the west coast, where the river Ulla flows into the Ría de Arousa; El Rosal (or O Rosal) extends from the west coast along the right bank of the river Miño, which divides Spain from Portugal; and Condado do Tea (*condado* simply means county) extends along the river further inland. Some of the westerly vineyards are almost at sea level, but the mountains above the Miño rise to 2,000 m and the average height of the vineyards is 500 m. In El Rosal the up-river vineyards are on terraces on the steep slopes of the mountains that rise above the river and the little rivers that flow into it.

**Climate**
This is dominated by the Atlantic. The Salnés valley is the coolest of the subzones with an average temperature of 13°C and few

extremes. The summers can be dry and very pleasant, but the proximity of the Atlantic gives a rainfall of 1,500 mm. El Rosal has a slightly higher average temperature of 14°C but also a higher rainfall of 1,400 to 2,000 mm. In either place the summer temperature does not rise above 30°C. Condado de Tea is less influenced by the Atlantic and has more extremes of temperature, freezing in the winter and going as high as 40°C in the summer, with an average of 13 to 15°C, and is generally also wetter, with an average rainfall of 1,300 to 2,000 mm. Sunshine averages 2,200 hours per year.

## Soils
In the Salnés valley and El Rosal the soil is alluvial over the local pinkish granite. In the Condado do Tea granite and slate appear on the surface with light, granitic soils.

## Grapes
Authorized white varieties: Albariño (90 per cent), Loureiro Blanco (Marqués), Treixadura, Caiño Blanco and Torrontés. Albariño grapes are the most expensive in Spain.

Authorized red varieties: Brancellao, Caiño Tinto, Espadeiro, Loureiro Tinto, Mencía and Sousón.

## Planting
Traditionally on pergolas with the vines widely spaced: 3 m apart and 4 m between rows. They are pruned long, with seven *brazos* (arms) per vine and with one *pulgar* (pruning bud) and ten *yemas* (fruiting buds) per *brazo*. There can be as many as seventy bunches of grapes on a vine. There is now, however, a move to use a modification of the Geneva Double Curtain method of training, known as *silvo*, and other pruning methods are being tried experimentally. This may eventually make mechanical harvesting possible in the flatter vineyards. There are 600 to 1,600 vines per ha depending on the size and steepness of the site. The damp climate gives rise to fungal problems, but the local authorities give every assistance in monitoring so that treatments are kept to a minimum.

## Vineyard area
1,768 ha at the last count, but increasing within the limits of what the EU allows.

## Authorized yield
Albariño 71.5 hl/ha. Others 87.5 hl/ha. In practice, however, the yield is usually 50 to 60 hl/ha.

## Wines

Although some red wines are made (with the abnormally low minimum alcohol level of 9.5°), all the important wines are white. The Albariño whites are 100 per cent varietal with a minimum alcohol of 11.3°. Others sold as varietals must have at least 85 per cent of the named variety. Val do Salnés must be at least 70 per cent Albariño. Condado de Tea must have a minimum of 70 per cent Albariño or Treixadura vines, or of the two combined, and the rest authorized varieties. El Rosal must have the same combination of grapes. All the whites other than Albariño must have a minimum of 10° but usually work out at 11–12.5°. *Rosados* do not fall within the DO but some good ones are made.

## Production

41,877 hl (1996/7).

## Vintages

These wines are generally drunk young, so vintage information is not of much value. Most recent vintages have been good; 1995, 1996 and 1997 very good.

Galicia is the wettest, coolest part of Spain where vines are grown and is near the limit of where vines *can* be grown. It is so green, fertile and beautiful in the Miño valley (on both sides of the border, though in Portugal it is called Minho) that it looks like a vision of the Garden of Eden. The fresh, slightly sparkling *vinhos verdes* from Portugal became well known in the 1960s, though many that were exported were prepared specially for foreign markets and were very different from those found in Portugal. The best were made from Alvarinho and Loureiro grapes, especially the former. In Spain these are the Albariño and Loureira Blanca. There were stories that Galicia produced fresh, light, acid wines like *vinhos verdes* but these were never seen in the rest of Spain, not even in the north, though this can partly be accounted for by the famous Galician thirst. Perhaps the stories had been handed on by word of mouth from generation to generation, for there had indeed been a flourishing wine trade, but this began to collapse with the arrival of oidium in 1851, when the vineyard area went down from 13,398 ha to 4,079 ha and much of the population left; and then mildew came in 1885 and phylloxera in 1899, so that in a hundred years the vineyards were reduced to little more than a third of what they had been. By the

1970s these two varieties had almost died out in Galicia. It was the old story: such vineyards as remained grew quaffing wines of no quality produced from high yielders like the Palomino and the Alicante. Then a revolution happened. Spain at that time had plenty of good red wines, and a few good white ones, but there were no fresh, light, delicate whites. The technology to produce such wines, even in a hot climate, was available and, as can be seen from many sections of this book, people started to use it. In the quest for light wines, someone happily thought of Rías Baixas. In the late 1970s and 1980s, leading bodegas from other parts of Spain such as Rioja and Penedés started to move in. Then came the smart money. Restaurateurs from Madrid, and local businessmen who had made fortunes from tinned fish or plastics, wanted vineyards. By 1988 the wines were good enough for a DO to be created, and the growers aspired to produce Spain's leading white wine. They may well have done so, though other districts would no doubt hotly dispute it. They have certainly produced something unique that has caught on to such an extent that it is Spain's most admired and most expensive white wine.

The Albariño vine is by far the most important. Unfortunately it is a low yielder, which is probably why it went through such a period of neglect. The traditional way of growing it is on *parrales*, pergolas with granite uprights and a canopy of wires, which look so attractive when the vines are in leaf that they add materially to the illusion of being in the Garden of Eden. It produces varietal wines that are light and fragrant but so acid and astringent that they can be mouth-searing, especially when very young. This is a style that is sought after, though, and many growers retain the acidity by avoiding the malolactic fermentation altogether or by using it only on a proportion of the crop, as they find that it not only reduces acid but also aroma and flavour. In the absence of a malolactic fermentation, the malic acid of the grapes often gives a rather appley element to the nose and flavour. Although it is generally recommended that these wines be drunk within the year, as they spend time in bottle the cutting edge becomes more blunted, and some would say that after a year, or at most two years, in bottle they are at their most attractive. The odd bottle that has been kept for several years (usually accidentally) can become remarkably smooth and fills out in flavour, but this only applies to the best, especially varietal Albariños; others just grow dull. Some people, however, prefer

A typical modern bodega

blended wines to the varietals, and if the blended wines lack the unique penetration of the Albariño, they add layers of complexity; often they are more immediately appealing. In El Rosal, which is the smallest of the areas but the one with the oldest tradition of wine growing, Loureiro is the most popular grape and gives a herbal element to the scent. In Condado del Tea, the Treixadura gives a flowery element but the Torrontés can make for rather bitter wines.

With bodegas springing up and new vineyards coming into production, it is not surprising that a lot of experiments are going on. No two wine makers do exactly the same thing. But one thing they all have in common: a wish to keep everything cool. The grapes are moved quickly into the press houses to avoid heating by the sun, and one extreme measure that is being adopted is to use cold water instead of air in the inflatable bag of the horizontal wine presses. Cold maceration is usual. It goes without saying that fermentation is in temperature-controlled stainless steel. Then comes the question of oak. Very often there is none, but some have a few months in oak, usually American but Galician and French are being tried. Whether oakiness is or is not attractive in Albariño wines can only be a matter of opinion.

The word *pazo*, which appears in many of the names, is best translated as 'grange'.

## Some leading bodegas

### Agro de Bazán

It is not easy to pin down an exact date for the foundation of this bodega. Feasibility studies started in 1979 and work on the estate began in 1980, when trees were felled to make room for the vineyard, which was planted in 1981. The bodega was built in 1988, just in time for the vintage, and the first wines were sold in the following year. It is all very new and completely up to date, the creation of a Galician entrepreneur, Manuel Otero Candeira, whose fortune is based on tinned fish. He set up the winery in a most beautiful position at Tremoedo in the Salnés valley; and he set it up with immense enthusiasm, which is justified by the very high quality of the wines. There are 11 ha of Albariño vines and no other variety is used. There is no malolactic fermentation, giving wines of great fragrance, the acidity being controlled by maceration and tank-ageing. The wines (and also the tinned fish) are sold under the name Granbazán. The standard wine is Granbazán Verde, so called because it comes in a green bottle of a Rhenish shape. Granbazán Ambar comes in a brown bottle and is made from free-run juice, giving it an unusually generous flavour behind great freshness. It is exemplary. Granbazán Limousin is likewise made from free-run juice, but only in the best years, and spends a year in Limousin oak followed by six months in tanks before bottling. It is one of the very few wines of the district actually intended for ageing. There is also a brandy and the company has wine interests in Chile.

### Pazo Baión-Comercial Oula

Also in the Salnés valley, this 40 ha estate has 33 ha of Albariño, the largest single vineyard of this variety. Also known as Granja la Fontana, its great house is described by its owners as 'an English-style building with architectural hints of a French château'. It is certainly unique. It was recently acquired by the Freixenet Group, of Cava fame, and produces one of the best varietal Albariños under the name Vionta and a second, very good varietal Albariño under the name Pazo de Baión.

## Pazo de Barrantes

There can be few estates more beautiful than this one, which has been in family ownership for generations, passing to the Conde de Creixell through his mother in 1982. It forms part of Dominios de Creixell, the other part being the great Rioja house, Marqués de Murrieta. The ancient *pazo* in the Salnés valley has been beautifully restored and is also the headquarters of the Fundación Creixell which, amongst other things, has a considerable Graham Greene archive; he used to stay there. But although the estate has existed for centuries, it has entered the commercial production of Rías Baixas wines much more recently. There is an 8 ha vineyard of Albariño vines which are trained in a new way, using three wires. The first vintage was in 1991. Pressing is very slow, with only light pressure, so the grapes are in the press for three to four hours, but there is no separate maceration. There is then a slow fermentation at 15 to 18°C. They use tall, slender, light green Italian bottles that are very elegant but not so easy to store. About half the wine is subjected to a malolactic fermentation but nevertheless the acidity is distinctly on the high side. It is bottled at 10°C to retain some dissolved carbon dioxide. They are expert wine makers and although the wine is already very good, it is likely to evolve further in stature.

## Bodegas Castro Martín

This bodega, founded in 1981 and with a 10 ha vineyard of Albariño at Puxafeita-Ribadumia in the Salnés valley, sells excellent varietal wines under the name Casal Caeiro.

## Adegas Das Eiras

This modern bodega, founded in 1990, exemplifies the influx of capital and wine-making skills into the area. A 70 ha vineyard was planted which enjoys the equable maritime climate of El Rosal, and which is now reaching maturity. Everything is spotless, and in wine making the emphasis is on keeping things cool. There is a cold maceration at 8–10°C, cool hydromatic bag presses are used, and the fermentation is at 17°C. The results are excellent. Abadía de San Campio is a varietal Albariño, the exceptionally good Terras Gauda is 75 per cent Albariño, 15 per cent Loureira Blanca and 10 per cent Caiño Blanco, and there is a further version of Terras Gauda, the Etiqueta Negra (Black Label) with the same grape mix but fermented in French oak; its high price is justified by an extra dimension of flavour.

## Palacio de Fefiñanes

Founded in 1904, this bodega in a sixteenth-century palace at Cambados, in the extreme north-west of the area, is the oldest in the DO and pioneered Albariño grapes. It provides two good wines: 1583 Fefiñanes and Fefiñanes Oro, the latter oak-aged for a year.

## Granja Fillaboa

A family-owned bodega founded in 1986 at Fillaboa-Salvaterra do Miño, it has 24 ha of Albariño vines. Its wine, sold under the name Fillaboa, is very good.

## Lagar de Fornelos

Founded in 1982 in El Rosal, this bodega was bought by La Rioja Alta in 1988. It began with 7 ha of Albariño vineyard, but in the 42 ha estate there have been massive levellings and plantings, trained *en espaldera*. While most of the land near by is granite, here there is an outcrop of slate and mineral-rich sand. Only Albariño grapes are used: in 1985 80 per cent came from its own vineyard, 10 per cent from other growers in the same zone and 10 per cent from the Salnés valley. The fermentation is at the very low temperature of 15°C and is not subjected to a malolactic fermentation, but nevertheless is not excessively acid, producing a very attractive, well-balanced wine. It is bottled just before shipment and sold under the name Lagar de Cervera. The bodega also produces brandy.

## Adegas Galegas

A modern company formed in Meder-Salvaterra do Miño, in the Condado de Tea, by twelve growers who between them have 40 ha of Albariño, Treixadura and Loureira situated in various areas of the DO. Its wines are amongst the best. Don Pedro de Soutomaior is a varietal Albariño, as is the excellent Dionisos; Bouza Grande is 50 per cent Treixadura, 30 per cent Albariño and 20 per cent Loureira. Veigadares is 85 per cent Albariño, 10 per cent Treixadera and 5 per cent Loureira, cask-fermented. It is unusual in producing a red, Señorío de Rubios, which is also cask-fermented and made from 50 per cent Espadeiro, 30 per cent Gran Negro and 20 per cent Caiño.

## Bodegas Limeres Rodríguez-La Val

Founded in 1985, this bodega is as up to date as it is possible to be, and is rapidly becoming one of the major growers, with three vineyards, one of 4 ha around the bodega at San Miguel de Tabagón in El Rosal, one of 32 ha at Salvaterra and one of 25 ha at Las Nieves, both in Condado de Tea. The 4 ha vineyard, growing 80 per cent Albariño, 10 per cent Loureira and 10 per cent Treixadura, was established well before the bodega was founded, but that of Salvaterra was only planted in 1990 and is now entering maturity. The bodega makes two wines of excellent quality: La Val, which is a varietal Albariño, and Viña Ludy, made from 80 per cent Albariño and 10 per cent each of Loureira and Treixadura.

### Bodegas Marqués de Vizhoja
This small bodega at Arbo has 13 ha of Albariño vines as part of a 135 ha estate. It started selling its excellent wine in 1988 under the name Torre La Moreira.

### Robaliño
Another recent foundation at Arbo, dating from 1991, this bodega has established a very good reputation with its varietal Albariño, Liñar de Vides.

### Pazo San Mauro
In a countryside of beautiful estates, this one, in the Condado de Tea, stands out – and so do its wines. Near Salvatierra de Miño, it extends from the banks of the river to a height that gives wonderful views over Portugal. At the bottom there is a sandy beach, facing an inviting island in the river, and it rises to cross the Vigo–Madrid railway lines, ascending the mountainside to a chapel at the top dedicated to San Mauro, the patron saint of the wounded, built in 1582 on a site where there had been a chapel since the thirteenth century. The present owner, a businessman from Vigo, bought the estate in the 1960s from a canon of Túy cathedral. At that time there were vines but no Albariño, and the house was in ruins; it was beautifully restored in 1991. Old vines of the Treixadura, Torrontés and Loureiro varieties still remain at the higher levels of the estate, which also grows apples and kiwi fruit. Land was cleared and a new Albariño vineyard established in 1988 on unusually sandy soil and in a well-sheltered position. The vines are grown on *cordon simple*. At present there are 30 ha but the vineyard is being expanded. There is a modern winery. There are two wines, Pazo San Mauro, which is

a varietal Albariño, and Condado Domiño, made from 60 per cent Albariño, 20 per cent Treixadura, 15 per cent Torrontés and 5 per cent Loureira.

## Santiago Ruiz

It is a pleasant change to find a bodega that has been going for years and years, and has thus become legendary. The buildings themselves date from the seventeenth century. The bodega even has an agreeable little museum of wine making. It was founded at El Rosal in 1882 by the great-grandfather of the present owner who, a hundred years later, and describing himself as a young Galician of eighty-five, brought it up to date by installing stainless steel. Despite its antiquity it owns only a very small vineyard but buys from growers all around the village. The wine is made typically from 70 per cent Albariño, 20 per cent Loureira and 10 per cent Treixadura, and is unusually fruity and complex, with a good balance of acidity well removed from the searing character of some of its rivals. It also produces a most agreeable non-DO *rosado*.

## Bodegas Salnesur

This cooperative was founded in 1988 at Cambados to enable the local growers to benefit from the newly created DO. They did it on a splendid scale and it has a huge tower with a view of the island of La Toja on one side and vineyards on the others. It has 375 members in the Salnés valley, many of whom planted new vineyards that are just reaching maturity – which goes for most of the Albariño vineyards throughout the region. Everything is stainless steel and, as usual, the emphasis is on cool wine-making. The must from the pneumatic presses is cooled in a heat exchanger before entering the settling tanks, and is fermented at 16°C. All the wine then undergoes a malolactic fermentation. The wines are very good. Condes de Albarei Clasico is a varietal Albariño, the best version, sold as Condes de Albarei Enxebre, made from very ripe grapes grown in the oldest vineyards and free-run must. Condes de Albarei Carballo Galego is an Albariño cask-fermented in Galician oak. They also make liqueurs.

## Pazo de Señorans

This small bodega in Paradela-Meis was founded in 1989. It has an 8 ha Albariño vineyard. Its wines are very good. It also makes brandy.

## Valdamor

A recently formed cooperative, Valdamor shows how these organizations have changed their image in the more prosperous regions. This has 308 members dedicated to growing top-quality Albariño vines in the area of Xil en Meaño in the Salnés valley. The installations are completely modern and produce two wines, one fermented normally and the other barrel-fermented.

## Bodegas de Vilariño-Cambados

Founded in 1986 by 280 Albariño wine growers in the Salnés valley, some years ago this would no doubt have been a cooperative, but nowadays it prefers to be described as a company with 280 shareholders. Between them they have 1,000 parcels making up 150 ha. They keep themselves closely supervised, with a school for wine growers, two agricultural engineers working in the vineyards, and five meteorological stations. Only the best grapes command the highest prices and all are Albariño. It goes without saying that the plant is modern stainless steel and the bodega is built on a vertical plan so that the wine can be moved by gravity. Fermentation is at about 16°C, and in most years the wine is given a full malolactic fermentation, though this may be reduced to a half in very good years. Its wines are amongst the best. About 80 per cent is sold as Martín Códax, the name of a thirteenth-century Galician poet and troubadour. The second wine (which is also good) is sold as Burgans. There is also a small production of Organistrum, named after an extinct medieval musical instrument, depicted in stone on the portico of the cathedral of Santiago de Compostela; it is fermented in Allier oak, which gives it complexity without making it too oaky. They also make liqueurs.

## Pazo de Villarei

Founded in 1993, this bodega at San Martiño de Meis is a member of the great Bodegas & Bebidas group. It has a very modest 1 ha vineyard and buys in the rest of its needs from carefully supervised local growers. It produces very good varietal Albariños, one of which is fermented in new American oak.

# RIBEIRA SACRA

## Geography

Ribeira Sacra means 'sacred river bank', a country of Romanesque monasteries. The DO is so new that no official map yet exists, but the area is clearly defined in five subregions. Listed in the order of the official regulations, these are: Amandi, on the right bank of the river Sil and stretching inland towards Monforte de Lemos; Chantada, on the right bank of the river Miño; Quiroga, on the right bank of the river Sil towards Ribeiro; Ribeiras do Miño, on the left bank of the river Miño opposite Chantada; and Ribeira do Sil, on the left bank of the river Sil. The best vineyards are on the south-facing slopes – a better word for some of them would be precipices – at an altitude of 200 to 500 m. But the area is at the limit for cultivation of the vine and none is found above 400 m except in sites that enjoy special microclimates.

## Climate

The picture is an extremely complicated one, with the rivers twisting to give many microclimates, depending on the exposure and height of the vineyards. In the valley of the Sil, rainfall is 700 mm and the mean temperature 13.2°C. In the valley of the Miño the rainfall is 900 mm and the mean temperature 13.9°C.

## Soils

There is again great variety, with plutonic acid rocks, Silurian slates, and schist.

## Grapes

Preferred red varieties: Mencía, Brancellao, Caíño, Loureira Tinto, Sousón, Merenzao, Ferrón and Espadeiro.

Permitted red varieties: Mouratón, Negreda and Alicante.

Preferred white varieties: Loureiro, Treixadura, Godello, Dona Branca (Doña Blanca), Albariño and Torrontés.

Permitted white variety: Palomino.

Of all these, the most widely planted at the present time is Mencía, occupying 25 per cent of the vineyard area.

## Planting

Very flexible – indeed, the regulations say 'do whatever works best' – but usually Guyot or double cordon Royat; 2,500 to 4,000 vines per ha.

**Vineyard area**
At present less than 1,500 ha, but suitable sites are available to extend this to as much as 6,500 ha in the future.

**Authorized yield**
Preferred red varieties: 61.75 hl/ha. Preferred white varieties: 68.25 hl/ha. Other varieties: 77 hl/ha.

**Wines**
Reds and whites. To be labelled as monovarietal they must be made from at least 85 per cent of one of the preferred varieties, the remaining 15 per cent to be of other preferred varieties, and have a strength of at least 11°. Generic wines must contain a minimum of 60 per cent preferred varieties and have a strength of at least 10°. At present the bulk of the production is red.

**Production**
The figure for 1994–95 was only 7,000 hl, but a good year might produce 25,000 hl.

**Vintages**
1994 6, 1995 6, 1996 6, 1997 4.

In referring to the beauty of the landscape around Spanish vineyards one stands the risk of being accused of exaggeration, but no one could exaggerate the beauty of this one. Many of the best, terraced slopes are very steep so that viticulture and vintaging are difficult; but they also have a very fine exposure to the sun, which must make them potentially amongst the best vineyards in the world. They have not yet come anywhere near to realizing their potential. Even now, white wines from the Albariño grape show greater ripeness and less acidity than their neighbours in Rías Baixas, with real complexity and enormous length. The red wines are not yet notable, but on such sites it seems likely that really fine wines will emerge. Most of the wine making is still on a very small scale, but the smart money is beginning to arrive.

*Some leading bodegas*

**Adegas Moure**
This modern *adega* (bodega) was founded in 1984 at O Saviñao and is one of the few to export. It produces an exceptionally good

varietal Albariño and a highly praised varietal Mencía. These are marketed under the name Abadía de Cova.

**José Manuel Rodríguez González**
His varietal Mencía, sold under the name Décima, has been highly praised.

**Ubalda López Díaz**
He produces another highly praised Mencía under the name Mezquita.

# RIBEIRO

## Geography
Ribeiro joins on to the better-known area of Rías Baixas, but is further inland to the east, in the beautiful valley of the river Miño above the point where it forms the border between Spain and Portugal. The commercial centre is the delightful little town of Ribadavia, where the river Avia flows into the Miño. The river Arnoia, flowing from the east, joins the Miño a little further down. The vineyards are in the river valleys and on the slopes above them, at heights varying between 100 and 350 m, and many are on terraces.

## Climate
Humid and relatively cool, influenced by winds blowing along the valley and from Portugal. Temperatures rise to 36°C in summer and fall as low as −4°C in winter, with an average of 15°C. The rainfall is very low by Galician standards, at 800 to 1,000 mm, and there are 1,800 hours of sunshine.

## Soils
Generally sandy and alluvial over granite, but better soils for quality wines are found on the higher levels.

## Grapes
Recommended red varieties: Caiño, Ferrón, Sousón and Brancellao.
   Permitted red varieties: Garnacha Tintorera (Alicante), Mencía and Tempranillo.
   Recommended white varieties: Treixadura, Godello, Lado, Loureiro and Albariño.

Permitted white varieties: Palomino (Jerez), Torrontés, Macabeo and Albillo.

## Planting
Traditionally on pergolas, but these are dying out, and most are now grown pruned and trained by the Guyot or Silvo/Espada methods. Generally 1.3 m between vines and 1.8 m between rows; 7,000 vines per ha.

## Vineyard area
3,100 ha.

## Authorized yield
91 hl/ha, though in practice 50 hl/ha is more realistic.

## Wines
Whites between 9° and 13°. Reds between 9° and 12°. There is also a special category unique to this area: *enverado*. This is a relic of the days when white grapes were picked in August, before they were ripe, to get acidity, but such wines are now rarely made. Their strength is between 8° and 9°.

## Production
149,850 hl.

## Vintages
1994 6, 1995 6, 1996 6, 1997 4.

According to the fourteenth-century French chronicler Froissart, John O'Gaunt's archers were put out of action for two days after drinking Ribeiro's 'ardent wines' and it is said that the same fate befell the Napoleonic troops in the Peninsular War. But until recently the story became rather sad. There was the usual trouble with phylloxera and then the equally usual reaction: quantity instead of quality. Depressing white wines were made from the Palomino and equally dim, or even worse, reds from the Alicante. Such wines are still to be found and should be assiduously avoided. Although the DO was set up in 1952 the story continued as before, one of cheap bulk wines. Then, in the 1980s, things began to change. The neighbouring DO Rías Baixas was having a marvellous success, in terms of both quality and profitability. Anyone looking around could have seen that Ribeiro was capable of competing, and they looked. The bodega to show the way forward was the cooperative – most unusual! It produced some wines of real quality, and it goes on making them. This showed what could be done and, as in so much of Spain at that time, capital was waiting to be poured in. The result was the arrival of new bodegas and new enologists producing wines of excellent quality from the best local varieties grown on the higher terraces. If the whites do not have the searing penetration or the finesse of their neighbours from Rías Baixas, they are nevertheless fresh, light, fragrant and, at their best, delicious. The reds do not quite measure up to them, but nevertheless they are excellent to drink, with plenty of fruit and body rather than complexity or elegance. All should be drunk young.

## Some leading bodegas

### Bodega Alanís
Founded as a family bodega in 1910, it started bottling in 1970. It is now part of the great Bodegas y Bebidas group and specializes in white wines from local varieties. It is thoroughly modern and its wines are very well made. Gran Alanís is made from Treixadura, Torrontés and some Palomino and is very good, but the San Trocado, which omits the Palomino, is better.

### Bodegas Campante
One of the new wave of bodegas, founded in 1988, it owns 6 ha of vineyard and makes both white and red wines. The wines are sold under the names Campante, Gran Reboreda and Viña Reboreda. They also blend table wines.

### S.A.T. A Portela
Another of the new bodegas, founded in 1987, this is likewise completely up to date. It makes red and white wines under the name Señorío de Beade. Its best white wine is sold under the name Beade Primacia.

### Emilio Rojo
This relatively small bodega, founded in 1987, has 2 ha of vineyard. Its eponymous white wine, made from 50 per cent Lado, 25 per cent Treixadura, 10 per cent Albariño, 10 per cent Loureira and 5 per cent Torrontés, is much praised.

## Bodegas Vilerma
Founded in 1988, this bodega gets its grapes from a vineyard planted ten years earlier. It makes a good, light white wine from Lado, Torrontés, Albariño, Loureiro and Treixadura.

## Viña Mein
A small bodega founded by a lawyer from Madrid in 1987, in an old farmhouse surrounded by 2 ha of vineyard. It makes its good white wine, Casal de Mein, from 65 per cent Treixadura, 10 per cent Loureira, 10 per cent Godello, 10 per cent Albariño and 5 per cent Torrontés.

## Vitivinícola del Ribeiro, Sociedad Cooperativa
Although most of its wines do not aspire to excellence, this is the cooperative that led the way. It was established in 1968 and began to bottle wines under the name Pazo two years later. In this it was a pioneer. It now has 800 members with 750 ha of vineyard, producing half the wines of the DO, and it goes without saying that the grapes it can draw upon are variable in quality, but it is guiding its members towards the best. It has modern equipment and its best white wines are very well made. Amadeus is made from 85 per cent Treixadura and 15 per cent Torrontés. Viña Costeira is made from 60 per cent Torrontés and 40 per cent Palomino.


# VALDEORRAS

## Geography
Although in Galicia, this area borders on Castilla-Léon, with which it has much more in common than with the other Galician vineyards. Its centre is the little town of Barco de Valdeorras (or O Barco) on the river Sil, which flows into the river Miño northeast of Ourense (or Orense). The vineyards are in the river valley and on the hillsides on either side at a height of 240 to 300 metres. The best wines come from the slopes and are mostly between O Barco and A Rúa. The doubling up of the names is in order to give the version of each name in the Galicians' own Romance language. There is at present no official map of the DO but one is planned.

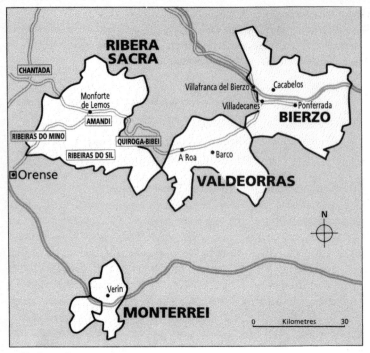

Inland north-west

## Climate
Well inland, the area is influenced by both the continental and the Atlantic weather systems. It has a relatively high rainfall of 850 to 1,000 mm, but that is a good deal lower than is found in some places to the west; it is one of the driest parts of Galicia. Temperatures can reach as high as 44°C in the summer and go down to −4°C in the winter, with an average of 11°C. There are 2,500 hours of sunshine a year.

## Soils
In the river valley the soils are alluvial but in some places there is limestone underneath, while the hillsides contain a lot of slate, which makes cultivation difficult as it tends to slide down, but it gives excellent wines from the Godello grape.

## Grapes
Recommended red variety: Mencía.

Permitted red varieties: Garnacha Tintorera (Alicante), Gran Negro and María Ardoña (Merenzao).

Experimental red varieties: Cabernet Sauvignon, Tempranillo and Merlot.

Recommended white variety: Godello.

Permitted white varieties: Palomino and Valenciana (Doña Blanca)

Experimental white varieties: Lado, Moscatel de Grano Menudo, Riesling, Chardonnay and Gewürtztraminer.

## Planting
Generally *en vaso* on the slopes and *en espaldera* on the plains, with a spacing of 1.6 to 1.8 m between rows. *Espaldera* is taking over in the modern commercial vineyards. Maximum density 4,000 vines per ha.

## Vineyard area
2,000 ha, but of these only 1,500 are actually planted.

## Authorized yield
56 hl/ha on the slopes and 70 hl/ha on the plains.

## Wines
Reds, whites and *rosados* with a minimum strength of 9°. Traditionally made to be drunk as *jóvenes*, but there are some *crianzas* and the best reds are considerably stronger than the minimum, typically 11.5° and going up to 12.5°.

## Production
48,165 hl.

## Vintages
As these wines are generally made to be drunk young, an assessment of older vintages is irrelevant. Nineteen ninety-three was a poor year but other recent vintages have been good or very good, particularly 1997.

This area has yet to come into its own but is well on the way. It is one of those places that came to grief with the arrival of phylloxera, for which various dates are given ranging from 1882 to 1911. Before then there were 8,000 ha of vineyard. Whatever the date may have been, there can be no doubt about the result: that excellent local grape the Godello all but disappeared, and growers went in for quantity rather than quality, planting lots of that dull grape (for table wines) the Palomino, with Garnacha Tintorera, Gran Negro (producing very dark wines of little quality) and even hybrids. The results were drunk locally but there was no national market, and so far as export markets were concerned, Valdeorras simply did not exist. The DO was set up in 1957 but did not produce any immediate effect. However, the Consejo Regulador has since been at the forefront in conducting experiments to find the best varieties, methods of viticulture and techniques of vinification. In the 1970s there was a hot dispute over whether still to go in for quantity or to look for quality. At that time the government was encouraging the planting of French varieties, but after much experiment the more enlightened growers decided to look for quality and to go back to the Godello. Experiments are still continuing enthusiastically, as the list of experimental varieties given above shows, but the Godello won an enthusiastic following and deserved it. The main snag was that there were practically no Godello vines, so that cuttings had to be taken, then propagated, and good clones had to be chosen and propagated further. The results, to the amazement of those who deplored the whole exercise, have been completely successful, but it has taken time; and it has been complicated by the fact that there are few large-scale growers, most of the vineyards being very small and peasant-owned. They are deterred by the fact that the Godello is a shy yielder and is hard to harvest. There are now 350 ha of Godello vineyards but, to put it in perspective, this is still only a small part of the whole. A similar story can be told about the red Mencía, which is also a great success; so much so that Valdeorras looks as if it will soon be as well known for its red wines as for its whites – a very odd thing to happen in Galicia.

Before the move to quality, practically all the wines were made by cooperatives and sold in bulk for drinking in Galicia. Now much of the wine, whether made by cooperatives or by private bodegas, is sold in bottle, and although there is a steadily increasing export trade, the local market is still by far the most important one.

The move towards quality and the higher prices that would come with it brought investment, and the major bodegas are now as well equipped as any, with computer control of cold fermentations, ultra-cooling, cold microfiltration and so on. Fermentation temperatures were experimented with and 18 to 19°C was found to be best. The move towards quality has also brought about a considerable rise in grape prices, so the peasant growers make a living.

No one would claim that Valdeorras grows world-class wines, but nevertheless they are thoroughly good and their excellent value has led them on to the shelves of English supermarkets. Although *rosado* is permitted in the DO, very little is made. About 80 per cent of the production is white. The best wines are the varietal Godellos, which are dry, fragrant, fresh, fruity and, at their best, delicious, with excellent length; and the varietal Mencías, which are rather lightweight but thoroughly sound table wines, to be drunk young with great pleasure. Good, cheaper wines of both colours are made by blending these grapes with others. It is these that are generally found in the English supermarkets. Those that do not contain the noble grape varieties are unexciting and are sold locally or cheaply in Spanish supermarkets. Quality is going up more rapidly than marketing skills, and this is an area to watch.

## Some leading bodegas

### Bodegas Godeval S.A.T.
It is hard to imagine a bodega in a more beautiful place than this. It was founded in 1985 and in 1988 moved into a restored monastery dating from the ninth century, formerly of the military order of the Knights of St John of Jerusalem, in an exquisite, tranquil valley. They make their wine from their own 17 ha vineyard, planted exclusively with Godello, pruned to give a very low yield. Everything is completely up to date here and they are dedicated wine makers. The result is a modest production of just one excellent white wine: Viña Godeval.

### Bodegas Medorras
Founded in 1984, this bodega has had considerable success in the export markets. At present it has 12 ha of vineyard, planted with Godello, Mencía and Cabernet Sauvignon. It makes good red and white wines. The whites are sold under the name Godellón, the top wine being Godellón Oro, and the reds under the name Viña Ladera.

## Os Cinco Irmans
This bodega was started in 1987 by two doctors, and its young Godello is thoroughly sound.

## Joaquín Rebolledo
With 15 ha of vineyard, this model bodega was created by a lawyer in his family estate. His red and white wines are very highly praised, the reds going up to a *reserva*, and he is unusual in making varietal Merlots and Cabernet Sauvignons.

## Cooperativa Santa María de los Remedios
Although its sales are mostly local, this cooperative makes some good wines. Started in 1959, it now has 332 members who between them own 250 ha of vineyard. Its best white is Arume Godello and its best red is sold under the name Medulio.

## Bodegas Señorío S.A.T.
This is a most impressive bodega. It was founded in 1988 by a group of professionals whose object was to produce first-class wine by controlling the wine making from the vineyard to the bottle, but it is now essentially run by one family. They acquired 20 ha of vineyard, which is planted with the classic varieties *en espaldera*, save for one small part which is experimental and is planted with all sorts of things. Other grapes are bought in from local growers who are supervised by the enologist. Wine making is exemplary. They make a complete range of wines, including a minimal amount of *rosado*, but for all practical purposes the production is 80 per cent white and 20 per cent red. There are three ranges. The top white is Valdesil, a varietal Godello, and the top red is Valderroa, a varietal Mencía. Both are very good indeed. The most unusual wine is Vannereida, a varietal María Ardoña, which has a delightful and most unusual nose coupled with length and complexity, but it has to be drunk young and the last vintage was drunk entirely by the family. On the next level down are the rather cheaper Montenovo red, made from equal parts of Mencía and Garnacha, and Montenovo white, made from equal parts of Godello and Palomino. The noble varieties are dominant and the wines are excellent value. Finally there is the Valmaior range, which is multivarietal and are sold as good, cheap wines in Spanish supermarkets.

## La Tapada S.A.T.
One of the youngest bodegas, it has 9 ha of vineyard and has acquired a very good reputation for its whites, which are varietal Godellos and include one that is barrel-fermented. They are sold under the name Guitián.

# 7
## *The Levant*

Wine has been grown here, as in most of Spain, since at least as far back as Roman times. The old kingdom of Valencia covered the areas that were to become the provinces of Valencia, Alicante and Castellón and here grew 'Vinos Valencianos'. They have long had a flourishing export trade and at the end of the nineteenth century benefited, as did so much of Spain, from the phylloxera catastrophe in France. In 1889 there were 247,423 ha of vineyard. But phylloxera duly found its way here, like nearly everywhere else, and by 1922 there were only 152,841 ha. The position of the vineyards changed too, and for the better. Before phylloxera, vines flourished in the fertile soil of the coastal plain, but these were turned over to more profitable uses, notably orange groves and orchards of almonds, while the vineyards were replanted in the hills, where they still are.

Most of the vineyards in the Levant today are in the autonomies of Valencia and Murcia but one – Almansa – is in the east of Castilla La Mancha. It makes more sense, though, to consider it as part of the Levant than as part of La Mancha. As many holiday-makers and colonies of foreign residents have found, the Levant is a most agreeable part of Spain. The coast is washed by the warm Mediterranean sea and there is lots of sunshine. The holiday-makers rightly enjoy the sound local wines, and indeed they are so sound and such good value that the bodegas there became pioneers in the export trade, which they have retained and expanded. This is the second largest vineyard area in Spain and third largest in the world, the ports of Valencia and Alicante handling 45 per cent of Spain's wine exports – though these, of course, include wines grown elsewhere. And apart from wine there is a very large trade in table grapes and raisins. But no one would suggest that any really great wines are grown here. For those, one must look elsewhere. That is not to say, though, that this part of Spain has missed out on the wine revolution. Far from this being so, the best bodegas were amongst the first to install modern technology. They are as well equipped as those anywhere and their wines are just as well made, but modern enology has not yet spread to all the bodegas, and especially not to all the cooperatives, so it is easier to buy a disappointing bottle here than it is in most places. There are plenty of good wines, though, and the best from this region are undoubtedly the sweet Moscatels.

# ALICANTE

## Geography
The province of Alicante lies at the south of the autonomy of Valencia. The city itself is a flourishing port and industrial centre dominated by the remains of two Moorish castles, but there is not much of the old town left. It has a long tradition of wine growing and, like Valencia, grows many other things as well. The DO vineyards are separated into two distinct regions. The northernmost subzone, La Marina, stretches inland from the coast around Denia. The southern subzone, Clásico, includes the city itself, though part of the old vineyard area in what was once described as the garden of Spain has been swallowed up by development; then it stretches north and west as far as the foothills of the central Meseta and crosses the border of the province of Murcia, though the wines grown there are made and matured in the province of Alicante. It has borders with the DOs of Valencia, Yecla, Almansa and Jumilla. The lowest vineyards are just above sea level, the highest, around Albanilla in Murcia, go up to 400 metres.

## Climate
Vineyards by the coast enjoy a Mediterranean climate, but this gets more continental inland. In the northern subzone the average temperature is 15.3°C but in the south it is 18°C. Throughout most of the year there is no rain at all. Rainfall is unpredictable and, when it does come, is generally heavy, varying between the wide limits of 200 and 500 mm. The average sunshine is 2,400 hours. This climate makes it a wonderful place to winter in, but in summer it can be very hot; grapes can easily become raisins.

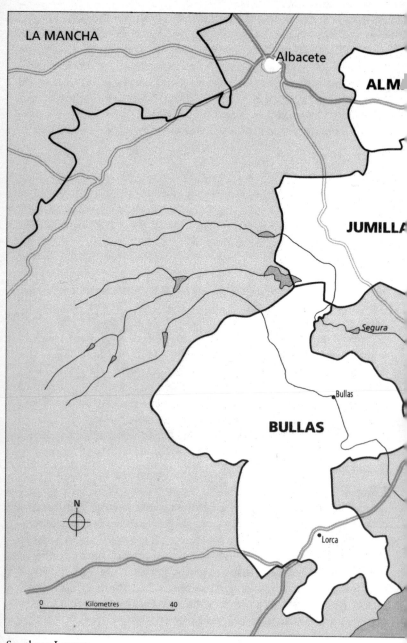

Southern Levant

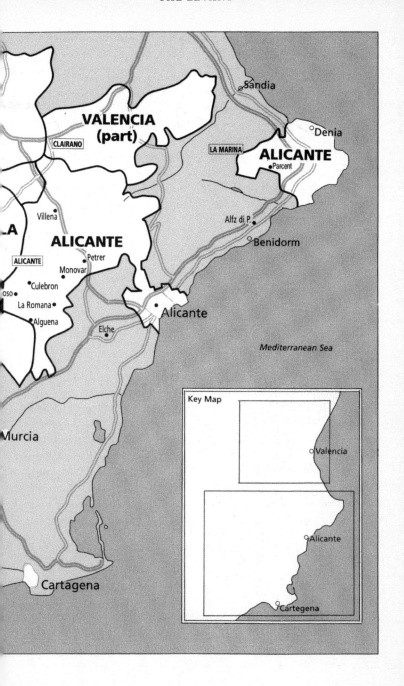

VALENCIA
(part)

CLAIRANO

LA MARINA

ALICANTE

Sandia

Denia

Parcent

Villena

ALICANTE

ALICANTE

Petrer

Monovar

Culebron

oso

La Romana

Alguena

Elche

Alfz di P.

Benidorm

Alicante

Mediterranean Sea

Murcia

Cartagena

Key Map

Valencia

Alicante

Cartegena

## Soils
There are some alluvial soils by the coast, but for the most part they are stony, dry and chalky, with some clay in places.

## Grapes
Authorized red varieties: Monastrell, Garnacha Tinta, Garnacha Tintorera, Tempranillo and Bobal.

Experimental red varieties: Cabernet Sauvignon, Merlot, Syrah and Pinot Noir.

Authorized white varieties: Merseguera, Moscatel Romano, Macabeo, Planta Fina and Airén.

Experimental white varieties: Riesling and Chardonnay.

The Monastrell is the most widely planted of the red varieties and, of the white varieties, Planta Fina is beginning to disappear and Airén to take its place.

## Planting
Pruned *en vaso* in the cooler districts and *en cabeza* in the hotter ones. Both square and rectangular patterns are used.

## Vineyard area
17,154 ha.

## Authorized yield
Reds 35 hl/ha, whites 49 hl/ha.

## Wines
Most are sold as *jóvenes* but there are some reds up to *reserva*. The minimum strength for red and *rosado* wines is 12°, for whites 11°. But there are also some special wines. Red *doble pasta* (see below) is made, with a minimum strength of 12°. White Licor Moscatel must be made from 100 per cent Moscatel and have a minimum strength of 15°. The unique Fondillón, which is described in the text below, must be made from 100 per cent Monastrell, have a minimum strength of 16° and be aged for at least eight years.

## Production
Approximately 100,000 hl, but the figure given for a good year is 326,371 hl.

## Vintages
1980 5, 1981 5, 1982 7, 1983 4, 1984 5, 1985 4, 1986 4, 1987 6, 1988 4, 1989 5, 1990 6, 1991 5, 1992 4, 1993 5, 1994 5, 1995 5, 1996 5, 1997 5.

Alicante used to be associated with rather dim table wines that were pleasant enough to drink but little more; there were rumours of a legendary wine called Fondillón, which could never be found, and there were sweet Moscatels that were out of fashion. There have been great changes here as in the rest of Spain. The dim wines are still to be found but modern wine making, though far from universal, is now firmly in place. Cold-fermented white wines are fresher and more fragrant than those of the past, and the best sweet white wines, made from the Moscatel grape, are amongst the best anywhere, but the real revolution has happened with the reds. Here one must, perhaps rather reluctantly, thank the imported experimental varieties. The best of the reds today are those in which an admixture of Cabernet Sauvignon adds backbone and structure. They can be excellent. The astonishing thing is that they are not better known. There are also special lusty red and *rosado* wines known as *doble pasta*. In this method the must is run off after about twelve hours' maceration and fermented to make a *rosado*. The lees are left in the vat, which is then topped up with more grape pulp that is fermented on two lots of lees. This results in very full-bodied wines that can go up to 18° alcohol. *Doble pasta* wines are still made and are exported in bulk for blending, as they always have been.

Alicante's unique wine, though, was and is Fondillón. It is made exclusively from the Monastrell grape mostly grown in the Valle de Vinalopó to the north-west of the city. From the sixteenth century until well into the nineteenth it was regarded as one of Europe's great wines, to be served at the tables of the aristocracy. It was certainly well known in England, though imports do not appear to have been large. In the seventeenth century it was generally priced above sherry and was one of the most expensive wines imported. In his play *The Honest Whore* (1604), Thomas Dekker made one of his characters say, 'You'll bleed three pottles of Alicant, by this light, if you follow 'em.' Gervase Markham (1568–1637) in his *English Housewife*, where he gave remedies for all the ills that may befall wine, thought it worthwhile to include Alicante: three or four gallons of 'stone honey clarified' were to be added to 'Alligant that be brown hard'. And William Salmon in his *Compleat English Physician* (1693) wrote '*Alicant*. It is a delicate red, Stomach Wine, strengthens the Tone of the Stomach, stops Vomiting, causes a good Appetite, stops Fluxes of all sorts, restores the tone of the Bowels, and is excellent against a Tabes, Phthisick and spitting of Blood.' A remarkable wine indeed! And in the same century the English fleet put into Alicante to buy it to ward off the scurvy. These descriptions and others elsewhere suggest it was Fondillón that was being referred to. One shipper who opened a London office in 1876 listed seventeen qualities, nine dry and eight sweet, the oldest coming from a *solera* laid down in 1811. It disappeared at the end of the century and was not seen for fifty years. A few casks were preserved, though, in private bodegas. Then, at the end of the 1940s, Salvador Poveda Luz, whose family had a bodega in Monóvar, set about recreating it, guided by local traditions and the wines that were still to be found. It is now made by many of the leading shippers. But it is an expensive wine to make well and its eclipse may well have been a result of the booming trade with the French, in which the Alicante growers fully joined, following the phylloxera disaster in that country. French families came in and settled, everyone grew rich, and exports from Valencia increased from half a million hl in 1877 to 8 million in 1882. But Fondillón was not what the French were looking for.

Traditionally Fondillón was made by selecting the best and ripest grapes and then drying them in the sun, further to increase the concentration of sugar; they sometimes lost as much as half their weight. Then they were pressed and put with their skins into oak vats where a tumultuous fermentation was followed by a slow one, the whole, including the skin contact, lasting thirty days and producing a deeply coloured, very alcoholic wine of 16 to 18°, astringent with tannin and with 6 to 8° Baumé of sugar. The wine was then aged, usually using the *solera* system. Old barrels, covered with cobwebs, were kept in the *sacristía*, to be tapped only on special occasions.

Nowadays things are slightly different. The best grapes are selected to give the greatest strength and they are either left for a long time on the vine (left too long in this climate they can become raisins) or occasionally are sunned. The wine is made with only a small period of skin contact, to produce a *clarete*, avoiding the old astringency, and the wine is then aged, sometimes, in exceptionally good years, as vintage wine but usually in *soleras*. As it ages it oxidizes, the redness disappearing and being replaced by a pleasant amber. It must be aged for at least eight years, and peaks at about twenty – or the equivalent produced by a carefully regulated *solera* in which never more than 20 per cent is withdrawn from the oldest scale in a year. The alcoholic strength is between 16 and 18°. The sweetness depends on the initial sweetness of the grapes, and some wines can be completely dry, others moderately sweet, between 0 and 4° Baumé. They have an agreeable oxidized nose, rather like a light oloroso sherry. The dry versions make good aperitifs, the sweeter kinds being dessert wines which, both in colour and in style, call to mind old, browning tawny ports.

## Some leading bodegas

### Bodegas Alfonso Crianza de Vinos
A family bodega founded in 1872 and now in the sixth generation, it has 40 ha of vineyard, planted entirely with Monastrell, and a small museum. It specializes in *rancio* wines and makes a good vintage Fondillón. Its red Siglo XXI Gran Reserva is quite unlike anything else, having a touch of sweetness and plenty of tannin, but leaning towards *rancio*; it reminds one of the best wines of the past.

### Bodegas Cooperativas de Alicante (BOCOPA)
This macro-cooperative was founded in 1987 to bring together eight Alicante cooperatives which, between them, account for over half of the DO wine, grown by 3,000 members. It introduced modern wine making and its wines are, at the least, well made and good value. Some are much more than that. It uses the trade names Marina Alta, Viña Alcanta, Viña Alone (Alone is Greek for Alicante), Viñacantil and Marqués de Alicante. The very sound Viña Alone red is made from 70 per cent Monastrell and 30 per cent Tempranillo. The Moscatel Alone is a good, luscious example. The top red, Marqués de Alicante, is made from equal parts of Tempranillo, Monastrell and Cabernet Sauvignon; it is very well balanced and is worth seeking out. Fondillón Alone 1970, despite apparently bearing a vintage year, is made from a *solera* laid down in 1970.

### Bodegas Brotons
A comparatively small bodega, founded in 1955, it has 40 ha of vineyard, which supply about half its requirements, the rest being bought in. Most of its wines are sold locally under the names Caserío Culebrón and Dormilón, and it specializes in reds and *rosados* from the Monastrell grape, but it also makes a well-regarded Fondillón, matured by the *solera* system.

## Bodegas García Carrión

This old-established bodega, dating from 1890, operates on a large scale with all sorts of products, including fruit juices and wines sold in tetrapacks. It has 90 ha of Monastrell vineyards. It is actually in Jumilla but buys wines from various places and produces Alicante DO wines, sold under the names Castillo de San Simón, Covanegra and Montelago. Following the style of Jumilla, its best wines show ageing potential. Its unusual and delicious Castillo de San Simón is worth seeking out.

## Bodegas Gutiérrez de la Vega

Founded in the late 1970s, this bodega operates on only a small scale, but nevertheless its wines are amongst the most highly regarded in the district. They are sold under the names Casta Diva, Viña Caballeta, Viña Alejandria, Rojo y Negro and Viña Ulises. The Muscats sold under the Carta Diva mark include a dry one that really is dry and a good, unusual sweet one, Cosecha Miel.

## Bodegas Enrique Mendoza

A bodega of modest size, founded in 1989, it has 75 ha of vineyard and produces very highly regarded wines mostly from French varieties: Chardonnay, Cabernet Sauvignon, Merlot, Pinot Noir and Shiraz. Other wines are made by blending with Spanish varieties including Tempranillo. They are sold under the names Enrique Mendoza, Viña Alfas and Savia Nova. The varietal Cabernet Sauvignons, going up to *reservas*, are impressive, as is the Viña Alfas Selección, the 1994 being made from equal parts of Cabernet Sauvignon, Merlot and Pinot Noir.

## Salvador Poveda

A completely up-to-date family bodega with 150 ha of vineyard. Apart from its own name, it sells wine under the names Cantaluz and Viña Vermeta. Its white wines include, rather improbably, a Riesling. Its red Viña Vermeta Reserva is a varietal Monastrell and shows what good wines this grape can produce. The bodega is particularly noted for its vintage Fondillón.

## Primitivo Quiles

A family bodega with deep roots in the district, it has been growing grapes since 1780. It is particularly noted for its *rancio* and Fondillón wines, made from renowned *soleras*. It also makes a very good Moscatel.

# ALMANSA

### Geography
Although Almansa is physically at the extreme east side of La Mancha and should therefore strictly be considered in the context of that province, in terms of wine and of scenery it has much more in common with the Levant, bordering Alicante and the Murcian DOs Jumilla and Yecla. It is not contiguous with the La Mancha DO and is a long way from its centre. It is a countryside of small hills, like its neighbours, and totally unlike the vast plain of La Mancha. The vineyards lie at heights between 700 and 1,100 m but tend to favour the flat land at the bottom of the hills.

### Climate
Continental semi-arid, with summer highs of 40°C, winter lows of –8°C and an average of 13°C. The rainfall is between 300 and 400 mm mostly falling as heavy showers in spring and autumn. There are 2,800 hours of sunshine.

### Soils
Permeable, infertile and with a high lime content.

### Grapes
Authorized red varieties: Monastrell, Cencibel (Tempranillo) and Garnacha Tintorera.
   Experimental red variety: Cabernet Sauvignon.
   Authorized white varieties: Merseguera and Airén.
   The vast majority of grapes are red, with the Monastrell in the lead and producing the best wines; the Garnacha Tintorera comes a close second in quantity and a poor third in quality.

### Planting
Vines trained *en vaso* and planted in the *marco real* or *tres bolillo* patterns, with a maximum density of 1,600/ha.

### Vineyard area
6,100 ha.

### Authorized yield
Monastrell 21 hl/ha, Garnacha Tintorera 35 hl/ha, Merseguera 38.5 hl/ha.

## Production
85,963 hl (1994/5), but 120,000 hl are hoped for in a good year.

## Vintages
1985 6, 1986 5, 1987 5, 1988 5, 1989 7, 1990 5, 1991 5, 1992 6, 1993 6, 1994 6, 1995 6, 1996 5, 1997 6.

The town of Almansa is an agreeable little place with some good buildings, including an impressive castle, one of the last to be built in the reconquest. Indeed, the place has spent rather too much of its history as a battleground, including a major battle in the War of the Spanish Succession. Most of the wines from here are made with rather primitive equipment and taste like it, yet there is something rather special about them. The best red wines are unusually well balanced and can even be elegant. The Monastrell, in particular, is a vine that holds out great promise. The problem with this DO is that it has been slow to attract investment, though the cooperatives are now installing stainless steel. Its traditional trade has been in vast blending wines, sent to the coast and shipped from Alicante. But even though nothing as yet suggests that it is ever likely to move into the league of top-quality wines, its potential for producing very attractive wines is manifest. Its emergence into the export market is entirely thanks to one shipper: Bodegas Piqueras.

### Leading bodega

### Bodegas Piqueras
A family bodega dating from 1915, it has no vineyards of its own but has to buy everything in from growers whom it can supervise. It produces most attractive wines which it sells under the name Castillo de Almansa. The reds are the best, from *crianza* upwards, matured in American oak, and are made from about 75 per cent Cencibel and 25 per cent Monastrell. A slightly cheaper range called Marius contains a minor proportion of Garnacha Tintorera but tastes at least as good.


## BULLAS

### Geography
The southernmost of the Mediterranean areas for DO table wines, in the province of Murcia, it actually reaches the Mediterranean

coast for a short distance just north of Aguilas and stretches inland into the hills, with its northern border joining Jumilla. It is sparsely populated but includes two charming little towns: Bullas itself and Lorca. It is sparsely planted with vines, too, and most of the vineyards are well into the hills. There are three subzones: the westernmost, rising from 500 to 800 m; the central, round Bullas, at a height of 500 to 600 m; and the north-eastern at 400 to 500 m.

## Climate
From Mediterranean to continental as one travels north and west, semi-arid with summers going up to 40°C and frosts in winter. The average temperature is 15.6°C, with 350 mm rainfall and 2,900 hours of sunshine.

## Soils
The vineyards are mostly in the valleys between the rivers, on sandy and sometimes alluvial soil.

## Grapes
Recommended red variety: Monastrell.
    Authorized red variety: Tempranillo.
    Experimental red varieties: Cabernet Sauvignon, Garnacha, Merlot and Syrah.
    Recommended white variety: Macabeo.
    Authorized white variety: Airén
    Of all these, the Monastrell is hugely predominant.

## Planting
No information is currently available save that the density is 900 to 2,200 vines per ha.

## Vineyard area
3,500 ha are currently registered for the DO out of a total of some 5,500 ha.

## Authorized yield
49 hl/ha for red varieties and 56 hl/ha for whites.

## Wines
Whites 10 to 12.5°, *rosados* (exclusively from the Monastrell grape) 11 to 12.5° and reds 12 to 14°.
    In the past, production has been mostly of *rosados*, but the future is likely to lie with the young reds.

## Production

No statistics for total production are currently available, but sales of DO wines in 1994–95 amounted to 23,060 hl, and 34,100 are expected in a good year.

## Vintages

1994 6, 1995 5, 1996 6, 1997 6.

Although wines have been grown here since Roman times, they are only just beginning to emerge from total obscurity. They used to be of the usual Mediterranean type: alcoholic, heady, flabby, and mostly sold in bulk. A provisional DO was granted in 1982 and the full DO in 1994, but despite the enthusiasm of some local wine growers things have been very slow to get going. The DO wines are very difficult to find if you are there and impossible if you are anywhere else. Nevertheless, it has real possibilities. Wine makers are rapidly learning how well the Monastrell grape can perform in the hills behind the Mediterranean, and it should be possible to make some very good red wines; there are already experiments with *crianzas*. This is certainly an area to watch. At present, though, there are only two bodegas making and bottling DO wines: Carrascalejo, a family bodega founded in 1850, and Cooperativa Agrícola Nuestra Señora del Rosario, founded in 1950, which has 1,200 members and sells wines under the name Las Reñas. Both are in Bullas.

# JUMILLA

## Geography

Jumilla is bordered to the north by Almansa and to the east by Yecla and Alicante. Although most of the DO area lies within the province of Murcia, it extends westwards to areas in Albacete which form part of Castilla-La Mancha. It is also high, with the vineyards at between 400 and 800 m above sea level. There are no trees, other than some olives and nuts, and very little wildlife.

## Climate

This is continental and southern. In winter the temperatures fall to below zero but the summers are hot, sunny and arid. The temperatures rise to 40°C and sometimes higher, giving a yearly average of

15.5°C. The rainfall is very low and generally comes as heavy storms in late spring and late autumn. There are 3,000 hours of sunshine.

## Soils
Permeable, infertile, with sand, a high chalk content and large stones.

## Grapes
Authorized red varieties: Monastrell, Garnacha Tintorera, Tempranillo (Cencibel), Cabernet Sauvignon and Garnacha.

Experimental red varieties: Merlot and Syrah (neither yet officially permitted for DO wines, though Merlot probably soon will be).

Authorized white varieties: Airén, Macabeo and Pedro Ximénez.

The most important variety by far is the red Monastrell, which occupies 87 per cent of the vineyard. The most important white variety is Airén, but this only occupies 8 per cent.

## Planting
Grown as bushes *en vaso*, trained low, and planted in the *marco real* pattern with a minimum density of 1,100 and a maximum of 1,600 per ha, though there is now some intensive cultivation going up to 2,400. There are also some recent vineyards planted *en espaldera*. Irrigation of the vineyards is forbidden except in emergencies – there are many emergencies.

## Vineyard area
50,031 ha.

## Authorized yield
24.5 hl/ha for Monastrell, 28 hl/ha for the other varieties but, through drought and replanting, the actual yield is generally a good deal less. In 1993 it was 11 hl/ha.

## Wines
Reds:          Monastrell reds and *claretes*, 12.5° minimum.
               Reds and *claretes* other than Monastrell,
               12°minimum.
*Rosados*:     Monastrell, 12° minimum.
               Other varieties, 12° minimum.
Whites:        11.5° minimum.
Sweet wines:   12.5° minimum.

Wines sold as Jumilla-Monastrell must contain at least 85 per cent Monastrell.

The latest regulations of the Consejo Regulador only lay down minimum strengths, as above; but this is traditionally an area of strong or even massive wines, and although they are now being made lighter than they once were, whites can still go up to 15°, *rosados* and reds to 17°. *Doble pasta* wines (see Alicante, p. 233) are no longer dealt with in the DO regulations, but are still made.

Most of the wines are sold as *jóvenes*, but there is now a move towards *crianzas*.

## Production
273,442 hl (1994/5, but see text below).

## Vintages
1980 7, 1981 7, 1982 4, 1983 5, 1984 5, 1985 6, 1986 4, 1987 6, 1988 5, 1989 5, 1990 5, 1991 6, 1992 5, 1993 6, 1994 5, 1995 5, 1996 6, 1997 5.

The hills here are not very high or remote, and the soil, though rather sandy, is far from being the pure sand that phylloxera cannot get through, yet the aphid took a remarkably long time to arrive. The vineyards were free from it until 1989 and some have still not been replanted, but although it was a hundred years over-due, when it did come it wrought its usual havoc, even though some of the old vineyards had been replanted with grafted wines to increase yields. The figures speak for themselves. In 1989 67,379,200 litres of wine were sold. By 1993 it had fallen to 28,782,500 litres. But disastrous as this was, Spain was by then prosperous and it gave the chance of a fresh start. Wisely the grow-ers decided to stick largely with the Monastrell vine, which can produce remarkably good results here, but the addition of a small proportion of the French varieties has worked well. Fresh capital was attracted and new bodegas established, completely up to date. Unfortunately some of the old-established ones, faced with the enormous cost of replanting the vineyards, have not been able to keep up. The traditional trade was largely in powerful wines sold in bulk for blending, many of them made by the *doble pasta* method, but the demand for these has greatly declined and the move is towards lighter wines with more finesse. They can still be powerful and heady, though, and they have long had a devoted following in

Spain. Tasting them, one can well see why. Bulk wines, rather oddly, have found a market in Italy. But Jumilla, at the moment, is an area essentially of thoroughly enjoyable wines but not of great ones, though recently some of the *crianzas* have shown considerable distinction, and the Monastrell may yet show itself capable of producing something outstanding; wines made from it have already taken a great leap upwards in quality. Once the growers get their act together, very good things could result. It is an area, too, that can offer tremendous value for money and the supermarkets have been quick to recognize this; for instance, the well known 'flying wine maker' Peter Bright (an Australian based in Portugal) has made some excellent wines for Sainsburys. A rather odd wine, only found locally, is a sweet red from the Monastrell.

It is a pleasant place to visit, if you do not mind the heat. Jumilla is a most agreeable little town and the mountain views from the vineyards are spectacular.

## Some leading bodegas

### Bodegas y Viñedos Agapito Rico

Founded in 1989 by two growers, this is at present clearly the leading quality bodega in Jumilla and its wines are worth looking for. It makes only red wines and is entirely self-sufficient for grapes, having 70 ha of vineyard at a height of 700 m, planted with 25 per cent Monastrell, 25 per cent Tempranillo (Cencibel), 25 per cent Merlot and 20 per cent Cabernet Sauvignon, with 5 per cent other varieties. The vineyards were planted in 1983–84, before the bodega itself was founded, and after careful study of the soil and microclimates. They are irrigated by night, when necessary, using water from a reservoir fed principally from wells in the higher mountains and also by catching rain-water – when there is any. Everything is completely up to date here. Some of the wines are made by carbonic maceration and others traditionally, the *crianzas* and above being matured principally in French oak from Limousin and Allier, with a little American. Some box wine is made using Australian yeasts. The brand name is Carchelo, named after Monte Carche above the vineyards, and a little non-DO wine is made under the name Carchelito. The very good *joven* is made from equal parts of Monastrell and Merlot, the *crianza* from Monastrell, Tempranillo and Cabernet Sauvignon. One non-DO wine is made from equal parts of Cabernet Sauvignon and Monastrell, while another is a varietal Cabernet Sauvignon.

## Julia Roch e Hijos

A young bodega, founded officially in 1981, it really has a much longer history which can be traced back to 1870. It has an unusually large vineyard holding of 250 ha planted with Tempranillo (Cencibel), Monastrell, Cabernet Sauvignon, Macabeo and, experimentally, Syrah. Its sound wines – the *crianza*, made from Monastrell and Tempranillo and given a year in American oak, is the best – are sold under the brand Casa Castillo. There is also a Casa Castillo Vendimia Seleccionada, which is a varietal Tempranillo and is highly regarded.

## Bodega Señorío de Condestable

This was founded by the great Bodegas y Bebidas empire in 1968, when it took over a vast bodega then known as SAVIN. It operates on a grand scale, using the names Condestable, Señorío de Robles and Vilamar. It has raised the quality enormously, making varietal wines amongst others, and notably the varietal Monastrell.

## UTIEL-REQUENA

### Geography

Utiel-Requena lies inland, to the west of Valencia and a good deal higher, around the two towns that give it its name. Its vineyards are from 600 to 900 m above sea level, averaging 720 m, on an undulating plain surrounded by mountains.

### Climate

Although the area is near enough to the coast to be influenced somewhat by the Mediterranean, the climate is essentially continental, with a maximum of up to 40°C in summer and a minimum of −15°C in winter. The average is 13.9°C and, to put these extremes into perspective, the average for the hottest month, July, is 23.2°C and for the coldest, December, is 5.9°C; nevertheless the winters are long and cold, the summers relatively short. Quite recently a spring frost destroyed 40 per cent of the grapes. Rain falls mostly in spring and autumn, to the extent of 400–450 mm, and there are 2,500 hours of sunshine.

## Soils

These are very mixed, with the alluvial soils of the Magro valley in the north and with sandstone, marl and clay in the south, but there are also outcrops of limestone and the best vineyards are found on these.

## Grapes

Recommended red varieties: Tempranillo and Garnacha Tinta.
   Permitted red variety: Bobal.
   Experimental red varieties: Cabernet Sauvignon and Merlot.
   Recommended white varieties: Macabeo and Merseguera.
   Permitted white variety: Tardana (Planta Nova).
   Experimental white varieties: Chardonnay and Sauvignon Blanc.
   Despite its being only a permitted variety, the vineyards are largely planted with Bobal, though the Consejo Regulador is doing his best to get them replaced with Tempranillo. The experimental grapes are not officially permitted in DO wines.

## Planting

The square *marco real* pattern is used with 2.5 m spacing, and pruning is *en vaso*, with a density of 1,600 to 2,500 vines per ha.

## Vineyard area

39,916 ha.

## Authorized yield

Reds 45.5 hl/ha, whites 49 hl/ha.

## Wines

Reds up to *reserva*. Whites and *rosados* are made as *jóvenes*. There are also *doble pasta* wines (see p. 233). The minimum strength for all these wines is 10°. In addition there is a superior class of wines. The white Superior must be made from the Macabeo grape and have a strength of 10.5 to 12°. The *rosado* Superior must be made from the Bobal grape and have a strength between 10.5 and 12.5°. The red Superior must be made from Garnacha and Tempranillo grapes (though one suspects that there is often some Bobal there as well) and must have a strength between 12 and 13.5°. These Superior reds may be aged as *crianzas* or *reservas* with a few *grandes reservas*. *Crianzas* must be at least two years old with at least one spent in oak and *reservas* must be at least three years old with at least one in oak. There are also sparkling wines with a minimum strength of 11°.

## Production
129,096 hl (1992). A figure of 460,000 hl has been given more recently and 1,047,115 hl are expected in a good year.

## Vintages
1988 5, 1989 3, 1990 5, 1991 5, 1992 6, 1993 7, 1994 6, 1995 5, 1996 6, 1997 5.

Utiel-Requena is the largest of the three DO areas in the province of Valencia. It has a long wine-making history and there are medieval cellars still in the old part of Requena, which is a most enchanting little town; indeed, like some of the towns in the north, the whole place seems to be built above cellars carved out of soft sandstone. It also has an admirable little wine museum in a nineteenth-century round bodega. In the eighteenth century many of its wines were distilled, which made for easier transport, for the area was rather cut off from its principal market in Castilla and from the coast. Communications improved in the nineteenth century with a new road, now the N111, opened in 1847, linking Valencia to Madrid; and the railway line to Valencia was opened in 1887. All of this came in time for the district to benefit from the French wine crisis brought on by oidium and phylloxera. As in Haro, new bodegas sprang up around the railway station. Between 1850 and 1890 15,000 ha of vineyard were planted. The trade was not destroyed by the revival of the French vineyards and phylloxera did not get here until 1912, when it progressed relatively slowly, in part owing to the resistance to the parasite of the local Bobal vines. The vineyards continued to expand while they were being replanted, and by 1950 there were 40,000 ha, the same amount as there are today. There are vineyards everywhere there can be and the area gives the impression of being one great vineyard.

The local Bobal vine, which is not grown in many other places, is at once the strength and the weakness of the area. It does well in the higher vineyards where the summers are short and dry, and it is still by far the most widely planted vine here, producing attractive and successful *rosados*, and with the aid of the *doble pasta* method of vinification it can give strong and lusty reds. This method has long been declared to be in its death throes but it is still very much alive and provides bulk wines that are popular for blending, finding an improbable market in the vineyards of what used to be the east European Soviet bloc, and a more likely one in Valencia, to which DO they are admitted by special dispensation to beef up the rather thin local reds. Vinified in the ordinary way, its red wines are astringent, tannic and lacking in finesse but have the great advantage of being cheap and are often very good value for money. The best red wines made here, though, from the Tempranillo and the French varieties, particularly when they are blended together, show that Utiel-Requena can produce quickly maturing wines that are very attractive, even if they do not aspire to be in the front rank, and just a few wines age well in the medium term. For this reason the Consejo Regulador is encouraging growers to replace Bobal with Tempranillo. At the present time, though, the great majority of the wines are sold in bulk rather than in bottle.

## Some leading bodegas

### A. Y. M. Beltrán
Founded in 1940, this is one of the biggest vineyard proprietors with 150 ha. While most of its wines are sold in bulk, it bottles very well-regarded red and *rosado* wines under the name Viña Truquesa. The 1996 red *joven* was made from 60 per cent Tempranillo and 40 per cent Bobal, while the 1994 *crianza* was made from 85 per cent Tempranillo and 15 per cent Garnacha.

### Coviñas Sociedad Cooperativa
This large cooperative was formed in 1965 by amalgamating sixteen cooperatives in a new, modern building. It makes a very full range of good wines sold under the names Peñatejo, Enterizo, Viña Enterizo, Vendimia Inicial and Requevin. They go up to *grandes reservas*.

### Vicente Gandía Pla
See the section on Valencia below. It has a fine 75 ha vineyard, Finca Hoya de Cadenas, in Utiel-Requena, planted mostly with Tempranillo and occupying the most suitable ground on an estate that also includes almond and olive trees, with a delightful house dating from 1820. Further supplies are obtained from the local cooperative which also makes the wines from its own grapes. The wines include very good Tempranillo and Sauvignon varietals. Other varietals

may well be produced in the future. Their Utiel-Requena wines are sold under the names Floreal, Hoya de Cadenas and Marqués de Chive. The excellent Hoya de Cadenas Reserva 1989 was made from 85 per cent Tempranillo and 15 per cent Garnacha.

### Cavas y Vinos Torre Oria
A well-established bodega dating from 1897, it is one of the few to produce Cavas, and good ones, too. It has a modest vineyard holding of 5 ha but buys in and produces a complete range of well-regarded Utiel-Requena wines sold under the names Torre Oria, Villa Iñigo and Marqués de Requena. The 1992 red *crianza* was made from 80 per cent Tempranillo and 20 per cent Garnacha.

### Bodegas Schenk/Cavas Murviedro
This bodega will be discussed in the section on Valencia. It has built a fine new winery in Utiel-Requena and has a close relationship with the Cooperativa Valenciana de Viticultores, which has 350 members. It has persuaded the local growers to prune short in the interests of quality and the strength of the wine has gone up by half a degree. It buys casks from Château Pichon Lalande and uses them from the third to eighth year of age. It makes wines up to *crianza* level but no *reservas*. Its varietal Tempranillo *crianzas* are very good.

## VALENCIA

### Geography
Valencia is a modern, thriving city, the third largest in Spain, and the port is the largest in the amount of wine it handles. The vineyards are divided into four subzones: Valentino to the west of the city, which includes Cheste (formerly a separate DO); Alto Turia to the north-west of the city; Clariano, which is quite separate, in the extreme south of the province, bordering on Alicante; and Moscatel de Valencia, to the south-west of the city. Each of these subzones, however, can be further subdivided. Valentino is the biggest, with about 60 per cent of the vineyards, planted on slopes between 100 and 550 m above sea level. Subdivisions include Campos de Liria at 175 m and Serranía at 550 m. Alto Turia, at 400 to 700 m, is hilly and has some 10 per cent of the vineyard. Clariano can be divided

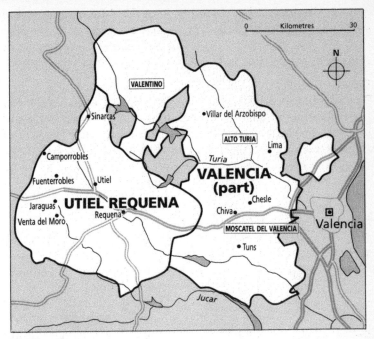

Northern Levant

into two parts: the eastern and the western, the vines being planted on terraces at between 160 and 650 m above sea level with an average of 350 m. Moscatel de Valencia to the south-west of the city, is rather scattered and only accounts for a small amount of the vineyard; it has outposts in Valentino. The height varies from 100 to 400 m. All these heights should be regarded as very approximate as no two sets of official figures agree.

**Climate**
Down by the coast it is Mediterranean and moderate, but with the odd local feature that it can be unexpectedly cold at night, even in summer, so that temperature fluctuations of 30°C between day and night are not uncommon. Most of the vineyards are 30 km or more inland, where the climate is more continental, rising to 35°C in summer and going down to −5°C in winter. In Valentino the mean temperature is 14°C, in Alto Turia it is 12.5°C and in Clariano it is 15°C. The rainfall is lowest in Alto Turia, where it averages

460 mm, and highest in parts of Valentino at 550 mm, though it varies a lot between the various subzones and Campos de Liria has only 280 mm. There are 2,700 hours of sunshine. The whole can be regarded as arid or semi-arid.

## Soils
The lower parts of Valentino have brown or reddish-brown soils with limestone; higher up they are brown and contain limestone. Alta Turia has rather sandy soil but with some chalk. In Clariano the soils are rather similar to those of Valentino, but in the Valle de Albaida there is clay in the subsoil.

## Grapes
Recommended red varieties: Monastrell, Garnacha Tinta, Garnacha Tintorera and Tempranillo.

Authorized red variety: Forcayat (in Clariano only).

Experimental red variety: Cabernet Sauvignon.

Recommended white varieties: Macabeo, Merseguera, Malvasía, Planta Fina de Pedralba, Pedro Ximénez and Moscatel de Alexandría.

Authorized white varieties: Planta Nova and Tortosí.

The red Bobal vine is widely grown but is not authorized for the Valencia DO save for some wines grown in Utiel-Requena (see above). It is idle to suggest, though, that none is used.

## Planting
In hot areas the vines are pruned *en vaso*, keeping the grapes close to the ground to protect them from the heat. The square *marco real* pattern is used, 2.5 m apart where it is hottest and 2.25 m where it is less hot. Where it is merely warm, they are pruned *en cordón* and planted in a rectangular pattern 3 by 1.75 m. The vine density is 2,500 per ha in Clariano and 2,000 elsewhere.

## Vineyard area
16,149 ha.

## Authorized yield
Reds 49 hl/ha, white Alto Turía 45.5 hl/ha, other whites 56 hl/ha.

## Wines
There is a complicated range of wines with different regulations for the four subzones.

Valentino. White wines are made from Merseguera, Planta Fina,

Pedro Ximénez and Malvasía. They come in all shades of sweetness from bone dry upwards and must have a minimum strength of 11°. *Rosados*, *claretes* and reds are made from both Garnachas and must likewise have a minimum strength of 10.5° for *rosados*, otherwise 11°. *Licoroso* and *rancio* wines are made from Moscatel and Pedro Ximénez and must have a minimum strength of 15°.

Alto Turia. Dry whites from Merseguera with a minimum strength of 10°.

Clariano. Dry whites from Merseguera, Tortosí and Malvasía with a minimum strength of 10°. *Rosados*, *claretes* and reds from Monastrell, Forcayat and the two Garnachas with a minimum strength of 11°.

Moscatel de Valencia produces what its name suggests. The minimum strength is 10° unless the wine is a *licoroso*, when it is 15°.

The whites, *rosados*, *claretes* and many of the reds are made as *jóvenes* but some of the reds are given ageing. There is now a move, though, towards *crianzas*, which use the new plantings of Tempranillo and Cabernet Sauvignon. This style of wine has only just begun to develop. The very sweet *licorosos* and the *rancios* can be classified as *reservas* after twenty-four months in American oak and twelve months in bottle.

There are also some *espumosos* with a minimum strength of 11°.

The Valencia DO back label may also be applied to wines containing up to 30 per cent of wines made from the Bobal grape in neighbouring Utiel-Requena.

In the past the wines, especially the reds, have tended to be a good deal stronger than the minimum, and when they have fallen short they have been legally strengthened with wines from Utiel-Requena, but currently the grapes are being picked before they are overripe and this will bring the strength down to meet modern tastes. However, the taste for stronger wines will still undoubtedly continue and there are those who would simply combine the two DOs into one.

**Production**
625,000 hl.

**Vintages**
1987 6, 1988 4, 1989 4, 1990 4, 1991 5, 1992 5, 1993 6, 1994 6, 1995 5, 1996 6, 1997 5.

Valencia is a delightful place to visit. It is a buzzing industrial city and the centre of the orange trade; but for the most part its wines are not distinguished. There are few small bodegas, the trade being in the hands of big operators, including cooperatives, which supply them as well as selling direct. They sell agreeable wines in enormous quantities at very attractive prices to fill the shelves of Spanish stores and of supermarkets all over the world. They were the pioneers of the export trade, efficient and commercial. They also sell table grapes, grape juice and dry Moscatel to Italy for making *spumante*. Vast quantities of wine are sold in bulk, particularly to France, Germany and Italy. This is a wholesale trade with wines coming from all over the place and should be considered as quite apart from the DO. Few of their DO wines rank highly by absolute standards but some of the Moscatels do. These come in all styles from light, sweet and slight to massive and memorable.

## Some leading bodegas

### Anecoop Sociedad Cooperativa

Wine forms only part of the activities of this cooperative, which was established in 1975 as a cooperative of cooperatives. With its headquarters in Valencia, it is a very large business indeed, mainly concerned with selling fruit and vegetables produced by 132 members, some of which are as far away as Sevilla and Navarra. Its wine side is a cooperative of nine cooperatives, the total membership of which must be enormous, and in 1993–94 it sold 210,729 hl of wine in more than sixteen countries, most of it in bulk. No doubt it sells yet more now. Although it does much to supervise how the wines are grown and made, results at present appear to be variable. One of its cooperatives is La Baronía de Turís, founded in 1920 and now supplied from 1,460 ha of vineyard. Its wines include young reds and *rosados* made from Garnacha, and whites, both dry and medium dry, made from Malvasía. These are sold under the names Barón de Turís and Racó de Turís; the wines are the same but different names are used in different markets. Other names include Cañamar and Baronía. It has *soleras* for maturing Moscatels and dry white wines. Its Moscatel Turís is a good example of the modern, light style. Many of its wines are sold as table wines without DO. Amongst others it also sells wines from Cooperativa Vinícola Chivana (Castillo de Chiva), Cooperativa Cheste Vinícola (Castillo de Cheste), Cooperativa del Villar (Cerro Gordo and Laderas), Pedralba Vinícola Sociedad Cooperativa (Barón de Pedralba, Planta Fina and Valentino) and Cooperativa Vinícola de la Viña (Juan de Juanes, Moreral and Torre Tallada).

## Vicente Gandía Pla

This family bodega, now in its third generation with the fourth coming along, was founded in premises on the dockside at Valencia in 1895. In 1992 it moved into new premises at Chiva, which are an inspired piece of architecture and equipped with all the most modern wine-making techniques. Apart from its Valencian wines from Alto Turia, it also produces a complete range in the DO Utiel-Requena. Its wines are amongst the best from both areas and are made on a grand scale with a very large proportion exported. Its Valencian wines are sold under the name Castillo de Liria and there is a complete range including whites from the Merseguera grape vinified in all degrees of sweetness. The Moscatel is particularly good; it received the Masters of Wine Certificate of Excellence. About 60 per cent of its wines are bottled, the remainder being sold in bulk to Switzerland, Germany, Norway and Sweden. Its vineyards are exemplary.

## Bodegas Schenk/Cavas Murviedro

The Schenk empire (which seems the right word for it) is Swiss-owned, with wine interests in Switzerland, Burgundy, Baden-Baden and Italy as well as in Spain, and sells its wines internationally, with offices in several countries. The Swiss company was founded in 1893 and created its Valencian bodegas in 1927. It is also active in Utiel-Requena and Alicante and its wines are undoubtedly amongst the best. The white Cavas Murviedro *joven* is made from equal parts of Merseguera and Moscatel; the Moscatel is harvested first but kept unfermented so that the two varieties can be fermented together, and the Moscatel comes through strongly in the resulting dry, surprisingly light wine. A varietal Tempranillo from the Clariano district shows great potential. Their reds extend up to a good *crianza* and they make a big-bodied red under the name Los Monteros. The name Estrella is used for a very good, modern-style Moscatel. The name Castillo Murviedro is also used.

# YECLA

## Geography
A small inland enclave surrounding the town of Yecla in the province of Murcia, it is surrounded by the DOs of Alicante, Jumilla and Almansa. It is the only DO in Spain to have the odd distinction of containing but a single municipality. The vineyards are on gentle hills at a height of 400 to 700 m, surrounded by higher hills and mountains, giving some most attractive views. It includes a small subzone, Campo Arriba, to the north, which can have its name on the label and is noted for producing a more intense style of wine.

## Climate
Southern continental. It is far enough inland to be hot in summer and cold in winter, but far enough south for the winters not to get too cold. The average temperature is 15°C with an average summer high of 35°C, though it can go up to 42°C, and an average winter low of 5°C, though it can go down to −10°C. The rainfall is 300 to 350 mm and it very rarely rains, but when it does it comes down in torrents; and there are 3,000 hours of sunshine.

## Soils
Mostly chalky over limestone with sandy topsoil and clay in some areas, particularly in the south-east. There are many big stones.

## Grapes
Recommended red variety: Monastrell.
   Permitted red variety: Garnacha.
   Experimental red varieties: Tempranillo, Cabernet Sauvignon, Merlot and Syrah.
   Authorized white varieties: Merseguera, Macabeo and Airén.
   Experimental white variety: Sauvignon Blanc.
   Of all these, Monastrell is by far the most important, occupying 80 per cent of the vineyard.

## Planting
Grown mostly *en cabeza* but some of the newer vineyards are grown *en cordón*, planted in a rectangular pattern with 2.5 m between vines and 3.5 m between rows. Some of the newest vineyards of all, however, are being planted *en espaldera*. Maximum vine density 1,600/ha.

**Vineyard area**
12,000 ha with 7,000 ha actually under vine.

**Authorized yield**
For Monastrell grapes in the Campo Arriba subzone 17.5 hl/ha. For other varieties and elsewhere 28 hl/ha.

**Wines**
Red Yecla Campo Arriba: 14 to 16°.
Clarete Yecla Campo Arriba: 14.5 to 16°.
Red Yecla: 12 to 14°.
Rosado Yecla: 11.5 to 14°.
White Yecla: 11.5 to 13.5°.
Red *doble pasta* Yecla: 14 to 16°.
Whites go up to *crianza* and reds to *gran reserva*.

**Production**
10,700 hl but higher figures are expected in the future.

**Vintages**
1990 5, 1991 5, 1992 5, 1993 5, 1994 5, 1995 6, 1996 6, 1997 5.

It may seem odd that the little enclave of Yecla has its own separate DO but it is firmly based on history. The wine growers have long had their own identity and they intend to keep it. For a long time the wine making has been in the hands of cooperatives. Most of the wine they made, and still do make, is strong and heady, sold in bulk for blending. The grapes were generally picked too late, giving wines of more than 13° which oxidized very quickly. Now, like the other Levantine districts, they recognize that this is a trade with little future and are moving into bottled wines that can be sold on their merits. The district as a whole has been hampered by the fact that there are practically no private bodegas. There are three cooperatives and two active private bodegas with a third being established. The bodega that has brought Yecla on to the international markets is Castaño. It has been a remarkable solo pioneering effort. Others are following and the potential that is undoubtedly there will be realized before very long. At present the best whites are remarkable achievements for wines grown so far south, fresh and with enough acidity. If the best reds lack subtlety and complexity, they make an excellent initial impact, with lots of fruit, and are most enjoyable.

## Leading bodega

### Bodegas Castaño

Generations of the Castaño family have been respected wine grow-ers. In 1985 the present generation took a great leap forward, built a fine new bodega, and equipped it with the latest technology. One is immediately impressed by their dedication and enthusiasm. They have three beautifully maintained vineyards in different parts of the DO: of 125, 90 and 75 ha. These provide them with 90 per cent of their needs. They make a wide variety of wines, 80 per cent of which are red. All three colours come as *jóvenes*, but the reds go up to *reserva* and the whites to *crianza*, with a barrel-fermented *joven*. At the beginning the grapes are sorted to see what class of wine they will be used for. All fermentations are temperature-controlled. Some of the reds are made by carbonic maceration, beginning at 25 to 30°C for the entire grapes and then at 20 to 25°C following pressing. Other reds are made by traditional methods and fer-mented at 23 to 25°C. Whites are fermented at 14 to 15°C and *rosados* at 15 to 16°C. Finally, some of the reds are made in giant autovinifiers at 25 to 28°C. American oak is used for ageing for between two months and six years. The wines are sold under the names Castaño, Viña Las Gruesas (which is the name of one of their vineyards), Pozuelo (which is the name of another), Castillo del Barón and Dominio Espinal. They continue to experiment with

different combinations of grape varieties. The white Viña las Gruesas 1995 was made from equal parts of Macabeo and Airén, while the barrel-fermented version, sold under the Castaño name, was made from 75 per cent Macabeo and 25 per cent Airén and given three months in barrel. The Viña las Gruesas *rosado* of the same year was made from 80 per cent Monastrell and 20 per cent Garnacha, given ten to twelve hours' maceration. The Castaño *tinto* was a varietal Monastrell, with 40 per cent carbonic maceration and 60 per cent traditional. The 1992 Pozuelo *crianza* was made from 70 per cent Monastrell and 10 per cent each of Cencibel (Tempranillo), Cabernet Sauvignon and Merlot, made in autovinifiers. The 1990 Pozuelo *reserva* was similarly made but with a grape mix of 80 per cent Monastrell and 10 per cent each of Cabernet Sauvignon and Merlot, and was given two years in wood. In 1997 they made a varietal Cabernet Sauvignon. These are all serious wines but, to pick just one, the barrel-fermented white is worth looking for.

# 8

# *The Centre of Spain*

---

Much of the centre of Spain is flat: a dull plain. The forests that filled it centuries ago have long since been cut down, and the result has been to create something of a desert: broiling hot in summer and desperately cold in winter. Until the 1970s the only wines of any note grown there were those of Valdepeñas, which were nationally distributed and very agreeable, but they were essentially wines one drank when one could not afford Rioja, and they had no enthusiastic following. Most of the vines in the central plain produced thin white wines in large quantities that were distilled for brandy. Modern wine making has changed all that. Good quality and very good-value wines are now grown all over the place. The transformation has been remarkable and many of the wines are now well worth seeking out. This applies especially to the modern wines of Valdepeñas.

## VINOS DE MADRID

### Geography

The area is divided into three subzones: San Martín de Valdeiglesias, Navalcarnero and Arganda. San Martín de Valdeiglesias is to the west of the city of Madrid and slightly south, joining the DO of Méntrida, a landscape of gentle hills that rise into the Sierra de Gredos. Navalcarnero is also to the west and nearer to the city, likewise joining the DO of Méntrida. Arganda is south-east of the city, joining the DO of La Mancha. The vineyards vary in height from 522 to 800 m. Wines from different subzones cannot be mixed.

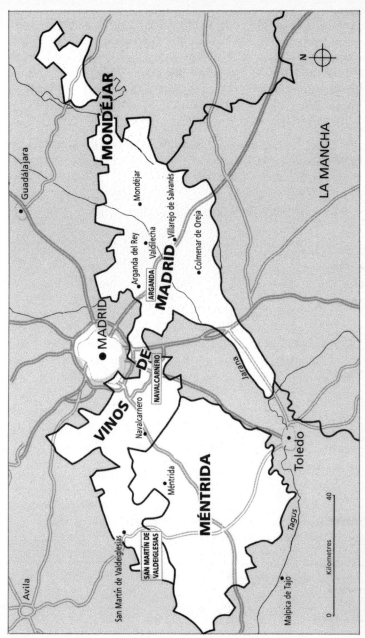

Vineyards near Madrid

## Climate

This is continental and given to extremes, rising to 40.7°C in summer and falling to –8.2°C in winter, with an average of 13.7°C and 2,800 hours of sunshine. The difference in microclimates between the three subzones is illustrated by their rainfalls: 461 mm in Arganda, 529 mm in Navalcarnero and 658 mm in San Martín de Valdeiglesias.

## Soils

Again, there are substantial differences between the subzones. In San Martín de Valdeiglesias it is brown over granite and slightly acid. In Navalcarnero it is poorer in quality, covering a subsoil of sand and clay. In Arganda it is richer, with clay/marl over granite, and there is limestone in some places.

## Grapes

Authorized red varieties: Tinto Fino, Tempranillo (Cencibel) and Garnacha.

Authorized white varieties: Malvar, Albillo and Airén.

Although listed separately, the Tinto Fino is generally regarded as a clone of the Tempranillo. In San Martín de Valdeiglesias the principal grapes are Garnacha and Albillo, in Navalcarnero they are Garnacha and Malvar, and in Arganda they are Tinto Fino and Malvar, though there is also a good deal of Airén. Other varieties are grown experimentally, notably Macabeo, Chardonnay, Jaén and Cabernet Sauvignon.

## Planting

Most of the vineyards are planted in the *tres bolillos* pattern, though others are used. The vines are generally pruned *en vaso*, though there is some use of Guyot and *cordón doble*.

## Vineyard area

San Martín de Valdeiglesias 3,821 ha, Navalcarnero 2,107 ha, Arganda 5,830 ha. These figures should be compared with a total 23,957 ha planted in the area as a whole.

## Authorized yield

Airén and Malvar 56 hl/ha, others 35 hl/ha.

## Wines

Reds, *rosados* and whites. The minimum strengths are as follows: reds 11.5° in Arganda, 12° in the other subzones; *rosados* 11° in

Arganda, 11.5° in the other subzones; whites 10° in Arganda, 11° in the other subzones. Some of the reds are *claretes* and contain a proportion of wine from white grapes. Practically all the wines are *jóvenes* but the first *crianza* red was released in 1992 and there are now *reservas*, with a movement towards greater ageing. *Crianza* reds have to be aged for a minimum of two years of which six months have to be in *barricas*, *reservas* have to have three years and one year, and *grandes reservas* have to have a minimum of two years in *barrica* and three in bottle. White and *rosado reservas* have the same ageing as red *crianzas*, while *grandes reservas* must be aged for a minimum of four years of which at least six months is in *barrica*.

## Production
3,848,588 litres (1992) with DO out of a total of 38,478,516 litres.

## Vintages
1987 7, 1988 3, 1989 5, 1990 5, 1991 5, 1992 5, 1993 6, 1994 7, 1995 6, 1996 6, 1997 6.

Madrid was chosen in 1561 by King Philip II to be capital of Spain. At 646 m above sea level it is the highest capital in Europe and, as far from the sea as it is possible to be, of all Spanish cities it suffers from one of the nastiest climates. It had the inestimable advantage, though, that it was small, unknown, and not associated with any of the old kingdoms that were being united to form the modern Spain. It was not chosen for the excellence of its wines, although as in almost every part of Spain, wine had been grown there since Roman times. The bars of Madrid provided a captive market and the vineyards around the city produced large quantities of cheap bulk wines to satisfy the demand. In the nineteenth century, however, the railways brought competition. Nevertheless, at the beginning of the twentieth century there were 30,000 ha of vineyard. Then the story developed as in so many parts of Spain, save that here phylloxera arrived late. It reached San Martín de Valdeiglesias in 1914 and then wrought its inevitable devastation, with the usual result that the vineyards were replanted with varieties calculated to give large yields of alcoholic wines, notably Garnacha and Airén. Tempranillo was brought in, though, by a native of the Rioja in 1930 and showed that the vineyards were capable of producing much better wines.

The transition from bulk wines to good bottled wines started in the 1970s. The demand for bulk wines fell, and Spain's increasing prosperity meant that the market was shifting towards quality. In 1981 a movement was started to create a DO, which finally came about in 1990. At that time there were only two or three bodegas bottling wine and the new Consejo Regulador had to create a quality wine region virtually from scratch. There was very careful selection of the wines that were allowed to carry the DO label and the majority were rejected, as the figures above demonstrate. Those that did qualify began to show that good quality wines could indeed be produced, especially reds made from Tempranillo, and Arganda is generally the best of the three zones. Bodegas started to use modern methods and production rose from 72,000 bottles in 1986 to 2,183,200 in 1995. Even so, no one would suggest that this is one of Spain's fine wine areas; it does, however, produce good wines at very attractive prices, the reds, at present, being distinctly more attractive than the whites. It is an area worth watching, as quality is likely to go on improving.

## Some leading bodegas

### Bodegas Ricardo Benito

Founded by Felipe Benito Alvarez in 1940, this bodega in Naval-carnero was developed by his son Ricardo Benito Lucas and is now in the third generation. It has 90 ha of vineyard planted with Garnacha, Tempranillo and Malvar, and also buys from local growers. It is one of the most active in the export markets and one of the few to make a *reserva*; Señorío de Medina Sidonia 1990 was made from 90 per cent Tempranillo and 10 per cent Garnacha, fermented at 25°C and given twelve months in American oak, while the 1992 vintage was a varietal Tempranillo with sixteen months in oak. Its *crianza*, Tapón de Oro, made from 80 per cent Tempranillo and 20 per cent Garnacha, was first sold in 1992. The same name is used for an excellent *joven* from Garnacha made by carbonic maceration and for a barrel-fermented white from 95 per cent Malbar and 5 per cent Macabeo. A second range of *joven* wines is made under the name Castizo. Ranges of non-DO wines are sold under the names Ricardo Benito and Torre Estrella.

### Bodegas Francisco Casas

This bodega was also founded in Navalcarnero in 1940 and is also active in the export markets. Under the name Tochuelo it sells a very pleasant red made from 70 per cent Garnacha and 30 per cent Tempranillo, a *rosado* made from 100 per cent Garnacha and a white made from 100 per cent Malvar. A second range of wines is sold under the name Pintón.

## Bodegas Castejón
A family bodega at Arganda del Rey. It was founded in 1959 and has 33 ha of vineyard planted with Tempranillo, Malvar and Jaén. It also buys grapes in. Its good red Viñadul *crianzas*, made from 80 per cent Tempranillo and 20 per cent Malvar, are fermented at 25°C, spend twenty-four months in vats, twelve months in oak and twelve months in bottle. The same trade name is used for a *rosado* made from Tempranillo. Another red is sold under the name Viña Valducar. The name Viña Rey is used for a light red *joven* made from equal parts of Tempranillo and Malvar, and for a white, which is a varietal Malvar fermented at 18°C.

## Bodegas Jesús Díaz e Hijos
Founded in 1900, this bodega in Colmenar de Oreja, in the Arganda subzone, is one of the most highly regarded in the DO. It has 60 ha of vineyard and buys in locally. Its red *crianza*, Valdealcala, which has nine months in American and French oak, is made from 85 per cent Cabernet Sauvignon and 15 per cent Tempranillo, and a white, sold under the same name, is a varietal Macabeo. It also has a barrel-fermented Chardonnay, which it sells under the name Convento de San Bernardino. Its normal range of wines uses the company name as trade mark, the red being 80 per cent Tempranillo, 10 per cent Malvar and 10 per cent Cabernet Sauvignon, the *rosado* 70 per cent Tempranillo and 30 per cent Malvar, and the white a varietal Malvar.

## Vinos Jeromín
Founded in 1954, this bodega in Villarejo de Salvanés, in the Arganda subzone, has established a good reputation and some export sales. It owns only one small vineyard, planted with Cabernet Sauvignon, and buys in the rest of the grapes. It has some stainless steel and also uses *tinajas* for fermenting small quantities, controlling the temperature by heat exchangers. Fermentation is at 17°C for whites, 25–27° for *joven* reds and 28° for *crianzas*. The wines intended for ageing are given a malolactic fermentation but not the *joven* wines. *Crianzas* are given six months in oak and a year

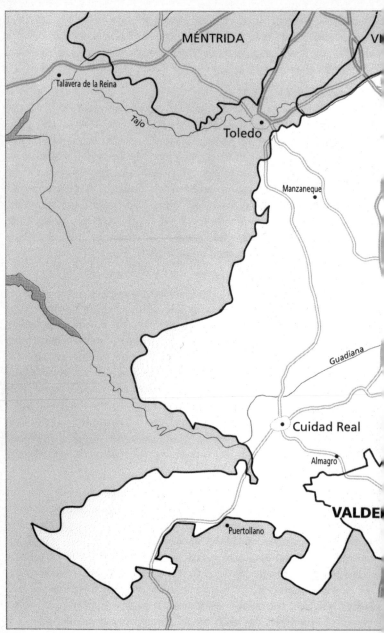

Central Spain

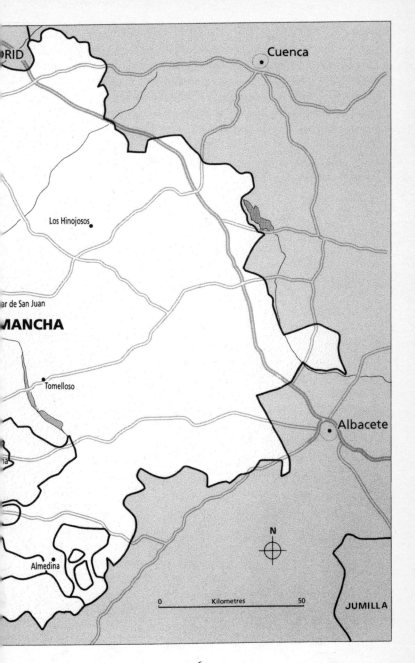

in bottle, *reservas* a year and two years. It produces an unusually wide range of wines. The varietal Cabernet Sauvignons, a *rosado* and a red, together with a varietal white Malvar, are sold under the name Puerta del Sol. They are good wines and go up to *reservas*, including a white. Its Puerta de Alcalá range are all varietal, with the exception of the *rosado*, which is a blend of Tempranillo and Malvar, the reds, going up to a *reserva*, being Tempranillo and the whites Malvar. The Vega Madroño and Puerta Cerrada ranges are all made from more than one grape, the reds being Tempranillo and Garnacha, the *rosados* Malvar, Tempranillo and Garnacha, and the white Malvar and Airén.

## Bodegas Orusco
This family bodega in Valdilecha, in the Arganda subzone, was founded in 1896. It has 11 ha of vineyard, planted with Tempranillo and Malvar. It sells a complete range of wines under the names Main, Viña Main and Viña Orusco.


# LA MANCHA

## Geography
La Mancha is a huge, slightly sloping plain in the middle of Spain. It is in the southern part of the Meseta, a high plateau between the Sierra Morena and the river Tajo, and is the largest DO, stretching from the DO Vinos de Madrid in the north to Valdepeñas in the south, which it practically surrounds. The slope is invisible to the eye but the height is 489 m in the north and 645 m in the south. Steps are being taken to refine and subdivide this great area in the year 2002, but the present plans may well change.

## Climate
This is continental. It is very hot indeed in the summer (the highest recorded temperature is 44.2°C) and very cold in the winter (the lowest recorded temperature is –22°C) but the average is more reasonable at 13.5 to 14.8°C. The average rainfall is 300–400 mm, with rain falling mostly in the winter. There are 3,000 hours of sunshine and 200 cloudless days. It has been sensibly described as high and dry. The hot, dry climate over the grape-growing season results in the vines being remarkably healthy and needing the minimum of attention.

## Soil
Mostly red-brown sandy clay but with some limestone and chalk.

## Grapes
Authorized red varieties: Cencibel (Tempranillo), Moravia, Garnacha, Cabernet Sauvignon and Merlot.

Authorized white varieties: Airén, Pardillo, Verdoncho and Macabeo.

Some other varieties are being grown experimentally, including Chardonnay.

## Planting
The density varies between 1,200 and 1,600 per ha, depending on how much water there is. They are planted in a square, or *marco real*, pattern with 2.5 metres spacing and are pruned *en cabeza*, to keep them close to the ground, avoiding evaporation and limiting the penetration of sunshine.

## Vineyard area
176,386 ha until 2002, when new regulations are expected to reduce it.

## Authorized yield
White wines 39 hl/ha, red wines 32.5 hl/ha. But in practice the yields are a good deal less: in 1993, 17 hl/ha.

## Wines
Nearly all are *jóvenes*, but in the future there may be more *crianzas*, especially from the imported vine varieties. Whites must be between 11° and 14°, but are tending towards the former and come in all degrees of sweetness from very dry to very sweet. *Rosados* must be between 11° and 15°. Reds must be between 11.5° and 15°. Some sparkling whites are also made.

## Production
4,647,500 hl (1992).

## Vintages
As these wines are mostly made to be drunk young, a review of past vintages would not be sensible. There have been no recent failures.

The most famous native of La Mancha is undoubtedly Don Quixote. His ghost haunts the place and there are still plenty of windmills, including some that were there in his day, though some of the more affected have been created in his memory. In the days when he took his tilts, though, it was rather different. There were many fields of grain to feed the windmills and there were far more trees. Now there are very few and they get fewer every year as water is pumped out of the subsoil, starving them of nourishment, and used to cultivate crops that would be better grown somewhere else. Happily, though, this does not apply to vines, which are famous for being able to flourish in impossible places. Scenically it is a very dull plain, an area to hurry through. But those who do so miss some charming towns and villages. Almagro, for instance, is a delightful town with a *parador* built into an old monastery and two enchanting theatres, one of which, dating from the sixteenth century, must be one of the oldest in the world still in use, the other a little early nineteenth-century gem. Tembleque, with its wooden galleries around the Plaza Mayor, has not changed for hundreds of years.

Forty-three per cent of the surface of La Mancha is vineyard, and if Spain has 17 per cent of the world's vineyards, La Mancha itself

Windmills in La Mancha

has 7.3 per cent. It is Spain's largest DO. In sheer quantity it is very important, but not all the grapes go into making wine. Some are eaten, others – quite a high proportion – go to make wine that is distilled to make *holandas*, which are matured in the sherry bodegas and elsewhere to provide Spain's justly popular brandies. Nevertheless, there is a lot of wine, and in the past much went into the 'wine lake', while the local growers tried to dissuade EU bureaucrats from pulling up their vineyards. The wine used to be dreadful, but that is no longer so. And perhaps it was not always so; when Captain George Carleton published his memoirs in 1728 he was strong in praise of Manchegan 'Vino Sainte Clemente'.

In 1966 a Consejo Regulador was appointed to look after La Mancha, Almansa and Méntrida, but that did not work as there were obvious conflicts of interests. In 1970 they were split up, and at much the same time big money started to flow in. La Mancha is so dry that the vines are unusually healthy, calling for remarkably little work in the vineyards. The large corporations saw that this was the place where bulk wine could be made economically, and they made it well, led by Rumasa, then the largest quality wine producer in Spain. All this came as a revelation to the locals, mostly cooperatives. The secrets, of course, were early picking and cold fermentation. The Airén grape, in particular, was transformed. It had been regarded as a bulk producer for distillation, giving flat and unattractive wines. With the yield limited, the grapes picked earlier, kept cool and lightly pressed, and the fermentation controlled, it proved capable of giving rather attractive wines. The malolactic fermentation is usually avoided, to retain acidity. And the newcomers brought in the French varieties which imported backbone and structure to the reds. No one would suggest that this is a district for great wines, though some of them can be very attractive. What it does brilliantly is to produce decent, agreeable wines in large quantities that can be sold at affordable prices.

### Some leading bodegas

#### Campo Almaina
A very small bodega producing first-class varietals from Airén, Garnacha and Cencibel, established at Almedina in 1973.

## Bodegas Ayuso

This is a large family-owned bodega founded in 1947. Its white wines include the unusual semi-sweet Armiño, a varietal Airén, and Viña Q, a dry varietal from the same grape. It is particularly noted for its Estola range, the reds being varietal Cencibels, going up to a *gran reserva*.

## Bodegas Centro Españolas

A sparkling new bodega founded at Tomelloso in 1991 by fifteen shareholders, the buildings being even more recent. It has 220 ha of local vineyard, most of which was planted in 1986 before the company itself was formed, supplying about 70 per cent of its needs. It is unusual in producing about 80 per cent red wines, and all its wines are sold in bottle. Seventy-five per cent is exported and major customers include the UK supermarkets. The intention is to produce more wines with oak ageing, mostly in American oak but with some French. There are already successful *crianzas*; *reservas* and *grandes reservas* are planned. The wines are good, consistent and excellent value. It uses a large number of trade names. Verdial red is a varietal Tempranillo and Verdial white is a varietal Airén. Fuente de Ritmo is also a varietal Tempranillo given six months in American oak. Rama Corta is a good red made from 75 per cent Tempranillo and 25 per cent Cabernet Sauvignon. Allozo reds are varietal, and include a Tempranillo *crianza* given one year in American oak and a Cabernet Sauvignon. The same trade name is used for varietal *jóvenes*, both white and red. Other trade names include Rama Corta, Varal and Tempranal. It also makes a brandy sold under the name Casajuana.

## Cooperativa Nuestra Señora de la Cabeza

A modern cooperative in Pozo Amargo. Its bottled wines, sold under the name Casa Gualda, have established a good reputation and include a Cabernet Sauvignon.

## Cooperativa Nuestra Señora de Manjavacas

A modern cooperative in Mota del Cuervo. Most of its wine is sold in bulk but a proportion is bottled and sold under the name Zagarrón, which has established a good reputation.

## Cooperativa Nuestro Padre Jesús del Perdón

This cooperative in Manzanares was founded by a group of local wine growers in 1954. It has been the most active in the export trade and its activities have been fully justified by its sound wines. It is one of a group of three cooperatives, the others being in Rioja and in Penedés; the latter houses its export office. Its 500 members own 3,000 ha of vineyard, about 80 per cent being of white vines, mostly Airén but with some Macabeo; the reds are Cencibel and Cabernet Sauvignon. There has recently been a major reconstitution and replanting. The soil here is rather chalky and some of the vineyards are over the underground bed of the river Guadiana. It bottles 40 per cent of its wines, which is a high proportion for a cooperative in this area. Must is extracted under minimum pressure, and that from the pressing, which is about 40 per cent, goes to distillation. The white wines are fermented at 18°C, the reds at 25°C. Its wines, whites, *rosados* and reds, are sold under the names Yuntero, Mundo de Yuntero and Lazarillo. The whites include a Yuntero that is barrel-fermented. The *rosado* is made from equal parts of Cencibel and Garnacha. The reds include Lazarillo and Yuntero varietal Cencibels. The Yuntero range goes up to *reservas*, matured in American oak, the red *crianzas* and *reservas* containing up to 25 per cent Cabernet Sauvignon. The white Mundo de Yuntero is organically grown. Other names used include Casa la Teja and Viña Tomar.

### Cosecheros Embotelladores
In the late 1960s fourteen local wine growers with 300 ha of vineyard between them got together. They make their own wines but combined to form a central bodega in Noblejas to which they are delivered. The wines have established a good reputation and are sold under a number of names: Cuevas Reales, El Juglar, Longeve and Viña Donante. Their white Cuevas Reales is remarkably northern in style.

### Bodegas Cueva del Granero
A big bodega in Los Hinojos with 500 ha of vineyard; it is active in the export markets, producing a complete range of sound wines, including varietal Cabernet Sauvignon reds.

### Evaristo Mateos
This bodega in Noblejas produces a wide range of wines under several names: Aldehuela, Evaristo, Sembrador and Vega Tinteña. The Sembrador range goes up to a *reserva*, which is very good.

## Bodegas Julián Santos

A family firm dating from 1900 and now in the third generation, this bodega is fascinating in that it has moved with the times yet has not abandoned the traditional trade. It is unusual in making more red wine than white. It is backed by two vineyards, amounting to 700 ha, and buys also from local growers. It saw the quality revolution coming and joined in, making its first quality wines in 1984 and installing a bottling plant three years later. It has a good quantity of stainless steel but still retains *tinajas* and cement fermentation tanks, though these are now temperature-controlled in the usual way, by lowering stainless-steel heat exchangers into them. Whites and *rosados* are fermented at 18°C, reds at 25°C. At the lowest end of its range there are non-DO wines packaged in cartons and sold under the names Viña Anta, Castillo de Ainhoa and Bartizan. A cheap range of DO wines is sold under the name Citadel. The best wines are sold under the name Don Fadrique, which is reserved for a small proportion of the production, up to the level of *grandes reservas* matured in American oak. The best reds are mostly varietal Cencibels but include a varietal Cabernet Sauvignon.

## Bodegas Torres Filoso

A family bodega in Villarrobledo dating from 1921; its best wines are sold under the name Arboles de Castellejo. They include a varietal Chardonnay with six months' oak ageing and a red *crianza* made from equal parts of Cencibel and Cabernet Sauvignon. There are also varietals from Cencibel and from Cabernet Sauvignon.

## Vinícola de Castilla

As modern as can be, this was founded as a model bodega by Rumasa in 1976, when it was the largest producer of quality wines in Spain, and it led the way to the remarkable improvement of Manchegan wines. After its dispossession by the state, the La Mancha operation was acquired by private shareholders. It owns no vineyards but buys in from local growers: Cencibel, Airén, Viura, Cabernet Sauvignon, Merlot and a small amount of Chardonnay. The French varieties are used principally for wines at the top of the range. The reds are fermented at 20 to 25°C and the *rosados* and whites at 14 to 16°C. The modern equipment includes a Vinimatic installation for making reds. There are underground cellars for maturing the *crianzas* and above in American oak. *Reservas* are given fifteen to sixteen months in oak and two to three years in bottle, *grandes reservas* three years in oak and six in bottle. In the past there used to be more white wines than reds but at present they are made in roughly equal quantities. Apart from producing a considerable number of buyers' own brands for supermarkets, the wines are sold under various names. Sound wines offering good value are sold as Finca Vieja, Viña del Castillo and Gran Verdad. Varietal wines – the red from Cencibel, the *rosado* from Garnacha and the white from Airén – are sold under the name Castillo de Alhambra. Castillo de Manzanares is a medium-priced range, a red varietal Cabernet Sauvignon and a white varietal Viura. The next range is Señorío de Guadianeja, which includes a semi-sweet white and which goes up to Cencibel and Cabernet Sauvignon varietal *grandes reservas*. Other wines at the top of the range are sold under the name Selección and are blended from a number of varieties, the white 1994 from 50 per cent Viura, 30 per cent Airén and 20 per cent Chardonnay, the red 1993 from 60 per cent Cencibel, 20 per cent Cabernet Sauvignon and 20 per cent Merlot. Sparkling wines are also made in small quantities and sold under the name Cantares. It is all rather bewildering, but tasting them demonstrates that all are good value and excellent examples of what can be produced in a given price range, including the top. The varietal Cencibels are well worth seeking out.

### Vinícola de Tomelloso
This large cooperative at Tomelloso, founded in 1986, has access to 2,200 ha of vineyard and has established a good reputation for its wines, many of which are varietal or have 10 per cent of a second variety. Most are sold under the name Abrego, but there is also a varietal Macabeo sold under the name Añil, and the top wines in the range are sold under the name Torre de Gazate, including a Cabernet Sauvignon *reserva*.

### Viñedos Mejorantes
Established at Villacañas as recently as 1994 with 186 ha of vineyard, this bodega's wines have been highly praised. Names used include El Portillejo, Viña Sabiñar, Viñedos Mejorantes and Señori de Hergueta. It is clearly one to watch.

# MÉNTRIDA

### Geography
Near the great city of Toledo, partly in the province of Madrid but mostly in that of Toledo, it adjoins the DO Vinos de Madrid. There are some hills to the north-west but most of the area is dull and flat. The height of the vineyards is 200 to 500 m.

### Climate
Right in the middle of Spain, it is continental and given to extremes: 40°C in the summer and −4°C in the winter, with an average of 15°C. There is a rainfall of 400 mm, mostly in the autumn and winter, and 2,800 hours of sunshine.

### Soils
Some sandy, some clay, and a little limestone.

### Grapes
Garnacha, Tinto de Madrid (Tinto Basto) and Cencibel (Tempranillo or Tinto Fino). Garnacha is vastly predominant but Cencibel is encouraged for newly planted vineyards. Some Cabernet Sauvignon is grown experimentally.

### Planting
Generally rectangular and pruned *en vaso*, but other methods are being tried.

### Vineyard area
12,931 ha.

### Authorized yield
Cencibel 28hl/ha, others 42 hl/ha.

### Wines
Red and *rosado*, with minimum strengths of 12° and 11.5° respectively. Most are *jóvenes* but there are some *crianzas*.

### Production
41,160 hl (1994–95).

### Vintages
In the nature of things, details of vintage years are not relevant. Recently they have all been good.

By no stretch of the imagination is Méntrida a fine wine area, though the potential is there, as has been demonstrated by the Marqués de Griñón, whose vineyards (see p. 189) are on the edge of it but who, understandably, will have nothing to do with the DO. Traditionally the wines were enormous and heady, the *rosados* 13 to 18° and the reds 14 to 18°, made from overripe grapes (the growers were paid according to sugar) by the *doble pasta* method (see p. 233). The market for these heavy wines has gone, and in 1991 new and lower levels of acceptable strength were introduced. It was a vicious circle: the wines were bad so they fetched very low prices, and the prices were so low that no one could afford to modernize to produce good wines. Moreover, the locals had developed a taste for oxidized Garnacha and continued to be willing to buy it. Now, at last, things are beginning to change and there is some stainless steel installed, but most of the wines are still notably unsubtle and there is practically no export trade. Some of the bodegas, however, are trying to improve things and in future notably better wines may be expected. It would at present be premature, or even absurd, to attempt a list of leading bodegas, but some of the better wines are being made by the Cooperativa Vitivinícola San Isidro at Camarena, whose wines are sold under the name Bastión de Camarena, and especially by José María Cases Llop, founded in 1981 at Quismondo, who uses the names Gran Viñedo, Plazco and Quismo, and who is beginning to export.

# MONDÉJAR

## Geography
This is the only significant wine-growing area in the province of Guadalajara and lies to the south-east of the town. There are two parts, one centred around Mondéjar and the other around Sacerdón, and until it received DO status very recently it was known as VdlT Sacerdón-Mondéjar or Mondéjar-Sacerdón, to taste. It is contiguous with Vinos de Madrid and just touches La Mancha. It is gently undulating.

## Climate
Fully continental, with very hot summers and very cold winters. The average temperature is 18°C and the rainfall 500 mm.

**Soil**
In the north it is red over lime and clay. In the south it is brown and chalky. Neither sort is very fertile.

**Grapes**
Recommended red varieties: Cencibel and Cabernet Sauvignon.
   Permitted red varieties: Tinto de Madrid, Garnacha and Jaén.
   Recommended white varieties: Malvar, Macabeo and Torrontés.
   Permitted white varieties: Pedro Ximénez.

**Planting**
Maximum density 1,200 vines per ha.

**Vineyard area**
3,000 ha.

**Authorized yield**
In terms of grape production, 6,000 kg/ha for white varieties and 5,000 kg/ha for reds.

**Wines**
Mostly reds but with some whites, including sweet ones. Most are sold as *jóvenes* but there are some *crianzas*.

**Production**
7,000 hl of DO wines out of a total of about 35,000 hl.

**Vintages**
The first DO vintage, 1996, was classed as good, as was 1997.

This area has never been noted for fine wines, most being sold in bulk to the bars of Madrid or drunk locally. In these very early days of the DO it is impossible to know how it is likely to develop. Out of the five bodegas, the leader at the moment is Bodegas Mariscal; given the impetus of the DO it could achieve good things.


## VALDEPEÑAS

**Geography**
The DO of Valdepeñas is almost entirely surrounded by that of La Mancha. It is a plain with small hills, 700 to 800 m above sea level.

The best vineyards are in the western area of Los Llanos (the plains) and in the northern area of Las Aberturas (the openings).

## Climate
This is continental. It is very hot in the long summer, reaching up to 42°C, and falling in winter to −10°C. The vines are sometimes damaged by frost. The average temperature is 16°C. The rainfall is 250–400 mm, mostly in the spring and autumn, but sometimes there is a deluge and floods, as in 1979. The average sunshine is 2,800 hours. Over the grape-growing season the weather is hot and dry, making the vines easy to tend.

## Soil
Valdepeñas means 'valley of stones', and the soil is indeed stony, light in colour from almost white to faintly red light brown, and shallow, but the subsoil is chalky and retains moisture well deep down. There is little or no clay.

## Grapes
Authorized red variety: Cencibel (Tempranillo).
   Experimental red varieties: Cabernet Sauvignon, Merlot, Pinot Noir and Garnacha.
   Authorized white variety: Airén (Valdepeñera).
   Experimental white varieties: Macabeo and Chardonnay.

## Planting
The vineyards are planted in the square, or *marco real*, pattern with 2.5 m spacing and normally 1,600 vines per ha, the limits being 1,400 and 2,300. The Airén vines are pruned *en cabeza* and the Cencibel *en vaso*.

## Vineyard area
32,752 ha, of which 30,546 are in production.

## Authorized yield
Cencibel 28 hl/ha, Airén 42 hl/ha. In practice the better growers work with a much lower yield of 22 hl/ha.

## Wines
There are four colours. White is made from Airén grapes and has a strength of 11–13.5°. *Rosado* is made from Cencibel or (more usually) from a mixture of wines from both varieties and has a strength of 11.5–14.5°. Light red (*clarete*) is made by mixing wines from

both varieties, but with a minimum 20 per cent Cencibel, and has a strength of 11.5–14°. Red is from Cencibel, though a little Airén may be added, and has a strength of 12.5–15°. Many are made as *jóvenes* for immediate drinking, but other wines are matured for two years and there is a substantial number of *reservas* and *grandes reservas* which are supposed to be varietal Cencibel, though in practice minor proportions of other varieties are often included.

**Production**
907,311 hl (1992).

**Vintages**
1987 6, 1988 6, 1989 7, 1990 6, 1991 6, 1992 5, 1993 7, 1994 5, 1995 6, 1996 7, 1997 5.

Valdepeñas, like so many Spanish vineyards, traces its history back to the Romans. In the remote past it grew white wines but the reds started as long ago as the twelfth century, when black grapes were introduced by monks from Burgundy, which may help to reinforce the theory that Cencibel is remotely related to Pinot Noir. By the end of the eighteenth century, Valdepeñas was on the Royal Road between Madrid and Andalucía, and its wines regularly travelled in both directions, as they still do. They were highly regarded in Madrid and production was as high as 4 million litres. The area got a fillip in 1861 when the railway arrived and provided easy transport not only to Madrid but to the ports. It was one of the last districts to be hit by phylloxera, which did not come until 1911, when it had its usual devastating results, but by then the remedy was well established and the vineyards soon recovered.

Valdepeñas has long had a reputation for making good wines that offer excellent value. Forty years ago, if you were giving a party you had Rioja if you could afford it and Valdepeñas if you had to set your sights a little lower. They were the two wines distributed nationally. In those days, though, the town of Valdepeñas was rather a run-down place, producing wines that were easy and agreeable to drink but noticeably lacking in aroma. Now, with the introduction of modern techniques and cool fermentation, the aroma is there and the wines are notably better. The reds are robust and can be positively heady, but the best are excellent and can achieve real complexity of flavour, while the *claretes* – made with a mixture of red and white grapes – the red grapes usually being present in a far higher proportion than the 20 per cent required by the regulations – have a very pleasant fragrance and an agreeable balance. There are good *rosados*, too, and if the white wines are overshadowed by the others, they are nevertheless fruity and sound, if still sometimes rather lacking in acidity. The run-down town has become a prosperous city. If the wines of Valdepeñas no longer have the special position they once had, it is simply because so many world-class wines have emerged in the rest of Spain – wines that often did not exist twenty or thirty years ago. Valdepeñas wines are not world class, but they are nevertheless very good and remain excellent value.

## Some leading bodegas

### Casa de la Viña

Remote in the countryside, this great estate of 2,850 ha was bought by the Bodegas y Bebidas group in 1987 and its history as a major wine maker dates only from then. The buildings used once to be a farm and stockyard. They are deceptive. From the outside everything looks ancient, but once you are inside you see that the plant is as modern as can be. The vineyards are remarkable. From the bodega they extend for 6 km, making a total of 980 ha, 950 ha of Cencibel and 30 ha of Airén. Not surprisingly, it is completely self-sufficient for grapes. The 'cellar' is above ground, but it is impressively cool, and there is plenty of new American oak, with 20 per cent being replaced each year. It claims to press the grapes within ten minutes of picking them. Its red, *rosado* and white wines are all first class. The *crianzas* and above are given plenty of ageing – well above the legal minimum. For instance, the 1989 *gran reserva* was bottled in March 1995 and then given eighteen months in bottle before sale, when it still showed considerable ageing potential. At the other end of the age scale, the bodega makes an excellent red *joven*.

### Miguel Calatayud

To make wine in Valdepeñas and to have as one's surname the name of a major and totally different wine-growing area might invite confusion, but once the facts are appreciated there need be no problems. Miguel Calatayud set up his business in 1940 and moved into his present premises, in the middle of the town of Valdepeñas, ten years later; it remains a family business, now run by his son. He has 60 ha of vineyard, 40 ha of Cencibel and 20 ha of Airén, which supply 15 per cent of his needs, the rest being bought in. Walking into the bodega gives the impression of stepping into the past, as it retains a massive installation of earthenware *tinajas*. There is stainless steel as well, but this is only used for making the cheaper wines. The best wines are still fermented in the traditional way but with the modification that heat exchangers can be lowered into the *tinajas* for temperature control. However unfashionable the method, the wines, red, *rosado* and white, sold under the names Vegaval and Vegaval Plata, are very good and go up to *grandes reservas*, the *crianzas* and above being matured in American oak. A new and completely up-to-date plant is now being installed, though, and wines from the 1998 vintage onwards may be fermented in stainless steel. There are also plans to introduce varietal Cabernet Sauvignons, Merlots and Macabeos. They sell non-DO wines under the name Viña Almazán.

## Bodega Los Llanos/Cosecheros Abastecedores

Bodegas Los Llanos was founded in Valdepeñas by the Caravantes family in 1875. In 1971 they sold it to Cosecheros Abastecedores, a large company with wine interests in other parts of Spain. It was then moved in 1979 to a completely modern bodega in the country. The old premises are now a museum. They have 300 ha of vineyard, mostly planted with Cencibel, with minor plantings of Cabernet Sauvignon, Garnacha and Macabeo, which provides about 15 per cent of their needs, the rest being bought in from local growers. Although the Cabernet Sauvignon can give very good wine, they favour Cencibel, which is better adapted to the very dry climate. The whites are fermented with selected yeasts at 18°C, the reds at 22°C. The oak used for ageing the *crianzas* and above is mostly American but there is some French; new casks are bought every year and the old ones thrown away when they are twelve years old, giving an average cask age of six years, the wines being divided between casks of different ages and blended together before bottling. This is one of the most active bodegas in the export market and its wines are well known and appreciated in the UK. Sound *joven* wines are sold under the names Armonioso and Don Opas. *Crianzas* and above, going up to *grandes reservas*, are sold under the names Señorío de Los Llanos and Pata Negra. The Pata Negra *gran reserva*, a varietal Cencibel, is very good and has considerable ageing potential, with qualities of aroma and flavour that show just how good a Valdepeñas can be. Another excellent *gran reserva*, made from 85 per cent Cabernet Sauvignon and 15 per cent Cencibel, is sold under the name Loma de la Gloria. There is also an excellent varietal Cabernet Sauvignon.

## Luis Megía
A family-owned bodega founded in 1947, it was bought in 1989 by the Group Collins, an Hispano-Japanese enterprise. It has become one of the leaders in the area and is noted for its reliable wines. Its *reservas* and *grandes reservas* are certainly worth seeking out. It sells a complete range under the names Islero, Luis Megía, Don Luis Megía, Marqués de Castañaga and Duque de Estrada.

## Bodegas Real
Although established as recently as 1989, this small bodega has an unusually large holding of 350 ha of vineyard, growing Cencibel, Cabernet Sauvignon, Macabeo, Chardonnay and Airén. It already has a very good reputation, selling its red wines, aged in French oak, under the name Vega Ibor and its white under the name Viña Luz.

## Felix Solis
This is a very large enterprise and indeed claims to be the largest wine maker in Spain that is still family-owned. It was founded in the 1940s but its real growth has been in the last twenty years, with the introduction of oak ageing and development of the export markets. It is very strong in the UK, where it supplies large quantities of supermarket wines. It owns 600 ha of vineyard, planted entirely with Cencibel apart from 20 ha of Cabernet Sauvignon, but this is only enough to supply 8–10 per cent of its needs, the rest being bought in. Apart from its DO wines, it has a very large trade in table wines. Its DO wines, which are good, are sold under the names Los Molinos and Viña Albalí. These include a varietal Cencibel that is labelled with the alternative name Tempranillo, as this is better known to most drinkers, and a varietal Cabernet Sauvignon.

# OTHER WINES

### Antonio Gallego Herreros, Bodegas Brujidero

One thing can be said with absolute certainty about this bodega in Villanueva de Alcardete: it is unique. It is also hard to find, preferring anonymity. When found, at first sight it is clearly old-fashioned, with rows of concrete *tinajas* making it look like Ali Baba's cave, but closer examination shows that they are fitted with heat exchangers for cold fermentation. The eye soon wanders from the *tinajas*, though, to look at other things. There are cabbalistic signs, strange arrangements of obscure artefacts, and patterns of evident but enigmatic symbolism. The eponymous proprietor claims to be an alchemist and probably is. The bodega was set up by an ancestor, Antonio Herreros Duclos, of Roman descent on his father's side and of French descent on his mother's, in 1790 and has been in family ownership ever since, the present proprietor inheriting it through his mother. Some of his wines are superb and most of the others are good or, at the very least, interesting; they are certainly unlike anyone else's. They surprisingly include a *flor* wine, which is not at all bad and is certainly unique. Beneath the bodega, which was built in 1921, there is a cellar of very old wines. Much of his wines are sold in bulk to other shippers, and he is experimenting with wines from the Malvar grape, which look promising. But his best wines are made from the red Brujidero grape and sold under the Brujidero name. He claims that this grape comes from old, ungrafted vines that the phylloxera missed and that no one else has. He tried vinifying it in an old-fashioned clay *tinaja*, but this was not a success, as it burst in sunder, taking its support with it. Vinified now in the new, cement, temperature-controlled *tinajas*, it is excellent and is certainly one to seek out. There is also a very good, odd, rather brown, slightly sweet *rosado* version. These fascinating wines do not carry the DO. They can be bought in Toledo.

### Manchuela

This considerable area used to form part of a vast DO that included Almansa, La Mancha and Méntrida, but when this was reorganized to give separate DOs to those three areas, Manchuela got left out. This was deliberate, as its wines did not rate highly, most of them sold in bulk or distilled. The chief town is Albacete, and it is surrounded by La Mancha, Utiel-Requena, Almansa and Jumilla. At

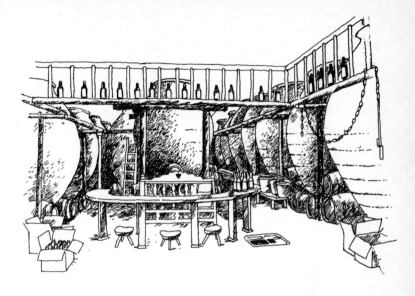

Brujidero

present it is holding rather precariously on to a DOp classification. Many grape varieties are grown but the predominant one is Bobal. The principal source of bottled wine is the Cooperativa Unión Campesina Iniestense in Iniesta.

## Marqués de Griñón, Dominio de Valdepusa

See p. 189.

## Sierra de Alcaraz

This newly recognized VdlT in the western part of the province of Albacete is producing such good wines that its promotion may only be a matter of time. The growers want a DO Altos de Bonillo, but it is early days yet. Uninhibited by tradition, it is growing French varieties, and although some of the Spanish traditionalists may be inclined to look askance, their appeal is undeniable. There are two leading shippers, both in El Bonillo. Bodegas Baronía, which sells its wines under the names Baronía and Viña Consolación, produces varietals from Chardonnay and from Cabernet Sauvignon, with a red *crianza* from 60 per cent Cabernet Sauvignon and 40 per cent Tempranillo. The bodega that is making the biggest mark in the export markets, however, is Manuel Manzanique, a boutique winery whose first vintage was in 1992. The 34 ha vineyard, Finca Elez, about 900 m above sea level, is planted with Chardonnay, Viognier, Cabernet Sauvignon, Merlot and Tempranillo, on sandy clay with limestone. It has a Chardonnay cask-fermented in Allier oak, and reds up to *reserva*, with a grape mix of 70 to 85 per cent Cabernet Sauvignon, 8 to 20 per cent Merlot and 7 to 10 per cent Tempranillo. The 1994 *crianza* was very successful, in a rather New World style.

# 9
# *Extremadura*

Extremadura (or Estremadura) is in the middle of that enchanting part of Spain that adjoins Portugal along the north–south border. A lot of it is hilly or even mountainous, but other parts are flat. The city of Mérida was once the capital of the Roman province of Lusitania and the Roman remains there are wonderful. The province of Badajoz contains some of the best vineyards, the others being in the province of Cáceres. There is some beautiful countryside and some enchanting little towns, like Jerez de los Caballeros.

The Romans, of course, planted vines there and the area went on growing large quantities of very sound table wines, which in the last ten years have flowed steadily into UK supermarkets, yet until very recently there were no DO wines. There were six VdlTs, though: Tierra de Barros, Cañamero, Matanegra, Montánchez, Ribera Alta del Guadiana and Ribera Baja del Guadiana. These have now all been combined into a single DO: Ribera del Guadiana.

## RIBERA DEL GUADIANA

**Geography**
Despite their combination into a single DO the six areas really need to be considered separately. Tierra de Barros (much the most important) surrounds the city of Badajoz, most of the vineyards being on either side of the river Guadiana in the direction of the Portuguese border. The countryside here is fairly flat and 300 to 350 m above sea level. Cañamero is far away to the east, in the province of Cáceres and up in the hills of the Sierra de Guadalupe at altitudes of 600 to 800 m. Matanegra is further south and centred around the town of Zafra. Montánchez is in the Sierra de Montánchez, in the

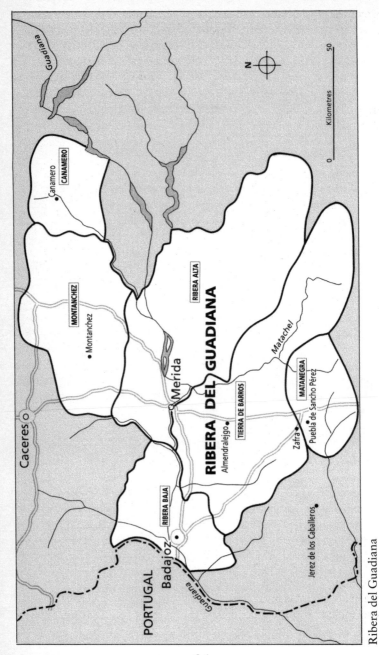

Ribera del Guadiana

province of Cáceres, north-east of Badajoz and south-east of Cáceres. Ribera Alta del Guadiana and Ribera Baja del Guadiana are both in the province of Badajoz, the former upstream on the river Guadiana and to the east of Mérida, and the latter to the west of the city of Badajoz by the Portuguese frontier. Thus the area as a whole covers a lot of ground, and joining the six original subdivisions into a single DO may be regarded as a matter of administrative convenience rather than of geographical logic, though all the areas run into one another with the exception of Cañamero.

## Climate

With such a wide area there are naturally variations. Tierra de Barros is very hot in summer and fairly dry, with a rainfall of 350 to 450 mm. Cañamero has a generally rather temperate climate but is rather wet, with a rainfall of 750 to 800 mm. Matanegra is likewise temperate but no statistics are available. Montánchez has a more continental climate, hot in summer and cold in winter, but with a smaller rainfall of 500 to 600 mm. No statistics are available for the two Riberas.

## Soils

*Barros* means clay, and the vineyards of Tierra de Barros are on fairly flat, fertile ground. In Cañamero the vineyards are on slaty hillsides. In Matanegra the soil is similar to that in Tierra de Barros. In Montánchez it is dark and acid. In Ribera Alta it is very sandy. In Ribera Baja it is muddy clay but the best vineyards are in rather shallow, not very fertile soil.

## Grapes

Authorized red varieties: Garnacha, Tempranillo, Bobal, Cabernet Sauvignon, Graciano, Mazuelo, Merlot, Monastrell and Syrah.

Authorized white varieties: Alarije, Borba, Cayetana Blanca, Pardina, Macabeo, Chardonnay, Chelva, Montúa (or Mantúa), Malvar, Parellada, Pedro Ximénez and Verdejo.

These many varieties include some that are found nowhere else in Spain. The most widely planted are Tempranillo (37.2 per cent), Pardina (22.3 per cent), Cayetana Blanca (11.5 per cent), Macabeo (7.2 per cent), Garnacha (5 per cent) and Montúa (4.1 per cent). Also included in the statistics of planting, but not authorized, are Garnacha Tintorera (2.4 per cent) and Eva (1.4 per cent).

## Planting

Either *en vaso*, spaced 2.75 m in *marco real*, or *en espaldera*, spaced 2.75 by 1.5 m.

## Vineyard area

The whole area covers 1,666,400 ha but the vineyard area is 87,450 ha, and of this only 3,487 ha are registered for the DO. No figures for the area of vineyard in Cañamero are given in the Consejo Regulador's statistics but as those given for the other areas add up to the right total it would appear that none is registered as yet. The figures for the other areas are: Tierra de Barros 2,540 ha; Matanegra 139 ha; Montánchez 102 ha; Ribera Alta 224 ha; Ribera Baja 432 ha.

## Authorized yield

Not stated.

## Wines

Reds, whites and *rosados* in that order of importance. Sparkling wines are also made in the district, including a DO Cava, but that does not form part of this DO and is considered separately. The Consejo Regulador does not as yet appear to have laid down minimum strengths, but in the previous districts these were 11° for reds and 10° for whites and *rosados*.

## Production

43,374 hl (1997).

## Vintages

As the DO was not created until 1997 there can be no assessment.

Several years must pass before this new DO begins to show what it is capable of, and there will have to be a good deal of replanting with approved varieties and experiment to see what can be made. The principal area is Tierra de Barros, which got DOp status in 1979 and, with Bodegas Inviosa leading the way, after a few years was making wines good enough to earn a place in the export markets. There are now some very good wines, with the grapes picked early enough for there to be ample acid, and vinified in the modern way. That being said, most wines produced are not within the DO at all, as yet, and are rustic: bulk wines for drinking locally or for distilling. Some are also distinctly odd; for instance Montánchez used to produce a heavyweight red that actually grew some *flor*.

Some white wines are matured in the sherry style, using *criaderas* and *soleras*. It would be a pity to lose such curiosities but there is no immediate sign of their demise. The bodegas see the future, though, in producing wines with an appeal that enables them to compete nationally and internationally. It is hoped that they will not be tempted too much by international vine varieties and manage to produce some good and interesting wines from some of the unique local vines. Such wines do exist.

## Some leading bodegas

### Bodegas Castelar
Founded in 1963 at Hornachos, this bodega has established a good reputation, particularly for red and white *jóvenes*.

### Bodegas Inviosa
Established as long ago as 1931, this family-owned bodega occupies attractive premises in the middle of Almendralejo and was the first to move with the times, making wines that have earned a safe place in the export markets as well as in Spain. It is in the leading area of Tierra de Barros, where it has 300 ha of vineyard. It is unique in Extremadura in producing an excellent Cava, but that belongs to another chapter. Its table wines are sold under the name Lar with various additions. These go up to *grandes reservas*, matured in American oak. Its Lar de Barros wines include a varietal Macabeo white, a *rosado* made from 75 per cent Tempranillo and 25 per cent Garnacha, a delicious red *joven* made from Tempranillo, and a red *reserva* made from 80 per cent Tempranillo, 15 per cent Garnacha and 5 per cent Graciano. Lar de Oro is used for varietal wines from Chardonnay and from Cabernet Sauvignon. Lar de Lares is used for very good red *grandes reservas*, the 1987 vintage made from Garnacha, Tempranillo and Graciano, the 1991 predominantly Tempranillo.

### Bodegas Medina
This is also a family-owned bodega that was likewise founded in 1931, but at Puebla de Sancho Pérez in the district of Matanegra. It has 66 ha of vineyard, which includes an area where it is experimenting with ten varieties for red wine; its main holdings, however, are of Cabernet Sauvignon and Montúa. It makes a vast range of wines, sold under several names and featuring different

grape mixes. Its top wine is the very good red Jaloco, made from 50 per cent Cabernet Sauvignon, 35 per cent Tempranillo and 15 per cent Garnacha, given four years' oak ageing. The red Marqués de Badajoz is made from 60 per cent Tempranillo, 25 per cent Cabernet Sauvignon and 15 per cent Garnacha, also very good and given two years' oak ageing. The red Jaloco Zafra is made from 85 per cent Tempranillo and 15 per cent Garnacha. It also makes light reds that include some white grapes, sold under the names Pitarra del Abuelo, Viña Luz and Costa Brava. Its white Marqués de Badajoz is made from 50 per cent Cayetana, 30 per cent Viura and 20 per cent Montúa. There are several other *rosados* and whites.

### Bodegas S.A.T. Santiago Apostel

This bodega in Almendralejo, founded in 1979, has a substantial vineyard holding of 250 ha. Its wines are good and include an unusual white varietal Cayetana, barrel-fermented and sold under the name De Payva. Other wines are sold under the name Doña Francisquita.

### Viña Extremeña

Another large bodega in Almendralejo, this is also of recent origin, founded in 1970. The family owns 1,000 ha of vineyard which are cultivated without herbicides or chemical fertilizers. It makes all three colours of wine under a variety of names: Castillo de Valdestrada, Corte Real, Monasterio de Tentudia, Montaraz, Palacio de Monsalud, Palacio de Valdeinfante, Valdegema, Vega Adriana, Viña Almendra and Viña Extremeña. Five different names are used for varietal Tempranillo *reservas*, all from Tierra de Barros but differing in the methods used for ageing. Well, there is nothing like experiment, but this extends to the drinker. Some of these marks do not seem to differ very much from others, but the general standard is very high. It regularly enters its wines in competitions and is proud of having won many medals.

# 10

# *Andalucía*

———

Thanks perhaps to *Carmen*, the very name of Andalucía conjures up romantic visions of wild gypsy girls, bulls, flamenco dancing, roses and music. Oddly enough, there is an element of truth in the legend. It was here that the Moorish civilization in Spain reached its high point. It can be savoured in the exquisite buildings and gardens that survive in the glorious cities of Granada, Córdoba and Sevilla, in the houses with their patios, and in the *pueblos blancos*, the white villages dotted throughout the countryside. To say that it is the most beautiful part of Spain would be controversial, as there are many other areas with their vociferous champions who would dispute the honour. It is my own favourite, though. The great river Guadalquivir, which is navigable all the way up to Sevilla and beyond, is a seam of history flowing through a lively world. Along it the *conquistadors* set sail to conquer the New World, and along it they brought their treasures back. On the right bank of the estuary, where it meets the Atlantic, lie the *marismas,* which house one of the world's greatest nature reserves, the Coto Doñana. At the other extreme there are the mountains of the Sierra Névada. There is still something Moorish about the people who live there. I remember with joy walking by night through the streets of Sanlúcar de Barrameda when all my Spanish friends broke out spontaneously into singing and dancing flamenco. It is hard to imagine a pleasanter place to live in.

Wine has been grown here since before the time of the Romans and, because the sea borders it on two sides, has been exported from time immemorial. One of its wines is amongst the first to be mentioned in English literature. Chaucer's father was a leading wine merchant in London, and when his son wrote of wine he knew what he was talking about. In the *Pardoner's Tale* (*c.* 1390) he wrote of the wine of Lepe:

> Now keep ye from the white and from the red,
> And namely from the white wine of Lepe,
> That is to sell in Fish Street or in Chepe.
> This wine of Spain creepeth subtilly
> In other wines, growing fast by,
> Of which there riseth such fumositee,
> That when a man hath drunken draughtes three,
> And weneth that he be at home in Chepe,
> He is in Spain, right at the town of Lepe,
> Not at the Rochelle, nor at Bordeaux town.

'Fumositee' is a beautiful word; its meaning is so clear that no lexicographer would need to define it. Lepe lies within the area now defined as Condado de Huelva, but alas there are no longer vineyards there.

Although Andalucía always has, and still does, grow table wines, its speciality has always been the strong, usually fortified wines that Chaucer knew. These are now known as *vinos generosos* and (for sweetened wines) *vinos generosos de licor*. They are grown principally in four Denominaciones de Origen: from west to east, Condado de Huelva, Jerez-Xérès-Sherry y Manzanilla de Sanlúcar de Barrameda, Montilla-Moriles and Málaga. The first to receive the distinction of its own DO was Jerez, in 1933. Until then no very clear distinction was drawn between them. The prosperous merchants of Jerez used to bring in wine from their neighbours for blending with their own and even, in the more remote past, from Málaga. There was nothing in the least wrong about that. Unlike the notorious blending of Burgundy with Algerian, it was blending like with like, all grown in the same general area of Spain and according to a tradition dating back for centuries. However, delimitation is now the thing and the regulations have been tightened up over the years so that they are now very strict indeed. It is doubtful whether the consumer has benefited or suffered, but the new regime has certainly made life more difficult for the growers in Condado de Huelva and Montilla-Moriles.

These powerful wines have had their ups and downs in the scales of fashion and at the moment it must be admitted that they are having a down. The shippers have brought this on themselves, at

The Sherry Country

least to some extent, by having become too commercial, which has cost them their quality image. The fact remains, though, that the wines are amongst the finest in the world. At the moment, because the demand has been reduced, they are also astoundingly good value for money. They are due for a great revival.

## SHERRY (DO JEREZ-XÉRÈS-SHERRY AND MANZANILLA-SANLUCAR DE BARRAMEDA)

### Geography

The vineyards fall within a carefully defined area as shown on the map, but the best of them lie within a triangle with the towns of Jerez de la Frontera, El Puerto de Santa María and Sanlúcar de Barrameda at the apexes. These names are generally shortened to Jerez, Puerto and Sanlúcar.

### Climate

This is Atlantic, not Mediterranean, but being so far south is a law unto itself. Although it can be rather damp in winter and distinctly too hot for comfort at the height of summer, the Sherry country has a thoroughly pleasant climate to live in and one that is excellent for growing vines. The average temperature is 17°C with a maximum rising to 44°C and a minimum as low as −5°C, but these extremes are very rare and there is no frost problem. The climate is moderated by the nearness of the sea. The mean maximum is 23°C and the minimum 11°C. The total rainfall is about 650 mm but there are years of drought and periods of deluge. The mean humidity is surprisingly high at 66 per cent, but this varies considerably according to the two prevailing winds. The Poniente, from the west, is cool, not very strong, and humid: it can raise the humidity to 90 per cent. The Levante, from the south-east, is horrible, strong and hot: it can reduce the humidity to 30 per cent. These figures come from the meteorological station, which is in the vineyards and rather more exposed to extremes than are the towns. In particular Puerto, near where the River Guadalete flows into the sea, is cooler, and Sanlúcar, on the estuary of the River Guadalquivir, is cooler still. These differences influence the development of the wines in the bodegas. It is very sunny, with some 3,000 hours of sunshine.

## Soils
There are three kinds. The finest is *albariza,* so called because under the sun it looks almost as white as snow. It usually contains about 60 per cent chalk and can go up as high as 80 per cent. It reacts like a sponge to water and can absorb as much as 34 per cent by weight, which it then retains under a surface that does not crack in the sun. The next quality is *barro,* which is found in the valleys and looks brown, or even reddish owing to the presence of iron; it is only about 10 per cent chalk. The third kind is *arena*, which is sandy with a more yellowish-red tinge brought about by iron. There are few vineyards on the second kind and practically none on the third.

## Grapes
Once there were perhaps as many as a hundred varieties, and a survey in 1868 listed forty-two, but now there are only three: Palomino Fino (Listán), which accounts for about 95 per cent, Pedro Ximénez and Moscatel. The latter two are grown to produce sweet wines.

## Planting and pruning
There are two traditional patterns for planting: *marco real,* which consists of squares, and *tres bolillo,* of equilateral triangles. From the 1960s, however, these patterns were abandoned and the vines planted in rows with about 1.1 m between the vines and 2.3 m between the rows, to allow for mechanical cultivating. Traditionally the vines have been grown as bushes but recently they have been cultivated *en espaldera.* This makes life easier and allows canopy control in the interests of quality. The maximum density of planting allowed is 4,100 vines per ha. The method of pruning for bush vines is to leave one long branch (the *vara* or stick) with eight to ten 'eyes' to bear the crop and a stub (*pulgar* or thumb) with one or two eyes for the following year. Hence it it known as *vara y pulgar.*

## Vineyard area
10,326 ha (1996)

## Authorized yield
80 hl/ha, but this is liable to revision downwards.

## Wines
The denominación covers two distinct styles of wine: sherry and manzanilla – hence its compound name. There are two basic

classifications: *vino generoso* (15 to 22°), where the wines are bone dry, and *vino generoso de licor* (17.5 to 22°) for wines that are off-dry to sweet. In addition, there is sweet *vino dulce natural*, made by partial fermentation of Pedro Ximénez or Moscatel grapes. But each of these names encapsulates a bewildering variety of wines with many subtleties, and the list is too long to be usefully summarized. They will be described in the main text.

### Production
882,000 hl (1996).

### Vintages
The production of vintage wines is minuscule and these are selected only from the best vintages. There tends to be little difference between vintages anyway, and these are evened out by the method of maturation, so vintage years are irrelevant.

Sherry is beyond doubt one of the greatest wines in the world and at the moment, because the pendulum of fashion has swung against it, it is exceptional value. If asked about Spanish wines, this is the one people always think of first, for it has a remarkable history and was the first Spanish wine to become established on the export markets. It has already been mentioned that the Andalusian wine of Lepe was well known in Chaucer's time and Sherry has a continuous history from that day to this. The origin of the name goes back to a much earlier period, though. In AD711 the Moors won Andalucía by defeating the ruling Visigoths at the battle of Guadalete. Despite their religion the Moors grew wine and Jerez became prosperous. It was called Seris, a name later corrupted to Jerez by the Spanish and to Sherry by the English. In 1264 Jerez was reconquered by the Christians under King Alfonso X and its modern history dates from then. The suffix *de la Frontera* was added in 1380 by King Juan I in recognition of its services as one of the frontier towns between the two kingdoms. Old records show that Sherry was being exported to England from the beginning of the fifteenth century, and one of the more specific ones records that in 1485 it was shipped from Puerto de Santa María to 'Plemma, which is in the kingdom of England' – presumably Plymouth. Shortly afterwards, in 1492, Christopher Columbus discovered America and he set forth on his third journey, to discover Trinidad in 1498, from Sanlúcar de Barrameda. His ships were well provisioned with the local wines, so it is safe to say that Sherry was being drunk in the New World right from the very beginning. When Magellan set out to circumnavigate the world in 1519 he spent more on Sherry than on armaments.

English merchants have long travelled the world in search of trade and have settled where trade was to be found. William Ostrych from Bristol was living in Sanlúcar as early as 1523, and in 1530 he and his fellow English merchants petitioned King Henry VIII to grant them a charter, which he did, with a detailed constitution. They had their own church of St George, which still stands in Sanlúcar. By Elizabeth's reign Sherry sack was established as a firm favourite. The word 'sack' comes from the Spanish verb *sacar*, to draw out or export, and was used for Spanish wines generally. When Drake 'singed the King of Spain's beard' by setting fire to the Spanish fleet as it lay at anchor in the bay of Cádiz in 1587, he remained for three days and made off with 2,900 casks of wine – though the figure may be somewhat exaggerated. Perhaps he helped to make the wine popular, and if so his theft has been repaid many times over. In 1598 it received its most famous tribute from Shakespeare, through the mouth of Falstaff:

A good sherris-sack hath a twofold operation in it. It ascends me into the brain; dries me there all foolish and dull and crudy vapours which environ it; makes it apprehensive, quick, forgetive, full of nimble, fiery and delectable shapes; which deliver'd o'er to the voice, the tongue, which is the birth, becomes excellent wit. The second property of your excellent sherris is the warming of the blood; which, before cold and settled, left the liver white and pale, which is the badge of pusillanimity and cowardice: but the sherris warms it and makes it course from the inwards to the parts extreme. It illumineth the face, which, as a beacon, gives warning to all the rest of this little kingdom, man, to arm; and then the vital commoners and inland petty spirits muster me all to their captain, the heart, who, great and puffed up with this retinue, doth any deed of courage; and this valour comes of sherris. So that skill in the weapon is nothing without sack, for that sets it a-work; and learning, a mere hoard of gold kept by a devil till sack commences it and sets it in act and use ... If I had a thousand sons, the first humane principle I would teach them should be, to forswear thin potations and to addict themselves to sack.

*Henry IV, Part 2, Act 4, Scene 3*

He said it all.

Sherry has been with us ever since, but it has had its ups and downs. In the ups, when sales are buoyant, the merchants have repeatedly become over-confident and the quality has suffered, with the inevitable consequence that a down has followed. One of these downs lasted practically throughout the eighteenth century, but towards the end of that century restrictive practices that had lowered the quality were done away with and merchants flocked in from England, Scotland, Ireland and France. Their descendants are still there and the families will be mentioned in the accounts of the leading bodegas that trade today. In the nineteenth century the trade reached a climax. In 1864, 43.41 per cent of the total wine imports to Great Britain were Sherry and sales peaked at 68,467 butts (each containing 108 gallons) in 1873. But thereafter things went into a decline. There can be no doubt but that some awful wines were shipped, and to add to the miseries came the inevitable arrival of phylloxera in 1894. At that time Sherry was largely taken as a wine with food, and lighter wines were coming into vogue. The idea of taking an aperitif came on the scene surprisingly late. The days of high prosperity had gone.

In 1910 the Sherry Shippers' Association was formed in London. The shippers pooled their resources and launched a generic advertising campaign, certainly one of the first if not the first. But perhaps the greatest fillip of all came in the 1920s when Carl Williams, of Williams & Humbert, gave the first Sherry party, and the idea caught on. The craze for cocktail parties was just beginning, but the more discriminating began to take Sherry instead. Eventually the whole ethos that had produced the cocktail vanished, but the taste for Sherry remained and went from strength to strength. The Spanish Civil War had surprisingly little effect on the trade: things were quiet in the Sherry country. But the Hitler war made a big impact; little wine was exported in 1941, 1942 or 1943 and there was considerable hardship in a period when things were very grim throughout Europe. After the war things steadily got better. One of the postwar phenomena has been the remarkable rise in the Netherlands market, which started to take off in the mid-1960s. It remains one of the largest. The graph of sales throughout the world went up and up, reaching a dramatic peak of 1,519,852 hl in 1979. Then it started to go down, and although there were false dawns the fall proved to be inexorable. In 1996 it was 741,934 hl. The trade had been extremely prosperous when sales were a good deal lower, but when the graph was going up the shippers had projected it ever upwards and had committed themselves to enormous expenditure, planting vineyards and buying expensive new premises and equipment. Many of the smaller ones went to the wall. The reasons for this fall are complicated. Who can analyse the caprices of fashion? But there can be no doubt that some atrocious sherries were being shipped at the height of the boom and that cannot have helped. There has been an elaborate reconstruction plan. Surplus wine has been disposed of and many hectares of vineyard have been grubbed up. The shippers must now look to the future.

The vinification of Sherry has moved with the times. Not so very long ago the grapes were pressed by foot (though the feet were in specially designed boots) in wooden *lagares*, which were found in all the vineyards. From the lagar the must was run off into oak casks, where it fermented so rapidly that this first stage was known as the tumultuous fermentation. The casks were then transported to the bodegas in the Sherry towns, where the fermentation was completed and the maturation took place.

The bodegas are remarkable and beautiful buildings. Large and very high, they have often been described as 'cathedrals of wine', and anyone who has seen them will know how just the description is. There is very good reason why they are so high: to keep the temperature down in that very hot climate. Happily, most of the traditional buildings remain and fine examples can be seen in Jerez at old-established bodegas (the term is also used for the companies which own them) such as Domecq, González Byass, Harveys, Sandeman, Williams & Humbert, and Valdespino, in Puerto de Santa María at Osborne and Luis Caballero, and in Sanlúcar at Barbadillo and Hidalgo. This is not a complete list; most of the great names have them and some have no other sort. But some of those in the middle of Jerez have been pulled down in the name of progress, to make way for high-rise blocks, and others will undoubtedly follow. They are being replaced by modern and not very beautiful buildings on the edge of the town, one of which is partly underground. This does not detract from the quality of the wine, though, as the new buildings are well insulated and the edge of the town is cooler.

Nowadays the grapes are pressed in modern horizontal presses and everything is computer-controlled. Only the free-run must (*mosto yema*), with a maximum of 70 litres of must per 100 kg of grapes, is used for making Sherry. For the most part fermentation takes place in stainless steel at temperatures varying between 22 and 30°C depending on the kind of wine being produced, while some shippers go as high as 34°C. A small proportion is still fermented in cask, though; Valdespino makes nearly all its wine in this traditional way and González Byass uses it for 20–30 per cent of its wines. The first fermentation is rapid and is all over in a couple of days, by

A Sherry bodega

which time 95 per cent of the sugar has been converted into alcohol. This is followed by a further slow fermentation in tanks or in American oak casks that lasts for forty or fifty days. So all Sherry begins by being bone dry. This is only the beginning, though: its character and flavour are not yet at all developed and it is known as *mosto,* or must – a term that is also confusingly applied to the unfermented juice.

At this point the wine begins to develop. It is all put into American oak casks of 120 gallons capacity, which are filled only about five-sixths full so that there is a substantial air space over the surface of the wine, and very loose bungs are used, which keep dust out but allow air to circulate. Those wines that are destined to develop as finos start to develop *flor,* which is a thin layer of yeasts of the genus *Saccharomyces.* It looks rather like a layer of cream cheese. These yeasts protect the wine from oxidation and profoundly affect the nature of its development, giving a form of biological maturation. These wines receive a light fortification with a mixture of equal parts wine and grape alcohol to bring their strength up to 15° or so. Those wines that do not grow much *flor,* or any at all, are fortified to 17° or so. The *flor* is very sensitive to the level of alcohol and this kills it off, leaving the wines to develop by an oxidative maturation to become olorosos. It is also sensitive to temperature and grows best in the spring, when the vines flower, and in the autumn, when the vintage is gathered in – coincidences that led to a certain amount of mythology. It grows least abundantly in Jerez, which is the hottest of the sherry towns, and most abundantly in Sanlúcar, which is the coolest. Consequently the finos of Sanlúcar are the lightest and most pungent. They are known as *manzanillas.* Those from Jerez are the most robust.

Although a very small number of casks are matured apart as vintage wines – known as *añadas,* or wines of the year – Sherry is almost entirely matured in an unusual way: the *solera* system, or fractional blending. This works by adding younger to older wine and leaving it for a while. If a shipper has a cask of mature wine of a style that he likes and he draws some of it off – typically a third – then fills the void with a younger wine of the same style and leaves it for some time – typically six months – he will find that the cask is back where he started: the young wine has taken on the character of the older one and tastes exactly the same. Of course this is not done with just one cask. There may be perhaps a hundred in the *solera* (a term that is applied to the casks in the final stage of the process as well as to the process as a whole) and these are fed by a similar number of casks of slightly younger wine. These constitute the last scale in the *criadera* of wines that is used to feed the *solera*. This in turn is fed by the wine in another scale of the *criadera*, which may only have two or three scales or as many as twenty. The exact number depends on the style of the wine being made and the speed with which it is moved from one scale to another: operating a *solera* properly is rather complicated and calls for considerable skill. When the wine made is a fino, growing *flor*, there is another aspect to it. *Flor*, being a yeast, requires nutrients. These are found in the young wine, and as some of it finds its way into the older wine, the *flor* is kept nourished and growing.

As a fino grows old the nutrients are used up and so the *flor* grows weaker and eventually disappears. The biological ageing process is then replaced by an oxidative one. The wine grows darker in colour and begins to acquire a totally different aroma. It is then called an amontillado because it resembles the wine grown in Montilla-Moriles (see below) where wines of this kind originated. With great age, wines that are not growing under flor get stronger, as the water evaporates off quicker than the alcohol in the cool, dry atmosphere of the bodega. An amontillado can grow to be as strong as 22° and its flavour can become so strong that it is magnificent – but practically undrinkable. A little of such a wine in a blend, though, can result in something that is marvellous. Thus a true amontillado is the product of long, patient ageing. It must therefore necessarily be expensive. A cheap amontillado has to be spoof. The word is much misused. With olorosos there is no *flor* but otherwise the effects of age are similar. In between amontillado and oloroso there is another style known as *palo cortado*, meaning cut stick, from the mark that the bodega foreman puts on the casks to identify it. It has the bouquet of an amontillado with the flavour of an oloroso. There is not very much of this as only a few casks develop in this special way, so again the real thing is necessarily expensive. It is a wine of great finesse, much sought by connoisseurs. It can be imitated, relatively cheaply and quite well, by blending amontillados with olorosos.

All Sherries are therefore by nature completely dry. It has often been written that finos are dry, amontillados medium and olorosos sweet. This is complete nonsense. If a Sherry is sweet it is because it has been sweetened. It is a pity to sweeten a fino, as this robs it of its elegance and its fine impact. It must be admitted, though, that not all finos are elegant. Deficiencies are masked by sweetening and the result can be an acceptable wine that is easy to drink and less of an acquired taste than the real thing. Amontillados, *palo cortados* and olorosos take to sweetening wines very well, though, and the results are those exquisite dessert Sherries that are amongst the joys of wine drinking. Several wines are used for sweetening. The basic one nowadays is *mosto concentrado rectificado*, which is must concentrated under low pressure and treated to remove flavours other than sugar. Sweet and very light in colour, such preparations are used throughout the EU and have had to be used in Spain since it joined. The traditional sweetening wines have lots of flavour and impart something of their own to the blend. There are three of these and all are made in much the same sort of way. The great one is Pedro Ximénez (or PX), made from the grape of that name. It is naturally sweet, and the sweetness is concentrated by drying the grapes in the sun, then pressing them and running the must into casks containing a quantity of grape alcohol, so that when the alcoholic level reaches that at which the yeasts cease from bringing about the fermentation there is still plenty of sugar left: a wine called a *mistela*. A similar traditional wine is made from Moscatel grapes. A more recent innovation is a wine made from the usual Palomino Fino grapes in the same way. The first two are both very strong in flavour and are matured in *soleras*, gathering distinction as they age. They are regularly bottled as single varietals and the *soleras* of them are amongst the most precious possessions of the bodegas. The fine dessert wines are made by blending these with dry wines of different styles and ages to produce the kind required.

The wines from Sanlúcar de Barrameda are something slightly apart. As has been mentioned, *flor* grows there particularly abundantly and as the climate is slightly cooler it flourishes all the year round. As a result the finos have a character that is all their own and are given the name *manzanilla*, which means camomile. Beware! If you ask for a manzanilla in northern Spain, where Sherries are little understood, you are likely to be given a cup of camomile tea, which is said to be good for the digestion. As the wine ages, in the same way as in the other Sherry towns, it becomes a *manzanilla pasada* and then a *manzanilla amontillada*. Likewise there is *manzanilla olorosa*, though it is usually sold simply as oloroso. The local *palo cortado* is called *Jerez cortado*. All have their own particular style, which can be described as the manzanilla tang. Some people detect a certain saltiness and ascribe this to the nearness of the sea, but this is nonsense: there is no salt in them. It is a fair description, though.

Some Sherries are straight *solera* wines but others are blended and sold under fancy names. In addition there are a number of recognized descriptions. These are:

*Abocado*. Sweetened.

*Amontillado*. True amontillados are as described above, but unfortunately the name has been widely bastardized by the trade, especially in the United Kingdom, and has come to signify simply a wine of reasonably full body and moderately sweet. If you buy a cheap amontillado it will be that sort. A young amontillado is amber or very light brown, becoming darker with age. Minimum strength 16°, maximum 22°.

*Amoroso*. The name suggests 'loving' but the origin is different and is derived from the name of a vineyard. However it now means a soft, fairly sweet wine, usually based on oloroso.

*Brown*. Brown Sherries used to be very popular, especially in Scotland, owing to their warming nature. They are not often found nowadays as a result of the fashion for light wines. They are olorosos that are sweetened to a high degree and their colour often enhanced by the addition of specially prepared concentrated wines.

*Cream*. These popular wines are largely based on olorosos, blended to be sweet but not to have too deep a colour.

*Pale cream*. A comparatively recent invention based on fino, blended to be sweet but very light in colour. Pale cream has been a great marketing success but is seldom found on the tables of those who really appreciate Sherry. Minimum strength 15°, maximum 19°.

*Fino*. The lightest style of Sherry, which has already been described. The best are bone dry. These are the ones that appeal to Sherry lovers, but their strong impact tends to put newcomers off, so some are sweetened, which robs them of their finesse but enables cheaper wines to be used. The lightest wines are the colour of hay, which with greater age becomes more like straw. Minimum strength 15°, maximum 18°.

*Fino amontillado*. A wine passing from the first style to the second. As a further refinement, when the wine is a little older still the words may be written the other way round.

*Manzanilla.* A fino matured in Sanlúcar. The colour is as for fino. Minimum strength 15°, maximum 19°.

*Manzanilla pasada.* A manzanilla that has acquired age and is about to become an amontillada.

*Medium.* Any sort of Sherry moderately sweetened.

*Milk.* A sweetened oloroso traditionally associated with merchants in Bristol.

*Oloroso.* In its natural state this is bone dry and has already been described, but nevertheless, even in a straight *solera* wine, there is usually a slight sensation of sweetness, brought about by traces of glycerine and other compounds formed naturally in the fermentation. Its flavour has been likened to walnuts. It takes very well to being blended with sweet wines. The colour begins at light brown and darkens with age. Minimum strength 17°, maximum 22°.

*Palo cortado.* This is rather rare and combines the aroma of an amontillado with the flavour of an oloroso. In colour it is dark amber or light brown. Minimum strength 17°, maximum 22°.

*Solera.* Practically all Sherry is made on the *solera* system but the name has been usurped occasionally by merchants and has been applied to sweetened olorosos.

*Vino de pasto.* Once quite popular, this name has largely fallen from use. In the days when most of the Sherries exported were sweet it was applied to a drier style of wine which nowadays would be sold as medium Sherry.

Before bottling, most Sherries are further fortified to shipping strength if necessary, microfiltered and ultra-cooled – their temperature reduced to a very low level and kept there for a period so that tartrate crystals are precipitated and do not appear in bottle. This process dates from the 1960s, when the markets demanded wines that threw no deposits, particularly the American market, which thought that there was something wrong with a wine that had crystals in it. This is rather a pity, as some flavouring elements are lost at the same time. When Sherry was generally shipped at high strength – 18° and upwards – there were no problems of stability but, with lighter wines becoming steadily more fashionable, the strength has gradually been reduced and the lowest now permitted is 15°. These low-strength wines, particularly if sweetened, require very fine filtration and sterile bottling. Ultra-cooling is not, however, used with the finest dessert wines, which do tend to throw a deposit in bottle and can advantageously be decanted.

Decanting should be avoided, though, with other Sherries unless they are going to be drunk right away, when a decanter can look attractive. The reason for this is that Sherry, like all wines, oxidizes in contact with the air. Finos also tend to deteriorate in bottle. Modern methods of stock control have helped a lot, as merchants no longer keep them for months or even years. A fino should ideally be drunk within three months of bottling and definitely goes off after a year. After opening it is best to drink them within three days though they last a week or more if kept cool in the door of a refrigerator. Sweet wines can be kept for several years and are all right for two or three weeks after opening. The finest dessert wines are actually worth laying down. They gradually become less sweet and acquire fascinating qualities of flavour and bouquet: a sort of agreeable mustiness. In the past the leading merchants used regularly to list old bottled Sherries, but this practice has largely disappeared owing to the modern demand for cash flow. They can be laid down privately, though, and to be worth while they need to be laid down for ten years and upwards. They should be cellared standing upright as strong wines tend to attack the corks.

In Spain Sherry is invariably served with *tapas*, morsels of food. These can be very simple: nuts, crisps, olives, slices of sausage and so on, though the best bars vie with each other in the range of tapas they offer. The fact is that Sherry tastes at its best if accompanied with a little food – and it need not be just a little. Fino is one of the few wines that will stand up to quite a vinegary hors d'oeuvres and tastes well with soup; but it is also good with fish – especially shell-fish – chicken, salads and so on. And of course it is superb as an aperitif. The other styles of Sherry, when dry, make excellent aperitifs, too, and the added weight of a fine dry amontillado, *palo cortado* or oloroso can be delightfully warming in a cool and damp northern climate. These wines can be excellent, too, with meats and other foods that are generally associated with red wines. The rich olorosos are best at the end of a meal, with cheese, a sweet course or dessert; they are marvellous with Stilton and with nuts.

Like every other good wine, an important part of the attraction of Sherry is its bouquet. To smell this, it is essential to serve the wine in decent glasses. The so-called Sherry glass, which looks like a thimble on a stem, is dreadful, and Elgin glasses, which go in towards the middle, are the worst of the lot. As with all other wines, the aromatic elements need to expand in the air space above the surface: there just has to be an air space. Tulip-shaped wine glasses are admirable and the Spanish *copita,* which is wide at the bottom and which gradually tapers towards the top, is ideal. Glasses should not be filled to more than about a third of their capacity, so that the aroma can expand and concentrate in an enclosed space.

The labels of many fino bottles state that the wine should be served cool. This is important. A good test for a restaurant is to ask if they have chilled fino. If they have, and serve it in the right glasses, one has got off to a good start. But it should not be frozen stiff, as this kills the flavour entirely. The door space of a refrigerator is generally about right. The other styles can be served at room temperature though many people like them very slightly cooled: cellar temperature of about 13°C is ideal.

## Some leading bodegas

### Herederos de Argüeso
An independent shipper in Sanlúcar producing excellent manzanillas.

### Manuel de Argüeso
This Sanlúcar house, with its excellent manzanillas, is a subsidiary of Valdespino, of Jerez, see below. Apart from manzanillas it sells an excellent Oloroso Viejo.

### Antonio Barbadillo
An independent house in Sanlúcar, this is one of the leading shippers. Founded in 1821, its bodegas, in the old bishop's palace, are amongst the most beautiful in the whole of the sherry towns. It may well have been the first shipper to sell a wine as manzanilla. Nowadays it provides a very extensive range and all its wines are excellent. The best known are its Manzanilla de Sanlúcar and Manzanilla Pasada Solear, but it produces good wines of all styles, including a fino, Príncipe Amontillado, a superb Palo Cortado de Obispo Gascón and Oloroso Seco. There is also a table wine (see below). It is even experimenting with sparkling wines. The Pedro Romero bodega is a subsidiary.

## Agustín Blázquez

Founded in 1795, it was acquired in 1973 by Domecq, but its wines are kept separate and so follow their own styles. They include a notable fino, Carta Blanca.

## B. Bobadilla

This Jerez house was acquired by Osborne, of Puerto de Santa María, in 1990, and is principally famous for its brandies. Its sherries include the excellent fino Victoria and amontillado Alcázar.

## Luis Caballero

This is still a completely independent family firm in Puerto de Santa María, dating from 1830 and known throughout Spain for its orange liqueur Ponche Caballero. If Sherry used not to be its main money-spinner it was nevertheless an important part of its business, though the wines were sold in the export markets under the name of Burdon. John William Burdon was an Englishman whose Sherry business was very large in the middle of the last century, but he died childless and it was sold to Luis de la Cuesta, who in turn sold out to Luis Caballero in 1932. Many relics of him, including his portrait, remain in the Caballero offices. The present Don Luis Caballero is a large and dynamic man who, amongst many other things, owns the local castle of San Marcos. His enthusiasm is for Sherries of the very highest quality, and his aim is to produce them. He has invented his own way of making fino, which he markets under the name Puerto Fino. The idea is to keep it as fresh as possible. A mature *solera* fino is blended with a small proportion of young wine growing vigorous *flor*, under which it remains until it is ready for bottling. The results are impressive and he claims that it has a longer shelf life. In 1990 he took over the Jerez house of Emilio Lustau, which was noted for its fine wines but which was too small really to be viable. With his enthusiasm and capital all went well. This name is now the one used on the export markets, and for the rest of the story see below.

## Croft Jerez

Croft & Co Ltd is one of the oldest companies in the wine trade. It was founded in 1678 as Phayre & Bradley in Oporto, and the name of Croft did not appear until 1736, when it was called Tilden, Thompson & Croft. One of the partners, John Croft (1732–1820) somehow combined his activities in Oporto with being a wine merchant in York, of which he became sheriff. He was a notable antiquary and in 1787 wrote an interesting little book on wines. Early in this century the company was bought by Walter and Alfred Gilbey. They had strong links with the González family who kept a bodega specially for them. In 1962 W. & A. Gilbey Ltd merged with two other companies to form International Distillers and Vintners, which was taken over by Watneys, the brewers, in 1968. Following another take-over bid it became a subsidiary of Grand Metropolitan, which in turn became part of Diageo. Croft Jerez was established in 1970 and was able to take over the *soleras* of old wine then held for them by González Byass. The new Croft bodegas were built on a magnificent scale on a greenfield site on the edge of Jerez. The company is now one of the most prominent shippers, having achieved an enormous commercial success with its Croft Original Pale Cream, which is to be found in all the supermarkets; but connoisseurs will seek out its Palo Cortado – one of the best examples of that rare style.

### José de Soto

This reputable small house, dating from 1771, has been acquired by the revived Ruiz-Mateos interests. It is best known in Spain for its liqueur Ponche Soto, but it has some very good Sherries including the fino Fino Soto, a good dry oloroso Don José and a slightly softened Amontillado Selecto.

### Pedro Domecq

This house has such a long and complicated history that a whole book could be written about it. It was founded in 1730 by an Irishman called Patrick Murphy. He was a bachelor and when he died in 1762 he left it to his friend Juan Haurie, of French descent, who greatly expanded it. But Haurie, too, was a bachelor, and when he died in 1794 he left it to his five nephews. From February 1810 to August 1812 Jerez was occupied by Napoleonic troops and, as a result of divided loyalties, when they left the Haurie family found itself completely ruined. One of their kinsmen was Pedro Domecq, whose family came from the French side of the Pyrenees, but who had been born in Jerez and was not tainted by the scandal. He took over the business in 1816 and appointed a brilliant agent in England: John Ruskin's father, John James Ruskin. From then onwards the business expanded rapidly. Pedro Domecq died as the result of an accident in 1839 and 8,000 people followed his funeral. The House of Domecq became pre-eminent in the Sherry trade and was protected from its vicissitudes by a very healthy parallel trade in brandy and, of late, by wine and brandy interests in Mexico. In 1984 it was taken over by Allied Lyons to form the giant corporation Allied Domecq, which in turn amalgamated with Grand Metropolitan to become part of Diageo. Harveys is a subsidiary of the same company, as are several other well-known names such as de Terry, and Croft, from the other side of the amalgamation, but Domecq, Harveys and Croft are at present kept separate. Domecq's wines include the renowned fino La Ina, and there are other wines of the highest quality that are harder to find; indeed, at present they do not seem to be interested in exporting them at all. They include two amontillados, Botaina and Bolivar; two *palo cortados*, Nelson and Capuchino; and three olorosos, Rio Viejo, MDV and Sibarita.

### Duff Gordon

Sir James Duff was British consul in Cádiz in the latter half of the eighteenth century and had certainly started to ship Sherry by 1767. He became a friend of Thomas Osborne, a merchant from Devon, and they worked closely together, moving the combined businesses to Puerto de Santa María. Duff died in 1815 and was succeeded by a kinsman Cosmo Duff Gordon, who retired in 1848. The Duff Gordon business was bought by the Osbornes in 1872, who kept the name in being. See Osborne below.

### José Estévez

This young company, with bodegas on the edge of Jerez, acquired the long-established and respected Marqués del Réal Tesoro bodega and, more recently still, the excellent fino Tío Mateo, which used to be sold by the old-established bodega Palomino & Vergara, closed down by Allied Domecq.

### Bodegas Garvey

William Garvey came to Spain from Ireland in 1780 and by 1798 had established his bodegas in Jerez, which were destined to become amongst the greatest. His main bodega building, the Bodega de San Patricio, was in its time the largest of all: a truly magnificent building. Alas, gone is the glory! It was pulled down in 1997. The site in the middle of Jerez had become too valuable. It has moved into new buildings on the edge of the city. It was bought by Ruiz-Mateos, then went into private ownership and suffered a considerable decline. It has now once again become part of the renewed

Ruiz-Mateos interests. Its wines have always been excellent and include the fino San Patricio, the amontillado Tio Guillermo, the *palo cortado* Special Reserve and the dessert oloroso Flor de Jerez. The group also includes José de Soto, M. Gil Luque and Hijos de Rainera Pérez Marín.

## González Byass

A whole book could easily be written about this great bodega. It was founded in Jerez in 1835 by Manuel María González Angel. It is still controlled and managed by his direct descendants. Robert Blake Byass was taken into partnership in 1855 and the Byass family retained its interest until 1988, when the González family acquired it. The bodega buildings are amongst the finest in Jerez and include a remarkable, and not very practical, building designed by Alexandre Eiffel of tower fame. Queen Isabella II visited the bodegas in 1862 but unfortunately chose to arrive long after the vintage was over. Nevertheless Don Manuel acquired a large quantity of grapes which had been preserved for eating, so he could show her everything. From them he made a very fine wine and bought an enormous cask from Heidelberg to contain it. This holds 3,500 gallons. Somewhat irreverently perhaps (because it contains thirty-three butts and Christ was thirty-three years old) it was called El Cristo, but perhaps because the present generation is more wary of blasphemy than was its predecessor, it is now called El Maestro, as the apostles used to call Jesus. It now has twelve apostles, each filled with the best possible examples of different styles of sherry. They are each named and are placed as the apostles were at the Last Supper according to the picture by Leonardo da Vinci. Judas does not appear: he is in the vinegar store. Their superb Tío Pepe (which means Uncle Joe and was named after Don Manuel's uncle) is the most famous fino in the world. Other wines of impeccable quality are: manzanilla El Rocío, Amontillado del Duque, Oloroso Seco Alfonso and the older oloroso Apostoles, the beautiful, opulent dessert Oloroso Muy Viejo Matusalém and the Pedro Ximénez Noé. They have also recently introduced some vintage (*añada*) wines, which cost the earth and are worth every penny.

## John Harvey

Harveys was founded in 1796 in Denmark Street, Bristol, by William Perry, who from the beginning concentrated on selling Sherry and Port. A few years later Perry took into partnership Thomas

Urch, whose sister Ann was the wife of a renowned sea captain, Thomas Harvey. Their grandson was John Harvey. The last director with the name Harvey was Jack Harvey who died in 1958. In the same year the business became a public company, and was later taken over by Showerings, the makers of Babycham, which became part of Allied Breweries and is now part of Allied Domecq. Despite having acquired a great reputation for sherry, Harveys had no presence in Jerez until it bought the family bodega Mackenzie & Co, a name that has now disappeared. Today it has extensive bodegas there in a beautiful garden, and great stocks of wine, which are kept separate from those of Domecq, but some of their activities, such as bottling, have been rationalized and moved to a single building. It is best known for its very popular dessert wine Bristol Cream. The executives have recently been altering the names and presentations of the wines, which is rather confusing. Bristol Cream now comes in a blue bottle, reflecting the tradition of Bristol glass, and its good fino has been renamed Dune. It used to ship a range of very high-quality wines under the name 1796, but this was phased out in 1997 and it is not yet clear what is to succeed it.

### Emilio Hidalgo
A small but well-established Jerez house – not to be confused with Vinícola Hidalgo of Sanlúcar – whose main business is exporting cheap wines to the Netherlands, but it has some *soleras* of fine wines which include the softened amontillado Tresillo.

### Vinícola Hidalgo
An old-established bodega in Sanlúcar producing wines of the highest quality, notable for the finesse and lightness of touch associated with the wines of that town. Going in for quality rather than quantity, its extensive vineyards include vines that are eighty years old. Its wines include: manzanillas La Gitana and Manzanilla Pasada; Fino Superior; Amontillado Napoléon; *palo cortado* Jerez Cortado; Oloroso Dry; and Pedro Ximénez Napoléon.

### Emilio Lustau
The Lustau family, now firmly Spanish, is of French descent and founded the bodega in 1896. It operated on a small scale producing high-quality wines in historic bodegas on the city walls of Jerez. The great breakthrough came in 1981, when the late Rafael Balao, the manager, had the brilliant idea of introducing his *almacenista* range

of wines. The word refers to the source of the wines, not to their style. An *almacenista* is a storekeeper or wholesaler. In all the sherry towns some enthusiasts, often professional men such as doctors or lawyers, have had their own small bodegas housing *soleras* of all the styles of wine. They never sold in bottle but in bulk to the shippers, who bought them as required for their blends, some relying on them extensively. However, the shippers all had stocks of their own and, as demand fell, their requirements from the *almacenistas* grew less. The wines were still there and their quality first-rate, but the quantity of each was quite small. It was these wines that Lustau bought, bottled and put on the market. The success was phenomenal, as connoisseurs came to realize how good Sherry could be. Some of the other shippers saw that there was a special market for wines of this class and started to sell them, too, to the benefit of all. It was clearly time for Lustau to expand. The younger members of the family had interests of their own and did not want to enter the business. As has already been noted, the bodega was sold to Luis Caballero in 1990, so it remains a family concern but owned by a different family. Apart from the *almacenista* wines there is also a range of fine quality Sherries from the combined resources of the two companies. These include Puerto Fino (described above), the manzanilla Solera Reserva Papirusa, the slightly softened Amontillado Bodega Vieja and Solera Reserva Los Arcos, Solera Reserva Peninsula Palo Cortado, Solera Reserva Don Nuño, the dessert wines East India Solera and Oloroso del Tonel, two Pedro Ximénez wines, Murillo and Solera Reserva San Emilio, and two Moscatels, Las Cruces and Solera Reserva Emilin. The *almacenista* range includes: Manzanilla Pasada de Sanlúcar (Manuel Cuevas Jurado), Manzanilla Amontillada (Manuel Cuevas Jurado), Amontillado Fino (Pilar Aranda), Amontillado del Puerto (José Luís González Obregón), Palo Cotado (Vides), Dos Cortados (R. Farfante), Oloroso Viejo (Vda. de A. Barrego) and Oloroso de Jerez Pata de Gallina (Juan García Jarana). The names in brackets are those of the *almacenistas*. It is a remarkable range of top-quality wines.

## Grupo Medina

This group is a recent phenomenon – and what a phenomenon! It was started in 1970 at Sanlúcar by the brothers José and Jesús Medina who demonstrated (as José María Ruiz-Mateos had done in the past) that it was possible to come in from outside the traditional families and international combines and to establish a company of the first rank. They took over the established small bodega of Luís Páez and their best-known manzanilla is Alegría. They now own a half share, the other half being owned by the multinational Dutch company Ahold. Most recently they bought the famous and old-established company Williams & Humbert (see below). Other subsidiaries include Juan Vicente Vergara and Bodegas Internacionales.

### Hijos de Rainera Pérez Marín
A small bodega in Sanlúcar noted for its manzanilla La Guita.

### Marqués del Real Tesoro
See José Estévez above, p. 310.

### Osborne
With its headquarters in El Puerto de Santa María, this is one of the most important companies in the Sherry trade, and is still family-owned. Best known for its range of brandies, its trade mark is the great black bull which, despite the ban on roadside advertising, is still to be seen adorning the hilltops of Spain; but the name Osborne has had to be painted out and the bulls are now classified as sculptures. Thomas Osborne arrived in Cádiz from Devon in 1781 to join a firm of merchants, and became an adviser to the Duff Gordon family (see above, p. 310). In 1833 he became a partner until he died in 1845. In 1872 the Osbornes bought out the Duff Gordon interests and they have owned the company ever since. Until 1890 all the wines were sold under the Duff Gordon name but in that year they decided to enter the Spanish market and to make brandy, which they did under their own name, as Duff Gordon is unpronounceable in Spanish and Osborne is easy – they just sound the last e. Their wines have always been good and a few years ago they introduced some very special ones. They ship an excellent manzanilla, fino Quinta, fino amontillado Coquinero, Amontillado Seco Solera AOS, Oloroso Bailén and three fine dessert wines: Premium Oloroso 10RF, Oloroso Solera India and Alfonso el Sabio.

### Sánchez Romate Hermanos
This old-established bodega in Jerez is still happily independent. Although it is best known for its high-quality brandies, it also has some excellent Sherries, such as its amontillado NPU.

# Sandeman Coprimar

George Sandeman was a member of an old and prominent Scottish family. In 1790 he left for London with the affirmed intention of making his fortune, which he abundantly did. His father lent him £300 and he hired a wine cellar. He began by selling Sir James Duff's Sherries but obtained the Pemartín agency in 1823. He died in 1841 and was succeeded by his nephew George Glas Sandeman. Pemartín went bankrupt in 1879, owing Sandeman £10,000, a very large sum of money in those days, and they took over his assets. In this way they established their bodegas in Jerez. It continued as a family firm for many years, then became a public company, until it was bought by the great multinational company Seagrams in 1980. Subsequently it changed its name to Sandeman Coprimar. For many years its wonderful trade mark of the don in the black cape was seen all over Spain, but although, when poster advertising was banned, González Byass got its little torero and Osborne got its great black bull classified as sculptures, which were thus allowed to remain in place, the don somehow got missed out, to the loss of all. The new management was keen to reduce the minimum strength of sherry from 15.5 to 15°, appreciating that the current taste of wine drinkers is for lighter wine and taking the view that a lower strength would allow the wine-driven flavours to show through rather than the alcohol-driven flavours. Their first wine in the new style is the fino Soléo, a name suggesting sunshine; it is slightly sweet and very light, and they recommend drinking it very cool and with food. Their *soleras* of old oloroso are second to none and they have some glorious wines, but these are not easy to find. Their amontillado Royal Esmeralda is old, distinctly sweet, and well worth laying down, as is their *palo cortado* Royal Ambrosante. Their dry oloroso El Corregidor and their rich dessert wines Royal Corregidor and Imperial Corregidor are all excellent.

# A.R. Valdespino

No one makes better Sherry. Nor does anyone have a longer history, as the Valdespino family credibly believes that it has been growing wine continuously since the Reconquest. When the actual bodega was established is obscure, but suffice it to say that it is amongst the oldest and its ancient bodega buildings, built on a modest scale, are the most beautiful in Jerez. Everything is totally traditional and it ferments 80 per cent of its wine in casks. It owns the bodega Manuel de Argüeso in Sanlúcar and so can draw on ample stocks of manzanilla. Its wines include: manzanilla Deliciosa; fino Inocente (a single vineyard wine); amontillados Tío Diego and Coliseo (which is magnificent but so old as to be attractive only to real aficionados); dry *palo cortado* El Cardenal; slightly sweet *palo cortado* del Carrascal; dry oloroso Don Gonzalo; an old dessert wine Solera 1842; and Pedro Ximénez PX Viejo Reserva Superior.

## Williams & Humbert

Alexander Williams was an ambitious clerk working for Wisdom & Warter (see below). He was told that he would never be taken into the partnership and decided to start up on his own. He married Amy Humbert and his father-in-law advanced the considerable sum of £1,000 on condition that Amy's brother should become a partner when he came of age. Mr Humbert wrote to his son: 'if the firm fails I shall lose my £1,000 and as to Williams and Amy all will be destruction. You must, therefore succeed.' They did. Founded in 1877, it rose to be in the big league, just behind Domecq, González Byass and Osborne. Its most famous and successful wine was, and is, Dry Sack – a medium Sherry but dry by the standards of the Sherry sack that was shipped in Elizabethan days. Another best seller in the days when heavier and sweeter wines were the vogue was Walnut Brown, a wine that went down particularly well in the challenging climate of Scotland. Like so many English family companies, it had to go public to avoid the ruin of death duties and succumbed to a take-over bid by Ruiz-Mateos in 1972. Following the appropriation of the Ruiz-Mateos empire by the Spanish state in 1983, it endured a period of rudderless state management until it was bought by Barbadillo in 1988, who sold it on to become part of Grupo Medina. It has some excellent wines. Its fino Pando was first shipped in 1878 and a story was once current, thanks to its name, that it was first shipped for the P & O Line, but this is complete nonsense; it was named after a man called Panadero who first supplied the wine (from Montilla) to establish the *solera*. Dos Cortados is excellent and Canasta Cream is one of the best cream Sherries.

## Wisdom & Warter

It is said that if you repeat the name often enough you go mad, and in the last century *Punch* was pleased to say that Warter made the wine and Wisdom sold it – which was true of the partners. Joseph

Warter came to work for the Haurie bodegas in 1852 and two years later left to set up on his own, taking Mr Wisdom into partnership. They prospered, though Mr Warter was a difficult man and made mistakes, the worst of which was to get rid of Alexander Williams. The bodega has long been a subsidiary of González Byass, but has always been left to its own devices and operates entirely independently under robust management. It has excellent wines: fino Olivar; Royal Palace dry amontillado and Amontillado Very Old Solera, which is softened and certainly very old; the softened *palo cortado* Tizon; and Viale Pedro Ximénez amongst them.

## MONTILLA-MORILES

### Geography
The two towns of Montilla and Moriles lie in the province of Córdoba and are surrounded by low hills in the area shown on the map. The 'Superior' zone is in the middle. It is roughly a square of 50 km. The wines may also be aged and blended in the city of Córdoba, but few are.

### Climate
Being well inland, this is distinctly continental, with cold winters and long, hot summers, so that temperatures can rise as high as 45°C in summer and fall to −5°C in winter, but the yearly average is a pleasant 17°C. It is also relatively high, from 300 to 600 m above sea level, so when the days are hot the nights can be cool. The average rainfall is 620 mm, most of which falls between November and April. There are 2,500 hours of sunshine.

### Soils
The best vineyards in the 'Superior' zone are *albariza*, similar to the best soils of Jerez, white to look at and high in chalk, though here they are generally called *albero*. Surrounding this zone there are the border areas, or *ruedos*, where there is less calcium and more sand, giving a higher yield of less delicate wines, usually olorosos.

### Grapes
The classic vine here is the Pedro Ximénez, which ripens fully and attains very high sugar levels. For making table wines the grapes are picked earlier. The other variety for *vinos generosos* is the Moscatel.

In addition, Lairén (Airén), Baladí and Torrontés are grown for table wines.

**Planting and pruning**
The vines are grown as bushes, mostly in the *marco real* or square pattern, and are pruned *a la ciega*, with a fruiting top and buds at each end. The maximum density of planting allowed is 3,600 vines per ha. Growing in bushes helps to protect the vines from the intense sun; if they were grown on wires it would be necessary to irrigate.

**Vineyard area**
Approximately 2,680 ha in the Superior zone and 10,630 ha in all, 4,000 ha having been pulled up in the last few years. Supply and demand are now in balance.

**Authorized yield**
60 hl/ha in the Superior zone and 80 hl/ha elsewhere. In practice, the yield is usually 20 per cent less.

**Wines**
There are three categories: *vinos jóvenes afrutados*, which are sold within a year of production at a strength of 10 to 12°; *solera* (formerly called *crianza*) wines, sold as 'Pale Dry', 'Medium Dry', 'Pale Cream', 'Cream' etc, at a strength of 13 to 15°; and higher strength *solera* wines sold everywhere as fino, amontillado, oloroso and Moscatel, with a strength of over 15°, classified as *vinos generosos*. The DO, however, unlike Jerez, has been broadened to include table wines, which will be described separately at the end of this section.

**Production**
311,465 hl (1996), of which 4,500 hl were table wines.

**Vintages**
These influence the table wines but there is not much difference as between one vintage and another; 1996 was good and 1997 excellent. For the *vinos generosos* any differences are evened out by the method of maturation, so vintage years are irrelevant.

In a country of beautiful vineyards, those of Montilla-Moriles are amongst the most attractive. It is a landscape of low hills and wide, delightful views. Montilla is a charming old town on a hilltop, with fine old houses, impressive bodegas like those of the sherry towns, and vines growing right up to the town walls. Moriles, in contrast, is rather a dump. While the Superior zone is largely planted with vineyards, the rest of the area is by no means a monoculture. There is mixed farming and many olive trees, with hilltop villages, which add considerably to the enchantment of the place. Generally speaking, the wines grown in the area of Montilla are light and of great finesse, while those grown near Moriles tend to be bigger. Some of the best wines are made by blending from the two styles. And the *vinos generosos* are very good indeed. The *jóvenes* are table wines and are considered below.

It is the tragedy of Montilla-Moriles that it has always, metaphorically speaking, lain in the shadow of Sherry. It is easy to see why. The Sherry shippers had easy access to the sea. Until 1933 no distinction was drawn between the two districts, so that shippers in the Sherry towns bought the wines and sold them throughout the world as Sherry. In the circumstances, there was nothing remotely wrong in doing so. The wines were Andalusian, very similar in style, and of equal quality. Some were used to feed the Sherry *soleras* and others were used in making the Sherry blends. Either way they added nuances of their own and increased the range of styles available. In particular, the Pedro Ximénez grapes attained a higher degree of ripeness in the warmer climate and were invaluable for the preparation of sweet wines. It is still legal to bring them into the Sherry DO and they are the best of their kind. The others, however, have been phased out and can no longer be sold as Sherry. Although Montillas had long been sold in Spain, in the export markets they lacked historical renown and have had to make their own way. It was an uphill task, recently made all the more difficult by that swing in the pendulum of fashion that, for the time being, has taken strong wines out of favour. This is a great pity, for the wines are of the highest quality and are unjustly underrated. They deserve better.

The difference in style between Montilla and Sherry is easy to detect but hard to describe. The clue lies in the word amontillado. Sherries of this style were so named because they resembled Montilla, but in fact it went much further than that: many of them in the past actually came, wholly or in part, from Montilla-Moriles, whose wines were used as described above. But anyone who knows what amontillado tastes like (that is to say real, bone dry, old amontillado, not to be confused with the commercial 'medium' wines that usurp the name) will have some idea of the difference between

Montilla and Sherry. Even in Montilla finos it is easy to detect a touch of the amontillado character.

The preparation of Montilla is so similar to that of Sherry that to set it out would be simply repetitive. There used to be one striking difference but it is now at least partly historical. In the past the wine used always to be fermented in *tinajas*. These are huge vessels, originally made of earthenware but for many years now made of concrete. They look like a stage set for *Ali Baba and the Forty Thieves*. A man could easily hide in one. At the time of the vintage they are a wonderful sight with the must fermenting and bubbles bursting from the brim. Today about half the wine is still fermented in this way, the other half being fermented in temperature-controlled stainless-steel tanks like everywhere else. These are more prosaic but the temperature control is a good deal better. But even after fermentation in stainless steel the wine is passed into *tinajas* to complete its slow fermentation before being fed into the *criaderas*.

Apart from this difference, what has been written about sherry applies. The bodegas look very similar, though in the hotter climate some of the more modern ones are air-conditioned. They all contain impressive structures of oak butts containing the *soleras* and *criaderas* of the *generosos*, which work in exactly the same way. The finos grow under *flor*, and have a similar *flor* nose with that subtle difference mentioned above. The styles they develop are the same, too: fino (15 to 17.5°), amontillado (16 to 22°), *palo cortado* (16 to 20°) and oloroso (16 to 20°), which are blended in the same way to make creams and dessert wines. There are also varietal wines of excellent quality made from Pedro Ximénez and Moscatel grapes (15 to 18°).

In the United Kingdom, though, there is a difference in the way in which the wines can be labelled and it is one that is a good deal less than fair. The Sherry shippers had long used the words descriptive of the styles to distinguish their own wines. When a Montilla shipper (now defunct) started to use them in England, the Sherry shippers brought a passing off action against him. It was never fought out. Lacking resources, he caved in and gave undertakings to desist. The Montilla shippers regard themselves as bound by this and anyhow do not want to invite devastatingly expensive litigation, so the words are not used. The Sherry shippers tried a similar action in Spain, but there they failed, as the Spanish courts held, on ample evidence, that the Montilla shippers had been using them for years. In 1999, however, an EU directive altered things and the terms can now be used. Previously they were described simply as dry, medium or cream, which was exasperating for the shippers and not very helpful to the drinkers.

There is another thing that differentiates them from Sherry: with the exception of the varietal dessert wines, they are not usually fortified. The reason for this is that the very ripe Pedro Ximénez grapes are full of sugar, with an average sugar content of 15° Baumé and a corresponding amount of alcohol when they are fermented. If the level of alcohol is too high, this can be corrected with wine from the other varieties. Finos are marketed with 15 to 17.5° alcohol and the amontillados and olorosos from 16 to 20°. An old oloroso can even go up to 22°.

As in the Sherry towns, the difficult market for *vinos generosos* has caused some respected names to disappear but others happily are flourishing. These include some small houses making excellent wines but for reasons of space only the bigger ones will be described.

## Some leading bodegas

### Alvear
This is undoubtedly the leading bodega and easily the strongest in the export markets. It was founded in 1729 by Don Diego de Alvear y Escalera, a member of a distinguished family that originated in Navarra. It is still owned and run by his descendants. His assistant was Carlos Bilanueva who put his initials CB on the casks containing the choicest wines, and they are now immortalized as a brand name. It is one of the largest wine growers, with 320 ha, but this is not enough to supply all its needs. It markets a very full range of top-quality wines, as well as brandies and vermouth.

### Gracia Hermanos
Founded in 1959, it became in the late 1980s a member of the same group as Pérez Barquero (see below) but is run independently. It is the market leader in Spain with its own distinguished range of wines and, in addition, vermouth, gin, vodka, rum and anis.

### Pérez Barquero
Founded in 1905, this is now part of a group that includes Gracia Hermanos (above). Although its bodegas are beautiful and old-fashioned, it is right up with modern technology and does all its fermentations in temperature-controlled stainless-steel tanks,

cooling the must in a heat exchanger before feeding it in for fermentation. Its wines are very good indeed, notably the Gran Barquero range. It has extensive vineyards of 125 ha.

Other bodegas producing high-quality wines include: Aragón y Cia.; Bodegas Montebello; Bodegas Robles; Bodegas Toro Albala; Cia. Vinícola del Sur (a subsidiary of Pérez Barquero); Conde de la Cortina (a subsidiary of Alvear); Delgado Hermanos; Moreno; Navisa Industrial Vinícola España; and Torres Burgos.

### Some wines to seek out

**Fino**

| | |
|---|---|
| Fino C.B. | Alvear |
| Fino Capataz | Alvear |
| Alvear's Fino | Alvear |
| Secunda Bota | Delgado |
| María del Valle | Gracia |
| Gran Barquero | Pérez Barquero |
| Selección de Robles | Robles |
| Fino del Lagar | Toro Albala |

**Amontillado**

| | |
|---|---|
| Carlos VII | Alvear |
| Pacorrito | Aragon |
| Montearruit | Gracia |
| Gran Barquero | Pérez Barquero |
| Viejísima Solera 1922 | Toro Albala |

**Oloroso**

| | |
|---|---|
| Pelayo | Alvear |
| Asunción | Alvear |
| Crian | Gracia |
| Gran Barquero | Pérez Barquero |

**Pedro Ximénez**

| | |
|---|---|
| Pedro Ximénez 1927 | Alvear |
| Pedro Ximénez 1830 | Alvear |
| Dulce Viejo | Gracia |
| Gran Barquero | Pérez Barquero |

# CONDADO DE HUELVA

## Geography

Vines used to be the predominant crop throughout the whole of the area shown on the map, but the amount planted has been declining for many years and there are now only isolated vineyards, most of them near Bollullos del Condado, Manzanilla (not to be confused with the Sherry) and Chucena. Lying in the province of Huelva, the DO extends down to the Atlantic and, at its eastern edge, just into the Parque Nacional de Doñana, where the marshes of the Marismas del Guadalquivir form one of the greatest nature reserves in Europe. The Sherry vineyards are on the other side of the estuary.

## Climate

Being so far south, this is as much Mediterranean as it is Atlantic, but the Atlantic breezes and the proximity of the sea have a moderating influence. The average temperature is 18°C with a maximum of 28°C and a minimum of 9°C, though it sometimes falls lower and frosts are not unknown. Rainfall is 500 to 800 mm, but is liable to Atlantic vagaries, with twice the annual average in 1996 after five years of drought. There are 3,000 hours of sunshine.

## Soils

There is a certain amount of *albariza*, mostly around Manzanilla and Chucena, which gives the highest quality and lowest yield, but most of the soils are reddish in appearance, consisting of sand and clay, with some *barros*.

## Grapes

The special local variety is the Zalema, whose high yield endears it to the growers, but which also results in rather neutral and diluted wines. They would be well advised to reduce the yield drastically but are disinclined to do so. Despite the efforts of the Consejo Regulador to replace it, the Zalema still occupies 80 per cent of the vineyards and is likely to stay that way. Next in importance are the authorized (and encouraged) varieties, the Palomino with its close relation the Listán, and the Garrido Fino. A very small amount of Moscatel is also grown but not for DO wines.

## Planting and pruning

The old vineyards are planted in a rectangular pattern with 0.6 m between the vines and 2.5 m between the rows. They are pruned in the same way as the traditional Sherry vineyards: *vara y pulgar*. This pattern makes mechanical cultivation, even with miniature tractors, difficult; it is one of the very few vineyard areas where horses can still be seen in regular use. They are slow and the plough is easily controlled, as the ploughman walks behind it, allowing safe cultivation right up to the vines. More modern vineyards are planted in rectangles with wider spacing of 3.25 by 1.5 m to allow for mechanical cultivation with possible mechanical picking in the future. A few are cultivated on wires. The maximum permitted densities are 2,500 per ha for bushes and 3,000 per ha for wires.

**Vineyard area**
6,000 ha (1997), a decline from a historic figure of 21,000 ha.

**Authorized yield**
70 hl/ha, but it is typically rather less, about 50 hl/ha.

**Wines**
Since 1984 the emphasis has been on *joven afrutado*, a light white table wine. Traditionally, however, the district has grown *vinos generosos*. These are of two kinds: the *pálido*, a fino style fortified to 15.5° and the *viejo*, an oloroso style fortified to 17° and which can go up as high as 24°.

**Production**
460,812 hl (1993).

**Vintages**
These are immaterial for the *vinos generosos*. For the table wines there is some variation from one year to another, but as they are intended to be drunk in the year they are made, there is no point in investigating the qualities of past vintages.

To visit the smaller bodegas in Condado de Huelva is to walk into a time warp. They are rather like the very smallest bodegas in Jerez forty years ago. Admittedly the larger ones and the biggest cooperative have such modern equipment as temperature-controlled fermentation tanks, stainless-steel storage facilities and the like, but these are largely used for the table wine, which will be discussed later in this chapter. The *vinos generosos* are made with loving care, as they have always been, and they have a loyal local following, but it is clearly a trade in decline and one fears that it may be in terminal decline. It needs a vigorous enthusiast with a great deal of money and marketing skills to put these wines on their feet again. Such people do exist and they are active all over Spain, making the new generation of table wines, but there is none here. And such a person looking at *vinos generosos* would be more likely to look at Sherry or Montilla. Many of the bodegas are in the enchanting little town of Bollullos del Condado but others are found throughout the area.

Wine has been grown here, as in almost all of Spain, from time immemorial. It had a rare moment of glory in the fifteenth century. The Monasterio de la Rábida lies near the coast at the western end of the delimited area. It was here that Christopher Columbus sheltered and prayed before he set off from an island near Palos de la Frontera to discover the New World. His ships were provisioned with the local wine and so it is probably safe to say that Condado de Huelva was the first wine to be drunk in the New World, even before Sherry; but no distinction was drawn between them in those days. Hence the badge of the modern Consejo Regulador bears the sail of a galleon and a bunch of grapes.

Condado de Huelva is suffering, like Sherry and Montilla, from the decline in popularity of wines of this kind – but more so, as they have never had a serious export market nor have they been distributed nationally in Spain. Up to 1933, when the Sherry district was delimited, their principal market was in the Sherry towns, where they were blended in with the cheaper grades of Sherry. Now they have lost even that market.

Condado is derived from *conde*, or count, so it is the County of Huelva. To the west there is the Río Tinto with its minerals, to the east there is the Coto Doñana, and to the south there are magnificent Atlantic beaches, full of holiday-makers at weekends. It is an agreeable countryside of mixed agriculture, olive trees, pines, cork oaks and, above all, strawberries. It is the strawberries that make the money, and as the vineyards decline, the strawberry fields increase, but whether this will continue at the same giddy pace is doubtful, as there are now so many of them that the price has gone down. Lepe, mentioned by Chaucer, is vineless and surrounded by strawberries. There is hope, though. Some of the new vineyards are very serious and the Andrade bodegas have one that is magnificent: a model of what a great vineyard should be.

There are two traditional kinds of *vinos generosos*. Condado Pálido is a fino style. The best are made from Palomino and Garrido

Fino grapes and are generally fermented without temperature control either in vats or in *tinajas*, known locally as *conos*. They are then aged in American oak butts for a minimum of two years and fortified to a strength of between 14 and 17°. They are frankly rather feeble things compared with the finos of Jerez or Montilla and have been likened to the *pálidos* of Rueda – themselves a dying species. They are pleasant in the local bars but one would not seek them out. The other kind is Condado Viejo, usually from Zalema grapes. Fermented in the same way, they can attain a natural strength of as much as 15°. They are matured on ullage in oak casks for the same minimum time and are fortified to as much as 23°. The best of them are much older. Matured on ullage by oxidation in the *solera* system, they resemble oloroso Sherries and can be very good, especially when slightly sweetened. Shippers usually have a cask or two of really old wines and these can be very good indeed, vast in flavour and with considerable depth. These really are worth seeking out but are rare. There are also some good *palo cortados*. Although most of the olorosos are vinified from Zalema grapes, some of the best are from the other varieties.

### Some leading bodegas

Bodegas Andrade (look for the dry oloroso Doceñero); José and Miguel Martín; Iglesias; Jaime Oliveros; Vinícola del Condado (look for fino Mioro and oloroso Botarroble); and A. Villarán (look for *Solera* 1934).

## MÁLAGA

### Geography

The city of Málaga lies on the coast and is a port and a holiday centre. All Málaga wine is matured here. The vineyards, however, are split between two totally distinct areas. The smaller is on the coast, around and behind Estepona. It grows mostly Moscatel grapes. The second, which is much larger, includes Málaga itself and stretches to the east and north right up into the mountains. This is further subdivided into three areas. Molina is to the north-west, around the town of that name, growing mostly Pedro Ximénez. The second is Axarquía, which lies along the coast between Málaga and Nerja and stretches inland to the border of the province of Granada, where the vines are mostly Moscatel. The third, and smallest, is Mountain, right up in the north around Cuevas de San Marcos, where the grapes are predominantly Pedro Ximénez.

## Climate
Down by the coast it is Mediterranean and most agreeable, with an average temperature of 18.5°C and 3,000 hours of sunshine. But up in the mountains it is distinctly continental: hot in summer and bitterly cold with frosts in winter. The average rainfalls are 400 mm in Axarquía, 550 mm in Molina, and as much as 810 mm in the Mountain, where the average temperature is only 13.2°C, but the whole area has recently been experiencing the droughts and deluges noted in the rest of Andalucía. In the mountains there are wide temperature variations between day and night. Some of the Axarquía vineyards are as high as 2,000 m.

## Soils
In so large an area it is not surprising that these are bewildering in their variety. Around the coast it is alluvial, with clay, quartz and mica. In Molina it is ferruginous clay with chalk. In Axarquía it is gravelly with chalk. In the Mountain it is mainly limestone with thin layers of sand and clay in the subsoil.

## Grapes
The predominant, traditional grape is the Pedro Ximénez, here known as the Pedro Ximén. The only other authorized variety is the Moscatel. But others are found.

## Planting and pruning
Mostly grown in squares (*marco real*) of 2.25 m, though more recent plantings have been 3 by 1.5 m and some Pedro Ximénez is grown on wires.

## Vineyard area
890 ha.

## Authorized yield
70 hl/ha in Antequera, Archidona, Campillo and Estepona; elsewhere 45.5 hl/ha.

## Wines

Seven types of wine and eight descriptive terms are recognized. The types of wine are:

*Lágrima.* Literally 'tears': wine traditionally made from free-run must, but nowadays coming from a first, very light pressing.

*Seco.* Wine that has been fermented out so that it contains less than 5 grams per litre of sugar. Wines of this kind are often referred to as olorosos, which is a perfectly fair description but is unofficial. The strength varies from 13.5 to 23°.

*Abocado.* Fairly sweet with 5 to 50 grams per litre of sugar.

*Semiseco.* The same as *abocado*.

*Dulce.* Sweet wine with 600 grams per litre of sugar but more usually 150 to 225 grams.

*Dulce Pedro Ximén* and *Dulce Moscatel. Dulce* varietal wines.

*Dulce Lágrima.* A *dulce* made from *lágrima* must.

The descriptive terms are:

*Blanco.* White
*Dorado.* Golden
*Rojo-Dorado.* Red-gold
*Oscuro.* Dark
*Negro.* Black (in fact very dark)
*Crema.* Cream
*Pajarete.* Semi-sweet

## Production

49,000 hl.

## Vintages

Because of the way the wine is matured these do not matter.

Málaga is a sad story, for its wines were once very popular. Now they are sharing in the fate of all *vinos generosos* and are doing so to a high degree; although they are sold throughout Spain they do not have much of a presence on the export markets, which is a pity, for they can be very good. In Elizabethan times they were known as Malaga-(or Maligo-) sack and were rivals to sherris-sack. In the seventeenth century they were helped by having a customs rebate denied to wines shipped through Cádiz. When Sherry suffered a serious decline in the eighteenth century, Málaga flourished and enjoyed a golden age. The best wine was sold as Mountain, which is where it came from. Elegant silver decanter labels so inscribed are now, alas, seldom used for their original purpose. The decline set in during the nineteenth century and has gone on ever since. Thomas George Shaw went to Spain in 1844 and when he published his book *Wine, the Vine and the Cellar* twenty years later he wrote: 'I saw some of the dark, old "mountain", which used to be well known as a forenoon or liqueur wine; but which may be said to be now entirely forgotten.' The story has not changed. Málaga had the doubtful distinction of being the first Spanish vineyard to be invaded by phylloxera, in 1876, and the destruction became almost total. From 32.5 million litres in 1880, production had practically disappeared by 1886. But apart from phylloxera, Málaga was already in a decline. In the hundred years from 1878 to 1978 the vineyard area decreased to one-tenth. Through lack of enterprise or of capital they were not immediately replanted. Moreover, those that were replanted had other calls on their fruit: raisins and table grapes, particularly the Moscatel. These rival trades are still flourishing and their products are in healthy demand, competing with the wine shippers. Then there were other catastrophes. One of the best export markets was Russia, but this collapsed with the Revolution. Then it suffered grievously in the Spanish Civil War, when nearly all the wine was taken by the troops, most of it stolen. Spain was bankrupt and potential export markets had, for the time being, gone. Málaga rose from its ashes but never really got going again and is now suffering the ravages of fashion. Many of the shippers went bankrupt, one of the greatest losses having been the old-established house of Scholtz Hermanos, which made some of the finest wines. Their stocks were bought by Larios.

The vineyards are in the areas already described and most of them are small, though some of the shippers have substantial estates, notably López Hermanos, which has 250 ha. No new vineyards are being planted. Even so, and despite the wine's decline in popularity, there is a shortage of Pedro Ximénez and up to 10 per cent of the total requirement is allowed to be brought in from Montilla-Moriles. To make the traditional sweet wines the grapes are dried on esparto-grass mats in the sun, which is very labour-intensive, especially as they have to be covered over to avoid dilution by dew or rain, so that the practice has disappeared from the Sherry vineyards; and the shrivelling of the grapes results in a very low yield. The sugar content is so high, though, that it does not all ferment out and gives a sweet wine called *vino maestro* (literally master wine). Sweet wines are mostly made as *mistelas*, by stopping fermentation by adding alcohol and are called *vino tierno* (literally soft wine). *Dulce natural* is made from a fifty-fifty mixture of the two. Another agent used for blending is *arrope*: must boiled down to a third of its volume to make a dark syrup. The leading shippers, who aim at more subtle styles of wine, avoid using too much of this as it imparts a burnt taste.

All Málaga has to be matured in bodegas within the city. It can attain 15° naturally but is usually fortified to 18°, using *vino borracho* (literally drunken wine) made from a mixture of equal parts wine and alcohol, before maturation. The permitted range is 15° to 23°. Maturation has to take place for at least two years in oak casks but these are generally full, so the oxidation is gradual. It is usual to draw out about a third of the wine at a time and to fill in the void, but a full *solera* system is only used for making the oldest and most expensive wines. The styles and the descriptive words are listed above. The modern drier, lighter wines are never really likely to catch on; they have too many rivals that are more exciting. Recently a 'pale cream' style has been introduced which has already found favour in Spain and may succeed in the export markets. The old-style dessert Málagas can be very fine, though, and it is these that are well worth seeking out.

Despite the decline there are still several bodegas and two of them are outstanding.

### The leading bodegas

#### Larios

This is a very big concern, now a subsidiary of Pernod Ricard, and is famous for its gin and other spirituous drinks, but it also produces some excellent Málagas. Benefique oloroso is one to look for.

#### López Hermanos

This bodega owned by the de Burgos López family was founded towards the end of the nineteenth century: alternative dates of 1885 and 1896 are provided. Whichever may be true, it is old-established and successful. Amongst its fittings are two vast casks made of red pine from the Russian steppes, dating from the time when Russia was the principal export customer. Trajinero Dry is only fairly dry but is a good example of its kind. The sweet Málaga Virgen has a very sweet impact but enough acidity to prevent it from being cloying and giving an unexpectedly dry aftertaste.

## OTHER WINES

Table wines are grown all over Spain and Andalucía is no exception. Most of them have no DO but two of the DOs have expanded their definitions to include them: Montilla-Moriles and Condado de Huelva. Throughout Andalucía summers are hot, and only ten or twenty years ago one would have expected the wines to be of a very southern style: lacking in acidity, with little fragrance, flabby and uninteresting. This is no longer so, thanks largely to the availability of controlled-temperature fermentation and the understanding that, to get the acidity that table wines require, the grapes have to be picked early. Although no great table wines have yet emerged, there are now plenty of very acceptable ones.

### Montilla-Moriles
The DO regulations include white table wines and these are the best grown in Andalucía. They were started in the late 1970s to mitigate the damage caused by the dwindling sales of *vinos generosos* and have been a great success. To make them, Pedro Ximénez grapes are picked early, in August, and the must is given a low-temperature fermentation at about 16°C, to retain the fruitiness. The resulting wines are light, fragrant and most agreeable. They are not wood-aged and are intended to be drunk young. Amongst the best are Alvear's Marqués de la Sierra, Delgado's Lagar de San Antonio and Gracia's Viña Verde. To avoid confusion with the Portuguese wine, this last is sold on the export markets under the name Viña Amalia.

### Condado de Huelva
The white table wine – *blanco joven*, or *blanco afrutado* – only forms a small part of the production but is likely to become more important. The principal grape is the local Zalema. Some growers would like to experiment with European classic varieties such as Chardonnay and Riesling but say, reasonably enough, that everyone is growing them and that they want to retain their individuality. It is a pity that the local grape is so negative. To make table wines the grapes are picked in August and the must is cool-fermented at 15

to 18°C though some go up to 20°C. They tend to have the style of a very dilute fino, and although they are pleasant enough drunk locally it is hard to be enthusiastic. There is not a lot to choose between the various shippers.

## The Sherry area

Owing to the decline in the Sherry market, quite a lot of the good *albariza* vineyards are now used for table wine which, because it calls for no maturation, is more profitable and is therefore here to stay. It has not, however, been incorporated into the Sherry DO. And apart from these vineyards, which could legally produce Sherry, a wide variety of grapes are grown for table wine in the same general area but outside the Sherry zone. There is much talk of creating a new DO, provisionally called Vino de la Tierra de Cádiz, and this name is already being used by a number of growers, but at present it is unofficial. An official VdlT zone of Cádiz, however, has already been created. As is shown in other parts of Spain, although the Palomino vine produces glorious Sherries, as a vine for table wines it is rather bland and negative. Good wines can be produced from it but none that is exciting.

The pioneer was Antonio Barbadillo, whose Castillo de San Diego is popular in Spain and has had a considerable success on the export markets. It remains to be seen whether other growers in the Sherry area will follow his example or will prefer to put their faith in the new 15° Sherries.

The exquisite little town of Arcos de la Frontera lies well outside the Sherry area but vineyards there can and do grow wines that are very similar. One grower there – Bodegas Paez Morilla – deserves special mention. It has a small bodega in Jerez, producing Sherry (and some remarkably fine Sherry vinegar) but its most interesting vineyard is in the hills outside Arcos. It started to produce white table wine in 1979 and, finding the wine from the Palomino to be rather negative, planted Riesling, which is hard to grow but which has certainly added another dimension to the wine, sold as Tierra Blanca. A large part of the vineyard is given over to red wine varieties, which include Tempranillo, Garnacha and Cabernet Sauvignon. Several other varieties, both red and white, are being experimented with. The red wine, sold as Viña Lucía, is agreeable but at present lacks intensity. Young wines drawn from the oak tasted very promising, though, and it looks as though these will get better as the vines age and techniques are refined. They are worth keeping an eye on.

### Aljarafe
This is a CV lying between Sevilla and Condado de Huelva, making similar wines from the same grape varieties.

### Bailén
This CV produces light red table wines from Cencibel (Tempranillo) and also grows the white Airén. Although in Andalucía, it can simply be regarded as an outlying bit of La Mancha.

### Contraviesa-Alpujarra
Wines from this CV, formerly called Costa-Albodón, are hard to find even if you go there. It lies in the mountains east of Granada and down to the coast. Traditionally it has made *rancio* wines, principally from the Jaén Blanco grape, but many other varieties are planted and it is moving into table wines.

### Laujar
The province of Almería is noted principally for its table grapes, but some strong whites, *rosados* and light reds are grown within this CV.

### Lopera
This CV, within the province of Jaén, produces wines somewhat like Montilla from Palomino grapes. They are not bottled but are sold in bulk for drinking in bars.

### Villaviciosa de Córdoba
A small CV of diminishing importance, growing Montilla-like wines near Cordoba.

# 11

## *The Islands*

———

The two groups of islands covered in this section – the Balearics and the Canaries – have little in common save that they are both Spanish. The former is in the Mediterranean, the latter in the Atlantic and much further south. Only one of the Balearics grows wines in commercial amounts: Mallorca. The Canary Islands have between them no fewer than eight DOs and two VdlTs. Another thing that they have in common is that they drink nearly all their wine themselves, assisted, if not overwhelmed, by the enormous number of tourists they have to cater for. Mallorca only exports a very small amount and the Canary Islands export practically nothing, though they are now making efforts to enter the export markets. However, the wines are interesting and many visitors drink them on the spot.

### MALLORCA

The Mallorcan language (Mallorquí, which is still widely spoken) is very similar to Catalán and the island has much in common with the neighbouring mainland, but the wines are very different, and although international vine varieties are grown, the best wines rely on long-established local varieties. There is one DO, Binissalem, one VdlT, Plá i Llevant de Mallorca, and a wine-growing area that is unclassified near Andraitx. Local wines are to be found on restaurant lists but are not so easy to find in the shops, as most of them are sold direct. At the beginning of the nineteenth century there were 35,000 ha of vines on the island. Late in the century these were wiped out by phylloxera and have never recovered. Today there are 2,000 ha. Once-famous vineyards, growing Malvasías on the west coast, have long since disappeared.

# BINISSALEM

## Geography
The vineyards are on a plain north of Palma at an altitude of 250–300 m, sheltered by the mountains from the northerly winds.

## Climate
Mediterranean, with hot summers going up as high as 35°C and fairly mild winters, though it can go down to freezing point. The average temperature is 16°C. There are 2,800 hours of sunshine and 500–600 mm of rainfall, mainly in the autumn.

## Soil
Not very fertile, with some limestone over clay.

## Grapes
Recommended red varieties: Manto Negro (DO red wines must contain at least 50 per cent) and Callet.

Permitted red varieties: Tempranillo and Monastrell.

Recommended white variety: Moll (DO white wines must contain at least 70 per cent).

Permitted white varieties: Parellada and Macabeo.

Several other varieties, including imported ones, are being grown experimentally.

## Planting
Traditional vineyards are planted in a rectangular pattern 2.4 by 1.2 m but some of the newer ones are on wires. There are 1,700 to 3,500 vines per ha.

## Vineyard area
312 ha officially, though a breakdown of the figures given for the separate vine varieties mysteriously adds up to 359.

## Authorized yield
52.5 hl/ha for Manto Negro, Tempranillo and Monastrell, 63 hl/ha for Callet, Moll and Macabeo, and 70 hl/ha for Parellada.

## Wines
Red wines must be matured for at least two years, of which at least six months must be in oak casks of less than 1,000 litres. They go up to *reservas*, which must have a year in the wood, and *grandes reservas* are possible in the future, requiring two years in the wood

and three in bottle. The maximum strength is 14°. White wines must have a minimum strength of 10.5° and a maximum of 13°, and *rosados* a minimum of 11° and a maximum of 13.5°. These are sold as *jóvenes* and are not given a malolactic fermentation.

## Production
7,500 hl.

## Vintages
1991 5, 1992 5, 1993 5, 1994 7, 1995 6, 1996 5, 1997 6.

Binissalem is the local spelling. In Castillian there is only one s, and going back to the Arabic root this is probably right. Over the years, though, it can be found spelt in all sorts of ways. The wines were highly regarded in Roman days and kept their reputation, so that Al Henderson in his *History of Modern Wines* (1824) wrote: 'The island of Majorca furnishes several wines of sufficiently good quality to bear exportation; among which those made in the district of Benesale, three leagues from Palma, are accounted the best, at least of the red growths. The vintage, however, is not treated in the most judicious manner; the grapes being fermented for fifteen or twenty days in deep stone cisterns, into which they are introduced at repeated intervals, so that the operation is frequently checked in its progress, and is seldom fully completed. When it is thought to have ceased, the liquor is drawn off into large tuns, containing five or six pipes each; and there the secondary fermentation, as might be expected, is often so violent as to burst the vessels, though made of olive staves four inches in thickness, and bound with hoops proportionally strong.' Wine production collapsed after phylloxera, which struck in 1891, but never disappeared and the wines of Binissalem retained a good reputation that was much abused. People who lived there used to import wines from the mainland which were of very mixed quality and sell them as the real thing, to the intense indignation of the local serious growers. This state of things happily ceased with the creation of the DO in 1991, thanks largely to the efforts of the very reputable grower José Ferrer, who still puts *auténtica* on his labels to distinguish his wines from the bogus ones.

Conditions nowadays are very different from those described by Henderson. The bodegas are full of gleaming stainless steel and the wines, which in the past were somewhat musty, are now completely clean. The whites and *rosados* are very acceptable and may well grow better as new techniques are mastered. In particular there are experiments with giving the whites wood contact and even wood fermentation. The best whites are unexpectedly light and have good acidity. The reds have long been worth looking for and might well have been sought out much more had people realized how well they age; though the quality of the corks used until quite recently did not encourage this. They are not wines that immediately call out for ageing, as some do, but given the chance to age do so very gracefully and gain a lot in complexity. A 1959 Ferrer Reserva had developed beautifully by 1972 but by 1992 had been let down by its cork. Nowadays the corks are much better.

## Bodegas

### José L. Ferrer (Franja Roja)

This bodega, which is by far the biggest, was founded in 1931 and for years was the only quality producer on the island. It has 70 ha of vines and still makes some of the best wines. Modest quantities are exported. Its red wines are particularly good. The 1994 *crianza* was made from 85 per cent Manto Negro and 5 per cent each of Tempranillo, Cabernet Sauvignon and Callet, while the 1992 *reserva* was made from 80 per cent Manto Negro with 10 per cent each of Tempranillo and Cabernet Sauvignon.

### Antonio Nadal Ros

A younger establishment, founded in 1960. It has 25 ha of vines. Most of its wines are sold in bulk but wines of all three colours are bottled. The reds go up to a *reserva*, sold under the name Tres Uvas and made from 70 per cent Manto Negro with 10 per cent each of Callet, Cabernet Sauvignon and Monastrell.

### Herederos de Hermanos Ribas

This small bodega has a history going back to 1711, but the present company dates from 1986. It has 45 ha of vineyards and sells about half of its wines in bulk. They include a good *rosado*, but perhaps the best is the red *crianza*; the 1994 was made from 70 per cent Manto Negro, 20 per cent Cabernet Sauvignon and 10 per cent Tempranillo.

### Jaume de Puntiro

This very small bodega was founded in 1980. It has 11 ha of

vineyards and sells about half its wine in bulk. These include good reds and whites. A small proportion is exported.

## PLÁ I LLEVANT DE MALLORCA

### Geography
The name means 'the plain and coast of Mallorca'. It covers the plain in the centre and east of the island and includes an area once known as Felanitx. It aspires to be promoted to DO status and, if it is, no doubt it will be carefully delineated and regulated, but this has not happened yet.

### Climate
As Binissalem.

### Soils
As the area is large there is a considerable variety, but they tend to be deep and reasonably fertile.

### Grapes
Preferred varieties for reds: Callet, Manto Negro, Tempranillo and Cabernet Sauvignon.

Preferred varieties for whites: Chardonnay, Prensal, Macabeo and Parellada.

Several other varieties are grown, however, including Shiraz, Monastrell and Pinot Noir for reds and Moscatel for whites.

### Vineyard Area
1,000 ha.

Some very good wines are grown in the relatively large and rather vague area. In the past the red wines were the most highly thought of and they can indeed be good, particularly combinations of Cabernet Sauvignon and Tempranillo, but Pinot Noir does not at present seem to come off; it is a difficult vine wherever it is grown. The white wines at present seem to be the best, notably Chardonnays and dry Moscatels. There are also some popular *rosados* and *agujas* (lightly sparkling white wines).

*Bodegas*

**Jaume Mesquida**

Founded in 1945, this was the first bodega to establish a reputation for imported varietals. It has 25 ha of vineyards and produces a wide range of wines that include a barrel-fermented Chardonnay and a varietal Cabernet Sauvignon.

**Miguel Oliver**

Founded in 1912, it has 10 ha of vineyards and has recently won awards with its Chardonnay and Dry Muscat. It makes a very good Callet which is given eighteen months in American oak; it has plenty of body and a flavour unique to this grape variety. Its range of wines also includes a varietal Manto Negro.

**Trevin**

Although the company was only founded in 1969, it is a well-established family business now in its fourth generation and exports a proportion of its wines.


## ANDRAITX

Florianopolis, which owns the Bodega Santa Catarina, is a Scandinavian investment dating from 1985. At present it has 10 ha of vineyards planted with French varieties: Chardonnay, Merlot, Cabernet Sauvignon and Pinot Noir. It plans to expand to 70 ha and has planted vineyards in the centre of the island, which is perfectly proper as it does not have any DO. All the red wines are aged in oak for up to two years and are notably complex. There is also a delightful Cabernet Sauvignon *rosado*.


## THE CANARY ISLANDS

The early history of the Canary Islands is fascinating, stretching back to before the Christian era, and in AD 150 Ptolemy put his meridian line through the isle of Hierro, at the edge of the known world. The Romans paid a visit and found the island of Fuerteventura to be full of wild dogs, so they called it *Insula Canum* (Dog Island), later corrupted to Islas Canarias in Spanish and Canary

Islands in English. Descendants of the dogs are still there. The islands were also known as the Fortunate Isles. Thereafter they disappeared into the mists of mythology, and although expeditions reached them in the thirteenth and fourteenth centuries, the first serious expedition took place in 1402. They were coveted by various powers but by 1496 were firmly Spanish and have been so ever since. It is at this time that the story of wine begins. It is said that the first vines came from Crete to produce the Malvasía of Lanzarote, known in England as Canary sack. When Sir John Hawkins made his second voyage to the West Indies in 1564 he recorded that the wines were better than any in Spain, and when Thomas Nicholas published *A pleasant Description of the Fortunate Ilands called the Ilands of Canaria* in 1583 he wrote glowingly of the wines of Gran Canaria and Tenerife, but of Hierro he said, 'there is no wine . . . but onely one vineyard that an Englishman of Taunton in the West Countrie planted among rockes, his name was John Hill'. When Shakespeare wrote *The Merry Wives of Windsor* (c. 1600) he knew Canary sack as well as sherris-sack, for the host of the Garter Inn was given the line, 'Farewell, my hearts: I will to my honest knight Falstaff, and drink canary with him.' By then it was so highly favoured that it became the usual *douceur* to be given by the Spanish to English officials from whom they expected a favour. In 1634 Lord Cottington and Sir Francis Windebank were each given a tun of Canary wine by the Spanish agent in London and the parliamentarians liked it as much as the royalists, for Giles Greene, chairman of the Navy Committee, received two casks in 1644. Not surprisingly, English merchants settled there, and in 1683 sought to ship wine direct to New England instead of via England, as wines were being 'clandestinely imported under the Notion of Madeira Wines'. By 1687 12,000 pipes were being exported to England annually but the trade had begun to decline. The wine was dear; it had fallen out of fashion; French wine had become the 'modish liquor'; and, not least, 'The much adulteration of it by the mystery of vintners and Coopers . . . having stoakt the cuntry with such trash brewed wines under the Notion of Canarys that the Gentry and others when [they] come to towne, come prepossessed with a Prejudice against that noble liquor Canary.' How often has a like story been told! But unlike Sherry, Canary disappeared for ever. When Cyrus Redding published his *History of Modern Wines* (1833) he wrote, 'Canary was once much drunk in England, and was known only by that name. The writer of this tasted some which was a hundred and twenty-six years old, it having been kept during all that period in the family cellars of a nobleman, with whom he happened to be dining, and who produced a bottle, its contents little more than a pint, as a *bonne bouche*. Its flavour was good, and it had ample body.' It must originally have been sweet and strong. *Sic transit gloria mundi.*

There have been great changes and they have all happened in the last few years. New wine makers have arrived and have brought modern equipment with them. Here, as in most parts of Spain, there are stainless-steel tanks and controlled-temperature fermentations. There is a new generation of light table wines of all colours which are delicious to drink locally. But some of the old pattern remains. The wines are generally expensive so there is never likely to be much of an export market, faced with the competition of the mainland; and the most exciting are still the sweet Malvasías. But the islands have the great advantage that they are remarkably free from disease and phylloxera has never struck. The result is that old varieties that have long since disappeared elsewhere are still to be found, and the visitor can find himself in a time warp, drinking wines that have not existed anywhere else for a couple of hundred years.

The islands are situated so far south that seasonal differences are not as marked as they are in Europe, though they can be significant in the higher vineyards, and there are many microclimates; nor is there much variation in the daylight hours, which range from a minimum of ten hours eleven minutes to a maximum of thirteen hours forty-nine minutes, and the weather is less affected by dramatic changes than it is, for example, in Madeira. The environment for wine growing is therefore most unusual.

There are seven main islands in the archipelago and five small ones, but wine growing is only significant on Tenerife, El Hierro, Lanzarote and La Palma.


## TENERIFE

Vinously this is the most exciting island. It has five DO areas and also grows VdlT wines. In alphabetical order these are:

# ABONA

## Geography

This is in the extreme south of the island, the vineyards varying in height from 200 to 1,600 metres (average 600) on the slopes of Spain's highest mountain, Mount Teide (3,715 metres). The area of the zone is 1,936 ha but only 935 ha are planted.

## Climate

Summer high 35°C, winter low −5°C. Average rainfall 400 mm, but much less in some vineyards; irrigation is allowed. There are 2,500 hours of sunshine.

## Soils

There are many. In the valleys there is clay, sand, limestone, marl and volcanic ash. At over 600 m they are volcanic, giving good wine but small yields.

## Grapes

Authorized red varieties: Bastardo Negro, Listán Negro, Malvasía Rosada, Negramoll and Tintilla.

Authorized white varieties: Bermejuela, Gual, Malvasía, Listán Blanco, Verdello and Sabro.

Listán Blanco accounts for about 60 per cent of the vines and Listán Negro for about 35 per cent.

## Authorized yield

70 hl/ha, but in practice much less.

## Wines

These are mostly white, but with some red and *rosado*; a minute amount is fortified. The minimum strength for white and *rosado* is 11.5°, for red 12° and for *vinos de licor* 15°. All are *jóvenes*.

## Production

Average is said to be 5,000 hl but this is probably an exaggeration.

Although first alphabetically, this area was the last to get official recognition and cannot as yet be regarded as of any great importance. It is really a combination of two quite distinct areas with the dividing line at 600 m altitude. All the wine is made in three cooperatives. The biggest of these is Vinícola Cumbres de Abona, founded in 1989, whose members own 300 ha. It makes only whites and *rosados*, including a fragrant white called Viña Peraza, and exports ecological wines to Germany and Switzerland.

## TACORONTE-ACENTEJO

### Geography
This area is on the north-west of the island, 23 km long. The main road from Santa Cruz de Tenerife to the tourist resort of Puerto de la Cruz passes through it. The vineyards are on north-north-west terraces facing the sea at between 200 and 800 m above sea level.

### Climate
The Atlantic influence gives a humid and temperate climate, occasionally disturbed by hot winds from Africa; the average temperature is 16°C, rising to 30°C in summer and falling to 12°C in winter. The rainfall is low, at 200–300 mm, but mists, light drizzle and heavy dew ensure that the vineyards are adequately watered. The relative humidity is 60 per cent. The average sunshine is 2,500 hours.

### Soil
Reddish, fertile loam with a little chalk over a volcanic subsoil.

### Grapes
Preferred red varieties: Listán Negro and Negramoll.

Preferred white varieties: Listán Blanco, Gual, Verdello, Malvasía, Moscatel and Vijariego.

Authorized white varieties: Marmajuelo, Pedro Ximénez and Torrontés.

### Planting
There is a unique local practice of trailing the vines along the ground and providing supports where necessary. New vineyards, however, are being planted on the double cordon system. The maximum density is 3,000 per ha.

### Vineyard area
The total vineyard area is 2443 ha but only 939 ha are in production.

### Authorized yield
70 hl/ha but in practice much less.

## Wines

Red, *rosado* and white wines are produced, most of which are *jóvenes* but there are now some *crianzas* and *reservas*. Some red wines are fermented in oak, some are made by carbonic maceration, and only the reds go through a complete malolactic fermentation. The most important production is of reds, accounting for about 90 per cent, some of which have a little wine from white varieties blended in. The whites are between 10° and 12.5° but some old-style whites are made at between 12° and 14°. The *rosados* are between 10.5° and 13°. The reds are between 12° and 14°. There are also some *vinos de licor* between 15° and 22°. Wines sold as varietal have to be 100 per cent of the variety named.

## Production
5,440 hl (1996).

This was the first district in the Canary Islands to get its own DO and it remains both the most important and the most ambitious. All the wines are pleasant and some are more than that. The whites are easy to drink, the *rosados* can be excellent, and the reds range from the passable to the impressive. Apart from the DO wines there is a special local wine which I must confess I have never tasted but would like to: *vino de tea*. *Tea* is the local name for the Canary pine; it also means firebrand and is used idiomatically to indicate intoxication. These are vinified from the Albillo and other varieties. They are fermented in 500 litre pine barrels and are often kept for years in troglodyte wineries so that they come to resemble *rancios*. They are not bottled but can be bought at the door or in bars.

### *Some bodegas*

### Afecan
A small, modern bodega founded in 1986, producing reds and whites.

### Cándido Hermanos
A small, modern bodega with 15 ha of vineyards, founded in 1989 and producing mostly reds but also some whites.

### Insulares Tenerife
A modern bodega founded in 1992, an S.A.T. acting as a cooperative for 500 growers and producing some of the best wines of all

colours under the name Viña Norte, including a most agreeable red made from Listán Negra and Negramoll. The reds include *crianzas*.

## Monje

A modern family-owned bodega, founded in 1956, with 14 ha of vineyard producing wines of all colours, including a notable red Monje de Autor *crianza*. Its white wines are good, too.

## VALLE DE GÜÍMAR

### Geography

The vineyards are on the arid south-facing slope of the volcanic Mount Teide, in a strip parallel to the coast along the motorway to Santa Cruz. It is really a continuation of the Abona region and has the same quality dividing line of 600 m above sea level, the best vineyards being above it. In all they stretch from 200 to 1,600 m.

### Climate

A summer average of 18°C and a winter average of 12°C. Rainfall is 400 mm. There are 2,900 hours of sunshine.

### Soils

The terrain is very varied but the soil is mostly volcanic.

### Grapes

Red varieties: Listán Negro and Negramoll, with some Malvasía Rosada.

White varieties: Listán Blanco (73 per cent of the vineyard), Forastera (14 per cent), small quantities of Malvasía, Moscatel, Gual, Vijariego, Marmajuelo, etc.

### Planting

This follows local traditions and many different styles of cultivation can be seen, but recently planted vineyards tend to be on wires.

### Vineyard area

The total area is 913 ha but only 276 are in production. These are the official figures but others are quoted.

### Authorized yield

70 hl/ha but in 1995 the actual yield was 13.33 hl/ha.

**Wines**
Mostly white *jóvenes*, but also *rosados* and reds, with some of the reds seeing oak.

**Production**
6,000 hl (1995).

This is not as yet an area to be taken very seriously, though some of the white wines grown in the higher vineyards can be good. Traditionally it was a place of small family vineyards producing old-fashioned wines. Now there is a cooperative movement and new technology is moving in, so some interesting wines may emerge. One of the leading producers is Viña Chagua, founded in 1969.

## VALLE DE LA OROTAVA

**Geography**
This is not a valley at all but a famously beautiful vineyard area on the western foothills of the volcanic Mount Teide, extending from near sea level to 800 m or more.

**Climate**
This is notably humid with rainfall of 650 mm and additional water from sea mists. A summer high of 28°C and a winter low of 8°C give an average temperature of 15°C, with 2,600 hours of sunshine.

**Soils**
Very acid and generally volcanic with some clay.

**Grapes**
Authorized red varieties: Bastardo Negro, Listán Negro, Malvasía Rosada, Moscatel Negro, Negramoll, Tintilla and Vijariego Negra.

Authorized white varieties: Bastardo Blanco, Gual, Forestera, Listán Blanco, Malvasía, Marmajuelo, Moscatel, Pedro Ximénez, Torrontés, Verdello and Vijariego.

In practice the two Listáns account for practically the whole of the planting and some of the other varieties are hardly found at all.

**Planting**
This is by a unique local method, along horizontal poles about 60 cm above the ground. It is known as *cordón* but is totally different from cordon training as usually practised. The density is 1,000 to 2,000 vines per ha.

**Vineyard area**
The total is 926 ha but only 338 ha are in production.

**Authorized yield**
70 hl/ha but as usual this is not achieved in practice.

**Wines**
These are mostly white *jóvenes* made with no malolactic fermentation; there are also reds, including some *crianzas*, but practically no *rosados*. There are also some sweet wines. The minimum strength is 11° for whites and *rosados*, 11.5° for reds and 15° for sweet wines. These are of two kinds: *vino dulce clásico* obtained from Malvasía and Moscatel grapes left to shrivel on the vine or partially dried by sunning; and *vino de licor* made by stopping the fermentation by the addition of alcohol. To be sold under a varietal name they have to contain 85 per cent of that variety.

**Production**
5,175 hls (1996)

Initially these wines were made by small growers who sold them in bulk, but now that technology is beginning to move in, more are being bottled and quality is on the up. They need to go a lot further, though, before anyone need seek them out. The two largest producers are Bodegas Montijo and S.A.T. Unión de Viticultores Valle de Orotava, which sells its wines under the name Valleoro.

## YCODEN-DAUTE-ISORA

**Geography**
The DO is on the western tip of the island with two distinct orientations: north and west. In the north there is a mountain range which at first descends steeply and then more gradually until it ends in a fairly flat, low plain. In the west it is much more irregular with mountains, ravines and cliffs. The best wines generally come from the higher vineyards.

**Climate**
This is one of the hottest parts of the island but it is impossible to characterize its climate as there are many different microclimates, depending on orientation and height, with west-facing vineyards being generally hotter and drier than those facing north, the former having a rainfall of 200–300 mm and the latter 400–500 mm. As

you get higher, the temperature goes down and the humidity up. Taking the area as a whole, the average temperature is 19°C with a maximum of 35°C.

## Soils
Here again there is considerable variation, but they are generally volcanic along the coast with some sand and clay inland.

## Grapes
Although there are many authorized varieties, the Listán Blanco accounts for 78 per cent of the vineyard and the Listán Negro for 20 per cent, leaving all the rest with 2 per cent.

Authorized red varieties: Bastardo Negro, Listán Negro, Malvasía Rosada, Moscatel Negro, Negramoll, Tintilla and Vijariego Negro.

Authorized white varieties: Bastardo Blanco, Bermejuela, Forastera Blanca, Gual, Listán Blanco, Malvasía, Moscatel, Pedro Ximénez, Sabro, Torrontés, Verdello and Vijariego.

## Planting
This is somewhat haphazard, with two local forms of cultivation, but some of the more recent vineyards have wires. Most of the vineyards are small and cannot be cultivated by machinery. The density is from 2,000 to 3,400 vines per ha.

## Vineyard area
The total is 1243 ha but only 650 ha are planted.

## Authorized yield
70 hl/ha, but the actual yield in the 1995 vintage was 8.75 hl/ha!

## Wines
Whites with a minimum of 11° account for 55 per cent, *rosados* with a minimum of 11.5° account for 30 per cent, and reds with a minimum of 12° account for 15 per cent of the table-wine production. All have a maximum strength of 14°. Most are sold as *jóvenes*. But in addition there is a small production of Malvasía Clásico made by sunning the grapes to produce a minimum of 45 grams of sugar per litre, with a minimum strength of 15° and a maximum of 22°.

## Production
About 2,250 hl.

Known in the past as Icod de los Vinos, this area has one of the longest wine-growing traditions in the islands and used to be noted for those rich Malvasías, which now form only a small part of its production. The tradition here has been for there to be a large number of very small family bodegas, making the wines as their grandfathers did and maturing them in chestnut casks until they were sold, but many of these have now disappeared. Although most of the bodegas are still quite small, they use modern technology to produce excellent wines. The *rosados* are particularly good. It is a very active, exciting and expanding area; in 1992 there were only seven bodegas registered with the Consejo Regulador, but three years later there were twenty-two. One of the leading producers is Bodegas Viñatigo, which produces a good white wine called Añaterve from a combination of Malvasía, Gual, Marmajuelo and Vijariego grapes, and an excellent Viñatigo Blanco Allier, oak-fermented but not over-oaked. The local cooperative, Viña Donia, has 125 members, with more than 600 ha between them, and is making good wines. This district is worth watching.

## EL HIERRO

This is the most westerly of the Canary Islands and also the smallest. For centuries, before the advent of Greenwich (after some fierce competition from other places, notably Paris), it had the distinction of being the site of zero longitude and has a long vinous history going back to the days of Canary sack; indeed, some of the wines it produces today may well show what that historic wine tasted like. Politically it is integrated with Santa Cruz de Tenerife and so its wines are generally considered as part of Tenerife. It has only 170 ha of registered vineyards and in 1995 production was only 648 hl. Although, unlike most of its bigger neighbours, it does have an export trade (to Venezuela), most of the wines are sold and drunk locally. The full details of the regulations are not, therefore, worth setting out. There are some very unusual white vine varieties, though, including the Vermejuela (or Bermejuela), Breval and Diego (local name for Vijariego), all of which may produce varietal wines. There are only three bodegas, which have modern equipment.

# LANZAROTE

## Geography

This is the most easterly of the islands: an astonishing place. In the 1730s there was a volcanic eruption that lasted for six years and left a vast expanse of black, solidified lava that grows nothing: the Timanfaya national park. While the DO covers the whole island, it is divided into three subzones: La Geria in the south, Tinajo/San Bartolomé in the middle, and Haría in the north. Its highest peak is La Peña del Chache, which only rises to 670 m. The vineyards are on the mountain slopes.

## Climate

Lanzarote being the nearest to Africa, this is unique. The temperature is very even: a mean minimum of 16°C and a mean maximum of 24°C with an overall mean of 23°C. The rainfall, averaging 150 mm, is very low; the rain falls irregularly, and when it does fall it is torrential, but the volcanic soil retains the moisture. The humidity is high, though, with a mean of 70 per cent, but when the east wind blows from Africa (and it can blow for a fortnight at a time) this goes down dramatically and the heat goes up. Even when this wind is not blowing, it is a very windy place. There are 2,700 hours of sunshine.

## Soils

Vines will not grow in the volcanic ash (*picón*), but the soils beneath it are fertile, ranging from sand to clay over limestone.

## Grapes

Authorized red varieties: Listán Negro (Negra Común) and Negramoll (Mulata).

Authorized white varieties: Burrablanca, Breval, Listán Blanco, Malvasía, Moscatel and Pedro Ximénez.

Other varieties, however, may be found in old vineyards. Malvasía is the dominant variety.

## Planting

This is extraordinary, and the only other vineyard practising anything remotely like it is Colares in Portugal. The vines have to be planted in the soil beneath the volcanic ash. To achieve this, great pits known as *hoyas* or trenches known as *sanchas pedrimentales* are dug. Some of these have to go down as much as six feet. One to three vines are planted in the bottom. Naturally this results in a very low density of planting: 200 to 600 vines per ha. It is then necessary to make a pile of stones, known as an *abrigo,* to protect the vines from the prevailing wind. Some of these are walls and others look like pyramids.

### Vineyard area
The total area of the zone is 3,567 ha but only 2,117 ha are in production.

### Authorized yield
35 hl/ha, but in practice this is never approached.

### Wines
All sorts are made: red (11 to 14.5°), *rosado* (11 to 14°), white (10.5 to 14.5°), *vino dulce clásico* (15 to 22°), *vino de licor* (15 to 22°) and even some sparklers. *Vino dulce clásico* is made by leaving the Malvasía or Moscatel grapes on the vine until they are practically raisins, or by sunning them. *Vino de licor* is made by stopping the fermentation by the addition of alcohol.

### Production
6,112 hl (1995) but normally higher.

This island is certainly unique in its wines and in the way it grows them. It is not surprising that many of the vineyards are forty years old or more. Planting is so labour-intensive that new vineyards are only likely because it is the traditional family occupation and nothing else will grow. It can be no wonder that the wines are expensive. Nowadays labour is drawn off into the flourishing tourist trade; but tourists drink wine. Most of the wine is white, and most of it is fairly or very sweet, from Malvasía grapes with some Moscatel. The many small proprietors used to vinify their grapes individually using old-fashioned methods, and the quality was generally not such as would appeal today. This was one of the homes of Canary sack. Such wines are still made, but now there are modern bodegas making lighter, more modern wines. The principal grape is still the Malvasía, though, and when this is vinified to give a dry wine the results are rather unusual: there is a striking degree of fragrance but a degree of sheer bulk which, even at 12°, detracts from the finesse. Nevertheless these wines make agreeable drinking and there are some good sweet and semi-sweet ones.

Two substantial bodegas are El Grifo, a family bodega over a hundred years old that led the way forward, and Bodegas Mozaga, which dates from 1880. El Grifo produces a good Moscatel matured on the *solera* system: Moscatel de Ana. Mozaga has a rival matured in the same way: Moscatel Mozaga, together with a good Malvasía Seco, a varietal Diego and a red made from Listán Negro.

## LA PALMA

### Geography
Like all the Canary Islands this is volcanic, but more volcanic than most, as the Teneguía volcano erupted as recently as 1971. It is dominated by La Caldera de Taburiente, an enormous volcanic crater. The vineyards are in three zones: Fuencaliente in the south, Hoyo de Mazo in the centre, and Norte de La Palma in the north. The vineyards are generally around the coasts, planted at altitudes from 200 to 1,200 m. The great rival crop is bananas and the best bodegas will not buy grapes from banana growers, not through prejudice but because the bananas take the goodness out of the soil and starve the grapes.

### Climate
The average annual temperature is 18–20°C, with a minimum of 13–16°C and a maximum of 23–24°C, but this gives only a small part of the story. There are wide variations and many microclimates. The humid north-east trade winds bring rain, particularly at altitudes between 500 and 1,500 m. At elevations below 300 m and on east facing slopes the climate is drier and can be semi-arid on the coastal strip. Fuencaliente is the most arid part of all. Drip irrigation is allowed.

### Soils
These are volcanic and rich.

### Grapes
Authorized red varieties: Almuñeco (Listán Negro), Bastardo Negro, Malvasía Rosada, Moscatel Negro, Negramoll and Tintilla.

Authorized white varieties: Albillo, Bastardo Blanco, Bermejuela, Bujariego, Burrablanca, Forastera Blanca, Gual, Listán Blanco, Malvasía, Moscatel, Pedro Ximénez, Sabro, Torrontés and Verdello.

Many of these, however, are little planted. The Listán Blanco accounts for 46 per cent, the Negramoll 41 per cent, the Malvasía 2 per cent and all the others 11 per cent between them, but the Gual and the Verdello are officially favoured. The Listán Blanco is not and its spread is discouraged. Part of its production, however, is eaten as table grapes.

## Planting
Some of the vineyards, especially in Fuencaliente, have to be planted in the way already described for Lanzarote. In the Norte de La Palma the planting is more normal though very varied: bushes, wires and even pergolas. Some of the vineyards are on terraces supported by dry stone walls. Generally vines are planted wherever they will grow.

## Vineyard area
The total area is 1,666 ha but only 592 ha are registered with the Consejo Regulador as being in production.

## Authorized yield
56 hl/ha, but the actual yield is very much less.

## Wines
Whites (11 to 14.5°), *rosados* (11 to 13°), reds (12 to 14°), Malvasía *clásico* (15 to 22°), Malvasía *seco* (14 to 16°) and *dulce* (15 to 22°). Wines sold as varietal (mostly Malvasía and Sabro) must have at least 85 per cent of the named variety. Malvasía *clásico* is made by late gathering or sunning and must have at least 45 grams residual sugar per litre. Two-thirds of the wine is white and almost a third red, with very little *rosado* and only small amounts of the others. In addition to these, a wine unique to the Canary Isles is grown in the area Norte de La Palma: *vino de tea*, similar to that described on p. 344.

## Production
5,440 hls (1996).

This very beautiful island is well known to holiday-makers, who drink their fair share of its wines. Agriculturally it is by no means a monoculture and has flourishing trades in bananas and avocado pears. Of the wines, whites predominate and come in all degrees of sweetness, grown mostly in Fuencaliente. The best reds are grown in Hoyo de Mazo and some of the *jóvenes* are made by carbonic maceration. The general standard is high and the sweet Malvasías can be delicious. This is helped by the maturity of the vines, 90 per cent of which are over forty years old. These fall within the ambit of the DO but in practice never get the certification as they are not bottled but are sold in bulk at the door to all comers. They have a strong local following and are said to be good for you.

## Principal bodegas

### Llanovid Sociedad Cooperativa
Founded in 1948, this cooperative is the largest producer. It is modern and well equipped. It sells its wines under the trade mark Teneguia. Most are whites, including a range of varietals, but it makes the others as well, apart from *tea*.

### S.A.T. Unión de Viticultores de la Villa de Mazo
This smaller but equally modern cooperative was founded in 1986 and has red wines as its principal production.

### Bodegas Carballo
A small, privately owned modern bodega, founded in 1990, that produces mostly whites, with some Malvasías.

## OTHER WINES

There are two official districts growing table wines (VdlT) and both may soon graduate to DO status.

Gran Canaria El Monte covers the whole of the island of Gran Canaria. All the vineyards are in the north-east of the island, in areas formerly known as Santa Brígida and San Mateo, where there are 450 ha of vineyard growing the usual bewildering variety of vines in volcanic soil. Red wines have a minimum strength of 12°, *rosados* and whites 11.5°, *vinos de licór* from 18 to 22°. Much of the production is *rosado* but the most highly regarded wine is the so-called Tinto del Monte (Mountain Red), which is notably robust. The best known producer is Bodegas San Juan del Mocanál.

La Gomera also covers the whole island, where there are 350 ha of vineyard in the north-west, likewise growing the usual bewildering variety of vines in volcanic soil. It has the same minimum strengths of 12° for reds and 11.5° for *rosados* and whites, but the most notable wines are powerful whites made from the Forastera grape – anything up to 15°. The reds tend to be lightened by the addition of white grapes.

# 12

# *Cava*

━━━━━━━

## Geography
Cavas are made in several of the leading wine-growing areas of
Spain but 95 per cent come from Cataluña, where they originated.
To satisfy the European DO laws, however, the precise vineyards
where they are grown have to be delineated. At the moment there
are in all 159 authorized municipal areas. These include: in Cat-
aluña, Province of Gerona, 5; Province of Barcelona, 63; Province
of Tarragona, 52; Province of Lérida, 12. In Aragón, Province of
Zaragoza, 2. In Navarra, 2. In La Rioja, Province of Logroño, 18.
In País Vasco, Province of Alava, 3. In the Province of Valencia, 1.
In the Province of Badajoz, 1. There is also a provisional one in the
Province of Burgos. The capital of the Cava trade is San Sadurní
de Noya (or San Sadurní d'Anoia) in the area that makes Penedés
table wines.

## Climate
As the vineyards are split between so many provinces and so many
areas within those provinces, it is impossible to generalize save to
say that grapes for Cavas are grown in the cooler sites and those
that produce the lightest wines within those areas.

## Grapes
Authorized white varieties: Macabeo (Viura), Parellada, Xarel.lo,
Chardonnay and Subirat-Parent (Malvasía Francesca).
   Authorized red varieties: Garnacha and Monastrell.
   Experimental red variety: Pinot Noir.
   In Cataluña the traditional mix is of the first three named white
varieties, which are officially considered to be the principal ones,
while in the rest of Spain there is more Viura. Macabeo contributes
freshness and acidity, Xarel.lo gives body and Paralleda gives

fragrance and finesse. The red varieties are used in making *rosados* (often sold with the French word *rosé*), save that Pinot Noir may be pressed quickly and used in white wines, as it is in Champagne, but this is at present very rare. There is much heated argument over the use of Chardonnay: the traditionalists claim that it is a foreign grape that will detract from the unique style of their very successful Cavas, which do not attempt to be Champagne but which are their own thing; the modernists say that it is a world variety that will improve the wines and add to their appeal.

### Planting
Traditional *en vaso* viticulture is giving way to growing on wires. Macabeo and Parellada vines are sometimes grown on the Royat principle, but Xarel.lo on the Guyot. There must be between 1,500 and 3,500 vines per ha.

### Vineyard area
31,897 ha.

### Authorized yield
White 80 hl/ha, red 53 hl/ha. An increase of 25 per cent may be allowed, but above that the must may not be used for Cava.

### Wines
The method of viniculture is essentially the same as that used in France for making Champagne. The wine has to spend at least nine months in bottle on its lees before it is disgorged and must achieve a carbon dioxide gas pressure of four atmospheres. The alcoholic strength of the finished wine lies between 10.8° and 12.8°. The wines are made in six different degrees of sweetness, according to sugar content:

| | |
|---|---|
| *Extra Brut*: | less than 6 gm/litre |
| *Brut*: | 6–15 gm/litre |
| *Extra Seco*: | 12–20 gm/litre |
| *Seco*: | 17–35 gm/litre |
| *Semi-Seco*: | 33–50 gm/litre |
| *Dulce*: | over 50 gm/litre. |

In practice the wines are usually matured for well over the minimum period (though one noted house has recently been questioned in this regard) and may well have as many as five years, or occasionally even more, in bottle.

**Production**

1,146,700 hl (1993).

Cava is undoubtedly one of the world's great sparkling wines and its popularity has been increasing every year. In 1980 there were eighty firms producing it; by 1994 there were 254. Spain is now the second largest producer of sparkling wines after France and most of them are Cavas. There were early attempts to produce wine in Spain on the model of Champagne, but these failed. The breakthrough came in 1872. Josep Raventós i Fatjó, who was born in 1825, got together with a group of friends, known as the Seven Sages, to try to create a good sparkling wine. He was already a leading wine grower and head of his family bodega Codorníu. In 1872 he laid down the first wine in his cellar for bottle fermentation and in 1879 the first six dozen bottles were sold. They were highly successful and by the time he died in 1885 he had effected further improvements with the aid of a French enologist. His descendants are still leading shippers.

But why Cava? The word *cava* means cellar, as does bodega, but a cava has to be underground. At first the wine was called *Champán* – Champagne – or, in Catalán, *Xampán,* but not unnaturally the French Champagne growers objected. At the time it was not as iniquitous as it may now seem, as the name was used generically for sparkling wine all over the world, and still is, for instance, in the USA. The first action was taken in England, where a criminal prosecution failed but a case in the Chancery Division, brought in 1959, succeeded in preventing the sale of any wine as 'Spanish Champagne'. However, things went on as before elsewhere until Spain joined the EEC in 1986, when the name had to be dropped throughout the Community and a new name, Cava, was found. In 1989 it was recognized by the Community, but to achieve this it had to have a geographical basis, and this was done by delimiting the areas in which it had traditionally been produced. The vast majority are in Cataluña, and of these most are in Penedés, but the name of Penedés cannot be used on Cava labels as it is a geographical origin limited to table wines. All Cava is made, however, by the method that used to be universally known as the *méthode champenoise* or, in Spanish, as the *método champañés.* Unfortunately – and perhaps rather churlishly, as it accurately described a method of preparation rather than a geographical origin – the French objected to this, too, and it had to go. Now it has to be called the *método tradicional.*

CAVA

In other words Cava is made in exactly the same way as Champagne, but in a different country and using different grape varieties. The grapes are picked early so that they have plenty of acidity, and often early in the morning before the heat of day. Then they are brought in for pressing as quickly as possible, to avoid oxidation, and are pressed quickly and very gently, often with the most modern presses using a continuously moving rubber band. The must is cold-fermented to produce base wines, which must have an alcoholic strength of between 9.5 and 11.5°. These wines are then blended the following year to produce *cupadas* (*cuvées*) of the various styles that the shipper needs for each of his Cavas. Sometimes, as in Champagne, reserve wines are added to form part of the *cupada*; these are older wines put on one side. The next task is to put the bubbles in. This is done by adding to each bottle a small amount of *licor de tiraje* (in French *liqueur de tirage*), which contains yeasts and grape sugar in wine. This causes a second fermentation inside the bottle, producing carbon dioxide which is dissolved in the wine: the bubbles. Four grams of sugar are needed to give the right pressure; in practice a little more is used, but the alcoholic strength of the wine must not be increased by more than 1.5°. The bottles are tightly sealed, originally using a cork held down with a strong steel clip or *agrafe*, but now more usually with a plastic insert held in by a crown cork. The giveaway (as with Champagne) is whether the top of the bottle has a lip for the crown cork to fit on to. Unfortunately, in addition to the bubbles this fermentation also creates a deposit, which would disfigure the wine if it were left in. However, the wine has to be left in contact with this yeasty deposit for at least nine months, and the best wines are left for a good deal longer, often for several years. This results in an autolysis of the yeast, absorbing flavouring elements, mostly amino acids, into the wine, which gives all wines made in this way a characteristic yeasty aroma.

When the contact is deemed to have been long enough, the deposit is removed. This is done by a process called *removido* (in French *remuage*). Various stories are told about how it originated, the most likely one being an adaptation of Mme Clicquot's kitchen table. Be that as it may, the bottles are inserted into holes in *pupitres*, literally meaning 'desks', and it is easy to see why they are so called: they consist of two heavy wooden boards with holes in, joined together at the top, forming an inverted V. Bottles are put

359

into the holes, at first practically horizontal, and are shaken by hand, which loosens the deposit on the wall of the bottle. This is done every day for several weeks and the bottle is moved each time into a slightly more vertical position so that it finishes up with the deposit down on the cork. A few of the very small bodegas still use this process, but nowadays it can be done much more quickly by the use of techniques invented in Cataluña and now rapidly being adopted in Champagne. The first technique was the *girasol* (literally sunflower), which is a metal cage containing about sixty bottles, initially at an angle of 45 degrees; this can be moved a little every day, which shakes the sediment down on to the corks in exactly the same way but with much less effort. The second method is the *giropalette*, which again operates with a large number of bottles, stored in a number of containers, which are moved every six hours in a pattern controlled by a computer. This is quicker, just as good, and involves even less effort, but the machine is relatively expensive.

The next and final step is the *degüelle* (in French *dégorgement*) to disgorge the deposit from the bottle. The necks of the bottles are dipped into a freezing solution. The bottles are then turned the right way up, the cork removed, and the sediment, encased in a little block of ice, blows out. At the same time the *licor de expedición* (in French *liqueur d'expédition*) is added. This may contain a number of things, and each bodega keeps its exact formulation secret, but essentially it consists of wine, sugar and perhaps a little alcohol. The amount of sugar added at this stage determines the style of the wine (see above). But the alcohol may not be increased by more than 0.5°. Small producers do this manually, but in the big bodegas the whole process is automated, the bottles being picked up at one end of the line and emerging at the other with their final corks (*tapones de expedición*) held in by a wire *bozal* (literally muzzle).

The most popular styles in Spain used to be the *seco* and the *semi-seco* but now there is a general move towards the *extra brut* and the *brut*. Wine snobs in particular eschew anything sweet. But they miss a lot. A small degree of sweet, softening down the flavour of the wine, can be attractive, especially in a northern climate, and wines with a degree of sweet, even *semi-seco*, often go down very well when drunk alone at a party. The *dulce* wines are perhaps most suitable for drinking with a Christmas pudding. Cava is best served, like Champagne, in flute glasses and, like Champagne, chilled, but definitely not frozen; if a Cava is too cold essential aromas and complex flavours are entirely masked. But Cava is not Champagne and does not pretend to be. The wines should be judged on their own, very considerable, merits.

## Some leading bodegas

### Albet i Noya
See Penedés. Vines are grown organically at their Can Vendrell estate at Costers de l'Ordal in Alt Penedés. The three main varieties are used together with Chardonnay in some of the blends, for instance in the *brut*, which contains 10 per cent along with equal quantities of the three principal varieties. *Semi-seco* and *dulce* wines are given a year in bottle on the lees, and two to four years for the remainder. They are disgorged by hand and sold immediately.

### Bodegas Bilbaínas
See Rioja. Although most famous for its Riojas, this bodega has long made a good Cava called Royal Carlton from a grape mix of equal quantities of Malvasía and Viura.

### Can Feixes
See Penedés. This bodega makes excellent Cavas sold under the name Huguet. The grape mix is 57 per cent Parellada, 23 per cent Macabeo and 20 per cent Chardonnay. This rather unusual mix gives the wines an exceptional degree of finesse.

### Can Ráfols dels Caus
See Penedés. The Cavas, which are good and are sold under the trade name Gran Caus, are unusual in containing minor proportions of Chenin Blanc. For instance, the 1993 *extra brut* had the grape mix 50 per cent Xarel.lo, 40 per cent Chardonnay and 10 per cent Chenin.

### Castell de Vilarnau
This bodega in San Sadurní de Noya makes only Cavas and is a subsidiary of the great sherry and brandy house, González Byass. The Cavas are of exceptional quality. The grape mix in the 1988 Brut Gran Reserva was 60 per cent Macabeo, 35 per cent Parellada and 5 per cent Xarel.lo.

### Castellblanch
A renowned Cava house in San Sadurní de Noya, using the names

Castellblanch, Gran Castell and Canals & Nubiola. Founded in 1906, it became part of the Freixenet group in 1984. It has a vineyard holding of 250 ha. The three principal grape varieties are used in varying proportions, typically 40 per cent each of Macabeo and Parellada with 20 per cent Xarel.lo. The Brut Zero, which has two to two and a half years on its lees, has a grape mix of 30 per cent Macabeo, 60 per cent Parellada and 10 per cent Xarel.lo, and is notable for its exceptional length. The top Don Lustros has four years on its lees. The wines are very good.

### Cavas Agusti Torelló/Torelló Llopart
The roots of the Torelló family as wine growers are said to go back as far as 1395, but Agustí Torelló Mata started making Cava in 1950 and entered the market in 1979. He is still in charge, assisted by his children, and it is very much a family bodega. The estate and 110 ha vineyard, Can Marti de Baix, are 5 km outside San Sadurní de Noya in the direction of Barcelona. Only their own grapes are used. A full range of very good Cavas is produced from the three traditional grape varieties and sold under the names Torelló, Agustí Torelló Mata, Aliguer and, at the top, Kripta, this latter being sold in a special 'traditional' bottle based on the shape of an amphora, which looks wonderful but has the disadvantage that it cannot be stood up; it is very expensive.

### Cavas Castillo de Perelada/Cava del Ampurdán
See Ampurdán-Costa Brava. This very reputable Cava house had the unfortunate distinction of being the supplier of the wines that were banned from sale in England as 'Spanish Champagne' following the litigation referred to above. In addition to Castillo de Perelada it uses the name Gran Claustro for its top wine. Most of the wines are made from the traditional grapes but there is also a varietal Chardonnay and the Gran Claustro 1992 contained 30 per cent Chardonnay.

### Cavas Hill
See Penedés. It makes a complete range of good Cavas using the traditional grapes.

### Cavas Llopart
This family bodega in San Sadurní de Noya with 25 ha of vineyard has been making Cava since 1887 and uses the trade names Llopart, Integral, La Mesa del Rey and Leopardi. Its wines are highly

regarded and sometimes include small proportions of Chardonnay in addition to the traditional varieties.

### Cavas Recaredo
Founded in 1924, a family bodega in San Sadurní de Noya with 26 ha of vineyard. Its Cavas are well regarded.

### Cavas y Vinos Torre Oria
See Utiel-Requena. From a rather improbable part of Spain, this bodega produces some good Cavas with some Macabeo, mostly from Parellada and Malvasía. There is an unusual semi-seco Rosado Extra.

### Cellers Grimau-Gol
See Penedés. This young bodega has already established a fine reputation for its Cavas, vinified from the traditional varieties, which it sells under the name Duart de Siò.

### Chandon
See Penedés. No one knows more about making Champagne than do Moët & Chandon. This, the Spanish branch of their widespread empire, set up at Sant Cugat de Sesgarrigues, makes good Cavas under the names Chandon and Masía Chandon. It aims at making good Cavas, not imitation Champagnes, and so uses the traditional varieties with only a little Chardonnay. On the export markets, no doubt to avoid chaos, it uses the name Torre de Gall.

### Codorníu
The seminal part played by Josep Raventós i Fatjó in creating Cava has already been described, and happily his bodega, now run by his descendants, remains a pre-eminent producer. It is not known when the Codorníu family started to grow wine, but in 1551 Jaime Codorníu left an established business to his heir. Just over a hundred years later, María Anna Codorníu married Miguel Raventós and the present owners are all descended from that union. When Josep Raventós decided to make sparkling wine, he was taking a huge risk. No one could be sure that really good sparkling wine could be made or that it would sell well if it were. The investment was enormous, beginning with digging vast underground cellars, but it paid off magnificently.

Happily, the family is as inspired in its judgement of art and architecture as it is in wine. When Josep's son Manuel decided to build a great new bodega in 1898 he tried to get the great Catalan architect Antoni Gaudí to design it, but Gaudí was too busy elsewhere and one of his rivals, Josep María Puig i Cadafalch did it instead, producing a range of art nouveau buildings that is absolutely outstanding, in a landscaped setting. It is now a National Monument. He was one of a group of Catalan architects designing some of the most interesting buildings in the world at that time, so that the province has become as much a place of pilgrimage for students of architecture as it has for lovers of wine. And the first advertising posters were painted by Casas, Utrillo and Junyent. That is flair!

The underground cellars are now said to be the largest in the world, stretching for 24 km on five levels – and still growing. It goes without saying that the wine making is immaculate. It begins in the vineyards. They have 1,200 ha of their own and are supplied by 1,000 growers, who receive a complete technical backup and are carefully supervised. No wine is bought in. The grapes are mostly pressed with the latest Italian Sernagiotto presses, but only the first, free-run juice is used for Cava, the rest being sold off to wine makers. All the traditional grape varieties are used, but Codorníu is uninhibited in the use of Chardonnay; for instance, the excellent Anna de Codorníu is made from 90 per cent Chardonnay and 10 per cent Perellada, and in 1998 they increased the proportion of Chardonnay in Cuvée Raventós from 70 to 86 per cent. Their excellent Brut Chardonnay, which is very Champagne-like, is almost wholly Chardonnay. This liking for Chardonnay has brought them into a strongly argued conflict with some of their rivals. The question is whether Cava should follow its uniquely Spanish style or go international. There is no easy answer and the market place will decide. As another step, Codorníu has developed its own clone of Parellada, called Montonega, and giving extra fragrance. The business is also experimenting with Pinot Noir.

The must is vacuum-filtered and then fermented in stainless steel at 15 to 18°C. The Cava is then made by the *método tradicional* described above. The wine is kept on its lees for one to five years, depending on the quality being made. The Codorniús were pioneers of mechanical disgorgement.

There is an unusually wide range of excellent wines, backed by a stock of 100 million bottles. In order of price, from the cheapest to the most expensive, these include: Gran Crémant Brut, Extra Brut, 1551 Brut Nature, Cuvée Raventós, Anna de Codorníu Brut Nature, Non Plus Ultra Brut Nature, Gran Codorníu and Jaume Codorníu. A further range is sold under the name Mas D'Anoia.

The group includes the Cava houses of Masía Bach and Rondel as well as Raimat (see below), and has an operation in California.

### Coll de Juny

Founded at San Sadurní de Noya in 1918, this bodega produces a complete range of well-regarded Cavas under the names Dama, Montesquius and Santacana Artesanal. The traditional grape varieties are used, the mix for Dama 1993 *brut* being 50 per cent Parellada, 30 per cent Macabeo and 20 per cent Xarel.lo.

### Cooperativa Vinícola del Penedés/Covides

See Penedés. Some of the wine from this cooperative is supplied to other Cava houses, but it also makes its own very good Cavas under the names Duc de Foix and Xenius. Some are made using the traditional grape varieties, but Chardonnay is also available from the members and the Duc de Foix Reserva Especial Brut 1992 was made from equal parts of Chardonnay and the three traditional varieties.

### Ferrer Mata

This family bodega in Subirats, founded in 1988, buys its wine in, made from the traditional varieties. Its Cavas, sold under the name Mas Ferrer, are well regarded, especially the Mas Ferrer Reserva Familiar Brut Nature.

### Freixa Rigau

This is also a family bodega, in Capmany, dating from the 1940s. It produces good Cavas under the name Oliveda.

### Freixenet

There are two great rivals in the market for Cavas: Freixenet and Codorníu. Both produce very complete ranges that rival each other for quality and value. For anyone arriving at San Sadurní de Noya by train, this is the first bodega they see, as its impressive buildings are next to the railway station. It is the leading Cava exporter and, with its subsidiaries, is the largest sparkling wine maker in the world. Still family-owned, it was founded by Pedro Ferrer Bosch at the beginning of the twentieth century. He was the youngest son of a family that had owned an estate called La Freixenada (in Catalan a plantation of ash trees) in the Alt Penedés since the thirteenth century. His wife was Dolores Sala Vivé, whose grandfather had founded a wine company which gave a basis for the new enterprise, in which she joined him. It was wonderfully successful. From the beginning it went in for imaginative advertising and was one of the first to use television. A galaxy of stars took part in its campaigns, including such names as Gene Kelly, Plácido Domingo, José Carreras and Paul Newman.

From the beginning the emphasis was on quality and the *método tradicional*, using the traditional grape varieties. The use of Chardonnay is generally disapproved of, though some (20 per cent) *is* used in the top, superb, Reserva Real. The range includes Carta Nevada, which became instantly popular when it was launched in 1941 in white frosted-glass bottles. Its most popular wine today, especially on the export markets, is Cordón Negro, sold in black frosted-glass bottles and made from 40 per cent Parellada and 30 per cent each of Macabeo and Xarel.lo. The Vintage Brut 1991 (made only in good years, so there was no 1992 or 1993) is made from 40 per cent Xarel.lo, 35 per cent Macabeo and 25 per cent Parellada. Cuvée D.S., a delicate and subtle wine, is named after Doña Dolores Sala, who was the wine maker and was killed by the communists in the Civil War; a very good *gran reserva*, it is made from the three traditional white varieties in the proportions 40 per cent each of Macabeo and Xarel.lo with 20 per cent Parellada. The Macabeo is selected for high acidity and the wine has five years in bottle before disgorgement, giving an excellent result. A new development is Monastrell Xarel.lo, made from equal quantities of the two grapes. The Monastrell is, of course, a black grape but careful wine making (as when using the black Pinot Noir in Champagne) results in there being only the least trace of colour, but the Monastrell is very evident in the nose and flavour, producing a fascinating and unique Cava. The very top of the range is Reserva Real, mentioned above.

The Freixenet empire is spread world-wide. In Penedés it includes Segura Viudas and Castellblanch, acquired in 1984 after the disappropriation of Rumasa, and René Barbier (quite separate from the company of the same name in Priorato). In the United States it has an estate in Sonoma. In France it actually owns one of the oldest

Champagne houses: Henri Abelé. It also has wine interests in Mexico and offices in many countries, including England. Its subsidiaries are left to go their own ways and make their own, quite distinct and competing, ranges of wines.

### Gramona

See Penedés. The Cavas produced by this family bodega, and made from the classic grapes, are amongst the best. There is a complete range and even the cheapest wine – Tira Extra Brut – is matured for eighteen months. The Gran Reserva Brut is made from 30 per cent Macabeo, 40 per cent Xarel.lo and 30 per cent Parellada. Tres Lustros Nature is made from 70 per cent Xarel.lo and given five years in bottle. The top wine, Celler Batlle, is a *brut* wine made from 80 per cent Xarel.lo and 20 per cent Macabeo and given at least six years in bottle. It is named after Doña Pilar Batlle Gramona, who was the mother of the third generation of the family. The Cavas from this bodega keep unusually well in bottle.

### Bodegas Inviosa

See Ribera del Guadiana. This is rather an oddball, in Extremadura, right across from Penedés in the west of Spain. It makes a Cava from Macabeo, given eighteen months in bottle and sold under the name Bonaval. It is quite unlike the usual run of Cavas but very good.

### Juvé y Camps

See Penedés. It is perhaps rather unfair to ask wine growers whose wines they would drink in a restaurant that did not have their own. If you ask Cava producers, various names are mentioned, all of which are included in this section; but one name that *always* comes up is Juvé y Camps. The wines are very well made from the traditional varieties, kept on the lees for thirty months to five years, and sold in numbered bottles. A typical blend is 40 per cent each of Macabeo and Parellada with 20 per cent Xarel.lo. The Reserva de Familia is especially worth seeking out.

### Langa Hermanos

See Calatayud. One does not normally look to Calatayud for a Cava, but those from this bodega, sold under the name J. Langa, are very good.

## Josep Masachs

See Penedés. The Cavas are well regarded, especially the Brut de Brut *gran reserva*. Other names used are Carolina and Louis de Vernier. Masachs wines are made entirely from their own grapes but grapes are bought in for the Louis de Vernier range.

## Marqués de Monistrol

See Penedés. This large and successful Cava house makes good wines, using the traditional varieties. In 1996 it was acquired by the great Rioja house Berberana. The *extra brut* Gran Tradición, made from 30 per cent each of Parellada and Xarel.lo with 40 per cent Macabeo, is unusually good, as is the *rosado brut*, made from Monastrell and Parellada. The excellent top wines are sold as Gran Reserva de la Familia.

## Mascaró

See Penedés. Although Antonio Mascaró Carbonell is most famous for his brandies, everything he makes is good, and not least his Cavas, which are certainly amongst the very best. They are made from his own grapes together with some bought in from other growers, but no musts or wines are bought in. The traditional varieties are used, with an unusually high proportion of Parellada.

## Masía Bach

See Penedés. The Codorníu group leaves Masía Bach to make an entirely separate range of wines, including very good Cavas. The Brut Nature is typically made of 35 per cent Macabeo, 25 per cent Parellada, 10 per cent Xarel.lo, 10 per cent Chardonnay and 20 per cent Reserva wines, while the Brut Chardonnay is 85 per cent Chardonnay with 5 per cent each of Macabeo, Xarel.lo and Parellada.

## Masía Vallformosa

See Penedés. Good Cavas are made, particularly the Brut and Brut Nature. The Gran Reserva Brut is a well-matured wine of considerable character.

## Antonio Mestres Sagües

This bodega in San Sadurní de Noya has 88 ha of vineyards and began to make Cavas in 1928. The wines are well regarded and a complete range is sold under names that include Clos Damiana, Clos de Nostre Senyor Coquet Mestres and Mas Via.

## Moli Coloma/Cavas Sumarroca

This family bodega, founded in 1986 at Subirats with 60 ha of vineyard, has already established a very good reputation for its Cavas, sold under the names Sumarroca and Claverol. They are made from the three traditional varieties together with Chardonnay. The very good *gran reserva* Sumarroca Chardonnay contains 15 per cent Parellada.

## Heretat Mont-Rubí

See Penedés. The Cavas are good.

## Nadal Cava

This family-owned bodega, established in 1943 at El Plá del Penedés, has 110 ha of vineyard planted with the three traditional varieties. It makes only Cavas and they are good, especially the *brut* and *extra brut* wines.

## Parxet

See Alella. Just up the coast from Penedés, this bodega is a good example of small being beautiful. Its Cavas are certainly good. Parxet Brut Nature is made from 40 per cent Pansá Blanca (a clone of Xarel.lo) and 30 per cent each of Macabeo and Parellada. Parxet Brut Nature Chardonnay is 80 per cent Chardonnay with 10 per cent each of Macabeo and Parellada. Parxet Rosé Brut is a particularly good *rosado* made from Monastrell. The bodega is rather given to original packaging and the Parxet Aniversario (an excellent Chardonnay) comes in a silver-coloured bottle. There is a complete range of styles.

## Raimat

See Costers del Segre. A subsidiary of the great Codorníu company, Raimat makes Cavas every bit as good as its parent – but different. Partly this is the result of an uninhibited use of Chardonnay. There are four wines: Brut Nature, made from 30 per cent Chardonnay, 40 per cent Macabeo and 30 per cent Xarel.lo; Blanc de Blancs, made from 30 per cent Chardonnay, 40 per cent Macabeo, 20 per cent Xarel.lo and 10 per cent Parellada; Chardonnay, made from 85 per cent Chardonnay and 15 per cent Parellada; and Gran Brut, made from 40 per cent Pinot Noir and 60 per cent Chardonnay. They are all amongst the very best Cavas.

## Josep María Raventós i Blanc

See Penedés. Raventós uses the traditional varieties plus Chardonnay to produce a range of very good Cavas sold under the bodega name, also Clos del Sarral and L'Hereu.

## Joan Raventós Rosell

See Penedés. This Cava house also is not shy of using Chardonnay, often in quite high proportions, which gives their very good wines an additional degree of finesse. The wine at the top of the range, Brut Reserva Heretat, which is made typically from 50 per cent Macabeo, 30 per cent Parellada and 20 per cent Chardonnay and matured for at least four years, is well worth seeking out.

## Rimarts (Ricard M. de Simon)

This small bodega which started up at San Sadurní de Noya in the 1980s has already established a good reputation for its Cavas, most of which are made using the traditional varieties, but the Reserva Especial was made from 70 per cent Chardonnay with 10 per cent each of the traditonal varieties.

## Rondel

A subsidiary of the Codorníu group, created by them at Cervelló in 1949. It is technologically advanced and produces a range of popular Cavas under the names Rondel and Parnas.

## Roura

See Alella. Apart from its table wines, this young bodega also makes good Cavas, particularly the Roura Reserva Brut Nature.

## Rovellats

This family bodega, now in its third generation, was founded at San Marti Sarroca in the Alt Penedés in 1934 and began making Cava in 1942. It has 210 ha of vineyard planted with the three traditional varieties and Chardonnay, which is not, however, used in all the blends. It is housed in a fifteenth-century *masía* which has grown vines for 500 years. The Brut Imperial is made from the traditional varieties and matured for at least two years. The Brut Nature, with a similar grape mix, is matured for at least four years. The Masía S. XV Gran Reserva contains 5 per cent Chardonnay. The excellent Chardonnay Brut Nature is made from 85 per cent Chardonnay and 5 per cent each of Macabeo, Xarel.lo and Parellada. The wines are good and the Masía S. XV especially so.

## Sadeve/Vinos y Cavas Naveran

See Penedés. Its Cavas, sold under the name Naveran, are well regarded and include a varietal Chardonnay, Chardonnay de Naveran Patricia. Its Brut Nature is made from 20 per cent Macabeo, 40 per cent Xarel.lo, 20 per cent Parellada and 20 per cent Chardonnay.

## Manuel Sancho e Hijas

See Penedés. Its Cavas, sold under the name Mont Marçal, are well regarded.

## Segura Viudas/Conde de Caralt

See Penedés. Although a member of the great Freixenet group, this bodega in San Sadurní de Noya is run entirely independently. It is one of the great names in Cava, or rather two of the great names, as it has two ranges, sold as Segura Viudas and Conde de Caralt. Both are of exceptional quality, the wines sold under the Segura Viudas label tending to be the more expensive. It produces no cheap wines, though, and concentrates on the top end of the market. Although the Conde de Caralt range includes a varietal Chardonnay *brut*, the three traditional varieties are relied on for nearly all the wines. Any of these wines is worth seeking out, especially the Segura Viudas Aria and their Heredad Reserva. Segura Viudas also supply buyers' own brands including excellent Cavas for Marks & Spencer and for Tanners of Shrewsbury.

## Jaume Serra

See Penedés. Good Cavas are made from the traditional varieties.

## Signat

A small bodega at Alella, founded as recently as 1987, producing Cavas that are very highly regarded.

## Jané Ventura

See Penedés. Good and reliable Cavas, especially the Brut Nature, made from the traditional varieties.

## Pere Ventura

See Penedés. The Cavas are very good and the Brut Imperial is well worth seeking out, even though it is not top of the range. It is made from 35 per cent Chardonnay, 35 per cent Xarel.lo and 30 per cent Parellada. More exotic are Llàgrima d'Or, made from 35 per cent each of Macabeo and Parellada with 30 per cent Xarel.lo, and Coupatge d'Honor, made from 45 per cent Chardonnay, 30 per cent Xarel.lo and 25 per cent Parellada.

# 13

# *A Guide to Vines*

———

Three things determine what a wine will taste like: the variety or varieties of the grapes used; where and how they are grown; and the way the wine is made. The first thing to do in assessing a wine in a blind tasting is to try and identify the grape. Of course it is more difficult if wines from more than one variety are blended together, as often happens, but even then one variety tends to predominate and, having identified that, one can often go on to see what has been put with it. But this is not an essay on blind tasting. The point is that the style of a vine often shines through and it helps to know what vines are grown where. The other factors matter enormously, too. On different soils and in different climates, the same variety of vine gives very different wines, yet they still have something in common, like members of a family. And a wine maker can use grapes from the same vine variety to produce wines that are totally different in style and in colour, depending on how he vinifies them.

Vines are very complicated things. There are often many different clones of the same variety, producing wines that vary conspicuously in style and in quality. Quantity and quality seldom go together. Some clones are better for the one, others for the other; and the site, the method of pruning and, not least, the weather affect both. Vines are very adaptable, too. When they are transplanted they try to adapt themselves to the new conditions. The Spanish Tempranillo – certainly one of the world's best black grape vines – grows thicker skins in hotter places and is often given different names. In Ribera del Duero it becomes Tinto del País and in Toro it becomes Tinto de Toro – though some would deny that this is in fact the same vine. And many authorities suggest that the Tempranillo may be the Burgundian Pinot Noir, transplanted to Spain centuries ago and developing its own character there. A form of DNA testing is being created for vines and some unexpected relationships may emerge when it has progressed further. Most vines originated in the Middle East and many have come to western Europe via Greece. Indeed, a very knowledgeable friend claims to have found the ancestor of the Cabernet Sauvignon in Greece. The search goes on. And new vines are created by crossing. Vines have to be propagated by cuttings; if you grow one from a pip almost anything may happen. Vines spontaneously mutate, too.

Complicated as the picture is, knowing what vines are cultivated where, and the various names they are given, lies at the root of understanding wines, and the purpose of this chapter is to throw some light on it.

In Spain the gender of the names of many vines appears uncertain: they can be masculine or feminine, depending on where you are and to whom you are speaking. The more usual gender, when this applies, is used in the list that follows.

## Afartapobres

Red. Once cultivated in Cataluña but now very rare indeed and regarded as a table grape.

## Agudelo

See Godello.

## Airén

White. Spain's most commonly cultivated grape and probably the commonest in the world. It covers vast areas of La Mancha where it used to give a very high yield, producing dull wines, many of them used for distilling and some for blending with the heavy reds which used to be grown there. It has been transformed, though, by modern wine making. Cultivated for a low yield, picked early enough to have sufficient acid, and given a temperature-controlled fermentation, it now provides fruity, aromatic and agreeable table wines.

Grown in: Alicante, Almansa, Bullas, Jumilla, La Mancha, Montilla-Moriles, Navarra, Valdepeñas, Vinos de Madrid and Yecla.

Other names: Lairén and Valdepeñera.

**Alamis**

See Pedro Ximénez.

**Alarije**

White. Popular in Extremadura.
Grown in Ribera del Guadiana.

**Albán**

See Palomino.

**Albarello**

White. A rare vine grown in Galicia, where it produces very aromatic wines.

**Albariño**

White. The leading vine in Rías Baixas, where it likes shallow, sandy soils and produces remarkably fragrant wines of great quality. Its cultivation is rapidly expanding. It was certainly growing in Galicia in the eighteenth century and there are various theories about its origin: some claim it was originally French and others that it is the Riesling, brought in by German monks.
Grown in: the Chacolís, Costers del Segre, Penedés, Rías Baixas, Ribeira Sacra and Ribeiro.
Other name: (in Portugal) Alvarinho.

**Albillo**

White. Capable of producing very good wines, this has been variously identified with the Pardillo and Viura, but if it be related to one or the other it now has a separate identity.
Grown in: the Canary Islands, Castilla-León, Cebreros, Bodegas Mauro, Ribera del Arlanza, Ribera del Cea, Cigales, La Palma, Ribera del Duero, Ribeiro and Vinos de Madrid.

**Alcañón**

White. This produces good, fragrant, light wines in Somontano, where it is thought to have originated, though some claim it is related to the Viura.
Grown in: Somontano.
Other name: Alcañol.

**Alcayata**
See Monastrell.

**Alicante**
See Garnacha Tintorera.

**Alicante Blanca**
See Garnacha Blanca.

**Almuñeco**
See Listán Negro.

**Aragón, Aragonés**
See Garnacha Tinta.

**Baladí**
White. Rare.
Grown in: Montilla-Moriles.

**Barbera**
Red. An Italian variety widely planted in other countries and being tried experimentally in Spain.
Grown in: Navarra.

**Bastardo Blanco**
White. Of Portuguese origin and may have arrived by way of Madeira.
Grown in: the Canary Islands.

**Bastardo Negro**
Red. Otherwise as for Bastardo Blanco.
Grown in: the Canary Islands.

**Bermejuela**
White.
Grown in: the Canary Islands.

**Blanquirroja**
See Subirat-Parent

**Bobal**
  Red. The fourth most commonly cultivated vine in Spain. It does well in arid and semi-arid places. If its wines tend to be rather rustic, they are notable for colour, tannin and acidity. It also makes good *rosados*.
  Grown in: Alicante, Los Arribes del Duero-Fermoselle, Manchuela, Ribera del Guadiana, Utiel-Requena and Valencia.

**Borba**
  White. Noted for its yield rather than for its quality, it is popular in Extremadura.
  Grown in Ribera del Guadiana.

**Brancellao**
  Red. A native of Galicia, this vine is capable of producing good wines but is very rare and in danger of disappearing, as the emphasis in that area is now on the very successful whites.
  Grown in: Rías Baixas, Ribeira Sacra and Ribeiro.
  Other name: (in Portugal) Brancelho.

**Brave**
  White.
  Grown in: the Canary Islands.

**Bujariego**
  White.
  Grown in: the Canary Islands.

**Burrablanca**
  White.
  Grown in: the Canary Islands.

**Cabernet Franc**
  Red. A top French variety now being grown on a small scale in Spain. In world reputation it is overshadowed by Cabernet Sauvignon, but produces a rather lighter style of wine that ages well and may well become more widely grown. See also Mencía.
  Grown in: Navarra and Penedés.

## Cabernet Sauvignon

Red. A top French variety grown world-wide. It is at present *the* fashionable red grape. It has long been grown in Spain, at Vega Sicilia, in what is now the Ribera del Duero (though it was not so named when the grape was introduced there) and in Rioja. It is now giving superb wines in Penedés. It provides plenty of backbone and blends well with other varieties (as Bordeaux has shown for years), in Spain notably with Tempranillo.

Grown in: Alella, Alicante, Almansa, Ampurdán-Costa Brava, Bierzo, Bullas, Calatayud, Campo de Borja, Cariñena, Cigales, Conca de Barberá, Costers del Segre, Jumilla, La Mancha, Mondéjar, Monterrei, Navarra, Penedés, Pla de Bages, Plá i Llevant de Mallorca, Priorato, Ribera del Duero, Ribera del Guadiana, Rioja, Rueda, Sierra de Alcaraz, Somontano, Tarragona, Terra Alta, Tierra del Vino, Toro, Utiel-Requena, Valdeorras, Valdepeñas, Valencia, Vinos de Madrid, Yecla, and in a number of leading bodegas producing non-DO wines, such as Bodegas Alta Pavina, Bodegas S.A.T. Los Curros, Finca Retuerta and Viñedos y Bodegas de Malpica.

## Caiño

Two versions: red and white. Neither of these Galician varieties is widely grown but each is capable of giving good wines.

Grown in: Rías Baixas, Ribeira Sacra and Ribeiro.

## Calagraño

White. This was one of the traditional varieties in Rioja, but is now prohibited there and is practically extinct. It was not highly regarded. But it may be the same thing as Cayetana Blanca (see below), and if so is by no means extinct.

Other names: Cazagal, Naves.

## Callet

Red. It is said to be a native of Mallorca, where it is still widely planted, but nowhere else. Its wines are highly coloured but with little extract.

Grown in: Binissalem and Plá i Llevant de Mallorca.

## Cañocazo

White. Once fairly common in the sherry vineyards, it is now very rare indeed and no longer authorized. It is grown, however, in Australia, where it is sometimes wrongly called Palomino.

## Cariñena
See Mazuelo.

## Carrega-Rucs/Carrega-Sums
See Escanyavelles.

## Catalan
See Mazuelo.

## Cayetana Blanca.
White. This grape is high yielding and not at all well thought of, though quite widely planted, generally not in DO areas; some of its wines are used for distillation. It may or may not be the same as the Calagraño formerly grown in Rioja.
Grown in: Ribera del Guadiana.
Other names: Cayazal, Jaén (but not to be confused with the red Jaén), Jaina and Nava.

## Cazagal
See Calagraño.

## Cencibel
See Tempranillo

## Cendrón
See Graciano.

## Chardonnay
White. If Cabernet Sauvignon is sweeping the world as a red, then Chardonnay, from Burgundy, is doing the same thing as the fashionable white. It is easy to grow almost anywhere. It is also unusually easy to handle, adapting itself to the tastes of the enologist by absorbing oak (often too much) and blending easily with the wine of other varieties, as Champagne found out years ago. Deplored by traditionalists, who would stick to the native varieties, but loved by the public, it has been a great success in Spain, particularly in the new regions which are uninhibited by

tradition. Controversy rages over its use in making Cavas but such use is authorized. It is increasing its hold and is undoubtedly there to stay, producing a remarkable range of very good wines.

Grown in: Alella, Alicante, Ampurdán-Costa Brava, Bierzo, Calatayud, Cariñena, Cava, Conca de Barberá, Costers del Segre, La Mancha, Navarra, Penedés, Pla de Bages, Plá i Llevant de Mallorca, Ribera del Guadiana, Rioja, Rueda, Sierra de Alcaraz, Somontano, Tarragona, Terra Alta, Utiel-Requena, Valdeorras, Valdepeñas, Vinedos y Bodegas de Malpica and Vinos de Madrid.

## Chelva
White.
Grown in: Ribera del Guadiana.

## Chenin
White. This very fine French variety, originating in the Loire, has spread all over the world, notably into California and South Africa. Like all other vines, but to a greater extent than some, it changes its character notably when transplanted. In Spain it is as yet rather tentative but is producing some very fruity and flavour-some wines.
Grown in: Alella, Ampurdán-Costa Brava, Cava, Navarra, Penedés, Priorato and Somontano.

## Cinsault
Red. This vine from the South of France is promising, not least because of its ability to thrive in hot places, but so far has made no headway and is only experimental.
Grown in: Navarra.

## Colombard
White. Originating in the Charente area of France, this variety has been very successful in California and also thrives in hot places, but in Spain it is only experimental.
Grown in: Navarra and Terra Alta.

## Crujillón
See Mazuelo.

**Diego**
See Vijariego.

**Doña Blanca**
White.
Grown in: Bierzo, Ribeira Sacra, Monterrei and Valdeorras.

**Escanyavelles**
White. Thought to be a white mutation of the red Monastrell.
Once grown in Cataluña but now almost extinct.
Other names: Carrega-Rucs, Carrega-Sums.

**Espadeiro**
Red. A native of Galicia. Very rare.
Grown in: Rías Baixas and Ribeira Sacra.

**Esquitxagos**
White. Found in Tarragona and Castellón. It may be a clone of
Mersegura.

**Ferrón**
Red. Not widely grown.
Grown in: Ribeira Sacra and Ribeiro.

**Fogoneu**
Red. Grown in Mallorca but not authorized for a DO. Produces
undistinguished young red wines.

**Folle Blanc**
White. This is the French Folle Blanche, once popular for making
wine to be distilled for brandy.
Grown in: Chacolí de Vizcaya.

**Forcalla**
See Viura.

**Forcayat**
Red. High yielding and not very good.
Grown in: Valencia.

**Forastera**
White.
Grown in: the Canary Islands.

**Gamay**
Red. The Beaujolais grape from France. In Spain only being tried experimentally.
Grown in: Navarra.

**Garnacha**
See Garnacha Tinta.

**Garnacha Blanca**
White. The Garnacha grapes are Spanish, probably natives of Aragón or Alicante. They crossed the border into France and have become very popular there as Grenache. The white vine is believed to be a mutation of the red. In Spain it is a popular grape, but usually found in blends rather than as a varietal, though Torres have produced an experimental varietal. It produces enough alcohol, but has to be vinified well if there is to be enough acidity, and is easily oxidized.
Grown in: Alella, Ampurdán-Costa Brava, Calatayud, Campo de Borja, Cariñena, Costers del Segre, Navarra, Penedés, Priorato, Rioja, Somontano, Tarragona and Terra Alta.
Other names: Alicante Blanca, Garnacha Blanca de Rioja, Garnatxa Blanca.

**Garnacha Gris**
White. Another mutant being grown experimentally in Penedés.

**Garnacha Peluda**
Red. Another mutant of Garnacha Tinta which crops more regularly, giving wines with plenty of alcohol but tending to be deficient in colour and to oxidize easily.
Grown in: Alella, Priorato and Terra Alta.
Other name: Liedoner Gris.

**Garnacha Roja**
Red. Yet another mutant.
Grown in: Cigales.

**Garnacha Tinta**

Red. Spain's most popular red vine and very well known also in France as the Grenache, it is the world's second most widely planted vine. It has been maligned in the past but this is the result of over-cropping, which is only too easily achieved. With the yield kept down it can produce great wines, as in Priorato; and Garnacha grown in Rioja Baja adds smoothness to many of the Rioja blends. The alcohol level can be almost dauntingly high. It also makes very good *rosados*. Care needs to be taken, though, to avoid oxidation.

Grown in: Alella, Alicante, Ampurdán-Costa Brava, Los Arribes del Duero-Fermoselle, Benavente-Campos, Bullas, Calatayud, Campo de Borja, Cariñena, Cava, Cebreros, Cigales, Conca de Barberá, Costers del Segre, Jumilla, La Mancha, Méntrida, Mondéjar, Navarra, Penedés, Pla de Bages, Priorato, Ribera del Duero, Ribera del Guadiana, Rioja, Somontano, Tarragona, Terra Alta, Toro, Utiel-Requena, Valdevimbre-Los Oteros, Valencia, Valdepeñas, Vinos de Madrid and Yecla, as well as by a number of bodegas making good non-DO wines.

Other names: Aragón, Aragonés, Garnatxa, Lladoner and Tinto Aragonés.

**Garnacha Tintorera**

Red. It is unusual in being a Teinturier, producing red juice. It is not, however, in the top-quality league. It is widely planted in France, where it was bred in the last century by Henri Bouschet who crossed Aramon, Teinturier de Cher and Grenache.

Grown in: Alicante, Almansa, Benavente-Campos, Bierzo, Jumilla, Monterrei, Navarra, Ribera del Guadiana, Ribeira Sacra, Ribeiro, Valdeorras and Valencia.

Other name: Alicante.

**Garnacha Trepat**

See Trepat.

**Garrido Fino**

White.
Grown in: Condado de Huelva.

## Gewürtztraminer

White. Although this variety is usually associated with Alsace, it originated in Italy, at Tramin, or Termano, in the Italian Tyrol. Its arrival in Spain, pioneered by Torres, is comparatively recent, and the wines retain their notable aroma when grown in Spain, while avoiding the excesses sometimes achieved in Alsace.

Grown in: Ampurdán-Costa Brava, Bierzo, Navarra, Penedés, Somontano and Valdeorras.

## Godello

White. This excellent vine, producing fine wines with a distinctive aroma, is a native of Galicia. After phylloxera, its vineyards were replanted with high-yielding varieties and it almost became extinct but was saved by the efforts of RE.VI.VAL (Reestructuración de los Viñedos de Valdeorras), formed in 1974 to bring the vineyards of Valdeorras back to their former distinction. This has been a great success and the variety is on the up and up.

Grown in: Bierzo, the Canary Islands, Monterrei, Ribeira Sacra, Ribeiro and Valdeorras.

Other names: Agudelo, and see also Verdello.

## Gotim Bru

See Tempranillo.

## Graciano

Red. A very high-quality, very low-yielding grape believed to be a native of the Rioja, where it is finding increasing favour. Its name is said to be derived from *gracia*, 'grace'. Its wines are not highly alcoholic and are tannic, rough and acid when young, but they are deeply coloured (though the colour tends to go brown with age), age very well and when mature show great fragrance and finesse, so they are used, for example, in Rioja *grandes reservas*.

Grown in: Navarra, Ribera del Guadiana and Rioja.

Other names: Morastell, Cendrón and (in France) Morrastel and Tanat Gris.

## Gran Negro

Red.

Grown in: Monterrei and Valdeorras.

**Grau**
Red. A native of Galicia and very rare.
Grown in: Valdeorras.

**Gual**
White.
Grown in: the Canary Islands.

**Hondarribi**
See Ondarribi.

**Horgazuela**
See Palomino.

**Jaén**
Red. A high-yielding vine of no great distinction.
Grown in: Contaviesa-Alpujarra, Mondéjar and Vinos de Madrid
See also: Cayetana Blanca.

**Jaina**
See Cayetana Blanca.

**Jerez**
See Palomino.

**Juan García**
Red.
Grown in: Los Arribes del Duero-Fermoselle.

**Juan Ibáñez**
Red. Not widely grown.
Grown in: Calatayud and Cariñena.
Other name: Miguel de Arco.

**Lado**
White. Although little grown it is well regarded, producing light, aromatic wines.
Grown in: Valdeorras.

**Lairén**
See Airén.

**Liedoner Gris**
See Garnacha Peluda.

**Listán**
See Palomino. But the vine grown under this name in Condado de Huelva would appear to be a different variety, sometimes called Listán de Huelva.

**Listán Negro**
Red.
Grown in: the Canary Islands.
Other names: Almiñeco, Negra Común.

**Lladoner**
See Garnacha Tinta.

**Loureira**
There are both red and white versions, respectively Tinta and Blanca. Natives of Galicia, both are rare, the red version very rare indeed, but give good wines.
Grown in: Monterrei, Rías Baixas, Ribeira Sacra and Ribeiro.
Other name: Loureira Blanca is also known as Marqués.

**Macabeo**
See Viura.

**Madrigal**
See Verdejo.

**Malbec**
Red. A French variety from Bordeaux, introduced into what is now Ribera del Duero during the nineteenth century and occasionally found elsewhere, but little grown.
Grown in: Ribera del Duero.

**Malvar**
White. This may be a clone of Airén, but it is distinctly different,

giving lower yields, ripening earlier and giving generally better wines (though modern practices have, as noted above, greatly improved the Airén).
Grown in: Mondéjar, Ribera del Guadiana and Vinos de Madrid.

## Malvasía
White. Originating in Greece and associated with the legendary Malmsey, this has been established as a Spanish favourite for centuries. It has been about the place long enough to develop distinctive clones and there is now really a family of Malvasías, some of which are listed below. Most, but not all, of the wines it gives are sweet and all have a distinctive aroma.
Grown in: Los Arribes del Duero-Fontanelle, Bierzo, Benavente-Campos, Calatayud, Canary Islands, Navarra, Penedés, Tierra del Vino, Toro, Valencia, Valdevimbre-Los Oteros.

## Malvasía de Alicante, Malvasía Francesa, Malvasía Riojana
See Subirat-Parent.

## Malvasía Rosada
Red.
Grown in: the Canary Islands.

## Malvasía de Sitges
White. Another clone.
Grown in: Penedés.

## Manto Negro
Red. A native of Mallorca, where it produces very good wines.
Grown in: Binissalem and Plá i Llevant de Mallorca.

## Mantúa
See Montúa.

## María Ardoña
See: Merenzao.

## Marmajuelo
White.
Grown in: the Canary Islands.

**Marqués**
See Loureira.

**Marsanne**
A white French variety.
Grown in: Rioja.

**Mazuelo**
Red. One of the basic red vines of Rioja, it is found in the oldest vineyards there and also in Navarra, and is thought to have originated there, but it is equally well known as Cariñena and is thought to have crossed the Pyrenees from the eponymous town (which does not grow much of it nowadays) to become well established in France, and in other countries, as the Carignan. In Spain it is low-yielding and difficult to grow. It gives wines that are rather variable in alcohol but which have high natural acidity and tannin, so that they require some time to mature, which makes them unpopular with bodegas selling young wines, but make them valuable for blending.
Grown in: Ampurdán-Costa Brava, Calatayud, Campo de Borja, Cariñena, Costers del Segre, Navarra, Penedés, Priorato, Rioja, Ribera del Guadiana, Tarragona and Terra Alta.
Other names: Cariñena, Catalan, Crujillón and, in other countries, Carignan.

**Mencía**
Red. It is now generally equated with the Cabernet Franc, and where it is grown it certainly produces excellent wines of a similar style.
Grown in: Benavente-Campos, Bierzo, Monterrei, Rías Baixas, Ribera del Alanza, Ribeira Sacra, Ribeiro, Valdeorras and Valdevimbre-Los Oteros.

**Méntrida**
See Tinto de Madrid.

**Merenzao**
See María Ardoña.

**Merlot**

Red. A major French variety from Bordeaux, widely planted around the world and now finding favour in Spain, where it is producing excellent varietals.

Grown in: Ampurdán-Costa Brava, Alicante, Bierzo, Bullas, Campo de Borja, Cariñena, Cigales, Conca de Barberá, Costers del Segre, Jumilla, La Mancha, Navarra, Penedés, Pla de Bages, Ribera del Duero, Ribera del Guadiana, Rioja, Somontano, Tarragona, Terra Alta, Utiel-Requena, Valdeorras, Valdepeñas and Yecla. Also in some non-DO vineyards producing good wine, such as Finca Retuerta.

**Merseguera**

White. One of the best white varieties, especially favoured in south-east Spain.

Grown in: Alicante, Almansa, Utiel Requena, Valencia and Yecla.

**Miguel de Arco**

See Juan Ibáñez.

**Moll**

White. It produces light, agreeable wines in Mallorca.

Grown in: Binissalem.

Other name: it is sometimes said to be the same as Prensal, but this doubtful.

**Monastrell**

Red. It is a Spanish variety, taking its name from Murviedro in Valencia, but has spread around the Mediterranean, especially in the south of France, where it is known as the Mourvèdre, and in many other world vineyards. It is easy to grow and very resistant to disease, even phylloxera, so it is sometimes found on its own roots. It needs sun but dislikes wind. It produces very fine wines noted for their colour and tannins (which can be rather aggressive in young wines) and plenty of extract, with a strong varietal aroma. Although they can be drunk young, and usually are, they age well and often need to breathe for a time before they can give of their best.

Grown in: Alicante, Almansa, Binissalem, Bullas, Calatayud, Cariñena, Cava, Costers del Segre, Jumilla, Navarra, Penedés, Plá

i Llevant de Mallorca, Ribera del Guadiana, Valencia and Yecla.
Other names: Alcayata, Monastre and Valcarchella. In France,
Mourvèdre. In California and Australia, Mataró.

**Montonec**
See Parellada.

**Montonega**
A fragrant clone of Parellada developed by Codorníu; see Cava.

**Montúa**
White.
Grown in: Ribera del Guadiana.
Other name: Mantúa.

**Morastell**
See Graciano.

**Moravia**
Red.
Grown in: La Mancha.

**Moristel**
Red.
Grown in: Somontano.

**Moscatel**
White. The basic name of a whole family of vines, of which there
are at least 200 recognized members. Otherwise known as the
Muscat or Muscatel, it has been known since at least Roman
times. It is said to have got its name from the fact that flies are
attracted by its sweet and fragrant juice, and was known to Pliny
the Elder as *uva apiana* (grape of the bees), but is more likely
to have got its name from originating in Muscat. Grown all
over Spain, and indeed all over the world, its hallmarks are the
sweetness and unique fragrance. It is the best possible table grape.
Although it is possible to make relatively dry wines from them,
most of these grapes are used for sweet dessert wines.
Grown in: Campo de Borja, the Canary Islands, Condado de
Huelva, Málaga, Montilla-Moriles, Navarra, Plá i Levant de

Mallorca, Sherry, Tarragona, Terra Alta and Tierra del Vino. But there are few places where you will not find one of the family growing on at least a modest scale.

### Moscatel de Alexandría

White. Said to have been named after Alessandria in Italy rather than Alexandria in Egypt, but this is doubtful. It is sometimes named specifically in DO regulations; if a specific clone is not named, this is likely to be the one grown – for instance in the districts named above.

Grown in: Alicante, Campo de Borja, Calatayud, Cariñena, Penedés, Sherry, Valencia.

Other names: Moscatel de Chipiona, Moscatel de España, Moscatel Gordo, Moscatel de Málaga and Moscatel Romano.

### Moscatel de Grano Menudo

White. The small seed muscat, the best kind of Moscatel for wine making, providing a special fragrance. One strain has the odd characteristic that it mutates easily, from pink to reddish brown and back again, but the one grown in Spain generally stays white.

Grown in: Navarra, Penedés and Valdeorras.

Other names: Moscatel de Grano Pequeño, Moscatel Dorado, (in France) Muscat Blanc à Petits Grains, Muscat d'Alsace, Muscat de Frontignan, (in Italy) Moscato d'Asti, Moscato Bianco.

### Moscatel Negro

Red.

Grown in: the Canary Islands.

### Moscatel Romano

See Moscatel de Alexandría.

### Mouratón

Red.

Grown in: Monterrei and Ribeira Sacra.

### Moza Fresca

White. It has been said to be a clone of Merseguera. It is not highly regarded and is often confused with Doña Blanca.

Grown in: Bierzo, Monterrei, Ribeira Sacra and Valdeorras.
Other name: Valenciana.

**Mulata**
See Negramoll.

**Müller-Thurgau**
White. A German cross grown experimentally in Penedés.

**Muscat d'Alsace**
See Moscatel de Grano Menudo.

**Nava**
See Cayetana Blanca.

**Naves**
See Calagraño.

**Negra Común**
See Listán Negro.

**Negra de Madrid**
Red. Although planted in a number of vineyards in central Spain, it does not come into any of the DOs.

**Negramoll**
Red. It produces good wines to be drunk young.
Grown in: the Canary Islands.
Other name: Mulata.

**Negreda**
Red.
Grown in: Ribeira Sacra.

**Ojo de Libre**
See Tempranillo.

**Ondarribi**
There are two versions: Ondarribi Zuri, which is white, and Ondarribi Beltza, which is red.
Grown in: the Chacolís.

## Palomino

White. This widely planted variety is most important in the sherry vineyards, which are practically monovarietal. There it gives a good yield and produces one of the greatest wines in the world. Planted in other places for table wines, it likewise gives a good yield but the wines are usually very second rate. Now that the emphasis throughout Spain is on quality it is beginning to be replaced in many areas.

Grown in: Los Arribes del Duero-Fermoselle, Benavente-Campos, Bierzo, the Canary Islands, Cigales, Condado de Huelva, Monterrei, Navarra, Ribeira Sacra, Ribeiro, Rueda, Sherry, Valdeorras, and Valdevimbre-Los Oteros, amongst other places.

Other names: Albán, Horgazuelo, Jerez, Jerez Fino, Listán, Palomino Fino, Palomino de Chipiona and Palomino de Pinchito, Seminario, Temprana and Xeres.

## Pansá Blanca

See Xarel.lo.
Grown in: Alella.

## Pansá Rosada

White.
Grown in: Alella.

## Pardillo

White. Although this is not a highly esteemed variety, if the yield is low and the must cold-fermented it can give very respectable wines.
Grown in: La Mancha, Ribera del Guadiana and Rioja.
Other name: Pardina.

## Pardina

See Pardillo.

## Parellada

White. This is Cataluña's best vine. Grown in poor soils and cool areas, it produces light, aromatic and elegant wines with ample acidity. If the soil is fertile, though, the yield goes up and the elegance down. It is one of the three traditional varieties for making Cava, but also makes very good, light white table wines.

Grown in: Ampurdán-Costa Brava, Binissalem, Cariñena, Cava, Conca de Barberá, Costers del Segre, Navarra, Penedés, Pla de Bages, Plá i Llevant de Mallorca, Priorato, Ribera del Guadiana, Tarragona and Terra Alta.
Other name: Montonec.

### Parelleta
Red.
Grown in Somontano, where it originated.

### Pedro Jiménez
See Pedro Ximénez.

### Pedro Ximénez
White. One of Spain's great vines, it is low yielding and gives musts rich in sugar but lacking in acid. The wines nevertheless age well and it is a major variety for fortified wines and *rancios*, as well as producing some very good table wines. In *vinos generosos* it is usually used for making sweet wines, but it can also be vinified to give quality dry wines.
Grown in: the Canary Isles, Jumilla, Málaga, Mondéjar, Montilla-Moriles, Penedés, Priorato, Ribera del Guadiana, Sherry, La Sierra de Salamanca and Valencia.
Other names: Alamis, Pedro Jiménez, Pedro Ximén, Ximencia.

### Peluda
Red.
Grown in: Terra Alta.

### Petit Verdot
Red. A Bordeaux variety. There it is noted for its colour and the robust nature of its wines, but it often does not fully ripen. In Spain it looks very promising and has given an excellent varietal.
Grown in: Finca Retuerta and Viñedos y Bodegas de Malpica.

### Picapoll
White. Originates in the French Languedoc, where it is known as Picpoul or Piquepoul, and where it also exists in a black version.
Grown in: Pla de Bages.

**Picudo Prieto**
Red.
Grown in: Benavente-Campos and Valdevimbre-Los Oteros.

**Pinot Blanc**
White.
Grown in: Navarra.

**Pinot Meunier**
Red. A French variety from Champagne.
Grown in: Terra Alta.

**Pinot Noir**
Red. This French grape is the leading red variety in Burgundy and Champagne, and has been tried in many countries with varying degrees of success. It is a rather difficult grape to grow and to vinify.
Grown in: Alella, Alicante, Bierzo, Cava, Conca de Barberá, Costers del Segre, Mallorca, Navarra, Penedés, Plá i Llevant de Mallorca, Priorato, Rioja, Somontano, Terra Alta and Valdepeñas. Also for some serious non-DO wines such as Bodegas Alta Pavina.

**Planta Fina de Pedralba**
White.
Grown in: Alicante and Valencia.
Other name: Planta Pedralba.

**Planta Nova**
White.
Grown in: Utiel-Requena and Valencia.
Other name: Tardana.

**Prensal**
White. Probably another name for Xarel.lo.
Grown in: Binissalem and Plá i Llevant de Mallorca.

**Prieto Picudo**
Red. Although this variety is noted for producing aromatic and agreeable wines, they are all local rather than DO wines.
Grown in: Castilla and León.

### Riesling
White. This is one of the great world varieties, though somewhat under a cloud at the moment owing to the self-inflicted eclipse of German wines.
Grown in: Alicante, Ampurdán-Costa Brava, the Chacolís, Navarra, Penedés and Valdeorras.

### Rosana
White.
Grown in: Penedés.

### Rousanne
White. French.
Grown in: Rioja.

### Royalty
Red.
Grown in: Navarra.

### Ruby Cabernet
Red. A Cabernet Sauvignon × Cariñena cross being grown experimentally in Navarra.

### Rufete
Red. It gives light wines that oxidize easily.
Grown in: Las Arribes del Duero-Fermoselle and La Sierra del Salamanca.

### Sabro
White.
Grown in: the Canary Islands.

### Samsó
Red. Not widely grown now.
Grown in: Penedés.

### Sangiovese
Red. Italian.
Grown in: Navarra.

## Sauvignon Blanc

White. One of the major French varieties, now being grown all over the world. It has a very distinctive aroma which can nevertheless exist in a number of forms depending on site, ripeness and microclimate, sometimes compared with grass and at other times with cats' piss. Happily in Spain the former prevails.
Grown in: Cigales, Costers del Segre, Penedés, Rioja, Rueda, Utiel-Requena and Yecla.

## Sémillon

White. One of the major French varieties now being grown experimentally in Navarra.

## Shiraz

See Syrah.

## Sousón

Red. A rare Galician variety.
Grown in: Rías Baixas, Ribeira Sacra and Ribeiro.

## Subirat-Parent

White. One of the Malvasía family, now falling out of favour.
Grown in: Penedés, Rioja and for Cava.
Other names: Malvasía de Alicante, Malvasía Francesa and Malvasía Riojana and Blanquirroja.

## Sunol or Sumoll

Red. Once popular in Penedés but now distinctly on the decline, it gives aromatic but very acid wines which make excellent brandies.
Grown in: Penedés and Pla de Bages.

## Syrah

Red. A classic variety from the Rhône Valley in France, it seems a natural to try in Spain, and is being experimented with in a number of places but has not yet started to be grown in large quantities.
Grown in: Alicante, Ampurdán-Costa Brava, Bullas, Calatayud, Campo de Borja, Jumilla, Navarra, Pla de Bages, Plá i Llevant de Mallorca, Priorato, Ribera del Guadiana, Rioja, Tarragona,

Viñedos y Bodegas de Malpica and Yecla. Also for good non-DO wines such as Finca Retuerta.
Other name: Shiraz.

## Syrah Blanc
White.
Grown in: Navarra.

## Tardana
See Planta Nova.

## Tempranillo
Red. This native Spanish vine is undoubtedly one of the world's great ones and Spain's best. It is not a high yielder but the quality of its wines is excellent: fragrant, deeply coloured tending towards purple, with lots of fruit, enough alcohol, acidity and the ability to age well with little tendency to oxidize. Its wines tend to contain a certain amount of glycerine, giving them an agreeable unctuousness. And it makes remarkably successful blends with other varieties. It has been grown for a long time and in many places, so that clones have developed their own characters producing, for instance, the thick-skinned Tinto del País. And it has many other local names such as Ull de Llebre in Penedés. There is a theory that it is descended from Pinot Noir vines imported from France centuries ago, while others would suggest the Cabernet Franc, but no such connections have been established. It is said to get its name from *temprano*, 'early', because it ripens earlier than the Garnacha, with which it is associated in Rioja.
Grown in: Alella, Alicante, Almansa, Ampurdán-Costa Brava, Los Arribes del Duero-Fermoselle, Bierzo, Binissalem, Bullas, Calatayud, Campo de Borja, Cariñena, Cigales, Conca de Barberá, Costers del Segre, Jumilla, La Mancha, Bodegas Mauro, Méntrida, Mondéjar, Monterrei, Navarra, Penedés, Pla de Bages, Plá i Llevant de Mallorca, Ribera del Arlanza, Ribera del Duero, Ribera del Guadiana, Ribeiro, Rioja, Rueda, Sierra de Alcaraz, La Sierra de Salamanca, Somontano, Tarragona, Terra Alta, Tierra del Vino, Toro, Utiel-Requena, Valdeorras, Valdepeñas, Valencia, Vinos de Madrid and Yecla. Also for good non-DO wines such as those of Bodegas S.A.T. Los Curros and Finca Retuerta.

Other names: Cencibel, Gotim Bru, Ojo de Libre, Tinta Madrid, Tinto Fino, Tinto del País, Tinto de Toro and Ull de Lebre. In Portugal: Aragonez and Tinta Roriz.

## Tinta Madrid
See Tempranillo.

## Tintilla
Black.
Grown in: the Canary Islands.

## Tinto Aragonés
See Garnacha.

## Tinto Basto
See Tinto de Madrid.

## Tinto Fino
See Tempranillo.

## Tinto de Madrid
Red. Quite widely planted but, rather curiously, not in Vinos de Madrid and in only two DOs.
Grown in: Méntrida and Mondéjar.
Other names: Méntrida, Tinto Basto.

## Tinto de Navalcarnero
See Garnacha.

## Tinto de Toro
See Tempranillo. But it is certainly a special clone and could be a separate variety.

## Tinto del País
See Tempranillo.

## Torrontés
White. Originating in Galicia, this variety has spread far.
Grown in: the Canary Islands, Mondéjar, Montilla-Moriles, Rías Baixas, Ribeira Sacra and Ribeiro.

**Tortosí**
White.
Grown in: Valencia.

**Treixadura**
White. A Galician variety that thrives in the mountains, giving good, highly aromatic wines.
Grown in: Monterrei, Rías Baixas, Ribeira Sacra and Ribeiro.

**Trepat**
Red. A productive variety that likes heat. Its area is declining.
Grown in: Conca de Barberá and Costers del Segre.
Other names: Garnacha Trepat, Trobat, Tropat.

**Trobat/Tropat**
See Trepat.

**Ull de Llebre**
See Tempranillo.

**Valcarchella**
See Monastrell.

**Valdepeñera**
See Airén.

**Valenciana**
See Doña Blanca.

**Verdejo**
White. Although it is said to have been brought from Africa by the Moors, this is now considered to be a native Spanish grape – and one of the very best, providing aromatic, big-bodied wines of great character. It can withstand extreme cold and drought.
Grown in: Los Arribes del Duero-Fermoselle, Benavente-Campos, Cigales, Navarra, Ribera del Cea, Ribera del Guadiana, Rueda and Toro.
Other name: Madrigal.

**Verdello**
  See Godello. But there is some doubt about this, as Verdello in the Canary Islands is said to be the same as the Madeira Verdelho.

**Vermejuela**
  See Bermejuela.

**Verdoncho**
  White. This is not considered to be a quality grape.
  Grown in: La Mancha.

**Verijadiego**
  See Vijariego.

**Vijariego**
  White. There is also a red version, Vijariego Negra.
  Grown in: the Canary Islands.
  Other names: Diego, Verijadiego.

**Viognier**
  White. French, originally from the Rhône.
  Grown in: Rioja and Sierra de Alcaraz.

**Viura**
  White. This is one of Spain's most important varieties, probably originating in Aragón, and is very widely grown. It is equally well known under its alternative name Macabeo. Highly productive, it can give wines of very high quality but needs careful handling. If it is unripe the wines can be over acidic and bitter. If it is overripe the wines are dull. But harvested at the right time and cold-fermented, it gives wines of ample acidity but good balance that age well.
  Grown in: Alella, Alicante, Ampurdán-Costa Brava, Binissalem, Bullas, Calatayud, Campo de Borja, Cariñena, Cava, Cigales, Conca de Barberá, Costers del Segre, Jumilla, La Mancha, Mondéjar, Navarra, Penedés, Pla de Bages, Plá i Llevant de Mallorca, Priorato, Ribera del Arlanza, Ribera del Cea, Ribera del Guadiana, Ribeiro, Rioja, Rueda, La Sierra de Salamanca, Somontano, Tarragona, Terra Alta, Utiel-Requena, Valdepeñas, Valencia, Vinos de Madrid and Yecla.
  Other names: Forcalla and Macabeo. In France, Macabeu.

## Xarel.lo

White. A Spanish, specifically Catalan, variety that is principally noted as one of the traditional varieties for Cava. It is generally grown in low-lying vineyards and gives aromatic wines with plenty of body, adding a useful dimension to the other varieties. In the past it tended to oxidize, but this problem has been overcome by modern vinification.

Grown in: Alella, Ampurdán-Costa Brava, Cava, Costers del Segre, Navarra, Penedés and Tarragona.

Other name: Pansá Blanca (but this is a specific clone).

## Ximén/Ximencia

See Pedro Ximénez.

## Zalema

White. A very productive variety that is easy to grow and much esteemed for those reasons in Huelva, but it gives rather dull wines and these are unlikely to improve unless it is replaced or, at the very least, its yield is drastically reduced.

Grown in: Condado de Huelva.

# Glossary

———

ABOCADO: slightly sweet.

ABV: the EU standard of measuring strength: alcohol by volume at 20°C. Formerly known as Gay-Lussac, after the French chemist who invented a volume alcoholometer. In this book the notation ° is used to indicate abv.

AFTERTASTE: the flavour that is detected after the wine has been swallowed.

AGRAFE: a steel clip used to keep the cork in a sparkling wine during its bottle fermentation and sometimes after the final corking.

AGUAPIE: must from the second pressing.

AGUARDIENTE: grape spirit.

AGUJA: a very slightly sparkling wine.

ALAMBRADO: a wire cage placed round a bottle, originally to prevent fraud.

ALBARIZA: the name given to the best soil in the Sherry district. It is white in colour and contains a high proportion of calcium.

ALLIER: a variety of French oak.

ALMACENISTA: a storekeeper; someone who makes wines and keeps them for onward wholesale sale.

ALMIJAR: the yard outside a vineyard building where, especially in the Sherry area, grapes used traditionally to be dried in the sun before being pressed.

AMONTILLADO: a style of Sherry obtained when fino is aged for a long time in the wood. It resembles wines formerly prepared only in Montilla. They are still prepared in Montilla and the term is used both for Sherries and Montilla-Moriles wines of the appropriate style.

AMOROSO: a term used chiefly in the UK for a type of light and slightly sweet oloroso Sherry.

AMPELOGRAPHY: the comparative study of the vine.

AÑADA: a vintage wine; a wine made from grapes grown in a single year.

AÑEJO: wine aged for not less than three years.

AÑINA: the fourth, in order of merit, of the four leading districts with albariza soil around Jerez.

403

APALEADOR: stick used for stirring wine during fining.

ARANZADA: a measure of area used in vineyards. One aranzada equals 0.475 hectares or 1.1737 acres.

ARENA: sand.

ARROBA: a measure of weight or volume which is confusing because it is different in different parts of Spain. In Jerez it is equivalent to about 11.5 kg or 16.66 litres.

ARROPE: a syrup used in blending Sherry, made by simmering down must to one-fifth of its original volume.

AUTONOMÍA (or AUTONOMA): Spain is a federation of seventeen autonomous areas, plus two offshore. These are further subdivided into *provincias*, or provinces, which themselves are subdivided into *comarcas*, or counties, which are yet further subdivided into *municipios*, or municipalities.

AUTOVINIFIER: a modern machine for making red wine, effecting maceration, fermentation and temperature control by means of a rotating stainless steel tank, rather like a cement mixer. Another form exists for making white wines but is seldom found in Spain. Also known as a Vinimatic.

BACKBONE: the combination of flavouring elements that provides a wine with structure.

BALBAINA: the third, in order of merit, of the four leading districts with albariza soil around Jerez.

BARRICA: 225 litre oak cask.

BARRO: clay.

BÂTONNAGE: a French term, now used in most wine-growing areas. The stirring of the lees with a pole.

BAUMÉ: a measure of the sugar in must, obtained by using a hydrometer. If a 15° Baumé solution is fermented right out it gives a wine of 16.4°. Very roughly, each degree Baumé results in a degree of alcohol on fermentation. Its inventor was Antoine Baumé (1728–1804), a French pharmacist.

BIOLOGICAL AGEING: the maturation of wine under a film of yeast cells, as with fino sherry.

BOCOY: an odd-shaped butt usually containing about 40 *arrobas*.

BODEGA: winery. The word is used in two ways: a wine making establishment or a building in such an establishment.

BOTA: butt. The usual size contains 500 litres (30 *arrobas*) but there are also special sizes such as Bota Gorda, which is used in sherry bodegas for storing and maturing wine and which contains 36 to 40 *arrobas*.

BOZAL: literally muzzle; the wire placed over the cork of a bottle of sparkling wine to stop it blowing out.

CABACEO: the formula for a blend of wine.

CAMPAÑA: season. The period from one vintage to the next.

CANASTA: a cane basket used in vineyards.

CARBONIC MACERATION: a method of vinification for red wine used all over Europe. Whole bunches of grapes are put into a sealed container from which oxygen is excluded, usually by adding carbon dioxide. The fermentation starts within the grapes themselves, which then begin to break under their own weight; a normal fermentation then follows. There are many variations in the technique. Known in Spanish as *maceración carbónica* and French as *macération carbonique*.

CARRASCAL: the second, in order of merit, of the four leading districts with *albariza* soil around Jerez.

CASCO: cask.

CASSE: a generic term for various kinds of wine disease.

CAVA: the best kind of Spanish sparkling wine, see Chapter 12. The literal meaning of the word is a subterranean cellar.

CEPA: vine.

CHAPTALIZATION: the process of adding sugar to insufficiently sweet must before fermenting it, when the sugar is converted into alcohol, to improve the balance of wines that would otherwise be deficient. It is used (and abused) widely in northern Europe but not normally in Spain where the sun gives musts that are sweet enough without it. It is named after the remarkable Frenchman Comte Jean-Antoine Chaptal de Chanteloup, who became Minister of the Interior and president of the Academy of Science. He did not invent the process but gave it his blessing.

CLARETE: a light-coloured red wine.

CLARO: a clear wine.

CLAROS DE LIAS: clear wine obtained from the lees of must.

CLAROS DE TURBIOS: clear wine obtained from filtering the lees of wine.

CLONE: a stock of vines raised by vegetative multiplication from a single parent.

COLOR, VINO DE: a wine used for deepening the colour of Sherry blends.

COLD FERMENTATION: fermentation in which the temperature is prevented from rising by cooling the must.

COMARCA: county; see autonomía.

CONO: name given to a tinaja in Condado de Huelva.

CONSEJO REGULADOR de la Denominación de Origen: A government official body appointed to supervise a specific recognized wine area.

CORDÓN SIMPLE: as its name suggests, the least complicated way of training a vine. A single cordón, or arm, grows from the top of the trunk and is trained horizontally along a wire.

CORREDOR: a broker who buys and sells wine.

COSECHA: harvest, vintage.

CRDO: Consejo Regulador de la Denominación de Origen.

CRIADERA: literally a nursery. A series of butts that are never moved and from which periodically wine is drawn to refresh a solera or another criadera, the wine drawn out being replaced by an equal quantity of younger wine drawn from another criadera or from a stock of añada wine.

CRIANZA: literally 'brought up'. Applied to a wine given oak ageing.

CUARTO (BOTA): quarter cask (¼ butt).

CUPADA: a blend of various wines (*cuvée* in French) prepared, for instance, as the base wine for a Cava.

DEPOSITO: vat.

DE: Denominación Específica. See p. 9.

DEGÜELLE: disgorging, in French *dégorgement*; the removal of the deposit formed during the bottle fermentation of a sparkling wine.

DEP: Denominación Específica Provisional. See p. 9.

DESFANGADO: literally 'demudding': the separation of must from heavy impurities before fermentation.

DO: Denominación de Origen. See pp. 8–9.

DOBLE PASTA: after fermenting one lot of wine, the skins are left in the vat and a second fermentation of wine is done on top of them, so that very deeply red wines are made, generally used for blending. See the descriptions of Valencia and Alicante.

DOUBLE CORDON: a system of pruning. Two horizontal arms, trained along wires, extend from the vine's vertical trunk, with shoots growing upwards from the arms.

DOC, DOCa: Denominación de Origen Calificada. See p. 9.

DOP: Denominación de Origen Provisional. See p. 9.

DULCE: sweet.

DULCE APAGADO: a form of sweet wine made by adding alcohol to unfermented must and then fermenting it.

EMBOTTELADO: bottled.

ENOLOGY: modern spelling of oenology, the science of wine making.

EN CABEZA: A method of pruning vines. Literally it means 'in a head'. The vine is cut down drastically so that the portion quite near the ground thickens to form a sort of head which sprouts a number of shoots (five or six) which are cut short and form a crown.

EN CORDÓN: a commonly practised way of training a vine in which one or more often two cordóns, or arms, grow from the top of the trunk and are trained along wires.

EN ESPALDERA: the method of training vines on a wire fence, which is rapidly increasing.

EN RASTRA: a system of training a vine in which several long arms grow in rather haphazard directions.

EN VASO: the most common method of pruning vines in Spain. The vine is grown like a bush and pruned short. Over a period of three years the pruning is done to leave a vertical trunk with two shoots sticking out an angle and leaving what looks like a vessel, or vaso, between them. Subsequently it may be allowed more shoots.

ENVERADO: looking ripe.

ESPALDERA: the structure of wires used for supporting vines in vineyards. This is to be contrasted with the traditional method, which grew them as bushes.

ESPIRRAQUE: a third, heavy pressing. The wine obtained from it is generally distilled.

ESPUMOSO or ESPUMANTE: sparkling.

ETIQUETA: label.

EXTRACT (or DRY EXTRACT): the non-volatile components of wine; the solids.

FINCA: a farm.

FINING: clarifying wine by precipitating out the colloids and particles which cause opacity.

FINO: fine. It is used to define a kind of Sherry on which *flor* has bred freely.

FLABBY: a wine lacking in acidity and grip.

FLOR: literally 'flower'; a film of yeast cells growing on the surface of certain wines, notably fino Sherries and Montillas.

FONDILLÓN: a strong, oxidized wine which is a speciality of Alicante.

GAY-LUSSAC: French chemist who invented a volume alcoholometer. See abv.

GENEROSO: alcoholically strong wines made mostly in Andalucía.

GENEVA DOUBLE CURTAIN: a system of growing vines using two parallel wires, one vine being trained along one wire and the next along the other. The trunks are tall and the grapes grow downwards from the wires.

GIRASOL: literally 'sunflower'; a device used for shaking down the deposit formed in the bottle fermentation of sparkling wines, handling a number of bottles at the same time instead of shaking them individually.

GIROPALETTE: an automated form of girasol.

GLYCERINE: the trihydric alcohol glycerol which is a natural product of fermentation and a major constituent of wines; it is rather sweet tasting and can give a sweet sensation in the mouth even when the wine contains no sugar.

GOBELET: in this system the vine is trained low and pruned to a goblet shape, hence the name, the shoots being cut back to form a crown.

GRAN RESERVA: The top grade of aged wine; a wine made in a good year and given a substantial period of ageing. See p. 9.

GUYOT: a common method of pruning named after its French inventor. Known in Spain traditionally as *poda de pulgar y vara* (thumb and stick pruning), but the French term is now commonly used. As its name suggests, the vine is trained to have one long and one short shoot. In the single Guyot method one long shoot is trained horizontally along a wire; in the double Guyot method there are two, one in either direction. In Spain the system is considered especially suitable in cool areas.

HECHO: literally 'made', but it is a term applied to wine that is fully mature.

HECTARE: the European measure of area: 100 ares or 10,000 square metres equal 2.471 acres.

HOGSHEAD: a cask holding 250 litres, half the size of a butt.

HOLANDAS: grape spirits that are matured in wood to become brandy.

INJERTA: grafting.

INOX: stainless steel.

JEREZ CORTADO: name given to palo cortado in Sanlúcar de Barrameda.

JOVEN: a young vine. See p. 7.

LAGAR: wooden wine press.

LAGO: its usual meaning is 'lake', but in a wine context it is the fermenting tank used traditionally by small wine growers.

LÁGRIMA: free-run must.

LEES: the cloudy and sometimes solid deposits that form at the bottom of casks of wine; they consist of yeasts, tartrate crystals and other matters.

LENGTH: the time that the flavour of a wine lingers in the mouth after it has been swallowed.

LÍAS: the lees of must or wine.

LICOR DE EXPEDICIÓN: the preparation added before the final corking of a sparkling wine to give it the necessary degree of sweetness and to top it up after the disgorgement; *liqueur d'expédition* in French.

LICOR DE TIRAJE: the mixture of wine, sugar and yeasts put into a bottle to bring about the fermentation inside the bottle in making sparkling wines by the método tradicional.

LIMOUSIN: a variety of French oak.

MACHARNUDO: the first, in order of merit, of the four leading districts with albariza soil around Jerez.

MACERACIÓN CARBONICA: see carbonic maceration.

MACERATION: contact between must or wine and grape skins.

MADERIZATION: the oxidation of white wines which causes them to turn brown and to have a smell that is somewhat reminiscent of Madeira – hence the name.

MAGNUM: a bottle containing twice as much as an ordinary bottle: that is, 1.5 litres.

MALIC ACID: an acid found in grape must and also in apples. It imparts an acid flavour (which is sometimes desirable) and an appley smell. When it is not required it is removed by means of a malolactic fermentation, which is an entirely natural process but is now controlled.

MALOLACTIC FERMENTATION: the bacteriological transformation of malic acid into the less aggressive lactic acid, with the evolution of carbon dioxide.

MANZANILLA: a form of Sherry matured at Sanlúcar de Barrameda. It also means camomile, and the unwary who ask for it in the parts of Spain where Sherry is not a usual drink are apt to be given a cup of camomile tea.

MARC: grape residues after pressing.

MARCO REAL: square pattern used in planting out vineyards.

MEDIA BOTA: hogshead.

MESETA: Spain's central plateau.

MÉTODO TRADICIONAL: the method used in producing Cava and some other sparkling wines.

MISTELA: a strong and sweet wine made by inhibiting the fermentation by adding alcohol, leaving natural sugars.

MITAD Y MITAD (MITEADO): a fifty-fifty mixture of alcohol and wine used for fortifying fortified wines.

MOSTO: must; the juice of grapes. It ceases being must and becomes wine as soon as fermentation is complete. In the Sherry country, however, the term is used more loosely, both before and after fermentation and until the wine has been racked from the lees.

MOSTO CONCENTRADO RECTIFICADO: a sweetening agent made from concentrated must.

MOSTO YEMA: free-run must.

MUNICIPIO: municipality; see autonomía.

MUST: see mosto.

MYCODERMA ACETI: a ferment that turns wine into vinegar.

OAK: several kinds of oak are used for wine casks. See p. 5.

OCTAVO: an octave (eighth of a butt).

OENOLOGY: the science of wine making. It is now usually spelled without the initial o.

OIDIUM: a fungoid parasite of the vine.

OLOROSO: fragrant. A term used to define a style of Sherry in which either there has never been much *flor* or in which the growth of *flor* has been stopped by the additions of spirit: a dark and full-bodied wine.

ORUJOS: grape skins; the spirit distilled from grape skins; *marc* in French.

OXIDATION: the interaction of oxygen with various chemical elements in the wine. Correctly used, this forms part of the normal process of ageing and is essential for the ageing of wines like oloroso Sherry. But if it is uncontrolled because oxygen gets at the wine or if the wine has been kept too long, it loses its edge of flavour, goes brown, and gets spoiled.

PAGO: a distinct, named vineyard.

PALMA: a high quality fino Sherry.

PALMA CORTADA: a rather stouter fino tending towards amontillado.

PALO: a stick. Also an iron rod with a brush attached used for fining wine.

PALO CORTADO: a rather full-bodied Sherry of a particularly good style.

PASADO: a wine, particularly a Sherry, that has developed with age.

PATA DE GALLINA: literally 'hen's foot'; a style of oloroso Sherry that is dry but tastes slightly sweet owing to the presence of glycerine.

PAXARETE: sweet wine partly consisting of Pedro Ximénez used for sweetening blends of Sherry and for colouring whisky.

PERSISTENCE: the lingering flavour of wine which persists after it has been swallowed.

PÉTILLANCE: the presence of a very small amount of carbon dioxide, which gives a slightly tickling sensation.

PH: hydrogen power. It is an inverse measure of acidity, 7 being neutral, anything above 7 alkaline and anything below 7 acid. All wines are acid to some degree and usually have a pH between 3 and 4.

PHENOLICS or POLYPHENOLS: a naturally occurring group of compounds based on phenol. They include tannins and important elements of colour and flavour.

PHYLLOXERA: the 'vine louse', an aphid; a destructive insect parasite of the vine, originating in America.

PLASTERING: the addition of gypsum to grapes to increase the acidity of the must.

PRENSA: wine press.

PRICKED: a wine tainted with acetic acid (vinegar).

PROVINCIA: province; see autonomías.

PUPITRE: literally 'desk'; the device used for holding sparkling wines while the deposit formed by the second fermentation in bottle is shaken down on to the cork.

QUERCUS: oak.
QUINA: quinine, sometimes used as a flavouring element in medicinal wines and the like.

RACIMO: a bunch of grapes.
RACKING OFF THE LEES: drawing the clear wine off the lees that have accumulated at the bottom of the cask.
RANCIO: a traditional type of wine, going back to Roman times, that is deliberately oxidized, sometimes in glass demijohns kept outside, which hastens the oxidation by the heat of the sun and the cool of night.
RAYA: a term used in classifying Sherry musts. Also a coarse form of oloroso Sherry.
RAYA OLOROSA: a light raya.
REDONDO: a descriptive term used to describe a wine that is 'round' or well balanced.
REMONTAJE: process used in making red wine. The must is drawn from the bottom of the fermentation vessel and pumped through the 'cap' of skins that forms at the top.
REMOVIDO: the process of removing the deposit formed during the bottle fermentation of sparkling wines; *remuage* in French.
RENDIMIENTO: By pressing grapes very hard one can usually get one litre of must for each kilogram of grapes but such pressure makes bad wine, so a *rendimiento* of between 65 per cent and 70 per cent is set for each district to limit production.
RESERVA: a wine given a substantial period of ageing. See p. 7.
RESERVA DE FAMILIA: family reserve.
RESERVE WINES: wines from a previous vintage or vintages put on one side for use in blending the base wine for high quality Cavas.
ROSADO: pink wine. In French *rosé*, a term sometimes used on Spanish wine labels.
ROYAT: a system of pruning known in France as Cordon de Royat, in which the vine is trained into a curve and then horizontally along a wire.

SACAR: to draw off wine from a cask.
SACK: a historic term used formerly to describe wines for export, notably Sherry Sack, Malaga (or Malligo) Sack and Canary Sack.
SACRISTÍA: the area in a bodega that contains the oldest wines kept for special occasions.

SANCOCHO: a syrup made in the Sherry district by simmering must until it is one-third of its original volume.

SANGRÍA: a long drink served in a jug and made basically from red wine and fruit with soda water or sparkling lemonade, sometimes sugar and (in Spain) a dash of brandy. Bottled versions are now available.

S.A.T.: Sociedad Agraria de Transformación; a company of growers more exclusive than a cooperative.

SECO: dry.

SHORT: a wine whose flavour rapidly disappears after it has been swallowed.

SOLEO: the process of increasing the sweetness of grapes by drying them slightly in the sun.

SOLERA: a series of butts that are never moved and from which wine is periodically drawn, whereupon the *solera* is refreshed with an equal quantity of wine from a *criadera*. This system is particularly used for Sherry and for Montillla-Moriles. Also used loosely to describe the complete unit, consisting of the *solera* itself and all its *criaderas*. The word may not properly be used to describe a style of wine.

STRUCTURE: the flavouring elements that combine together to make a complete wine.

TANNINS: naturally occurring polyphenols which give an astringent taste but which are essential elements in good red wines, contributing to their ability to mature and last.

TAPÓN: cork.

TEARS: The little drops of wine which cling to the side of a glass and descend very slowly. They are largely made up of alcohol and glycerine, and are mostly found in wines of good quality.

TENT: a style of wine formerly made at Rota in the Sherry area.

TINA: large wooden vat.

TINAJA: large jars, formerly of earthenware but more recently made of concrete, used for fermenting and storing wine. Tinajas are still used but are becoming obsolescent. The term is also used for earthenware jugs sometimes used in bodegas.

TOAST: the charring given to the insides of the staves when a barrel is made.

TOLVA: hopper in which the grapes are received at the bodega.

TONEL: a very large storage cask containing two, three, four or more butts.

TONELERO: cooper.

TRES BOLILLO: diagonal pattern used for planting out vineyards.

TURBIOS: the lees of wine, as opposed to lías, the lees of must.

ULLAGE: empty space in cask or bottle.

UVA: grape.

vc: Vino Comarcal (local wine). See p. 8.

vcprd: Vinos de Calidad Producidos en Regiones Determinadas, quality wines produced in specific regions. See p. 8.

vdlt: Vino de la Tierra; country wine. See p. 8.

vdm: Vino de Mesa; table wine. See p. 8.

varietal: a wine made from a single grape variety.

velo: surface film of *flor*.

vendimia: vintage.

venencia: an instrument consisting of a small silver cup on the end of a long whalebone handle (though now usually made of stainless steel and plastic) used for drawing small quantities of wine from casks for tasting; an alternative form is made of split bamboo.

vid: vine.

viejo: old.

viejísimo: very old.

vinimatic: see autovinifier.

viña: vineyard.

vino blanco: white wine.

vino común or vino corriente: wine of ordinary quality.

vino de crianza: wine given oak ageing. See p. 7.

vino de mesa: table wine.

vino de pasto: in Spain a pale, cheap table wine; in the UK a Sherry blended as an aperitif (but obsolescent).

vino de prensa: wine produced from must obtained by pressing the grapes.

vino de xérès: Sherry.

vino joven: young wine. See p. 7.

vino tinto: red wine.

viticulture: the cultivation of vine grapes.

vt: see VdlT.


yema: bud. See *mosto de yema*.

yeso: gypsum (calcium sulphate), a small quantity of which is traditionally used in areas making fortified wines; it is sprinkled on grapes before they are pressed to increase acidity.


zona de crianza: the area in which a DO wine may be matured.

zurra or zurracapote: a *sangría* made with white wine instead of red.

# GENERAL INDEX

415

# INDEX OF BODEGAS

# INDEX OF VINE VARIETIES

---

433

# INDEX OF WINES

---

*Where the name of a bodega is also used as a brand, this is not necessarily listed below. See the Index of Bodegas.*